Soviet Architecture, 1917-1962

A Bibliographical Guide to Source Material

Soviet Architecture 1917-1962

A Bibliographical Guide to Source Material

Anatole Senkevitch, Jr.

University Press of Virginia
Charlottesville

*X Z5944
.R9S45
FA
10-75*

ISBN: 0-8139-0415-3
Library of Congress Catalog Card Number: 73-75335
Printed in the United States of America

Preface

THIS book began eight years ago as a personal bibliographical index of material on Soviet architecture. That index began rapidly to expand in late 1968 as I undertook a two-year period of intensive research on the subject at the Library of Congress. In the course of my research, the need for such a bibliographical compendium became quite apparent. No comprehensive bibliography on Soviet architecture was available in any language, including Russian, save either for a few highly selective lists or for guides concentrating on peripheral fields. The decision was thus made to bring my bibliography to publishable form in order to help provide access to the wealth of available source material on the subject, a good deal of which is held by major American research libraries.

Although this bibliography contains over 1,000 titles of books and articles, it is selective and does not presume to exhaust the source material. Moreover, any initial attempt to provide bibliographical control for an area of architectural history which has had the benefit of so little prior scholarly delineation has other limitations that will become apparent to the serious reader. The scope of this book was constrained by the bounds of available information, the present state of research, and the knowledge and judgment of a single compiler. The selection and appraisal of titles had to proceed side by side with the task of ascertaining the total reservoir of potential literature on the subject. While the range of existing source material was being determined, interest in Soviet architecture, primarily the modern period, began to intensify, with a commensurate increase in the quantity and quality of material published in the Soviet Union and subsequently in the West. As a result, the bibliography continued to expand from the time the University Press of Virginia approved its publication in the summer of 1970 to the final completion of the manuscript two years later. Even then, my ongoing research on the subject uncovered much additional material from previous and current publications alike that could legitimately have been included in the bibliography. The compilation of a bibliography, however, is a never-ending process. The task of compressing the vast array of previously untapped material into a systematic conspectus of titles germane to the scope and intent of this bibliography is likewise bound to reflect some arbitrary judgments and errors of interpretation. This book, therefore, is intended primarily to satisfy initial bibliographical inquiries into the history and theory of Soviet architecture, either directly through specific citations or indirectly through reference to pertinent bibliographical and serial sources. I hope that, in providing greater access than is presently available to the enormous quantity of material published on the subject, the present work may facilitate an increase in the critical study of this subject matter by architectural historians, Russian area specialists, and other scholars whose pursuits might lead them to an interest in Soviet architecture.

Although the process of selecting and assessing the material to be included in the bibliography was my responsibility alone, the final preparation of a complex work such as this could hardly be the work of a single person. I owe lasting debts of gratitude for the counsel and support I have received at every stage in the preparation of this book. Professors Walter K. Hanak, Frederick D. Nichols, William B. O'Neal, and Thomas T. Hammond of the University of Virginia were good enough to read parts or all of the manuscript in its initial form as my master's thesis. I have benefited much from their judgments and their suggestions. I am also very appreciative of the grant from the Committee on Soviet Studies at Cornell University which aided in the completion of the final manuscript. The staff of the Olin and Fine Arts libraries at Cornell gave generously of their time in resolving last-minute bibliographical disparities. My thanks go also to Ms. Florence Sprague and Ms. Marian Dalton of Cornell University for helping prepare the index.

Most of my research was done at the Library of Congress during the years 1969 and 1970, where the unfailing kindness and cooperation extended me by the Library's staff made my task far easier and altogether more feasible than it would otherwise have been. I am indebted to Dr. Sergius Yakobson, Dr. Paul L. Horecky, and Dr. Robert V. Allen of the Slavic and East European Division for their encouragement and assistance, as well as for placing at my disposal the considerable resources of their division; Mr. Robert G. Carlton provided invaluable assistance in bibliographic research and generously gave me the benefit of his unique knowledge and experience in preparing and indexing Slavic bibliographies. I am also indebted to Mr. Dudley B. Ball and to his staff in the Stack and Reader Division for making it possible for me to work productively over prolonged periods with the vast amount of material deposited at the Library of Congress.

Finally, I wish to express my deep and abiding gratitude to my wife, Judith J. Senkevitch, who bore patiently with many prolonged absences in connection with the preparation of this work and gave fully of her considerable talents. I am especially indebted for her masterful service in helping type and edit the various drafts of the manuscript. She has, in a very real sense, been a constant and intelligent partner in this undertaking, and her encouragement and penetrating criticism have proven, as always, to be indispensable.

Contents

Introduction

THIS annotated bibliography is intended to serve students of Soviet architecture, as well as to aid institutions and individuals collecting material on the subject. Its aim is to present Russian and Western-language publications, chiefly in article and book form, which are relevant to the study of the history and theory of Soviet architecture from the Russian Revolution in 1917 to the aftermath of the de-Stalinization campaign launched in the mid-1950s by Nikita S. Khrushchev. Russian publications have been emphasized since they represent the core of the primary source material at the disposal of Western scholars. The bibliography concentrates, as does the literature itself, on developments within the Russian Soviet Federative Socialist Republic (RSFSR).

The use of primary source material, most of which is in Russian, presents certain difficulties for the Western student. More crucial than the obstacle of language is the problem of adequate accessibility to this material, much of which is naturally deposited in Soviet archives; although Soviet archival collections with material pertaining to the country's architectural activity are beginning increasingly to be tapped, access to foreign scholars still remains something of a problem.[1] Fortunately, there is available in the West a profusion of monographic and periodical literature published in the Soviet Union

[1]"In recent years," writes Patricia Kennedy Grimstead, "an increasing number of visiting scholars have found it possible to use Soviet archives and manuscripts collections. To be sure, there has been little opportunity for work on the revolutionary or the postrevolutionary period, and research on many prerevolutionary topics has been hindered for a variety of reasons. Yet, despite remaining difficulties, the recent advances are extremely significant. Although access possibilities are subject to change and to variation according to individual projects, prospects for serious research on many phases of the Russian past look much brighter than they have since 1917" (Grimstead, "Soviet Archives and Manuscript Collections: A Bibliographical Introduction," *Slavic Review*, 24 [March 1965]: 105; entire article, p. 105-120). Mrs. Grimstead's assessment has generally been affirmed by the few Western scholars who have used Soviet archives in their research on that country's architecture. Among the archives assayed in the above article, those important for material on Soviet architecture included the following under the Main Archival Administration: (1) the Central State Archives of the October Revolution, Supreme Organs of State Power, and Organs of State Administration of the USSR (TsGAOR), (2) the Central State Archives of Literature and the Arts of the USSR (TsGALI), (3) the Central State Historical Archives of the USSR in Leningrad (TsGIAL), and (4) the Central State Archives of Films, Sound Recordings, and Photographic Documents of the USSR (TsGAKFFD); other useful repositories mentioned in her article include the various collections of the Academy of Sciences and the manuscript collections in major Soviet libraries and museums.

during the period under consideration; few episodes of twentieth-century architecture have been documented as extensively in published form. Major research libraries in the United States are among the richest repositories outside the Soviet Union for published materials in this field.[2] These libraries include the Library of Congress, the New York Public Library, and the Columbia University Library System.

With the largest collection of Slavic materials in the Western Hemisphere, the Library of Congress in Washington, D.C., contains the most comprehensive assortment of publications relating to Soviet architecture. The collection provides a comprehensive assemblage of bibliographical and reference material and is especially rich in monographic and periodical literature dealing with various aspects of the subject. Of special interest are the serial holdings, which contain complete or, in a few instances, virtually complete sets of almost 90 percent of the professional and scholarly architectural journals, as well as of periodicals published in various allied fields, such as planning, housing, construction, art, literature, and culture.[3] Most of the holdings dealing with

---

More recently, Mrs. Grimstead surveyed regional Soviet archives in her article, "Regional State Archives in the USSR: Some Notes and a Bibliography of Published Guides," *Slavic Review*, 28 (March 1969): 92-115. She observes that "many of these archives rank with those of Moscow and Leningrad for the materials they contain pertaining to all phases of Soviet as well as prerevolutionary life and culture" (p. 92). The best English language guides to Soviet archives, Mrs. Grimstead's two articles are indispensable references for any Western scholar contemplating archival research in the Soviet Union. Her book on the subject is to be published in the near future.

[2]Still among the best general surveys is Charles Morley, "Major Russian Collections in American Libraries," *Slavonic and East European Review,* 29 (Dec. 1950): 256-266. "European scholars," he wrote, "may be surprised to learn that libraries in the United States possess some of the largest collections of Russian materials outside the U.S.S.R." (p. 256). This situation surely applies to the availability in major American libraries of published source material dealing with Russian and especially Soviet architecture. Morley's article evaluates, in order of their size, the Russian collections at the Library of Congress, the New York Public Library, the Harvard University Libraries, the Hoover Library on War, Revolution, and Peace at Stanford University, and the University of California Library at Berkeley. As will be seen in the discussion below, his list does not fully reflect the order of importance among those collections with holdings pertaining to Soviet architecture.

A brief survey of libraries containing material pertaining to Soviet architecture and city planning is contained in Maurice Frank Parkins, *City Planning in Soviet Russia* (Chicago, 1953), p. 133-135. The libraries investigated include the Widener, Architecture, Landscape Architecture and Regional Planning, and Law Libraries at Harvard University; The American Russian Institute Library (now dissolved) and the New York Public Library in New York City; the Library of Congress and the reference libraries of the State Department, the Department of Commerce, and the former Federal Housing Agency in Washington, D.C. An effective procedure for making a systematic search of the Library of Congress for material on the subject is outlined on p. 134-135, n. 1.

[3]This assessment is based on a survey, made in conjunction with compiling the present bibliography, of Russian serials germane to the history of Soviet architecture held by the Library of Congress, as compared to the total number of such serials that were ascertained to have been published in the Soviet Union during the period under

Soviet architecture have been incorporated into the general collection and brought under the control of the central card catalogue. A small body of publications, some of them dealing with the initial postrevolutionary years, remain uncatalogued and apart from the general collections; many of these titles may be identified through the central card catalogue, however, and access may be obtained by arrangement with the Slavic and Central European Division of the library. Of great value to the student of Soviet architecture is the Cyrillic Union Catalogue located in the Library of Congress. The Catalogue represents an attempt to list all the Slavic books available in the United States and to indicate the particular library in which they are located; though no longer kept current due to staff shortages, the Catalogue still provides the best centralized source for determining the location of a particular Soviet architectural publication in this country.

Second only to the Library of Congress in the quantity and quality of its Russian materials is the New York Public Library. The student of Soviet architecture will find the subject well represented in the library's collection of books, pamphlets, and serials. Of special interest are the holdings relating to the modern period. Equally noteworthy are its serial holdings, which happily include titles not held by the Library of Congress and thus round out virtually the full complement of available Soviet periodicals relating to that country's architectural development. Access to this material is provided by the Slavic Division Card Catalogue, which lists all of the library's Slavic holdings. An added feature of the Slavic Division Catalogue is the abundant references that it provides to individual periodical articles.

The Columbia University Library System, which includes the Avery Architectural Library, is another major repository for published sources relating to Soviet architecture. Its holdings, abundant in material relating to the modern period, include monographs and serials that are available in no other library in the United States. Inasmuch as the Columbia Library network has, to a large extent, integrated its program of acquisition with that of the New York Public Library, the two institutions combine to make New York City an outstanding center for materials relating to Soviet architecture.[4]

Several university libraries whose collections do not match the breadth of those mentioned above have nonetheless accumulated significant holdings in the area of Russian and Soviet architecture. Using the Andrew Dickson White

---

consideration. The latter measurement was made with reference principally to the two-volume compilation of Rudolf Smits, *Half a Century of Soviet Serials, 1917-1968* (Washington, D.C., 1968); scrupulously developed from primary Soviet sources, it lists close to twenty-eight thousand titles.

[4]These two major library centers in New York City are augmented by the General Library of New York University, which acquired the nucleus of the former American-Russian Institute Library. Portions of the latter collection, however, have also been acquired by several other university libraries.

Architectural Collection as its nucleus, the Cornell University Library in Ithaca, New York, has made notable strides in recent years to build up a solid collection of published source material in this area. The University of California at Berkeley, California, the Harvard University Library at Cambridge, Massachusetts, and the University of Virginia Library at Charlottesville, Virginia, have also amassed respectable collections on the subject.

Thus the general inaccessibility of Soviet archives and libraries to Western scholars has largely been ameliorated through the accumulation of a wealth of important published source material on Soviet architecture at major American research libraries.

Among other difficulties which the Western student is likely to confront, few are likely to prove as vexing as the problem of interpreting the proliferation of published material pertaining to the history and theory of Soviet architecture. Indeed, few episodes in the history of twentieth-century architecture seem so paradoxical as the evolution of Soviet architecture from the Russian Revolution to the aftermath of the de-Stalinization campaign. The dynamic innovations of the cosmopolitan modernists, who viewed contemporary architecture as an embodiment of the social ideals fostering the Revolution, contrast sharply with developments between 1932 and 1955 that injected classical and national traditions into architectural activity. Where the Soviet avant-garde had promoted modern architecture as the means for structuring an egalitarian society on the basis of modern technology and socialism, the Stalinist apparatus proceeded to transform Soviet architecture into an instrument of state propaganda intended to express in monumental form the projected grandeur of socialist culture in its specific Stalinist manifestation.

Modernist concepts were first advanced by the constructivists and the rationalists, the two principal Soviet architectural movements in the twenties. Though there were numerous areas in which their respective doctrines tended to converge, the two movements stressed different formal prerequisites for developing a viable contemporary architecture. Constructivists emphasized specific social, technological, and utilitarian prerequisites for architectural production, while the rationalists were chiefly concerned with establishing formal aesthetic criteria for the articulation and perception of architectural form in space.

The architectural manifestations of constructivism evolved around the work of the Vesnin brothers and the theoretical activity of Moisei Ginzburg. Stressing the integration of the latest scientific and technological achievements into a rational process of architectural design, Ginzburg's initial writings provide an important literary record of constructivist theory in the early twenties.[5] In late 1925 the constructivist movement was transformed into the

---

[5]The most important of Ginzburg's early publications for enunciating the principal tenets of the constructivist doctrine is his *Stil' i epokha* [Style and Epoch] (Moscow,

Society of Contemporary Architects (OSA) and proceeded to postulate the functionalist doctrine, which held that the structural and spatial composition of an architectural problem was to be determined by its functional solution; its aesthetic potential was correspondingly to be realized through the integration of the functional method of design with the latest industrialized building techniques. From 1926 through 1930, the Society published the journal *S.A.*, initials standing for Contemporary Architecture (*Sovremennaia arkhitektura*). An invaluable chronicle of constructivist activity during the last half of the decade, the journal enabled the movement to maintain an active forum by which to disseminate its views.[6] As one of the journal's chief editors, together with the Vesnin brothers, Moisei Ginzburg remained the principal constructivist theoretician, elaborating the fundamental tenets of the functionalist doctrine in a series of articles and editorials.

Constructivist writing, highly didactic in nature, exhibits two conspicuous characteristics. First, it exudes a tone of triumph and optimism stemming from the movement's interpretation of the Russian Revolution. Constructivists, like the Soviet avant garde in general, viewed the Revolution not so much as a political event as a pervasive social cataclysm which liberated society from the debilitating exploitation of man by man and which unleashed new socioeconomic forces for building an egalitarian society. Yet constructivist writing also reveals a conspicuous sense of moral righteousness stemming from the movement's conviction that its doctrine and work alone had

---

1924). The first manifesto of constructivism in Soviet arts, from which Ginzburg drew significant inspiration, is Aleksei Gan, *Konstruktivizm* [Constructivism] (Tver, 1922). Gan's treatise extolled the virtues of technology and socialism and underscored the constructivists' concern with transforming all realms of artistic activity into socially useful endeavors aimed at building an egalitarian, socialist society.

[6]The OSA was the only Soviet architectural movement to publish its own professional journal with regular frequency in the period 1926-30. The annual publications *Ezhegodnik MAO* (see **no. 69** in the Bibliography) and *Obshchestvo arkhitektorov-khudozhnikov; ezhegodnik* (**no. 71**) were published at very infrequent intervals. Moreover, reflecting the deliberative nature of their parent organizations, these journals concentrated on publishing the results of competitions sponsored by these societies and refrained from promulgating any particular doctrine. As regards other allied publications, *Stroitel'-stvo Moskvy* (**no. 80**) and *Stroitel'naia promyshlennost'* (**no. 77**) devoted considerable attention to the country's architectural activity during this period and therefore provide a chronicle vital to the understanding of that activity *in toto*. However, they were neither exclusively architectural journals nor the organs of any single architectural movement or organization. The only other publication comparable to *S.A.* in scope was *Izvestiia ASNOVA*. Yet only a single issue of the rationalist journal was ever published, and spokesmen for the movement had to rely on several other publications, discussed below, to disseminate their views. Thus *S.A.* may indeed be viewed as the only full-fledged professional architectural journal during this period whose unique purpose was proselytizing a singular doctrine and propagandizing the aims and activity of a single movement. Such a decided advantage, for example, surely cannot be overlooked in accounting for the OSA's rise to preeminence in Soviet architecture during the last half of the twenties.

succeeded in synthesizing the undiluted forces of technology and socialism, unleashed by the respective industrial and Russian revolutions, that were deemed essential for fashioning a viable contemporary architecture. Such an attitude did much to fuel the acrimonious polemical battle among contending architectural movements which erupted in the late twenties.

The rationalist movement received its prime impetus from Nikolai A. Ladovsky, who injected a novel emphasis into the rationalist doctrine by infusing it with a specific aspect of *Gestalt* psychology. Though determined, like the constructivists, to evolve a new architectural idiom through the use of the latest industrial materials and techniques, the rationalists sought primarily to establish verifiable scientific criteria for perceiving and articulating architectural form as the basis for architectural design, and as a means for orienting man in space. Ladovsky and the rationalists maintained that reason and intuition should govern architectural production, and looked to the new science of psychology to support their concepts. Basic geometric forms were not only the most useful but also the most steeped with a psychological connection to social ideals, inasmuch as they possessed the capacity for conveying ideological meaning. It remained the architect's task to optimize the perception of that meaning by articulating the essential geometric properties of architectural forms and imbuing them with a commensurate artistic and aesthetic aspect. Internal dissension within the movement, which in 1923 had organized into the Association of New Architects (ASNOVA), led Ladovsky to establish a splinter group in 1928. Calling itself the Association of Architects-Urbanists (ARU), this group extended Ladovsky's formal rationale to urban, as well as architectural, design.

The amount of writing produced by the rationalists is meager when compared to the vast corpus of constructivist theoretical and polemical literature. This dearth may be explained in part by the fact that ASNOVA's activity prior to 1926 revolved primarily around pedagogical work, which the group tended to emphasize as its most vital function. Concerted efforts to publicize the rationalist doctrine began only in 1926 with the publication of the Association's journal, *Izvestiia ASNOVA* [News of ASNOVA]. Yet only one issue of the journal ever appeared, and rationalists had to rely upon other Soviet serials for transmitting their views: these journals included *Sovetskoe iskusstvo* [Soviet Art], *Stroitel'stvo Moskvy* [Construction of Moscow], and *Stroitel'naia promyshlennost'* [Construction Industry]. The most active and articulate publicist of the rationalists was not Ladovsky but rather ASNOVA cofounder N. V. Dokuchaev.[7] His articles, while sometimes lacking the flourish

---

[7]To be sure, Ladovsky published two important articles articulating the basis for the rationalist doctrine; both appeared in the single issue of *Izvestiia ASNOVA*, published in 1926. However, Ladovsky refrained from either elaborating or proselytizing the rationalist doctrine. That task was assumed by N. V. Dokuchaev.

and cogency of Ginzburg's writing, nonetheless provide succinct expositions of the movement's specific rationalist principles. The writings of the rationalist movement under Ladovsky are generally less didactic than those of the constructivists: though lean, they reveal a strong predilection for an erudite rather than rhetorical deliberation of architectural problems. With Ladovsky's departure from ASNOVA, however, the latter's publication activity assumed a more distinctly polemical overtone in an apparent effort to gain a sense of parity with the increasingly influential constructivist, or functionalist, movement. On the other hand, Ladovsky and his colleagues in the ARU, for whom V. Lavrov emerged as the leading publicist, maintained a tone of detached restraint in elucidating their theoretical positions in print.

The fervor with which the constructivists and rationalists promulgated their respective doctrines was matched only by the spirited polemical battle that erupted between the two movements in the late twenties. Constructivists accused ASNOVA of excessive preoccupation with abstract theory at the expense of considering the means for its practical application. R. Ia. Khiger surfaced as one of the more virulent apologists of the functionalist doctrine and attacked the rationalists repeatedly for devising abstract canons of form without any regard for their underlying social and functional prerequisites. To the rationalists, on the other hand, the functionalist doctrine promulgated by the OSA represented a certain denigration of architecture into a sterile and mechanistic abstraction, shorn of its vital artistic and aesthetic aspects. In identifying architecture with engineering, members of ASNOVA asserted, constructivism had lost sight of the formal prerequisites that were indispensable for viable architectural design. F. Shalavin and I. Lamtsov assumed the lead in ASNOVA's attack on their rivals, challenging basic hypotheses of the functionalist doctrine and ridiculing the righteous constructivist presumption of superiority in architectural affairs.[8]

---

[8]Numerous articles were involved in the polemical campaign; of these, a few emerged as cornerstones in the acrimonious struggle between the two movements. The constructivists were the first to engage in criticism. The editorial "ASNOVA," *S.A.*, no. 2 (1926): 59, accused Ladovsky of formulating much too abstract a framework for the rationalist doctrine. In the following year, F. Shalavin and I. Lamtsov launched ASNOVA's counteroffensive in an article entitled "O levoi fraze v arkhitekture (k voprosu ob ideologii konstruktivizma)" [Concerning the Left Phrase in Architecture (On the Question of the Ideology of Constructivism)], *Krasnaia nov'*, no. 8 (1927): 226-239, which challenged the viability and appropriateness of the functionalist doctrine. A general rebuttal to that criticism was included in the OSA editorial, "Kritika konstruktivizma" [Criticism of Constructivism], *S.A.*, no. 1 (1928): 1-4. Shalavin and Lamtsov intensified their attack in 1929, however, in an article entitled "O putiakh razvitiia sovremennoi arkhitekturnoi mysli [Concerning the Directions in the Development of Contemporary Architectural Thought], *Pechat' i revoliutsiia*, no. 9 (1929): 49-69; this statement used much of the strident polemic introduced by VOPRA. Simultaneously, Khiger published a speech which he had delivered to the First OSA Congress. Entitled "Formalizm: ideologiia upadochnichestva v sovetskoi arkhitekture" [Formalism: Ideology of Decadence in

The modernists were united, however, in their uncompromising struggle against the elder or "Old School" architects, educated in the academic traditions of prerevolutionary Russian architecture, who had not fully accepted modern architecture. Despite concerted and sometimes vicious attempts by rationalist and especially constructivist publicists to challenge the viability of eclecticism,[9] the elder architects remained conspicuously aloof from the ensuing polemical campaign. By the late twenties, however, the united modernist front had succeeded in repudiating the trend toward academic eclecticism. Few of the elder architects failed to modify their work to conform to prevalent modern trends, at times with consummate skill.

Even as modern architecture was, to all appearances, attaining preeminence in the Soviet Union by the late twenties, conditions that had sustained a decade of unbridled cultural ferment were beginning to be eroded from within by Stalin's furtive campaign to eliminate all opposition to his emerging dictatorship. This gradual move toward greater centralized control, coinciding with the mass industrialization and collectivization campaigns, was accompanied by the formation of "proletarian" organizations within the various realms of the country's cultural activity. These organizations sought, under the guise of affirming Marxist dialectics, to unmask the "enemies of the proletariat" within their own ranks and to repudiate abstract theory as decadent manifestations of a bourgeois "art for art's sake" attitude. The All-Union Society of Proletarian Architects (VOPRA) was organized in 1929 as the beacon of the "Proletarian Episode" in Soviet architecture. The turgid writings of VOPRA members, especially those of art historian Aleksei I. Mikhailov and architect Arkadi G. Mordvinov, served further to inflame the polemical struggle being waged within the ranks of the Soviet architectural community. Constructivists and rationalists alike were denounced for their alleged detachment from the proletariat's struggle for survival and from the newly proclaimed goals of the Stalinist regime. "Leonidovism" (*Leonidovshchina*), a term which had initially been applied to rebuke the visionary work of the young constructivist Ivan Leonidov, began to be applied more broadly to renounce all architects whose

---

Soviet Architecture], *S.A.*, no. 4 (1929): 142-146, it represented a bristling condemnation of every fundamental aspect of the rationalist doctrine. The above articles provide an inadvertent chronicle charting the gradual but certain decline both in the level of deliberation among the modernist movements and in their standing in the Soviet architectural community.

[9]The rationalist position was summarized succinctly by N. V. Dokuchaev, "Sovremennaia russkaia arkhitektura i zapadnye paralleli" [Contemporary Russian Architecture and Western Parallels], *Sovetskoi iskusstvo*: Pt. 2, no. 2 (1927): 11-12. The constructivists launched a more intensive campaign, which revolved around two articles. The first was "Nasha deistvitel'nost'" [Our Reality], *S.A.*, no. 2 (1927): 47-50; the second, "Kak ne nado stroit'" [How Not to Build], *S.A.*, no. 2 (1928): 41-47, was a protracted attack both upon eclectic architects and upon government agencies commissioning their work.

work was deemed too abstract and utopian, or "unproletarian."[10] In truth, the emergence of VOPRA and its ability to attack the other architectural movements with impunity heralded the consolidation of architectural forces that affirmed the right of government intervention in architectural affairs and asserted the architects' responsibility to comply with official dicta and expectations in their work. The proletarian movement also produced a belated and unsuccessful effort by the modern movements to merge into a federation entitled the All-Union Architectural-Scientific Society (VANO) in order to meet the VOPRA offensive and accommodate the newly evolving official demands. Correspondingly, the constructivist journal *S.A.* ceased publication after 1930 and was superseded by the journal entitled *Sovetskaia arkhitektura* [Soviet Architecture], which provides an invaluable theoretical and professional chronicle of this crucial and transitional period. Its contents reveal the extent to which the strident rhetoric employed by VOPRA succeeded in undermining the position and prestige of the modern movements. Not least, the VOPRA campaign augured the tactics and rationale of the impending ideological realignment of the country's architectural community through the official replacement of all architectural organizations by the single Union of Soviet Architects in 1932.

In sharp contrast to the writing produced during the twenties, publication activity between 1932 and 1941 was aimed simultaneously at promoting the revival of classical and national traditions in the name of socialist realism and at repudiating all modernist trends as legitimate avenues for the continued development of Soviet architecture. Classical and national traditions, first sanctioned through the competition for the Palace of Soviets, were perceived as being uniquely disposed to imbue Soviet architecture with a universal appeal to the widest spectrum of the Soviet citizenry; it was these venerable traditions rather than the austere, machinelike aspect of modern trends, that were promoted by official spokesmen, such as former Commissar of Education Anatoli V. Lunacharsky, as being most suitable for propagandizing the grandeur of the Stalinist regime and dramatizing the anticipated material potentials of the socialist state.[11]

---

[10]VOPRA's methodology and rationale were outlined in its manifesto, "Deklaratsiia VOPRA [Declaration of VOPRA], *Pechat' i revoliutsiia*, no. 6 (1929): 125-128. Mikhailov's various articles appeared in book form, entitled *Gruppirovki sovetskoi arkhitektury* [Groupings of Soviet Architecture] (Moscow and Leningrad, 1932). It was Mordvinov who launched the infamous attack on excessive abstraction in modern Soviet architecture with his speech, "Leonidovshchina i ee vred" [Leonidovism and Its Dangers] , *Iskusstvo v massy*, no. 12 (1930): 12-15. For the resolution passed by the Fine Arts Department of the Communist Academy adopting Mordvinov's harangue, see *Sovetskaia arkhitektura*, nos. 1-2 (1931): 18.

[11]Though instrumental in having the avant-garde emerge as the principal exponent of Soviet art in the twenties, the first Commissar of Education Anatoli V. Lunacharsky

The tightening of ideological lines in Soviet architecture revolved around the pernicious campaign to discredit all modern movements in the wake of their enforced dissolution in 1932. Modernism in its various manifestations began singularly to be anathematized as "formalism"; leaders of the modern movements were ostracized for having steadfastly rebuked the inroads that the classical traditions had made during the several decades preceding the Revolution. Charges of "decadence" and "eclecticism" were leveled to refer to specific manifestations of formalism. "Decadence" replaced "Leonidovism" as the term used to insinuate the presence of unorthodox tendencies in the work of visionary Soviet modernists; highly abstract concepts were ridiculed as antithetical vestiges of bourgeois elements in Soviet society. "Eclecticism," on the other hand, was a term brandished more in its traditional sense to denounce the virtual replication of classical styles, a trend epitomized by the work of the elder architect Ivan V. Zholtovsky; implicit in this charge, however, was the apparent dissatisfaction with the forthright assimilation of classical forms without adequate regard for expressing appropriate ideological content.[12] In truth, the unrelenting drive to purge formalism from Soviet architecture advanced the requirement of resolute obedience to party dictates and promoted the ideological censure of all trends and personalities deemed to be in opposition to official expectations. The elaboration and defense of official positions, therefore, began increasingly to dictate the character of the writing produced prior to the outbreak of the Second World War. That character was defined chiefly by two former members of VOPRA. They were architect Karo S. Alabian and art historian Ivan L. Matsa, the latter having served as president of the proletarian group. Installed as executive secretary of the newly formed Union of Soviet Architects and editor of its journal, *Arkhitektura SSSR* [Architecture of the USSR], Alabian emerged as the

---

surfaced as the first official spokesman to criticize the works of modern architecture and to appeal for a revival of classical traditions. Two of his articles proved instrumental in auguring the rationale behind the reorientation of Soviet architecture. The first is entitled "Arkhitekturnoe oformlenie sotsialisticheskikh gorodov" [Architectural Design of Socialist Cities], *Revoliutsiia i kul'tura*, no. 1 (1930): 58-61; the second, "Rech o proletarskoi arkhitekture" [Speech on Proletarian Architecture], *Arkhitektura SSSR*, no. 8 (1934): 4-7. The rationale enunciated by Lunacharsky was embodied in the decree issued in 1932 by the Commission for the competition for the Palace of Soviets, calling for the infusion of classical traditions in entries submitted to subsequent rounds of the competition. See "Itogi velichaishego arkhitekturnogo konkursa" [Results of the Great Architectural Competition], *Stroitel'stvo Moskvy*, no. 3 (1932): 14.

[12] The ideological basis for the "formalist" charge was outlined in L. Rempel' and T. Vainer, "O Teoreticheskikh korniakh formalizma v arkhitekture" [On the Theoretical Roots of Formalism in Architecture], *Arkhitektura SSSR*, no. 5 (1936): 8-13. The range of transgressions included under the umbrella of the epithet of formalism was delineated by Karo S. Alabian, "Protiv formalizma, uproshchenchestva, eklektike" [Against Formalism, Vulgarization, and Eclecticism] *Arkhitektura SSSR*, no. 4 (1936): 1-6.

principal scribe and purveyor of the official party line in Soviet architecture; his articles and editorials represent a virtual codex of that policy, faithfully delineating the desired implications of seminal official pronouncements for architectural affairs. As head of the Cabinet of Architectural Theory and History in the newly formed Academy of Architecture, Matsa became the principal theoretician in architectural matters; he assumed the precarious task of translating the various expressions of official predilections into an acceptable theoretical and ideological program for Soviet architecture. Although Matsa's initial efforts seemed intended to allay the growing suspicion among Soviet architects that the new policy advocated little more than a wholesale classical revival, his later writings narrowed the field of acceptable styles to those emanating from classical traditions.[13]

The Second World War induced the Stalinist regime to relax its unremitting campaign to construct an awesome socialist culture. Critically depleting the country's material resources, the war likewise forced the Soviet architectural community momentarily to abandon the Stalinist grand design for classical monumentality in favor of devising ways to erect badly needed defensive, industrial, and housing facilities of maximum utility with minimum needs. The resulting emphasis upon experimentation with industrialized building techniques produced a discernible impact upon the architectural writing of the period. In a series of articles, Ivan Matsa minimized his prewar dogmatic advocacy of classical traditions. In its place, he began extolling the virtues of innovation and contemporaneity in architectural production, much as constructivist Moisei Ginzburg had done in the twenties.[14] The architect Andrei K. Burov voiced undaunted disaffection with the deleterious effects of the classical syndrome which had pervaded prewar theory and practice. He recommended emulating both contemporary Western and early Soviet modernist experience in developing a more rational approach to architectural design.[15] But the writings were too few and the period too brief to achieve any long-range reversal of prior trends. The period of wartime moderation deteriorated

---

[13]In his "O prirode arkhitektury" [On the Nature of Architecture] *Arkhitektura SSSR*, no. 3 (1935): 7-9, for example, Ivan Matsa conspicuously refrained from invoking classicism as the only viable source of inspiration. With his article entitled "O klassike i klassichnost'i" [On Classicism and the Essence of Classicism], *Akademiia arkhitektury*, nos. 1-2 (1935): 35-38, however, Matsa initiated fanciful argumentation asserting classicism as the only legitimate tradition for the continued development of Soviet architecture.

[14]See especially Matsa's article entitled "Traditsii i novatorstvo" [Traditions and Innovation], *Arkhitektura SSSR*, no. 1 (1941): 31-35, and "Stroenie arkhitekturnogo obraza" [Construction of an Architectural Image], *Arkhitektura SSSR*, no. 4 (1941): 45-50.

[15]Andrei K. Burov, "Na Putiakh k novoi russkoi arkhitektury" [On the Way to a New Russian Architecture], *Arkhitektura SSSR*, no. 4 (1943): 30-36.

rapidly following the end of the war. The regime sought to reimpose firm control over all realms of cultural activity, thereby militating against the continued relaxation of ideological restraints.

The Soviet victory at the end of World War II and the ensuing mutual distrust that mushroomed between the Soviet Union and its erstwhile allies were accompanied by a dramatic reversal of official wartime attitudes. The principal element of this reversal was the transformation of patriotic elements cultivated prior to the war into an unrelenting chauvinist rationale. Its fundamental motives were to proclaim the superiority of the Soviet system over capitalism and to assert the preeminence of Soviet culture. In architecture, this development fostered a renewed revival of classical and national motifs. Unlike in the thirties, however, special emphasis was placed upon the assimilation of native traditions as the basis for developing a superior national architecture. Wartime experimentation with advanced industrialized building techniques and commensurate modes of architectural production was virtually abandoned. Great importance was attached instead to creating unique architectural images that would express the exalted aspirations of Stalinist chauvinism in ever more monumental forms.

The drive to assert the superiority of Soviet culture was orchestrated by Andrei Zhdanov, secretary of the Central Committee and Stalin's lieutenant on the cultural front. Memorialized by the epithet "Zhdanovism" (*Zhdanovshchina*), the campaign was fueled by Zhdanov's "anticosmopolitan" decrees to eradicate all vestiges of adulation of the West. These decrees ostracized various segments of the cultural community for allegedly having acquiesced to Western culture, announced that the superiority of socialism had to be demonstrated boldly in all cultural matters, and exhorted Soviet writers and artists to resume work on creating a unique socialist literature and art.[16] Zhdanov's invective was faithfully conveyed to the architectural community by Karo Alabian. At the same time, articles and editorials in *Arkhitektura i stroitel'stvo* (Architecture and Construction) launched a ruthless campaign to purge all members of the Soviet architectural community who had at any time in the past expressed open admiration of, or made the slightest favorable reference to, any Western ideas or architectural models. Published during the crucial period from 1946 to 1950, the above journal briefly superseded *Arkhitektura SSSR* until the latter's resumption in 1951 and provides a vivid account of the tactical ploys used to bring all aspects of Soviet architecture in line with the Stalinist chauvinistic rationale. Terms such as "cosmopolitanism" and "bourgeois objectivism" abounded to insinuate alleged subservience to foreign influences. In its broadest context, "cosmopolitanism" was employed to imply an unpatriotic sense of internationalism, while the term "bourgeois

[16]Many of Zhdanov's decrees are translated and reproduced in the compendium entitled *On Literature, Music and Philosophy* (London, 1950).

objectivism" was applied to connote a preference for Western interpretations of historical phenomena. Episodes of Soviet modernism, meanwhile, were again viewed as bourgeois products of capitalist influences and subjected to merciless attack.[17] The writing produced during the postwar period in the field of architecture must thus be seen as a product unique to its day, professing the blatant chauvinist rationale operating in Soviet architecture and society at large in order to saturate the consciousness of the populace with a sense of the superiority of the Soviet order.

Developments after Stalin's death produced a notable impact upon the course of Soviet cultural policy. Compared to the Stalinist reign of terror, the tempo of post-Stalinist Russia evolved as one of relative ferment and change after the issue of succession was finally resolved with the rise of Nikita Khrushchev. Demolishing the Stalinist cult and denouncing its excesses in Soviet life, the Khrushchevian regime embarked upon a policy of controlled relaxation of ideological restraints. Although the cultural thaw soon encountered its limits, the regime nonetheless maintained its general determination to loosen the shackles that had stifled cultural development under Stalin.

In this period renewed efforts surfaced within the architectural community to abandon the classical and national predilections professed by the Stalinist grand design and to resume experimentation with advanced industrialized building techniques. Significantly, this reversal was not obtained through any didactic proselytization of social, aesthetic, or ideological ideals. Rather, it was given official impetus primarily as a result of crucial economic pressures that threatened to dissipate the country's postwar building resources and thereby make it all the more difficult to satisfy the country's accelerating housing shortages. The Soviet leadership was obliged to recognize the need for streamlining the building industry through fundamental reorganization

---

[17]Two articles proved instrumental in launching the purge. The first, entitled "Razoblachit' nositelei burzhuaznogo kozmopolitanizma i estestva v arkhitekturnoi nauke i kritike" [Exposing the Carriers of Bourgeois Cosmopolitanism and Aestheticism in Architectural Scholarship and Criticism], *Arkhitektura i stroitel'stvo*, no. 2 (1949): 7-10, outlined the indictment against all alleged transgressors and served to define the sense in which the terms cited above were employed to insinuate unpatriotic sympathies with the West. M. Rzianin intensified the attack in his "Uludshit' rabotu Nauchno-issledovatel'skogo instituta istorii i teorii arkhitektury Akademii arkhitektury SSSR" [For an Improvement in the Work of the Scholarly Research Institute of the History and Theory of Architecture in the Academy of Architecture of the USSR], *Arkhitektura i stroitel'stvo*, no. 3 (1949): 4-5. Among those censured for alleged collusion with those accused earlier, paradoxically, was Karo Alabian. David Arkin was singled out for the harshest criticism of all in a subsequent article by A. Peremyslov, "Ideolog Kozmopolitanizma v arkhitekture D. Arkin" [Ideologue of Cosmopolitanism in Architecture, D. Arkin], *Arkhitektura i stroitel'stvo*, no. 3 (1949): 6-9. The one historical and theoretical account of Soviet architecture epitomizing the Stalinist chauvinistic postwar rationale is Mikhail P. Tsapenko, *O realisticheskikh osnovakh sovetskoi arkhitektury* [On the Realistic Foundations of Soviet Architecture] (Moscow, 1952).

and the widespread introduction of industrialization processes.[18] The party's mandate for a commensurate reordering of priorities in Soviet architecture produced effects no less profound than those which had been obtained through the party's decision in 1932 to replace all existing literary and artistic organizations with a single body for each sphere of cultural activity. Unlike developments in 1932, however, the reorganization of the Soviet architectural community was not part of a larger campaign aimed at reorienting the thrust of literature and the arts as a whole. Nor was the party mandate inspired by any conscious predisposition to prescribe any particular styles, as had been the case following the competition for the Palace of Soviets. The intended subordination of formal criteria to building considerations operated to remove architecture from the purely artistic or cultural domain. The artistic aspect, once preeminent in the Stalinist formula for monumental grandeur, was deemed to be a function of building and economic expediency rather than of an independent complex of formal, aesthetic, or ideological criteria.

Though a general sense of uncertainty permeated initial attempts to determine a new course for Soviet architecture, there was general agreement that some form of adjustment was inevitable. The journal *Voprosy teorii arkhitektury* [Questions on the Theory of Architecture], issued by the newly reorganized Academy of Construction and Architecture, recorded the initial theoretical postulations and debates that followed in the wake of official action by the Khrushchevian regime to reorient priorities in Soviet architecture; abstracts of proceedings of various conferences convened to deliberate the implications of new directives were published in *Arkhitektura SSSR* [Architecture of the USSR]. The more established members of the architectural community counseled against moving too rapidly toward any radical change. The younger generation of specialists, on the other hand, began to press earnestly for a reversal of Stalinist policies, arguing that a fundamental revision of architectural method and rationale was imperative. This new architectural intelligentsia maintained that the full-scale deployment of modern technology sanctioned by the regime to industrialize the building industry and streamline architectural practice demanded the formulation of a commensurate new "materialist" aesthetic portraying architecture as a fundamental symbiosis of technology, utility, and economy. G. Gradov and K. A. Ivanov assumed the lead in proselytizing the essential elements of such

---

[18]The gist of Khrushchev's imperatives for reorganizing the building and architectural enterprise was outlined in his speech to the Conference of Builders and Architects in December 1954. See Khrushchev, *O shirokom vnedrenii industrial'nykh metodov, uludshenii kachestva i snizhenii stoimosti stroitel'stva* [Concerning the Widespread Introduction of Industrial Methods, the Improvement of Quality, and the Lowering of Construction Costs] (Moscow, 1955): for Eng. trans., see *Current Digest of the Soviet Press*, Feb. 9, 1955.

an aesthetic. Gradov argued against perpetuating obsolete classicizing aspects of the socialist realism doctrine. He called for reviving in Soviet architecture a genuine sense of contemporaneity and innovation predicated upon the potentials of contemporary technology.[19] Ivanov underscored the growing notion that architecture was an innate synthesis of technology and art; he asserted that its ultimate aim of providing shelter and an ordered sequence of spaces for continuous functions of human activity distinguished architecture from either pure technology or pure art.[20] Thus architecture succeeded in carving out an independent domain within Soviet culture, while at the same time regaining essential aspects of the technological and functional rationales that had been professed in the twenties. By the early sixties the new materialist aesthetic had gained widespread currency in Soviet architecture, and the Stalinist classical rationale was in turn officially laid to rest.[21]

A gradual exoneration of modern Soviet architecture and a corresponding repudiation of subsequent trends advanced in the Stalinist era accompanied the promulgation of the materialist aesthetic. To be sure, initial efforts to re-assess the historical and current significance of the modern movements proved overly cautious and inconclusive, no doubt reflecting a lingering trepidation at proceeding too precipitously with a full-fledged rehabilitation of Soviet modernism. Selim O. Khan-Magomedov, however, emerged as the steadfast champion of modern Soviet architecture through his appeals for rendering a more objective assessments of its achievements and, subsequently, through an impressive array of publications illuminating significant episodes and personalities of the phenomenon.[22] The solid article and monographic studies

[19] G. Gradov, "Sovetskuiu arkhitekturu na uroven' novykh zadach" [Bringing Soviet Architecture on a level with New Problems], *Arkhitektura SSSR*, no. 2 (1955): 4-8.

[20] K. A. Ivanov, "O materialisticheskom ponimanii prirody i spetsifiki arkhitektury" [Concerning the Materialistic Understanding of the Nature and Specific Character of Architecture], *Arkhitektura SSSR*, no. 10 (1955): 26-32.

[21] The demise of the Stalinist classical rationale was proclaimed by Aleksandr V. Vlasov in his keynote speech to the Third All-Union Congress of Soviet Architects. See Vlasov, "Otchetnyi doklad pravleniia Soiuza arkhitektorov SSSR" [Summary Report of the Administration of the Union of Architects of the USSR], in *Tretii vsesoiuznyi s'ezd sovetskikh arkhitektorov* [Third All-Union Congress of Soviet Architects] ((Moscow, 1962), p. 10-33.

[22] Khan-Magomedov's campaign was launched with an article entitled "Novatorstvo i konservatizm v tvorchestve arkhitektora" [Innovation and Conservatism in the Practice of the Architect], *Voprosy sovremennoi arkhitektury*, no. 1 (1962): 31-48. Two years later, he addressed a conference of Soviet architects, appealing for an objective reassess-ment of the constructivist movement and a recognition of its enormous contributions to Soviet architecture. See Khan-Magomedov, "Traditsii i uroki konstruktivizma" [Traditions and Lessons of Constructivism], *Dekorativnoe iskusstvo SSSR*, no. 9 (1964): 25-29. He has published prolifically on key architects and developments of the Soviet modernist movement.

published by Vigdariia E. Khazanova exemplify the extent to which Soviet architectural scholarship has progressed in the space of a decade.[23]

As may be seen from the above discussion, the highly diverse and often ambivalent attitudes operating in succeeding periods of Soviet architecture permeate the published literature pertaining to its historical and theoretical development from the Russian Revolution to the aftermath of the de-Stalinization campaign in the mid-fifties.

The writing produced in the twenties consists, for the most part, of highly reasoned discourses that, though usually proselytizing the doctrine or cause of a particular modern movement, were nonetheless free from external ideological manipulation. The prolific body of published source material produced in this period remains unsurpassed in the richness of historical evidence it provides on the Soviet modern movements. As the modernist preeminence began systematically to be eroded in the late twenties both from within and from without the architectural community, so the increasingly acrimonious polemic began to dissipate the caliber of critical and theoretical rhetoric.

Material published from the mid-thirties to the latter fifties, its tenor varying in accordance with the policy of the Stalinist regime at any given point in time, presents more of a problem. The chief criticism of the literature produced by even the most reputable of Soviet scholars during this period is that it was subjected to stringent control by the party; the Stalinist regime rejected historical and theoretical findings at variance with prevailing official attitudes and demanded both professional and intellectual support for the implementation of its immediate objectives. Yet, as in the case of writing from other periods, much of the material published in the Stalinist era was produced by leading figures behind the events described. Although considerable scrutiny and discretion must be exercised in interpreting this evidence, it nonetheless provides valuable insights into the operating realities that governed developments in Soviet architecture and life under Stalin.

Since Stalin's death the climate of scholarly inquiry has improved substantially. Dramatic strides have been made to develop an objective

---

[23] Among the most noteworthy of Khazanova's publications are the first two volumes in the Academy of Sciences series: *Iz istorii sovetskoi arkhitektury 1917-1925. Dokumenty i materialy* [From the History of Soviet Architecture 1917-1925. Documents and Materials] (Moscow, 1963); and *Iz istorii sovetskoi arkhitektury 1926-1932. Dokumenty i materialy* [From the History of Soviet Architecture 1926-1932. Documents and Materials] (Moscow, 1970). These two installments exemplify the increased use of archival research and corresponding effort to bring to light the wealth of material that for many years languished in obscurity in Soviet archives. Khazanova also published *Sovetskaia arkhitektura pervykh let Oktiabria, 1917-1925* [Soviet Architecture in the First Years Following October, 1917-1925] (Moscow, 1970), which provides the first solid scholarly treatment both of the modernist episode and of trends that preceded the Revolution.

historiographical record of the country's architecture in general and its modernist episode in particular. Although official censorship still acts occasionally to inhibit the investigation of certain aspects of Soviet architecture deemed sensitive by the regime, contemporary Soviet architectural writing has been marked by a return to a more objective frame of reference. The tone and quality of current argumentation is, for the most part, refreshingly undoctrinaire and yields a far richer and more balanced insight into historical circumstances than was the case in the preceding two decades. As a result, the Western student will, on the whole, discover in the recent flow of Soviet historical and theoretical literature a far more sophisticated and reliable account of Soviet architecture than was ever produced under the inordinately manipulative and self-serving auspices of the Stalinist apparatus.

Scope and Organization of the Bibliography

THE aim of this annotated bibliography is to present a nucleus of those Russian and Western-language publications, chiefly in article and book form, which are particularly relevant to the study of the history and ideology of Soviet architecture from 1917 to 1962. Russian publications have been emphasized because they represent the core of the primary source material at the disposal of Western scholars. Similarly, the bibliography concentrates, as does the literature itself, on the activity contained within the Russian Soviet Federative Socialist Republic (RSFSR), or the heart of European Russia.

CRITERIA FOR INCLUSION

This work does not attempt to provide a comprehensive bibliography for every major area of undertaking in Soviet architecture. Rather, it includes only those titles which relate to the history and ideology of Soviet architecture in one or both of the following ways: 1) the title provides an intrinsic contribution to the understanding of historical developments operating in Soviet architecture in general or of a particular architect, movement, or related phenomenon, and 2) the title derives either historical or theoretical significance from aesthetic debates or trends occuring in the development of Soviet architecture.

Works whose topical treatment of Soviet architecture is more purely technical or specifically professional have not been included unless such works serve to illuminate theoretical or historical problems. The reader seeking such information is advised to consult the bibliographies listed in Section I. In addition, articles simply describing and illustrating projects or buildings have also been omitted unless they treat the circumstances in which the projects were conceived. The reader who is concerned with such accounts will wish to consult the division in Section I listing periodicals, in which every known Soviet architectural journal has been cited.

LOCATION OF MATERIALS

The division on bibliographies and reference aids in Section I may be viewed as a list of basic bibliographic material consulted principally at the Library of

Congress and the New York Public Library. Other libraries whose collections were consulted include the Fine Arts Library at Cornell University, the University of Virginia Library, and the Avery Architectural Library at Columbia University.

Monographs and articles not located at the Library of Congress but clearly identified through cross-references within a wide range of critical literature and bibliographical sources were sought in other libraries in this country, as well as in the British Museum. For those comparatively few titles that could not be located in this manner, but whose existence and prominent role in Soviet scholarly and professional debates was otherwise verified, general descriptive annotations were developed from a cross section of published accounts and reviews in order to assure proper identification and access.

The following Soviet architectural periodicals, available at the Library of Congress, were examined for the entire periods of publicaton: *Akademiia arkhitektury* (**no. 61** below), *Arkhitektura i stroitel'stvo* (**no. 64**), *Arkhitektura Leningrada* (**no. 66**), *Arkhitektura SSSR* (**no. 67**), *Ezhegodnik MAO* (**no. 69**), *Obshchestvo arkhitektorov-khudozhnikov; ezhegodnik (* **no. 71**), *Problemy arkhitektury* (**no. 72**), *S.A.* (**no. 73**), *Sovetskaia arkhitektura* [1931-34] (**no. 74**), *Sovetskaia arkhitektura* [1951–] (**no. 75**), *Stroitel'stvo i arkhitektura Leningrada* (**no. 78**), *Stroitel'stvo i arkhitektura Moskvy* (**no. 79**), *Voprosy sovremennoi arkhitektury* (**no. 81**), and *Voprosy teorii arkhitektury* (**no. 82**). Of the remaining Soviet architectural journals at the Library of Congress, the holdings of *Stroitel'naia promyshlennost'* (**no. 77**) were reviewed primarily for the period 1923-32. The Library of Congress holdings of *Stroitel'stvo Moskvy* (**no. 80**) are sparse, and were therefore supplemented by a survey of the complete holdings at the New York Public Library, primarily for issues from the period 1923-33.

Examination of Soviet serial publications in allied fields, held at the Library of Congress, was generally less comprehensive. However, several serials contained important articles on problems affecting Soviet architecture and were examined more thoroughly. They include *Iskusstvo* [1923-28] (**no. 84**), *Iskusstvo v massy* (**no. 86**), *LEF* (**no. 87**), *Sovetskoe iskusstvo* (**no. 92**), and the *VOKS Bulletin* (**no. 93**).

A number of Western journals were also examined. British journals that contain periodic discussions of Soviet architecture include the *Architect and Building News*, the *Architectural Association Journal, Architectural Design*, the *Architectural Review*, the *RIBA Journal, The Studio*, and *Survey*. American journals provide less rewarding offerings on the subject. The *Architectural Record, Progressive Architecture*, and *Problems of Communism* contain occasional noteworthy articles; on the other hand, publications such as *T-Square* and *The American Architect* devoted a surprising amount of attention to the subject. Several French publications were found to offer significant material on Soviet architecture; these include *L'Architecture d'aujourd'hui*, *L'Architecture vivante*, *L'Art d'aujourd'jui*, and *Cahiers d'art* . Of those German periodicals available for examination, comparatively few treated Soviet architecture, although *Wasmuths Monatshefte für Baukunst* published numerous important articles by Soviet writers during the twenties; other German language periodicals in which cursory examination revealed material on Soviet architecture include *ABC* and the more recent *Deutsche Architektur* and *Der Aufbau*. Italian journals containing occasional descriptive accounts of Soviet architectural activity include *Casabella continuita* and *Rassegna di architettura*. The Mexican architectural journal *Arquitectura* displayed a keen interest in Soviet architecture during the thirties and forties.

Unfortunately, a number of architectural periodicals which may well have provided additional articles on Soviet architecture either are not on deposit in the Library of Congress, are not available in this country, or else simply were not accessible for systematic examination.

BIBLIOGRAPHICAL METHODOLOGY

The bibliographical format employed throughout the present work has, with few modifications, been adapted from the one observed by the Library of Congress[1] and especially the system devised by Dr. Paul L. Horecky, presently Chief and East European Specialist of the Slavic and Central European Division of the Library of Congress, in his two bibliographical guides to Russian and Western-language publications on Russia and the Soviet Union.[2] Entries for the serials in Section I have been adapted in large measure from Rudolf Smit's definitive compendium.[3]

The bibliographical entries include information deemed essential for adequate identification. The annotations are designed generally to evaluate the nature and content of the material and thereby to suggest its relevance to an analytical study of the history and theory of Soviet architecture. Abstracts of principal theses developed in a given work are occasionally summarized

---

[1] U.S. Library of Congress, General Reference and Bibliography Division, Bibliographical Procedures and Styles, *A Manual for Bibliographers in the Library of Congress,* comp. Blanche P. McCrum and Helen D. Jones (Washington, D.C., 1954 [reprinted 1966 with a list of abbreviations]).

[2] Paul L. Horecky, ed., *Basic Russian Publications: A Selected and Annotated Bibliography on Russia and the Soviet Union* (Chicago, 1962); see also his *Russia and the Soviet Union: A Bibliographic Guide to Western Language Publications* (Chicago, 1965).

[3] U.S. Library of Congress, Reference Department, *Half Century of Soviet Serials, 1917-1968, A Bibliography and Union List of Serials Published in the USSR,* comp. Rudolf Smits (2v., Washington, D.C., 1968). This supersedes his earlier work, *Serial Publications of the Soviet Union, 1939-1951.*

when the material is of particular significance to the consideration of the topic at hand. References to additional or supplemental material are provided when the author of the cited work has produced complimentary or auxiliary works. or when useful parallel works are known to exist. Similarly, a title may appear in more than one section or category of the bibliography, underscoring the relevance of the work to the investigation of more than one of the topics herein contained.

To make the bibliography more useful and usable as a research reference aid, the material has been grouped into specialized sections relating both to specific research tools and to the various periods and problems in the development of the history and theory of Soviet architecture. Material within each of these sections is arranged alphabetically. Monographs and articles are organized according to the author's nationality; works by Soviet writers are grouped in one category regardless of the language in which they may have been published. Such a division makes it easier to distinguish between Soviet and non-Soviet points of view. Not least, it provides a more ready access to literature published by Soviet writers, the core of the primary source material contained in this bibliography.

Section I identifies those research tools indispensable to the systematic investigation of source material on the history of Soviet architecture. It includes bibliographical and reference aids published in the Russian and Western languages. Also included is the identification of Russian language scholarly and professional journals of architecture and art that contain significant material pertaining to the history and theory of Soviet architecture. In the case of architectural periodicals, an attempt has been made to cite every known publication that has been and that continues to be published in the RSFSR. The list of journals in the allied fields of the Soviet arts, however, is not comprehensive; it includes only those publications known to provide significant discussion of important problems in the development of Soviet architecture. Similarly, only those Soviet newspapers published by the architectural and allied fields, or which otherwise contain articles of special importance to Soviet architecture, have been identified.

Section II identifies published documents that are basic to the history of Soviet architecture. These documents include both material of a purely architectural nature and official decrees and pronouncements by the Communist Party and the Soviet government setting forth policy for Soviet architecture.

Section III identifies major theoretical works in two primary categories. The first includes works analyzing the Marxist and Soviet systems of aesthetics, as well as official policies that affected the development of Soviet architecture. An understanding of Marxist aesthetics, especially within the framework of Soviet interpretation, is essential in order fully to appreciate many of the underlying schools of thought evident in Soviet architecture. Prime sources for Marxist and Soviet aesthetics are therefore cited, as are major works that interpret and apply these general systems specifically to architectural activity. At the same time, Soviet architecture has been affected profoundly by the purposes and expectations of the Communist Party and the general political and ideological forces within the country. For this reason, works analyzing pronouncements by Lenin and other Soviet leaders and the decrees enacted by the party and government are also cited. The second category within this section includes those works by Soviet architects and scholars having as their central theme, regardless of ideological orientation, either the postulation of a self-sustaining philosophy of architecture or the systematic analysis of architectural phenomena which clearly reflects or derives from a specific theoretical point of view.

Sections IV, V, and VI identify basic source material relating to the major phases and problems within the historical evolution of Soviet architecture. To provide optimum accessibility to the material included here, a distinction was made between writings providing general historical assessments and those concerned with more specific problems affecting the development of Soviet architecture. Section IV contains works surveying the history of Soviet architecture. A work is included in this category if its analysis of a particular period is sufficiently broad or comprehensive to include a substantial discussion of other periods as well. The remaining material is grouped by subsections chronologically according to historical periods. Section V contains material on the architectural movements that existed prior to 1932, inasmuch as they comprised the mainstream of Soviet architectural activity and thus produced the vast majority of literature emanating from this period. Section VI contains material examining the trends in Soviet architecture following the eclipse of modernism in 1932. It is subdivided into major categories according both to directives issued by Party and government officials and to major issues subsequently debated within the Soviet architectural community in the search for a new acceptable Soviet architectural style. These categories have generally been observed in subsequent historical analyses by Soviet and non-Soviet writers alike. Section VII lists writings by or about important Soviet architects. It contains both topical and descriptive material of historical or analytical importance in assessing the architects' individual roles in the development of Soviet architecture. The availability of published material has in great part determined the specific architects included here. Although Kasimir Malevich and Vladimir Tatlin were never architects, writings by and about them have been included because their work proved vital to the postulation of theories of modern Soviet architecture. Likewise, material relating to Nikolai Miliutin, who became an architect only in the forties, has been included because of its direct bearing on architectural affairs during the crucial transitional period in which he was editor of *Sovetskaia arkhitektura* (1931-34).

Transliteration of the Russian Alphabet

THE transliteration of Russian names and places used in the text follows generally the system devised by the Library of Congress, with some minor exceptions. Ligatures used when a single Russian letter has to be rendered by two Latin letters have been eliminated. The Russian letters Я, Ю, and Ц, for example, are rendered Ia rather than I͡a, Iu rather than I͡u, and Ts rather than T͡s. Likewise, accepted English usage has been observed in the spelling of Russian proper names that have obtained widespread currency in Western literature. Thus, *Moskva* is rendered Moscow; *Lisitskii*, as Lissitzky. The English equivalent of the Russian alphabet is:

Russian alphabet	English equivalent	As in	Russian alphabet	English equivalent	As in
А а	A a	*a*h	С с	S s	*si*t
Б б	B b	*be*	Т т	T t	*to*
В в	V v	e*v*er	У у	U u	*roo*t
Г г	G g	*go*	Ф ф	F f	*if*
Д д	D d	*do*	Х х	Kh kh	German a*ch*
Е е	E e	*yet*	Ц ц	Ts ts	ne*ts*
Ж ж	Zh zh	mea*s*ure	Ч ч	Ch ch	*ch*ild
З з	Z z	*z*est	Ш ш	Sh sh	*sh*oe
И и	I i	*see*n	Щ щ	Shch shch	ra*sh-ch*ild
Й й	I i	bo*y*	Ъ ъ	"	Indicates nonpalatization of a preceding consonant
К к	K k	ca*k*e			
Л л	L l	*l*et	Ы ы	Y y	b*u*ild
М м	M m	*m*any	Ь ь	,	Indicates palatization of a preceding consonant
Н н	N n	*n*et			
О о	O o	*ou*ght	Э э	E e	*e*cho
П п	P p	*p*ut	Ю ю	Iu iu	p*u*re
Р р	R r	*r*ing	Я я	Ia ia	*ya*rd

Soviet Architecture, 1917-1962

A Bibliographical Guide to Source Material

I. Bibliographies and Reference Aids

A. BIBLIOGRAPHIES

1. Soviet Publications

a. Architectural

1. Grabar', Igor' E., et al., eds. "Bibliografiia" [Bibliography]. In *Istoriia russkogo iskusstva* [History of Russian Art]. v. 11, Moscow, Izdatel'stvo Akademii nauk SSSR, 1957: p. 601, 613-614; v. 12, Moscow, Izd-vo Akademii nauk SSSR, 1961: p. 559-564; v. 13, Moscow, Izd-vo "Nauka," 1964: p. 373, 381-382.

    V. 11 covers 1917-34; v. 12, 1934-41; v. 13, 1941-45. Each volume provides both monographic and periodical publications on Soviet architecture. Includes sections on general works, individual architects, and categories of buildings and projects according to type.

2. *Iskusstvo vsem—Arkhitektura* [Art for Everyone—Architecture]. Leningrad, Ministerstvo kul'tury RSFSR, 1960. 11 p.

    A popular series of bibliographies on various realms of art that includes the present pamphlet on both prerevolutionary and especially Soviet architecture. Sparse coverage, but contains useful information on contemporary literature. Annotated.

3. Kaganovich, M. "Bibliografiia. Osnovnye izdaniia, vyshedshie v RSFSR v 1926-1932 gg." [Bibliography. Basic Publications Issued in the RSFSR in 1926-1932]. In *Iz istorii sovetskoi arkhitektury 1926-1932. Documenty i materialy (tvorcheskie ob'edineniia)* [From the History of Soviet Architecture 1926-1932: Documents and Materials (Creative Societies)]. Moscow, Izd-vo "Nauka," 1970. p. 175-198.

    Includes an extensive listing of books, arranged by year published, on architectural topics issued during the period covered. Works cover the prerevolutionary period, but emphasis is upon the modern period. Single most important checklist on architectural works published in the period.

4. Khazanova, Vigdariia E. "Osnovnaia literatura po voprosam arkhitek-
    tury" [Basic Literature on Questions of Architecture]. In *Iz
    istorii sovetskoi arkhitektury 1917-1925. Dokumenty i materiialy*
    [From the History of Soviet Architecture 1917-1925. Documents
    and Materials]. K. N. Afanas'ev, ed. Moscow, Izd-vo Akademii
    nauk SSSR, 1963. p. 233-234.
        A useful inclusive listing of basic literature on architecture
    published in the RSFSR 1917-25, including materials dated 1926
    but submitted to the presses in 1925.

5. Koblentz, I. N., and S. A. Rimsky-Korsakov. *Istochniki bibliografii
    stroitel'noi promyshlennosti i arkhitektury* [Sources of Bibliog-
    raphies on the Construction Industry and Architecture]. Moscow,
    Izd-vo Vsesoiuznoi knizhnoi palaty, 1941. 215 p.
        An exhaustive bibliography of bibliographies and materials.
    Provides excellent coverage of prerevolutinary architecture, but is
    sparse for the Soviet period and excludes works on the modernist
    period. A section was added just prior to publication treating
    works on various technical aspects of Russian and Soviet archi-
    tecture.

6. Lavrsky, N. *Ukazatel' knig i statiei po voprosam iskusstva* [Index of
    Books and Articles Pertaining to Questions of Art]. Moscow, Izo
    Narkompros, 1919. 150 p.
        Contains sections on painting, sculpture, and architecture. The
    latter section includes material on both prerevolutionary and
    Soviet architecture. Useful, though little material had yet been
    published on the Soviet period.

7. Leonidov, Ivan. "Sovetskaia arkhitekturnaia kniga za 30 let" [The
    Soviet Architectural Book in 30 Years]. *Arkhitektura SSSR*,
    nos. 17-18, 1947: 97-104.
        An overview of Soviet publications on architecture. Stresses
    general histories of world and Russian architecture and translations
    of architectural classics. Contains few citations of specific works
    relating to Soviet architecture, though useful as an appraisal of the
    nature and extent of Soviet architectural publications for the
    period cited.

8. Mikhailov, B. P. *Architektur der Völker der Sowjetunion.* Berlin, Henschelverlag, 1953. 99 p. illus. For bibliography, see p. 96-99.
    A listing of basic works on Russian and Soviet architecture and titles of the major architectural periodicals. Publications relating to the modern period are not included.

9. *Prospekt knig* [Prospectus of Books]. Moscow, Gosstroiizdat, 1952. 37 p.
    A listing of books on various architectural topics published generally 1948-51. Preponderance of works cited are purely technical in nature; no annotations. Of marginal usefulness.

10. *Russische Kunst: Malerei, Graphik, Architektur, Kunstgewerbe, Theater, und Musik.* Moscow and Leningrad, Gosizdat, 1926. 79 p. illus.
    A catalogue, in German, of recent Soviet publications on the arts. Annotated, with replicas of front cover and/or title pages. Includes few titles on modern Soviet architecture.

11. *Russkie arkhitektory i stroitel'i. Annotirovanyi ukazatel' literatury* [Russian Architects and Builders. An Annotated Index of Literature]. Moscow, Profizdat, 1952. 160 p.
    Coverage of Soviet period is cursory; contains a bibliography of works on a few established Soviet architects, including Fomin, Shchuko, and Shchusev. Also includes sections on Marxist-Leninist classics on city planning and building, as well as on related Party decrees and pronouncements.

12. Sushkevich, P. T. *Izdatel'stvo Akademii arkhitektury SSSR. Annotirovannyi katalog 1934-1944* [Academy of Architecture USSR Press. An Annotated Catalog for 1934-1944]. Moscow, Izd-vo Akademii arkhitektury, 1944, 167 p.
    Covers the first ten years' activity of the publishing house. Major sections include: 1) theory and history of architecture, 2) architecture of the people of the USSR, 3) Soviet architecture, masters of architecture, 4) cities and countries, 5) architectural design, and 6) list of periodicals. A useful guide.

13. Vinograd, Z. D., and N. E. Rogovin. *Bibliografiia po arkhitekture* [Bibliography on Architecture]. Moscow, Izd-vo Akademii arkhitektury, 1940. 196 p.

The first attempt at a comprehensive bibliographical index of
books on architecture in the Russian language after Lavrsky's
Ukazatel'. . . in 1919 (**no. 6**) and Voltsenburg's *Bibliografiia* . . .
in 1923 (**no. 15**).

14.   Vladimirsky, A. *Arkhitekturnaia kniga za XV let* [The Architectural
Book in 15 Years] . Moscow, Izd-vo Akademii arkhitektury, 1949.
433 p.

An annotated catalogue of architectural monographs and
periodicals published by the Academy of Architecture of the
USSR 1933-49. The book is divided into three parts: 1) "Soviet
Architecture," with sections on major buildings, architectural design, city planning, building technology, interior design, and serial
publications; 2) "Architecture of the USSR," with sections on
Russian architecture and the architecture of the national republics;
and 3) "The History and Theory of Architecture," devoted to
foreign architecture. A list of books published from January to
September 1949 is appended.

15.   Voltsenburg, Oskar E. *Bibliografiia izobrazitel'nogo iskusstva* [Biblio-
graphy of the Fine Arts] . Petrograd, "Knizhnyi Ugol," 1923.

Of special value in identifying material relating to the years of
artistic and architectural activity from the turn of the century to
1922. Annotated.

b. General

16.   Academy of Sciences of the USSR. Library. *Bibliografiia izdanii
Akademii nauk SSSR; ezhegodnik* [Bibliography of the Publications of the Academy of Sciences of the USSR; annual] . v. 1+
1956+ Moscow, 1957+

Useful for identifying material relating to Soviet architecture
and allied areas published by the Academy. Entries on this subject
are grouped under the heading "Institut istorii iskusstv" [Institute
of Art History] , the branch of the Academy responsible for
publications pertaining to architecture. An index to entries,
subject, and author is included, as is a list of journals, series, and
serials. Contents of monographs (but not of journals) also indicated.

For Academy publications prior to 1956, consult: *Annotirovannyi katalog izdanii Akademii nauk SSSR, 1934-37* (Moscow,
1938, 278 p.); *Izdaniia Akademii nauk SSSR, bibliograficheskii
ukazatel' 1930-33* (Moscow, 1931-36, 4 v.); *Novye izdaniia*

Akademii nauk SSSR (Leningrad, 1923-37); *Sistematicheskii ukazatel' izdanii Akademii nauk SSSR, 1917-25* (Leningrad, 1925, 127 p.); see also *Katalog izdanii Akademii nauk, 1726-1923* (Petrograd, 1912-24, 3 v.).

17. *Bibliografiia sovetskoi bibliografii* [Bibliography of Soviet Bibliographies]. v. 1+ Moscow, Izd-vo Vsesoiuznoi knizhnoi palaty, 1939+

Issues since 1939 except for 1940-45. A basic research tool listing printed bibliographies with more than thirty titles, either published separately or contained in Soviet books or periodicals; generally useful for identifying sources of material on Soviet architecture.

18. Bodnarskii, Bogdan S. *Bibliografiia russkoi bibliografii; bibliograficheskaia literatura* [Bibliography of Russian Bibliographies; Bibliographical Literature]. Moscow, "Bibliograficheskie Izvestiia," 1918-30, 4 v.

This bibliography covers 1913-25, 1929. Contains separate bibliographies as well as bibliographical lists in books and periodicals; of general use for material on Soviet architecture.

19. *Ezhegodnik knigi SSSR; sistematicheskii ukazatel'* [Annual of Books of the USSR; a Systematic Index]. Moscow, Izd-vo Vsesoiuznoi knizhnoi palaty, 1941+

Issued regularly beginning with the second half of 1941; prior to that, only for 1925-29 and 1935. An annual cumulation of monographs listed in *Knizhnaia letopis'* **(no. 20)**, except for standards, abstracts of dissertations, and similar material. Published in two volumes one covering the humanities and social sciences; the other, natural sciences and technology. A good source.

20. *Knizhnaia letopis'* [Book Annals]. v. 1+ Moscow, Izd-vo Vsesoiuznoi knizhnoi palaty, 1907+

Bibliography in Russian of current books, pamphlets, and, through 1960, abstracts of dissertations published in the USSR in all languages. Published weekly, with a monthly supplemental volume listing government publications and similar matter. A good source for material relating to Soviet architecture.

21. *Letopis' izobrazitel'nogo iskusstva* [Annals of the Fine Arts]. Moscow, Izd-vo Vsesoiuznoi knizhnoi palaty, 1934+ quarterly. Title varies:

1934-38; *Izo letopis'*; 1939-40, *Bibliografiia izobrazitel'nogo iskusstva*; 1942-44, no. 1/2, *Letopis' izobrazitel'nogo iskusstva velikoi otechestvennoi voiny;* 1944, no. 3 – 1966, *Letopis' izobrazitel'nogo iskusstva.*

Coverage of works on Soviet architecture useful through 1940 issues; thereafter, coverage is sporadic.

2. Non-Soviet Publications

a. Architectural

22.   Allen, Robert V. "The Fine Arts." In *Russia and the Soviet Union: A Bibliographic Guide to Western Language Publications*. Paul L. Horecky, ed. Chicago, University of Chicago Press, 1965. p. 377-378.

A guide to some of the leading works in non-Russian languages. Of rather limited scope in the area of Soviet architecture.

23.   "Architecture in the USSR. A Short Bibliography of Books and Periodicals." *RIBA Journal*, 3d ser., v. 48, July 1941: 158.

A brief guide to useful contemporary sources on Soviet architecture, accompanying an article on the same subject.

24.   Baxandall, Lee. *Marxism and Aesthetics. A Selective Annotated Bibliography: Books and Articles in the English Language*. New York, Humanities Press, 1968. 261 p.

A major listing of books and articles dealing with the arts and literature from a Marxist standpoint that are available in English, whether in the original or in translation. Organization is primarily by the author's nationality or language-grouping; the work is subdivided by topics according to artistic categories. Includes a brief section on, and random references to, Soviet architecture; but of far greater importance in presenting the vast scope of literature in the English language dealing with the broad range and interpretation of Marxist aesthetics.

25.   "Bibliografia." *Casabella continuita*, no. 262, April 1962: 63-64.

Of particular value in identifying both Italian works on Soviet architecture and Soviet works translated into Italian.

26. Davidson, Rita. "Planning, Housing, Architecture in the USSR." *Pencil Points*, v. 28, Jan. 1947: 132, 134, 136; v. 28, Feb. 1947: 82, 84, 86, 88.

   Includes pertinent articles drawn largely from wartime American and British professional planning and architectural journals, periodicals, newspapers, and books on deposit at the Regional Planning and Architectural Libraries of Harvard University.

27. De Feo, Vittorio. "Bibliografia." In his *URSS: Architettura 1917-1936*. Rome, Editori Riuniti, 1963. p. 78-80.

   A useful general guide to Italian works on Soviet architecture.

28. Gray, Camilla. "Selected Bibliography" and "Russian Bibliography." In her *The Great Experiment: Russian Art 1863-1922*. New York, Harry Abrams, 1962. p. 297-306.

   Includes citations of work on, or pertinent to, Soviet architecture in the Western and Russian languages

29. Hamilton, George H. "Fine Arts." In *Basic Russian Publications: A Selected and Annotated Bibliography on Russia and the Soviet Union*. Paul L. Horecky, ed. Chicago, University of Chicago Press, 1962. p. 237-244.

   A useful guide to some of the leading works in the Russian language. Emphasis is upon art, and architecture is treated only sporadically. Includes useful entries relating to socialist realism in the arts.

30. Kopp, Anatole. "Bibliographie." In his *Ville et révolution. Architecture et urbanisme soviétiques des années vingt*. Paris, Éditions Anthropos, 1967. p. 270-275.

   A general guide particularly useful for identifying French works. Poor organization; contains numerous errors in citations. Some improvement and additions made in the English translation: see **no. 355**, p. 261-267.

31. Parkins, Maurice Frank. "Bibliography." In his *City Planning in Soviet Russia; with an Interpretative Bibliography*. Chicago, University of Chicago Press, 1953. p. 127-240.

   An annotated list of over 800 available Russian and non-Russian titles dealing with Soviet national planning, city planning, and housing, as well as some of the closely allied subjects, such as architecture, building, cities, geography, population, transportation, and rural reconstruction. Gives a picture of the whole field through a coverage of principal works. The material is arranged by major topics. Preceding some sections is an introduction to the subject and to the treatment of the material. Sections dealing with Soviet architecture are less systematic and comprehensive than those on planning, but the work illuminates much useful material.

32.   Sharp, Dennis. *Sources of Modern Architecture. A Bibliography.* New York, George Wittenborn, 1967. 55 p.
      First appeared as two separate supplements to the *Architectural Association Journal.* Provides the main sources and authoritative supporting material concerned with the modern movement in architecture.
      Lists books and magazine articles, magazines concerned with the modern movement, and biographies of individual architects, with a bibliography of works by and about them. Material on Soviet architecture is very limited.

33.   U.S. Library of Congress. Slavic and Central European Division. *Russia, a Check List Preliminary to a Basic Bibliography of Materials in the Russian Language, Part 3. Fine Arts.* Washington, D.C., 1944. 38 p.
      A mimeographed list of 788 items, some of which relate specifically to architecture, containing citations of some relatively little-known titles. Listings not organized either chronologically or by subject. Less useful for material on Soviet architecture than for material dealing with the transition from the turn of the century to the Revolution of 1917.

34.   Willen, Paul L. "Bibliography." In his "Soviet Architecture in Transformation: A Study in Ideological Manipulation." Master's thesis. Columbia University, 1953. p. 228-239.
      A general list of material used in the preparation of the work. Contains useful information on some of the basic periodicals on Soviet architecture and cites some of the key articles relating to the period 1928-36.

b. General

35.   Horecky, Paul L., ed. *Basic Russian Publications: A Selected and Annotated Bibliography on Russia and the Soviet Union.* Chicago, University of Chicago Press, 1962. 313 p.

A highly useful guide to bibliographies and reference materials on the Soviet Union in the Russian language. Included are general bibliographies and reference books grouped into 15 categories, as well as bibliographies covering 25 specific subject areas, including architecture (see **no. 29**).

36.   ——. *Russia and the Soviet Union: A Bibliographic Guide to Western Language Publications.* Chicago, University of Chicago Press, 1965. 473 p.

A useful guide to bibliographies and reference materials on Russia and the Soviet Union in the West European languages. The work lists general bibliographies and reference books, as well as bibliographies dealing with specific subject areas, including the fine arts (see **no. 22**).

37.   New York Public Library. Slavonic Division. *A Bibliography of Slavonic Bibliography in English.* New York, 1947. 11 p.

Of a total of 132 entries, 69 refer to bibliographies of material about Russia and the Soviet Union, including the arts. Of general usefulness. Reprinted from the *Bulletin of the New York Public Library* for April 1947.

B. CATALOGUES AND SURVEYS OF LIBRARY HOLDINGS

38.   Avery Memorial Architectural Library. *Catalogue of the Avery Memorial Architectural Library.* Columbia University. Boston, G. K. Hall, 1958. 12 v.

Reproduction of the card catalogue of the library, which has one of the most significant holdings in this country on Russian and Soviet architecture. Material on Soviet architecture may be found under the subject heading "Russia–Architecture," with no division between the prerevolutionary and Soviet periods. Material also listed by title and author.

39.   British Museum Department of Printed Books. *General Catalogue of Printed Books.* London, 1965-66. 263 v.

Reproduction of the complete catalogue of the British Museum to the end of 1955. Although the Library has a significant holding on Russian and Soviet architecture, the catalogue provides no conventional listing of this material by subject; access to this material is provided only by author and title.

40. Library of the Graduate School of Design. Harvard University. *Catalogue of the Library of the Graduate School of Design at Harvard University.* Boston, G. K. Hall, 1968. 44 v.

Provides access to 140,000 volumes, pamphlets, bound periodicals, and theses by author, subject, and title under a single alphabetical sequence. Includes material relating to the history of Soviet architecture, under the sections: "Russia" (v. 35), "Akademiia Arkhitektury SSSR" (v. 1), and "Akademiia Stroitel'stva i Arkhitektury SSSR" (v. 1). Bibliographical data for some entries is incomplete.

41. New York Public Library Reference Department. *Dictionary Catalogue of the Slavonic Collection.* Boston, G. K. Hall, 1959. 26 v.

Reproduction of the card catalogue of the Slavonic collection of the New York Public Library, which holds, with the Library of Congress, the most important collection of material on Russian and Soviet architecture in this country. Material on Soviet architecture may be found under the subject heading "Russia–Architecture," with no division between the prerevolutionary and Soviet periods. Access is also provided by title and author.

42. U.S. Library of Congress. Processing Department. *Monthly Index of Russian Accessions.* v. 1+ Washington, D.C., 1948+

A finding list chiefly of Russian-language monographs and periodicals received by the Library of Congress and other American libraries and an index to the contents of Russian-language periodicals received. Especially useful for identifying current accessions on Soviet architecture. A cumulative author, subject, and periodical location index to the first three volumes is available as a separate publication.

43. U.S. Library of Congress. Slavic and Central European Division. *Cyrillic Union Catalog.* Located in the Slavic Room of the Library of Congress.

A card catalog of 708,000 entries in Russian, Ukrainian, Belorussian, Bulgarian, and Serbian reported to the Library of Congress by 185 major research libraries in the United States and Canada up to 1956. A wealth of material on Soviet architecture may be identified by subject, author, and title.

C. PERIODICALS

1. Bibliographies and Lists

a. Soviet Publications

44. Academy of Sciences of the USSR. Institute of Russian Literature. *Periodika po literature i iskusstvu za gody revoliutsii, 1917-1932* [Periodicals on Literature and Art for the Years of the Revolution, 1917-1932]. Comp. K. D. Muratov and ed. S. D. Balukhatov. Leningrad, Izd-vo Akademiia nauk SSSR, 1933. 344 p.

Lists serials published in the USSR in the Russian language from January 1917 to June 1932. Includes serials and newspapers published in the various realms of art, including architecture, as well as bibliographical sources and supplements to newspapers and periodicals. Full bibliographical data is included in majority of instances, including editors of publications. Very useful for providing data on early Soviet architectural serials.

45. Il'insky, Leonid K. *Spisok povremennykh izdanii za 1917-1918 gg.* [List of Serial Publications for 1917-1918]. Petrograd, Voennaia tipografiia, 1919-22. 2 v.

Though not complete, the principal source for periodicals and newspapers published 1917-18, including those few relating to Soviet architecture.

46. Kaganovich, M. "Bibliografiia. Osnovnye izdaniia, vyshedshie v RSFSR v 1926-1932 gg." [Bibliography. Basic Publications Issued in the RSFSR in 1926-1932]. See **no. 3.** p. 179-198.

Includes an extensive list of journal and newspaper articles, arranged by years published, on architectural topics issued by the Soviet press during the period covered. A basic checklist.

47. *Letopis' periodicheskikh izdanii SSSR* [Annals of the Serials of the USSR]. Moscow, Izd-vo Vsesoiuznoi knizhnoi palaty, 1933+

A listing of Soviet periodicals and newspapers current for the respective years published, with brief bibliographical data. Beginning with April 1, 1950, the annual volume was replaced by two annual publications: *Novye, pereimenovannye i prekrativshiesia zhurnaly i gazety* [New, Changed, and Discontinued Journals and Newspapers] and *Trudy, uchenye zapiski, sborniki i drugie prodolzhaiushchiesia izdaniia* [Transactions, Scholarly Communications, and Other Continuing Publications]. Of value in identifying Soviet architectural periodicals and journals.

48. *Periodicheskaia pechat' SSSR, 1917-1949; bibliograficheskii ukazatel'*
[The Periodical Press of the USSR; a Bibliographical Guide].
v. 1+ Moscow, Izd-vo Vsesoiuznoi knizhnoi palaty, 1955+

    A full listing of serial publications, excluding newspapers,
issued during the indicated period; useful in identifying those
relating to Soviet architecture.

b. Non-Soviet Publications

49. Sharp, Dennis. "Select List of Periodicals." In his *Sources of Modern
Architecture. A Bibliography.* See **no. 32.** p. 51.

    An abbreviated list of architectural periodicals concerned with
the modern movement, citing title (with changes noted), place of
publication, and dates of publication. Entries for numerous
periodicals are incomplete, and only one Soviet architectural
periodical is cited.

50. U.S. Library of Congress. Cyrillic Bibliographic Project. *Serial
Publications of the Soviet Union; a Bibliographic Checklist.* 2d ed.
Compiled by Rudolf Smits. Washington, D.C., 1958. 459 p.

    Lists 7,100 publications known to have appeared in the USSR
1939-57. Gives the Library of Congress holdings and call numbers
and indicates other American and Canadian libraries having the
serials. Includes holdings relating to Soviet architecture.

51. U.S. Library of Congress. Reference Department. *Half a Century of
Soviet Serials, 1917-1968. A Bibliography and Union List- of
Serials Published in the USSR.* Compiled by Rudolf Smits. Wash-
ington, D.C., 1968. 2 v.

    A monumental work which provides a bibliography and union
list of all known serial publications, including those on architecture,
appearing in the Soviet Union at regular or irregular intervals since
1917 in all except Oriental languages, except where Russian titles
or contributions may appear. An excellent source. Supersedes the
author's earlier work, *Serial Publications of the Soviet Union,
1939-1951* and all previous lists of Soviet serial publications prepared by the Library of Congress.

2. Indexes to Contents

a. Soviet Publications

52. "Bibliografiia. Izokritika posle postanovleniia TsK ot 23 aprelia
1932 g." [Bibliography. Criticisms of Art Following the Decision
of the Central Committee of the Communist Party, dated April
23, 1932]. *Iskusstvo*, no. 6, 1933: 157-158, 163-164.

Contains a compendium of material published in newspapers and periodicals, both architectural and general, following the resolution by the Central Committee concerning the reorganization of literary and artistic organizations. Included are a section on decrees, resolutions, declarations, and editorials responding to the decree and a section on architecture and other arts. A useful list for this crucial period.

53. *Letopis' gazetnykh statiei* [Annals of Newspaper Articles]. v. 1+ Moscow, Izd-vo Vsesoiuznoi knizhnoi palaty, 1936+ monthly.
Selected bibliography of current articles in large Russian-language newspapers; of some assistance in identifying articles relating to Soviet architecture.

54. *Letopis' zhurnal 'nykh statiei* [Annals of Articles in Journals]. v. 1+ Moscow, Izd-vo Vsesoiuznoi knizhnoi palaty, 1926+ weekly.
Bibliography of current articles and documentary and literary materials in about 1,400 selected Russian-language periodicals; useful in identifying articles relating to Soviet architecture.

55. "Sistematicheskii ukazatel' statei i materialov za 5 let" [Systematic Index to Articles and Materials in 5 Years]. *Arkhitektura SSSR*, No. 7, 1938. A special Supplement.
Provides an index to the contents of the Soviet architectural periodical *Arkhitektura SSSR* from the first issue in July 1933 to July 1938.

56. "Soderzhanie zhurnala *Akademiia arkhitektury* za 1934-1936" [Contents of the Magazine, *Academy of Architecture*, during 1934-1936]. *Akademiia arkhitektury*, no. 6, 1936: 66-67.
Provides an index to the contents of the periodical *Akademiia arkhitektury* from issue nos. 1-2, 1934, to issue no. 6, 1936.

b. Non-Soviet Publications

57. Avery Memorial Architectural Library. *Avery Index to Architectural Periodicals.* 12 v. Boston, G. K. Hall, 1963.
Provides an index to articles on Soviet architecture appearing in selected architectural and related periodicals, under title of "20th Century Architecture—Russia." Certain entries with French titles are attributed incorrectly to a periodical whose title is given in English as *Architecture of the USSR.* This is misleading for the Soviet architectural periodical *Arkhitektura SSSR* (no. 67) has been published only in the Russian language.

58. *Current Digest of the Soviet Press.* v. 1+ New York, Joint Committee
on Slavic Studies, Feb. 1, 1949+ weekly.

A selection of the contents of over 60 major Soviet newspapers
and magazines translated into English in full or objectively condensed. Offers weekly indexes to *Pravda* and *Izvestiia*; quarterly
cumulative indexes also cover the contents of major Soviet serial
publications printed in English, as well as translations appearing
in the journal *Soviet Studies*. Of some use in identifying material
relating to Soviet architecture.

59. Royal Institute of British Architects. *RIBA Annual Review of
Periodical Articles.* v. 1+ London, 1967+

Annual index of some 3,000 articles from approximately 220
architectural, building, and planning journals published in many
languages. Titles of articles published in foreign languages appear
only in English translation. For material relating to the history of
Soviet architecture, see especially the section "Architectural History: 20th Century." Not comprehensive on Soviet architecture
but contains useful citations.

60. U.S. Library of Congress. Processing Department. *Monthly Index of
Russian Accessions.* See **no. 42**

Parts B and C. Part B lists periodicals, with contents (in English
translation only) of selected periodicals through v. 13, no. 4,
July 1960. Part C is an alphabetical subject index to Part A and
selected periodicals in Part B. Of some use in identifying materials
on Soviet architecture.

3. List of Soviet Periodicals

a. Architectural

61. *Akademiia arkhitektury* [Academy of Architecture]. Moscow, 1934-
37. Organ of the All-Union Academy of Architecture. One double
issue 1934; bimonthly 1935-36; 3 issues 1937.

Provides theoretical discussion fostered by official directives
instructing the Soviet architectural community to assimilate the
classical heritage of the past. Includes scholarly papers on the
history of Russian and European classical architecture as a basis
for attempts to derive a new philosophy of Soviet architecture.

62. *Architectural Chronicle.* Moscow, 1944-46. Issued in English by
VOKS, the Society for Cultural Relations with Foreign Countries.

monthly. Title varies: *Soviet Architecture Chronicle, Chronicle of Architecture*. Cover title: *Architecture*.

Propagandizes both contemporary developments in Soviet architecture and current efforts to rebuild the cities and architectural monuments destroyed in World War II.

63. *Arkhitektura* [Architecture] . M. Ia. Ginzburg, editor. Moscow, 1923. Issued by the Moscow Architectural Society. 2 double numbers published, nos. 1/2 and 3/5.

Provides a review of the activity within the Moscow architectural group, including publications of discussions and competitions conducted by the Society.

64. *Arkhitektura i stroitel'stvo* [Architecture and Construction] . Moscow, 1946-50. Official organ of the Committee on Architectural Affairs under the Council of Ministers, USSR, and of the Administration on Architectural Affairs under the Council of Ministers of the RSFSR. Semimonthly 1946; 14 issues 1947; monthly 1948-50. Temporarily supersedes *Arkhitektura SSSR* (no. 67) until the latter's renewal in Nov. 1951.

Provides a review of Soviet architectural practice for the period covered. Especially valuable for illuminating the feverish debates that preceded and followed Zhdanov's criticism of the Soviet arts and the corresponding issuance of decrees by the Central Committee of the Communist Party criticizing the various segments of the Soviet cultural front. Valuable also for articles explaining the purges of leading personalities in Soviet architecture in the postwar period.

65. *Arkhitektura i VKHUTEIN* [Architecture and VKHUTEIN]. Moscow, 1929. Issued by the Moscow VKHUTEIN, or Higher State Artistic-Technological Institute. One issue.

A review of work by the students and faculty of the institute.

66. *Arkhitektura Leningrada* [Architecture of Leningrad] . Leningrad, July 1936-45. Organ of the Leningrad branch of the Union of Soviet Architects. 2 issues 1936; 3 issues 1937; bimonthly 1938-40; 3 issues 1941; publication suspended July 1941-43; one double issue 1944; one issue 1945; publication superseded in Dec. 1946 by *Stroitel'stvo i arkhitektura Leningrada* [Construction and Architecture of Leningrad] (no. 78).

Provides an excellent survey of developments in Leningrad architecture and analytical biographies of its leading architects. Comparatively free of the polemic sometimes evident in the material contained in the journal *Arkhitektura SSSR* for the corresponding period.

67. *Arkhitektura SSSR* [Architecture USSR]. Moscow, July 1933+ Official Organ of the Union of Soviet Architects. Issues 1933-41 called v. 1-9; issues 1942-47 called nos. 1 through 17-18, with with the subtitle *Sbornik* [Collection], and appeared irregularly; publication suspended 1948-October 1951; thereafter, it reappeared under the original title as the official organ of the Union of Soviet Architects, the Academy of Architecture USSR, and the Administration of Architectural Affairs RSFSR. Monthly thereafter.

Began publication after the 1932 decree abolishing individual architectural organizations and providing for the organization of the Union of Soviet Architects; the official professional Soviet architectural journal. From 1933-36, of particular value for articles covering both the numerous arguments against constructivism and other vagaries of modern architecture and the attempts to posit the new tenets for applying socialist realism to Soviet architecture; analysis of current work by Soviet architects is framed in a corresponding polemic. After 1936, the periodical provides an important review of contemporary Soviet architectural practice, including reviews of work by individual architects, historical analyses of developments in Soviet architecture, official proclamations affecting the practice of architecture, and continuing theoretical and ideological discussions of the goals and directions of Soviet architecture.

68. *Arkhitekturnyi arkhiv* [Architectural Archive]. Moscow, 1946+ Organ of the Institute of the History and Theory of Architecture of the Academy of Architecture of the USSR.

Provides collection of documents and material on prerevolutionary Russian and Soviet architecture.

69. *Ezhegodnik MAO* [Yearbook of MAO]. Moscow, 1928-30. Publication of the Moscow Architectural Society. 2 issues; no. 5, 1928, and no. 6, 1930.

Provides excellent survey of designs submitted to the Society's competitions, as well as of selected completed buildings. Excellent plates.

70.   *Izvestiia ASNOVA* [News of ASNOVA (Association of New Architects)]. Moscow, 1926. One issue.

Propagandizes ASNOVA's theoretical positions and provides a survey of work done by its members and followers.

71.   *Obshchestvo arkhitektorov-khudozhnikov; ezhegodnik* [Society of Architects-Artists; Annual]. L. N. Benois, ed. Leningrad. 3 issues, 1928, 1930, and 1935.

Continues the format and objective of its prerevolutionary counterpart. Issues published in 1928 and 1930 stressed projects of modern design.

72.   *Problemy arkhitektury. Sbornik materialov* [Problems of Architecture; a Collection of Materials]. Moscow, 1936-37. Issued by the Academy of Architecture of the USSR. 2 v., 2 parts in each volume.

Scholarly journal; attention devoted equally to problems of prerevolutionary architecture and the Soviet and contemporary periods.

73.   *S. A.* (Sovremennaia arkhitektura) [S. A. (Contemporary Architecture)]. A. A. Vesnin and M. Ia. Ginzburg, eds. Moscow, 1926-30. Bimonthly. Official publication of the Society of Contemporary Architects (OSA). Issued by the Central Administration of Scholarly Institutions, USSR. Last issue no. 6, May 1930; superseded in 1931 by *Sovetskaia arkhitektura* (no. 74).

Chronicles the various stages in the development of Soviet constructivism and the views of its leaders, particularly the theories developed by Moisei Ia. Ginzburg. Propagandized constructivism and functionalism in architecture; condemned classicism, eclecticism, and expressionism; and published those projects and buildings which best expressed the philosophy of constructivism and functionalism in architecture. Also published work of and articles by leading proponents of modern architecture in Western Europe and America.

74.   *Sovetskaia arkhitektura* [Soviet Architecture]. N. A. Miliutin, ed. Moscow, 1931-34. Bimonthly 1931-33; single issue 1934. Organ of the Section of "Sotsrasselenie," the Institute of Housing Construction, the Economic Komacademy, the Sector of Narkompros, and the Central Committee of the Union of Workers of Industrial and Communal Construction. Not to be confused with the periodical issued by the Union of Soviet Architects of the USSR, beginning 1951 (no. 75).

Began publication when all architectural movements except
VOPRA merged into the federative organization VANO. As interim
architectural publication following *S.A.* **(no. 73)** and generally
preceding *Arkhitektura SSSR*, it provides coverage of activity in
the Soviet architectural community for the crucial transitional
period, 1931-33. Of particular value for its articles that deal with
the pros and cons of constructivist and functionalist architecture
and analyze the philosophy and work of each of the architectural
movements; includes theoretical essays attempting to posit Marxist
criteria for a philosophy of Soviet architecture.

75. *Sovetskaia arkhitektura* [Soviet Architecture]. Moscow, 1951+Irregu-
     lar. Official organ of the Union of Architects of the USSR.
         Contains scholarly essays on various aspects of prerevolutionary
     and especially Soviet architecture, including biographical material
     on leading architects and their work.

76. *Sovetskaia arkhitektura; ezhegodnik* [Soviet Architecture; Annual].
     Moscow, 1949+ Issued by the Academy of Architecture of the
     USSR. annual. Issues 1949-55 called v. 1-7.
         Provides a summary, both pictorial and textual, of projects
     and buildings completed within the given year.

77. *Stroitel'naia promyshlennost'* [Construction Industry]. Moscow,
     September 1923+ Organ of the State Committee on Construction
     Affairs of the USSR. Monthly 1923-32; 10 issues 1933; monthly
     1934-35; 18 issues a year 1936-37; monthly beginning 1939.
     Publication suspended Nov-Dec 1930. Title changes: with no. 10,
     1958, becomes *Promyshlennoe stroitel'stvo* [Industrial Construc-
     tion].
         Contains much useful information dealing with various aspects
     of Soviet architecture. Most useful for 1923-33, when used by
     movements and groups other than the constructivists (the OSA)
     to disseminate their doctrines and to propagandize their activity.
     Also useful for evaluating actual technical progress in the con-
     struction industry in relation to the demands posed, first, by
     modern and, subsequently, by the officially prescribed modes of
     traditionally inspired architecture. After 1933, journal becomes
     substantially less concerned with architectural affairs.

78. *Stroitel'stvo i arkhitektura Leningrada* [Construction and Architec-
     ture of Leningrad]. Leningrad, July 1946+ Organ of the Executive
     Committee of the Leningrad City Soviet of Workers' Deputies, the

Leningrad Section of the Union of Architects of the USSR, and the Leningrad Board of the Scientific-Technical Society of the Building Industry of the USSR. 3 unnumbered issues 1946/47, dated July, Nov. 1946, and Oct. 1947; 2 unnumbered issues dated Jan., Feb., and one issue called no. 3(9) in 1948; 2 issues 1949; 3 issues a year 1950-52; quarterly 1953-59; monthly beginning 1960. Title varies: 1946-59 called *Arkhitektura i stroitel'stvo Leningrada* [Architecture and Construction of Leningrad]. Superseded *Arkhitektura Leningrada (*(no. 66).

Provides coverage of professional activity in the Leningrad architectural community, with few historical essays or analyses.

79. *Stroitel'stvo i arkhitektura Moskvy* [Construction and Architecture of Moscow]. Moscow, Nov. 1952+ Issued by the Executive Committee of the Moscow City Soviet. Monthly. Title varies: 1952-59, *Arkhitektura i stroitel'stvo Moskvy.*

Provides coverage of professional activity in the Moscow architectural community and includes occasional historical vignettes on Soviet architecture.

80. *Stroitel'stvo Moskvy* [Construction of Moscow]. Moscow, Sept. 1924-Feb. 1941. The organ of the Presidium of the Moscow Soviet (of Workers, Peasants, and Red Army Deputies). Monthly 1924-34; 18 issues 1935; semimonthly 1936-41. Superseded in 1945 by *Gorodskoe khoziastvo Moskvy* [City Management of Moscow].

Issues prior to 1933 particularly valuable as an active forum for architectural dialogue, the propagation of nonconstructivist views, as well as for general and official architectural criticism and commentary. For 1933-37, useful only as supplement to architectural serials. Subsequent publications became only marginally concerned with developments in architecture, concentrating more on municipal administration.

81. *Voprosy sovremennoi arkhitektury* [Questions of Contemporary Architecture]. Moscow, 1962+ Official scholarly journal of the Institute of Art History under the Ministry of Culture of the USSR and the Academy of Sciences of the USSR.

Contains essays that treat various aspects of Soviet architecture, including historical analyses of particular periods and problems. An excellent source for recent, more objective, and well-documented studies of the early period of modernism in Soviet architecture.

82. *Voprosy teorii arkhitektury* [Questions on the Theory of Architecture].
     Moscow, 1955+ Issued by the Institute of the Theory and History
     of Architecture and Building Technology under the Academy of
     Construction and Architecture of the USSR.
         Scholarly journal which emerged following the Party decree of
     November 4, 1955, concerning the elimination of excesses in
     design and construction and the intensification of theoretical
     work in order to improve the state of Soviet architecture. Pro-
     vides a record of investigations into the theoretical questions of
     Soviet architecture that reflect current assessments of historical
     problems and the formulation of new theories and policies to be
     implemented in Soviet architectural practice and scholarship.
     Especially useful for assessing post-1954 developments.

b. Allied Fields

83. *Dekorativnoe iskusstvo SSSR* [Decorative Art of the USSR]. Mos-
     cow, 1958+ Issued by the Union of Artists of the USSR. Monthly.
         Occasionally provides good articles dealing with personalities
     and issues in Soviet architecture, including those from the earlier
     periods of activity.

84. *Iskusstvo* [Art]. Moscow, 1923-28. Issued by the State Academy of
     Artistic Learning. 4 v. 4 parts each in v. 3-4 (1927-28).
         An excellent record of activities and developments in all the
     various Soviet arts, including architecture.

85. *Iskusstvo* [Art]. Moscow, 1933+ Organ of the Ministry of Culture
     of the USSR. Bimonthly 1933-55; 8 issues a year 1956-57;
     monthly beginning 1958. Publication suspended July 1941-Dec.
     1946.
         Useful for occasional articles providing criticism of, or expressing
     official policy in, Soviet architecture, as well as statements by
     Soviet architects on a variety of problems affecting their work.
     Not to be confused with **no. 84.**

86. *Iskusstvo v massy* [Art to the Masses]. Moscow, April 1929-May
     1932. Official publication of the Russian Association of Artists
     of the Revolution. 8 issues 1929; monthly 1930-31; 10 issues
     1932. Title changed in 1931 to *Za proletarskoe iskusstvo* [For a
     Proletarian Art].
         This official organ of the "proletarian" movement in Soviet
     art provided a forum for the most direct and vituperative criticism

by members of VOPRA of the Society of Contemporary Architects and for debates of the theories of proletarian art as propounded by the Association and its followers.

87. *LEF; zhurnal levogo fronta iskusstv* [LEF; the Magazine of the Left
Front of the Arts]. Vladimir V. Maiakovsky, ed. Moscow, March
1923-25. 4 issues 1923/24; 3 issues 1924/25. Superseded in 1927
by *Novyi LEF* **(no. 90).**
Organ of the early futurist and constructivist movements in
Soviet art and literature which published works relating to all the
arts. An important record of the period.

88. *Literatura i iskusstvo* [Literature and Art]. Moscow, Sept. 1930-31.
Organ of the Institute of Literature, Art, and Language. Monthly.
Superseded in 1932 by *Marksistsko-Leninskoe iskusstvoznanie*
(no. 89).
Contains interesting articles reflecting the growing skepticism
of modern architecture.

89. *Marksistsko-Leninskoe iskusstvoznanie* [Marxist-Leninist Knowledge
of Art]. Moscow, 1932. Issued by the Institute of Literature and
Art of the Communist Academy. 6 issues. Superseded *Literatura
i iskusstvo* **(no. 88).**
References to criticism of modern architecture, within growing
framework of Marxist dialectics.

90. *Novyi LEF* [New LEF]. Moscow, 1927-28. Superseded *LEF; zhurnal
levogo fronta iskusstv* [LEF; the Magazine of the Left Front of
the Arts] **(no. 87).**
Continued the program of its precursor, though of less direct
relevance to Soviet architecture.

91. *Pechat'i revoliutsia* [The Press and the Revolution]. A. V. Lunacharsky
and V. Polonsky, et al., eds. Moscow, May 1921-June 1930. 3
issues 1921; 5 issues 1922, called nos. 1-2 (5), 6-8; 7 issues 1923;
6 issues 1924; 8 issues a year 1925-27; monthly 1928-30. Superseded in Sept. 1930 by *Literatura i iskusstvo* **(no. 88).**
A journal of art criticism with reviews of literary and artistic
works and personalities, including those relating to Soviet architecture.

92.   *Sovetskoe iskusstvo* [Soviet Art] . Moscow, April 1925-28. Issued by
      the Main Administration on Artistic Affairs of the RSFSR. 9
      issues 1925; 10 issues 1926; 8 issues 1927; 7 issues 1928. Super-
      sedes *Khudozhnik i zritel'*. Superseded in 1929 by *Iskusstvo*
      (Moscow, 1929, 8 issues in all).
         Contains several important articles, including those by N. V.
      Dokuchaev, ASNOVA polemicist.

93.   *VOKS Bulletin.* Moscow, 1930-56. Issued by the "Vsesoiuznoe
      obshchestvo kul'turnoi sviazi s zagranitsei" [The All-Union Society
      for Cultural Relations with Foreign Countries] . Monthly 1930-
      31; 6 numbered issues and one unnumbered issue 1932; 10 issues
      1933-34. No data available on 1935-38. 3 unnumbered issues
      dated Jan.-March and 3 issues called nos. 4/5-6 in 1939; one
      unnumbered issue dated Jan./Feb. 1941; 8 issues 1942; monthly
      1943-45; bimonthly 1946; 1947-52, issues are numbered con-
      secutively 51-77; bimonthly 1953-55; 10 issues 1956. Title varies:
      VOKS; Socialist Construction in the USSR; 1934, nos. 7/8-9/10,
      VOKS Illustrated Almanac. Superseded in 1957 by *Culture and
      Life.*
         Contains occasional articles on Soviet architecture.

D. SOVIET NEWSPAPERS

1. Architectural and Related

94.   *Arkhitekturnaia gazeta* [Architectural Newspaper] . Moscow, Jan. 1,
      1935-39. 6 times per month. Organ of the Administration of the
      Union of Soviet Architects. As of March 1, 1939, published
      jointly with *Stroitel'nyi rabochii* under the title *Stroitel'naia
      gazeta* (no. 95).
         Provides a chronicle of daily events and developments within,
      or affecting directly, the Soviet architectural community. In-
      cludes articles and statements by Soviet architects.

95.   *Stroitel'naia gazeta* [Construction Newspaper] . Moscow, March 1,
      1939+ Superseded *Arkhitekturnaia gazeta* (no. 94).
         Continuation of format and objectives of its precursor (no. 94).

2. Allied Fields

96.   *Literaturnaia gazeta* [Literary Newspaper] . Moscow, 1929+ Organ
      of the Administration of Soviet Writers of the USSR.Daily. From
      Jan. 6, 1942-Nov. 1944, published jointly with *Sovetskoe iskusstvo*
      (no. 97) under the title *Literatura i iskusstvo* [Literature and Art] .
      Resumed publication under original title Nov. 7, 1944.

Contains dialogue on the nature and direction of the Soviet arts, with occasional specific references to developments in Soviet architecture.

97. *Sovetskoe iskusstvo* [Soviet Art]. Moscow, 1931+ Organ of the Ministry of Cinematography and the Committee on Art Affairs under the Council of Ministers of the USSR. Irregular. From Jan. 6, 1942-Nov. 1944, published jointly with *Literaturnaia gazeta* (no. 96) under the title *Literatura i iskusstvo* [Literature and Art].
Provides occasional articles on official views and discussions affecting developments in Soviet architecture.

3. General

98. *Izvestiia* [News]. Organ of the Presidium of the Supreme Council of the USSR. Petrograd, Feb. 28, 1917+ (with no. 46, 1918, transferred to Moscow). Daily.
Contains official proclamations and statements giving the government's position on matters affecting Soviet architecture, as well as reports on various problems and developments in the Soviet architectural community.

99. *Pravda* [Truth]. Organ of the Central Committee of the Communist Party of the Soviet Union. March 5, 1917-March 1918, published in Petrograd; thereafter in Moscow. Daily.
Contains articles reflecting the Party's position and attitude on matters affecting Soviet architecture. Includes reports on various current problems and developments in the architectural community.

100. *Trud* [Labor]. Organ of the All-Union Central Council of Labor Unions. Moscow, Feb. 19, 1921+ Daily.
Occasionally contains reports on various current problems and developments in Soviet architecture.

101. *Vecherniaia Moskva* [Evening Moscow]. Moscow, City Committee of the Communist Party of the Soviet Union and the Moscow Soviet, 1923+ Daily.
Contains reports on various current problems and developments in Soviet architecture.

E. ENCYCLOPEDIAS AND HANDBOOKS

1. Soviet Publications

102. *Bol'shaia sovetskaia entsiklopediia* [Great Soviet Encyclopedia]. 2d
      ed. S. I. Vavilov, chief ed. Moscow, Izd-vo Bol'shaia sovetskaia
      entsiklopediia, 1950-58. 51 v. illus.
         The basic encyclopedia of the USSR, which contains reference
      and biographical material, with frequent bibliographical references,
      useful to the study of Soviet architecture under "Architecture,
      RSFSR," "Architecture," and names of individual architects, etc.
      V. 50 contains general information on the culture and architecture
      of the Soviet Union. The first edition (1926-47; 65 v.; O. Iu.
      Schmidt, chief ed.) still retains its independent reference value
      and is useful for comparison with the second edition to determine
      the changes in policy and/or ideology.

103. Kaufman, Isaak M. *Russkie biograficheskie i bibliograficheskie
      slovari* [Russian Biographical and Bibliographical Dictionaries].
      Moscow, Kul'tprosvetizdat, 1955. 751 p.
         An important tool for biographical and bibliographical research
      that lists material chronologically under subject headings. Section
      on architecture contains useful material on the Soviet, as well as
      the prerevolutionary period.

104. *Malaia sovetskaia entsiklopediia* [Small Soviet Encyclopedia]. 3d ed.
      B. A. Vvedenskii, chief ed. Moscow, Izd-vo Bol'shaia sovetskaia
      entsiklopediia, 1958-61. 10 v. illus. 1st ed. 1928-31, 10 v.; 2d ed.
      1933-47, 11 v.
         Provides concise encyclopedic information useful to the study
      of Soviet architecture, with fewer discrepancies in date of infor-
      mation and in interpretation than the *Great Soviet Encyclopedia*
      (no. 102).

2. Non-Soviet Publications

a. Architectural

105. *Dictionnaire universel de l'art et des artistes.* Paris, Ferrand Hazan,
      1967. 3 v.
         A standard encyclopedia format provides synoptic information
      on the major styles of art and architecture, as well as biographical
      material on major personalities; moderate coverage of Soviet
      architecture.

106. *Encyclopedia of Modern Architecture.* Gerd Hatje, ed. New York, Harry Abrams, 1964. 336 p. illus.

  Contains generally useful reference and biographical material relating to modern architecture. Has a poor summary under "Soviet architecture," a superficial examination under "Constructivism," and a few brief biographies of Soviet architects and artists.

107. *Encyclopedia of World Art.* Prepared under the guidance and supervision of the Instituto per la Collaborazione Culturale. New York, McGraw-Hill, 1959-67. 15 v.

  A systematic and inclusive collection of exhaustive monographic studies prepared through a broad international collaboration of scholars. Material is prepared to present a major historical synthesis covering the arts of all periods and countries. The comprehensive study on the Soviet Union provides a good synopsis of Soviet architecture in all the major republics of the USSR. Divided by periods, with a good bibliography (see v. 14, p. 466-584). V. 15 serves as an index to the entire set.

108. *Larousse Encyclopedia of Modern Art.* Rene Huyghe, ed. London, P. Hamlyn, 1965. 444 p. illus.

  An encyclopedic guide to modern art—painting, sculpture, architecture, and the minor arts; contains useful information on the Soviet experience.

109. *McGraw-Hill Dictionary of Art.* Bernard S. Myers, ed. New York, McGraw-Hill, 1969. 5 v.

  A ready reference survey of the three-dimensional arts which provides biographies of major personalities as well as substantial articles on styles, periods, cities, buildings, museums, and definitions. A fair number of entries on Soviet architecture may be found under these categories. No index.

110. *Wasmuth Lexikon der Baukunst.* Berlin, Ernst Wasmuth, 1929-37. 5 v.

  An encyclopedia of architectural styles and personalities of major periods and countries. A brief survey of Soviet architecture is provided (see v. 5, p. 481-485).

b. General

111.   Institute for the Study of the USSR, Munich. *Biographic Directory of the USSR*. Wladimir S. Merzalow, ed. New York, Scarecrow Press, 1958. 782 p.

A biographical directory of contemporary Soviet personalities, including architects. Lists information on careers, published works, and major buildings in highly abbreviated fashion. Especially useful for data on individuals comparatively obscure in the mainstream of developments in Soviet architecture and for older generations of architects still alive at the time.

112.   Osteuropa-Institut, Munich. *Sowjetbuch*. 2d ed. Hans Koch, ed. Cologne, Deutsche Industrieverlags-Gesellschaft, 1958. 687 p.

A book of general and biographical information on the USSR prepared by German specialists. Contains essays on principal sectors of Soviet life, rosters of leading Party, government, and cultural officials, a 60-page biographical dictionary, and a good bibliography of Western European literature on the USSR. Includes some material under these categories relating to Soviet architecture.

113.   Utechin, Sergei V., ed. *Everyman's Concise Encyclopedia of Russia*. New York, Dutton, 1961. 623 p. illus.

In dictionary form, the work is of substantial reference usefulness for entries on Soviet architecture, allied arts, and cultural affairs, as well as for substantial biographical material on a number of important personalities. Some entries supply bibliographic references.

114.   *Who's Who in Soviet Social Sciences, Humanities, Art, and Government*. Comp. Ina Telberg. New York, Telberg Book Co., 1961. 147 p.

Biographical data on 700 persons, based upon information contained in the third edition of the *Malaia sovetskaia entsiklopediia* (**no. 104**). A useful source of information on current personalities in Soviet architecture, containing frequent bibliographical references to the works of those listed.

115.   *Who's Who in the USSR, 1961/1962*. Heinrich E. Schultz and Stephen S. Taylor, eds. Montreal, Intercontinental Book and Publishing Co., 1962. 963 p.

Expands, though does not completely supersede, **no. 114.**

F. OTHER REFERENCE TOOLS

116.   U.S. Library of Congress. Reference Department. *Russian Abbreviations: a Selective List.* 2d ed., revised and expanded. Comp. Alexander Rosenberg. Washington, D.C., 1957. 513 p.

An alphabetical list of Russian abbreviations, giving the words which they represent in full, together with English translations. Highly useful in deciphering the innumerable abbreviations employed in official Soviet terminology in the realm of architecture and planning.

G. HISTORIOGRAPHY AND SCHOLARSHIP

1. In the Soviet Union

117.   Academy of Architecture of the USSR. *Desiat' let Akademii arkhitektury SSSR* [Ten Years of the Academy of Architecture of the USSR]. Moscow, Izd-vo Akademii arkhitektury, 1944. 99 p.

A collection of essays by officials of the Academy, treating the history and activities of each of the institutes within the Academy. Includes a statement by David E. Arkin, director of the Cabinet on the Theory and History of Architecture, assessing the work of his department and projecting the work planned for the future (see p. 63-68). Also appended are lists of the publications by the Academy and its members for the period covered.

118.   Afanas'ev, K. N. "Ot redaktora" [From the Editor]. In *Iz istorii sovetskoi arkhitektury, 1917-1925 gg.* [From the History of Soviet Architecture, 1917-1925]. See **no. 138.** p. 5-6.

Speaks of the insufficiency of available general and pictorial material and documents relating to Soviet architecture. Points out that archives are insufficiently inventoried and indexed to provide adequate knowledge of, or access to, their holdings. Identifies some of the basic Soviet works dealing with the history of Soviet architecture.

119.   Arkin, David E., and Nikolai I. Brunov. *O rabotakh po istorii russkoi arkhitektury* [Concerning Work of the History of Russian Architecture]. Moscow, Izd-vo Akademii arkhitektury SSSR, 1946. 29 p.

Speech delivered at the 7th session of the Academy of Architecture of the USSR. A summary of the scholarship thus far undertaken by the Academy on the study of Russian architecture. Includes a brief review of work undertaken and planned on the Soviet period (see p. 29).

120.   Bylinkin, N. P. "Razvitie arkhitekturnoi nauki v SSSR" [Development
       of Architectural Scholarship in the USSR]. In *Stroitel'stvo v SSSR,
       1917-1957* [Building in the USSR, 1917-1957]. See **no. 228**.
       p. 713-749.
           The only known available competent introduction to the
       historiography and scholarship on various aspects of architecture
       and planning from the beginning of the twentieth century to
       1957. Interpretations reflect contemporary official thought. A
       highly useful work.

121.   ——. "O sostoianii zadachakh nauki v oblasti teorii i istorii arkhitek-
       tury" [Concerning the Problems of Scholarship in the Realm of
       the Theory and History of Architecture]. *Voprosy teorii arkhi-
       tektury*, v. 1, 1955: 5-24.
           A general survey of Soviet architectural scholarship. Concludes
       that Tsapenko's *O realisticheskikh osnovakh . . .* (**no. 233**) and
       K. K. Lagutin's *Arkhitekturnyi obraz . . .* (**no. 212**) remain the
       only significant works on the theory of Soviet architecture.

122.   Ivanov, K. A. "Osnovnye trebovaniia k sovetskoi arkhitekture na
       novom etape ee razvitiia" [Basic Requirements of Soviet Archi-
       tecture at the New Stage of Its Development]. *Voprosy teorii
       arkhitektury,* v. 1, 1955: 25-47.
           Provides a review of a number of important works by archi-
       tectural scholars, as well as vital decrees and pronouncements on
       architecture in order to arrive at a systematic framework of
       historical context. Also contains excellent references to comparable
       material from earlier periods to reinforce the analysis of existing
       scholarship and provides a current interpretation of these works.
       A highly useful source.

123.   Kroga, Irzhi (Kroha, Jiři). "Razvitie arkhitekturnoi mysli v sovetskom
       zodchestve" [Development of Architectural Thought in Soviet
       Architecture]. *Arkhitektura SSSR*, no. 1, 1968: 55-58.
           A concise, objective analysis of developments in modern Soviet
       architecture by a prominent Czech architect; outlines those areas
       most in need of investigation by historians and theoreticians to
       clarify the history of this period of architectural ferment. Reflects
       the current revival of an objective interest by Soviet scholars in
       this period. An excellent source.

124. Matsa, Ivan L. "Rabota komissii po istorii sovetskoi arkhitektury" [Work of the Commission on the History of Soviet Architecture]. In *Problemy arkhitektury. Sbornik materialov* [Problems of Architecture. A Collection of Materials]. v. 2, book 1. Moscow, Izd-vo Akademii arkhitektury, 1937. p. 39-42.

   Outlines the method and scope for beginning the preparation of a history of Soviet architecture, while alluding to the general problems involved with the insufficiency and disarray of existing material. Included in the preliminary plan were the decrees of the Party and the regime relating to architecture, pronouncements by leaders of the Party and the regime, the platforms of the various Soviet architectural organizations, a chronology of important events, and material relating to city planning and the construction of new cities. Unfortunately, the particular work proposed herein seems never to have been produced, though subsequent works have, in some measure, appropriated parts of the general scheme.

125. ——. "Vstupitel'noe slovo" [Introductory Remarks]. *Akademiia arkhitektury*, nos. 1-2, 1934: 7-8.

   Remarks delivered to the First Session of the Cabinet of the Theory and History of Architecture of the Academy of Architecture in June 1934. Matsa's comments outline generally the scope and function then foreseen for the study of the history and theory of architecture, including the application of Marxist-Leninist dogma to this work, and project the role of the Cabinet in the production and supervision of such work.

126. "Na vtorom rasshirennom plenume vsesoiuznogo orgkomiteta SSA" [At the Second Expanded Plenum of the All-Union Organizing Committee of the Union of Soviet Architects]. *Arkhitektura SSSR*, no. 12, 1935: 60.

   A synopsis of the plenum held on October 26-29, 1935, in Moscow. Includes a general critique of architectural historians, theoreticians, and others speaking out on theoretical questions of Soviet architecture.

126a. "O edinstve khudozhestvennoi kul'tury" [On the Unity of Artistic Culture]. *Dekorativnoe iskusstvo SSSR*, no. 1, 1967: 2-5.

   Proceedings of a round-table discussion among critics, historians, and theoreticians organized by the editorial board of the journal to discuss current issues in the theory of Soviet architecture and art. Participants included M. F. Ladur, editor of the journal, Ivan L. Matsa, G. A. Nedoshivin, B. I Shragin, A. I. Mikhailov, Selim O. Khan-Magomedov, E. A. Rozenblum, and L. N. Pazhitnov. An excellent commentary on the current state of Soviet architectural criticism and historiography.

The second part of the proceedings published as "O khudozhest-vennoi kul'ture 20-kh godov" [On the Artistic Culture of the Twenties], *Dekorativnoe iskusstvo SSSR*, no. 2, 1967: 29-31.

127.   "Organizatsiia rabot po sostavleniiu istorii sovetskoi arkhitektury" [Organization of Work on the Compilation of the History of Soviet Architecture]. *Arkhitektura SSSR*, no. 8, 1934: 68.

A plan for compiling a history of Soviet architecture as outlined by Prof. G. M. Ludwig, secretary of the Academy of Architecture. Notes the immense problems of preserving and compiling documents on Soviet architecture; identifies problems with documents related to specific projects.

128.   Peremyslov, A. "Ideolog kozmopolitizma v arkhitekture D. Arkin" [Ideologue of Cosmopolitanism in Architecture, D. Arkin]. *Arkhitektura i stroitel'stvo*, no. 3, 1949: 6-9.

In December 1947 the Architectural Society of Moscow criticized the "antipatriotic acts" of David Arkin. As secretary of the Union of Soviet Architects, he had prepared an article for the British journal *Architectural Review* (no. 454), for which he is charged with having written anti-Soviet propaganda. The entire range of his scholarly work is also brought to task as representative of an "unexemplary" behavior and attitude. He is criticized for having produced the monograph *Arkhitektura sovremennogo zapada* [Architecture of the Contemporary West] (Moscow, Gosizoizdat, 1932), containing essays on the philosophy and work of Le Corbusier, Frank Lloyd Wright, Bruno Taut, Walter Gropius, and other modern Western architects. Specifically, he is condemned for allegedly having used his high office to propagandize "cosmopolitanism" and "Americanism" in Soviet architecture and art.

129.   "Protiv formalizma v arkhitekturnoi praktike i nauke" [Against Formalism in Architectural Practice and Scholarship]. *Arkhitektura SSSR*, no. 10, 1954: 37-40.

A comprehensive account of recent meetings of the Academy of Architecture that provided a forum for intensive self-criticism of past errors by architects and administrators of the Academy, in response to the decree by the 19th Congress of the Communist

Party ordering the elimination of excesses in design and construction and a corresponding increase in the use of precast concrete elements. The Academy was under attack for failing to formulate a sound policy for Soviet architecture and for negating the technical aspects of architectural practice. A. G. Mordvinov, president of the Academy, was attacked in his capacity both as an architect and as chief administrator of the Academy for stressing the artistic aspect of Soviet architecture, at the expense of structural and technological considerations. B. Mikhailov observed that there has existed a struggle in Soviet architecture between realism and formalism, the latter including constructivism and its companion modern movement, but presently including also the trend of pseudo-classicism. An illuminating source documenting the extent of change in the official attitudes and demands on Soviet architecture.

130. "Razoblachit' nositelei burzhuaznogo kozmopolitizma i estestva v arkhitekturnoi nauke i kritike" [Exposing the Carriers of Bourgeois Cosmopolitanism and Aestheticism in Architectural Scholarship and Criticism]. *Arkhitektura i stroitel'stvo*, no. 2, 1949: 7-10.

Provides an excellent insight into the official interpretation at this time of all preceding scholarship and criticism on Soviet architecture, citing specific groups and personalities and criticizing their work.

131. Rzianin, M. I. "Uludshit' rabotu Nauchno-issledovatel'skogo instituta istorii i teorii arkhitektury Akademii arkhitektury SSSR" [For an Improvement in the Work of the Scholarly Research Institute of the History and Theory of Architecture in the Academy of Architecture of the USSR]. *Arkhitektura i stroitel'stvo*, no. 3, 1949: 4-5.

Contends that the Marxist development of theoretical questions in Soviet architecture and the problems of assimilating the architectural heritage were disregarded in the Institute because Karo Alabian, vice-president of the Academy of Architecture, did not maintain the Party line in architecture, supported a group of "bourgeois cosmopolitans" within the Academy, generated an incorrect direction for research work, and concealed criticism of the insufficiency in the work of the Academy. Condemns the insufficient struggle for ideology and party spirit within the ranks of the Academy, cites several works by established scholars to support these accusations, and admonishes the Academy to improve the quality of its work by eliminating all vestiges of cosmopolitanism, aesthetic formalism, and bourgeois objectivism

132.   Shaposhnikov, Iu. "Protiv lozhnogo istorizma v nauchnykh issledo-
       vaniakh" [Against False Historicism in Scholarly Research].
       Arkhitektura i stroitel'stvo, no. 2, 1949: 11-13.
          Contends that the Institutes of the History and Theory of
       Architecture and of City Planning under the Academy of Archi-
       tecture, as well as architectural historians, critics, and authors of
       doctoral theses in architecture and city planning, are devoting too
       much study to the history of ancient and foreign architecture at
       the expense of attention to the problems of contemporary Soviet
       architecture.

2. In the United States

133.   Dossick, Jesse J. *Doctoral Research on Russia and the Soviet Union.*
       New York, New York University Press, 1960. 248 p.
          A bibliography of 960 American, British, and Canadian disser-
       tations, arranged by fields. Section on architecture, p. 33-36,
       reveals that no doctoral dissertations were completed on Soviet
       architecture and refers to Paul Willen's observations on the state
       of American research on Soviet architecture (see **no. 136**).

134.   ——. "Doctoral Dissertations on Russia, the Soviet Union, and
       Eastern Europe Accepted by American, Canadian, and British
       Universities, 1969-1970." *Slavic Review,* v. 29, Dec. 1970: 766-
       776.
          Observes that no dissertations on Russian and Soviet architec-
       ture have yet been produced.

135.   Starr, S. Frederick. "Writings from the 1960s on the Modern
       Movement in Russia." *Journal of the Society of Architectural
       Historians,* v. 30, May 1971: 170-178.
          An overview of recent research and publications, Soviet and
       Western, on the modern movements in Soviet architecture and
       planning. Focuses upon several areas, including the arts and crafts
       and the classical revival, Russian traditions of planning and Wes-
       tern influences, relation of modern movements to the visual arts,
       ideologies of the modern movements, professional considerations,
       analysis of individual works and competition projects, and causes
       of the movements' decline. Contains useful material and insights.

136.   Willen, Paul. "Architecture and the Minor Arts." In *American
       Research on Russia.* Harold H. Fisher, ed. Bloomington, Indiana
       University Press, 1959. p. 164-175.

A useful though highly generalized survey of American research on Soviet architecture to date, suggesting general areas of inquiry and approaches to the study of topics hitherto insufficiently explored. Bibliographical references are included in "Notes" (p. 231-232).

137.   ——. "Architecture in the Soviet Union (A Report for the Use of Specialists in the Field of Architecture Planning to Visit the Soviet Union)." New York, Institute of International Education, 1963. Mimeographed. 14 p.

A general overview of Soviet architecture and planning from 1917 to 1962. Treats the historical background, the professional organization, architectural education, housing, construction techniques, city planning, and American scholarship on Soviet architecture (adapted from his earlier study, **no. 136**).

II. Documents

A. ARCHITECTURAL

138. Khazanova, Vigdariia E. *Iz istorii sovetskoi arkhitektury 1917-1925: Dokumenty i materialy* [From the History of Soviet Architecture 1917-1925: Documents and Materials]. K. N. Afanas'ev, ed. Moscow, Izd-vo Akademii nauk SSSR, 1963. 250 p. illus.

First attempt by Soviet scholars to compile historical and archival material on Soviet architecture. Contains valuable material, including little-known and heretofore unpublished sources relating to Soviet architecture 1917-25. Includes a list of the major architectural institutions and literature published in the RSFSR in 1917-25 and a list of abbreviations of words and titles.

139. ——. *Iz istorii sovetskoi arkhitektury 1926-1932. Documenty i materialy (tvorcheskie ob'edineniia)* [From the History of Soviet Architecture 1926-1932: Documents and Materials (Creative Societies)]. K. N. Afanas'ev, ed. Moscow, Izd-vo "Nauka," 1970. 211 p. illus.

The second in a series of published documents relating to the history of Soviet architecture (see **138**). Focuses on the theoretical problems, movements, and professional organizations in Soviet architecture in 1926-32. Contents developed from Soviet archives and from articles published in the Soviet press during that time. A bibliographical guide to basic literature published on the subject within the given period is appended (see **no. 3**). The single most important collections of documents and materials relating to modern architecture in the Soviet Union. Highly recommended.

140. Matsa, Ivan L., ed. *Sovetskoe iskusstvo za 15 let. Materialy i dokumentatsiia* [Soviet Art in Fifteen Years. Materials and Documentation]. Moscow and Leningrad, Ogiz-izogiz, 1933. 662 p.

An important collection of documents and materials relating to every realm of activity in the Soviet arts in 1917-32. Divided into three periods: 1) heroic communism, 2) rehabilitation, and 3) reconstruction. Important material on Soviet architecture contained in section 3, p. 521-552; includes declarations of ASNOVA, ARU, OSA, Union of Young Architects, and VOPRA, as well as important documents and decrees relating to the competition of the Palace of Soviets and other important competitions and developments in Soviet architecture. A valuable tool.

141. Union of Architects of the USSR. *Vtoroi vsesoiuznyi s'ezd sovetskikh arkhitektorov* [Second All-Union Congress of Soviet Architects]. Moscow, Gosstroiizdat, 1956. 394 p.

An abridged stenographic account of the speeches and proceedings of the congress held in Moscow in 1955. Provides valuable insight into contemporary views on the problems of socialist realism and classical decoration in Soviet architecture.

142. ——. *Tretii vsesoiuznyi s'ezd sovetskikh arkhitektorov* [Third All-Union Congress of Soviet Architects]. Moscow, Gosstroiizdat, 1962. 183 p.

An abridged stenographic account of the proceedings and speeches of the congress held in Moscow, May 18-20, 1961. Provides a valuable record of changes in emphasis and official outlook in Soviet architecture.

143. *Za sotsialisticheskuiu arkhitekturu* [For a Socialist Architecture]. Moscow, Izd-vo Akademii arkhitektury, 1937. 56 p.

A collection of vital Party pronouncements on Soviet architecture compiled for the delegates to the First All-Union Congress of Architects held in Moscow in 1937. Includes 1) the December 30, 1922, speech by S. M. Kirov on the construction of the Palace of Soviets; 2) the resolution of February 28, 1932, concerning the final design of the Palace of Soviets; 3) the Party resolution of April 23, 1932, concerning the reorganization of literary and artistic organizations; 4) the resolution of May 10, 1933, on the construction of the Palace of Soviets; 5) the Party resolution of October 14, 1933, concerning architectural education; 6) the Party resolution of July 10, 1935, on the general plan for the reconstruction of Moscow; 7) L. M. Kaganovich's speech of May 14, 1935, on the significance of the Moscow Metro; 8) the Party resolution of February 11, 1936, on improving construction and reducing its cost; and 9) the account of the All-Union Congress of Soviet Architects as contained in *Pravda* on June 15, 1937, and in *Izvestiia* on June 16, 1937.

B. PARTY DECREES AND PRONOUNCEMENTS

1. General Collections

144.   The Communist Party of the Soviet Union. Central Committee. *O Partiinoi i sovetskoi pechati: sbornik dokumentov* [On the Party and the Soviet Press: A Collection of Documents]. Moscow, Izd-vo Pravda, 1954. 697 p.

Includes decisions of the congresses and conferences of the Communist Party, important directives, instructions and letters of the Party Central Committee, and decrees and ordinances of the Soviet government that, through the years, have affected Soviet architecture. Of great use.

145.   *Kommunisticheskaia partiia Sovetskogo Soiuza v rezoliutsiakh i resheniakh s'ezdov, konferentsii i plenumov TsK* [Communist Party of the Soviet Union in the Decisions of the Congresses, Conferences, and Plenums of the Central Committee]. 7th ed. Moscow, Gospolitizdat, 1953-60. 4 v. (v. 1, 1898-1925, 252 p.; v. 2, 1925-53, 1204 p.; v. 3, 1930-54, 691 p.; v. 4, 1954-60, 639 p.).

The official edition of resolutions of Party congresses and conferences and of some of the resolutions of the Central Committee. Useful for documenting resolutions affecting Soviet architecture, though not all are included here.

2. Individual Decrees and Pronouncements

146.   "Iunskii Plenum TsK VKP(b) 'Ob organizatsii gorodskogo khoziaistva' " [June Plenum of the Central Committee of the VKP(b), "Concerning the Organization of City Management"]. *Sovetskaia arkhitektura*, no. 3, 1931: 1-3.

Decree, with analysis of its impact upon Soviet architecture; an outline of new services to be provided by Soviet cities and the role of the architectural and planning profession in helping to provide them. See also **no. 156.**

147.   Kaganovich, Lazar M. *The Construction of the Subway and the Plan of the City of Moscow.* Moscow, Cooperative Publishing Society of Foreign Workers in the USSR, 1934. 58 p., with a plan for the reconstruction of Moscow.

Speech delivered to the Plenum of the Moscow Soviet on July 16, 1934. Outlines the plan for the construction of the Moscow subway and defines the scope and means then envisioned for the reconstruction of the city and the ideological purposes to be served by such a project. An important document.

148. —. *Rech' na soveshchanii po voprosam stroitel'stva* [Speech at the Conference on Questions of Construction]. Moscow, Partizdat, 1935. 24 p.

Outlines the three main problems officially viewed as facing the task of construction in the Soviet Union: 1) creating a sound industrial system for organizing work, 2) increasing the mechanization and industrialization of the building industry, and 3) improving the quality of the work performed by the country's building brigades, imbuing them with the fervor of the "Stakhanov movement." Criticizes Soviet architects for stressing external appearance of a building, even though not always successfully, at the expense of its internal disposition and the corresponding quality of its construction. One of the main speeches suggesting the accent of the new policy by the official most responsible for the reorganization of the Soviet architectural profession at this time.

149. —. *The Socialist Reconstruction of Moscow and Other Cities in the USSR.* New York, International Publishers, 1931. 125 p.

The program by which Kaganovich, then head of the Moscow Soviet, proposed to administrate the reconstruction of Moscow, and in the process, reorganize the Soviet architectural community to make it more responsive to the tasks set forth by the Party and the government. An important document. See also **no. 158.**

150. Khrushchev, Nikita S. *O shirokom vnedrenii industrial'nykh metodov, uludshenii kachestva i snizhenii stoimosti stroitel'stva* [Concerning the Widespread Introduction of Industrial Methods, the Improvement of Quality, and the Lowering of Construction Costs]. Moscow, Gospolitizdat, 1955. 48 p.

Speech delivered by Khrushchev to the All-Union Conference of Builders, Architects, and Workers on December 7, 1954, directing the participants' attention to the need for decreasing construction and production costs and eliminating all decorative excesses in architectural design. The latter was prompted less by aesthetic considerations than by economic necessity. This speech provides the basis for further action to prosecute as policy the recommendations outlined herein.

151. *O general'nom plane rekonstruktsii gor. Moskvy: Postanovlenie SNK SSSR i TsK VKP(b)* [Concerning the General Plan for the Reconstruction of the City of Moscow: The Decree of the Soviet of People's Commissars of the USSR and the Central Committee of the All-Union Communist Party (of Bolsheviks)]. Moscow, Gospolitizdat, 1935.

Outlines in detail the scope of the measures taken in the reconstruction of Moscow and gives specific directions for the further development of Soviet architecture. See also *General'ny plan rekonstruktsii goroda Moskvy* [General Plan for the Reconstruction of the City of Moscow] (Moscow, Gospolitizdat, 1936).

152.   "O perestroike literaturno-khudozhestvennykh organizatsii" [Concerning the Reorganization of the Literary-Artistic Organizations]. *Stroitel'stvo Moskvy*, no. 4, 1932: 23.

Decree which disbanded all previous architectural organizations to form the Union of Soviet Architects, charged with supervising all further development of Soviet architecture to the prescribed formula of socialist realism. See also *Sovetskoe iskusstvo za 15 let* (**no. 140**), p. 644-645. For English translation, see "On the Reorganization of Literary and Artistic Bodies," *Soviet Culture Review*, no. 5, 1932: 21-22.

153.   "Ob arkhitekturnom obrazovanii" [Concerning Architectural Education]. *Stroitel'stvo Moskvy*, nos. 10-11, 1933: 35-36.

Contains the decree issued by the Central Committee of the Communist Party on the organization of the All-Union Academy of Architecture of the USSR, to open on January 1, 1934.

154.   *Ob uluchshenii proektnogo i smetnogo dela i ob uporiadochenii finansirovaniia stroitel'stva* [Concerning the Improvement of Designing and Estimating of Building Costs and of the Regulation of Financing Construction]. Moscow, Gospolitizdat, 1938.

Resolution of February 26, 1938, by the Council of People's Commissars. Includes a section charging the architectural profession with responsibility for more economical measures of design and construction.

155.   "Ob ustranenii izlishestv v proektirovanii i stroitel'stve" [Concerning the Elimination of Excesses in Design and Construction]. In *Postanovleniia TsK KPSS i Soveta Ministrov SSSR po voprosam stroitel'stva ot 23, 24 avgusta i 4 noiabria 1955 g.* [Decree of the Central Committee of the Communist Party and the Council of Ministers of the USSR on Questions of Construction, dating from Aug. 23 and 24, and Nov. 4, 1955]. Moscow, Gospolitizdat, 1956. p. 163-173.

Directs all further efforts in construction and design to increase the comfort and utility in all buildings and, especially, to eliminate all excesses. This decree finally put an official end to the trend in operation since 1932 and directed that beauty and expressiveness in design henceforth be achieved through purely architectural means: integral composition to be articulated by proportions and rhythm, and the architectural forms to be determined by the nature of new materials.

156. "Postanovlenie SNK SSSR 23 aprelia 1934 g. 'Ob uluchshenii zhilish-chnogo stroitel'stva' " [Resolution of SNK USSR of 23 April 1934, "Concerning the Improvement of Housing Construction"]. *Izvestiia*, April 24, 1934.

Directs improvement in housing design and construction.

157. *Postanovlenie Soveta narodnykh komissarov soiuza SSR i Tsentral'-nogo komiteta VKP(b) 11 fevralia 1936 g. "Ob uluchshenii stroitel'-nogo dela"* [Resolution of the Soviet of People's Commissars USSR and the Central Committee of the VKP(b), from Feb. 11, 1936, "Concerning the Improvement of Construction"] . Moscow, Gospolitizdat, 1936.

Directs improvement in all aspects of construction, including realistic correlation of design to construction demands, as well as adequate supervision of construction.

158. "Rezoliutsiia po dokladu Tov. Kaganovicha, priniata plenumom TsK VKP(b) 15 iunia 1931 g. 'O Moskovskom gorodskom khoziaistve i o razvitii gorodskogo khoziastva SSSR' " [Resolution on Commissar Kaganovich's Speech, as Passed by the Central Committee of the VKP(b) on June 15, 1931, "Concerning Moscow's City Management and the Development of City Management in the USSR"]. *Sovetskaia arkhitektura,* nos. 1-2, 1931: inside front cover.

Provides for reorganization of architectural work for more effective implementation of improvements to cities and states that the Party will reject architects from both the right (traditionalists) and the left (avant-garde) who fail to respond to present demands. See also *Za sotsialisticheskuiu rekonstruktsiiu Moskvy* [For the Socialistic Reconstruction of Moscow] (Moscow, Gospolitizdat, 1931).

159. Shushko, A. O. "Za sozdanie vysokokhudozhestvennoi sovetskoi arkhitektury" [For Creating a Highly Artistic Soviet Architecture].' *Stroitel'stvo Moskvy,* no. 12, 1934: 10-18.

Contains the decree, dated September 23, 1933, issued by the presidium of the Moscow Soviet on the creation of architectural studios under the Moscow Soviet's supervision and control. Lazar M. Kaganovich named to head the Architectural Planning Commission (ARKHPLAN) of the Moscow Soviet, created to administer these studios.

III. Theoretical Works

A. AESTHETICS AND IDEOLOGY IN SOVIET ARCHITECTURE

1. Soviet Publications

a. Monographs

160.   Academy of Arts of the USSR. Institute of the Theory and History
        of the Fine Arts. *Ocherki Marksistsko-Leninskoi estetiki* [Essays
        on Marxist-Leninist Aesthetics]. Moscow, "Iskusstvo," 1960.
        A detailed analysis of the roots of materialism and realism in
        world aesthetics, the development of contemporary Marxist-
        Leninist aesthetics, the formulation and bases of socialist realism,
        as well as its applications to various forms of art. For discussion
        on architecture, see p. 209-213. An important source for the
        aesthetics of Soviet architecture and art.

161.   ——. Scientific Research Institute on the Theory and History of the
        Fine Arts. *Marksistsko-Leninskaia estetika* [Marxist-Leninist Aes-
        thetics]. Moscow, "Iskusstvo," 1966. 442 p.
        A current reinterpretation of Marxist-Leninist aesthetics, in-
        tended as a text for institutes of higher education. Analyzes the
        major categories of aesthetic consideration. For section on archi-
        tecture, see p. 159-164. Assumes the contemporary argument
        that the use of architectural decoration no longer assures the
        beauty of a building. Argues that the building can no longer be
        treated merely as a symbol of beauty, but that its forms must be
        shaped by the functional designation of the building and by its
        ability to satisfy the needs of that segment of the population
        which it is designed to serve. Reflects the new "materialist"
        aesthetic.

162.   Academy of Sciences of the USSR. *Osnovy Marksistsko-Leninskoi
        estetiki* [Foundations of Marxist-Leninist Aesthetics]. Moscow,
        Gospolitizdat, 1961. 639 p.

A comprehensive, systematic analysis of the basic problems of Marxist-Leninist aesthetics. See p. 472-476 for analysis of the effects of architecture upon the varied role of aesthetics in the Soviet society. An important work, illuminating the aesthetic image projected for architecture under the formula of socialist realism.

163.   Berestov, V. F., L. F. Denisova, et al. *Iz istorii sovetskoi esteticheskoi mysli* [From the History of Soviet Aesthetic Thought]. Comp. V. Z. Rogovin. Moscow, "Iskusstvo," 1967. 523 p.

A collection of essays by numerous Soviet scholars on various aspects of Soviet aesthetic thought in the period 1917-32. Topics include Soviet aesthetic thought in the twenties (see **no. 192**), proletarian culture, the struggle with formalism and socio-criticism, realism in the art criticism of the twenties, Lunacharsky on the artistic image, and dialectics in the aesthetics of the twenties. Contains a comprehensive bibliography of Soviet works on aesthetics published during the period covered. The first competent scholarly attempt to characterize the principal aesthetic problems of the period and to illuminate important but little-known or forgotten factual material.

164.   Burov, Alexander I. *Esteticheskaia sushchnost' iskusstva* [Aesthetic Essence of Art]. Moscow, Gosizdat "Iskusstvo," 1956. 292 p.

Proceeds from the observation that Marxism-Leninism holds art to be a specific form of social consciousness and argues that 1) art, as any other form of consciousness, is a reflection of reality, and 2) it follows that art functions within the limits of general laws determined by the Marxist-Leninist theory of reflection and by all demands that stem from this theory. Surveys the major Marxist and socialist classics to develop the basis for this philosophy. A highly useful source for gaining an insight into the dialectic machinations of the Soviet aesthetics of the period. For German translation, see: A. I. Burov, *Das ästhetische Wesen der Kunst* (Berlin, Dietz Verlag, 1958, 331 p.).

165.   Chernishevsky, Nikolai G. *Esteticheskie otnosheniia iskusstva k deistvitel'nosti* [Aesthetic Relations of Art to Reality]. Master's thesis in 1855. Moscow, Goslitizdat, 1955. For English translation of the concluding portions of the essay, see: *Russian Philosophy*. v. 2. Ed. James M. Edie, James P. Scanlan, and Mary-Barbara Zeldin. Chicago, Quadrangle Books, 1965. p. 16-28.

A vigorous critique of Hegelian aesthetics, faulting its placing art above reality. To counter this separation of art from life, the work argues that the artist is not simply a passive recorder but, in his selection and creation, passes judgment on the reality he portrays. This gives art a moral dimension, as well as making it derivative from, and subservient to, life. Important as the first formal statement of the materialistic, utilitarian attitude toward aesthetics that may be viewed as a precursor of the motives of socialist realism in Soviet architecture and art.

166.   Dmitrieva, N. A., V. M. Zimenko, Iu. D. Kolpinsky, et al. *Ocherki Marksistsko-Leninskoi estetiki* [Essays on Marxist-Leninist Aesthetics]. Moscow, Gosizdat "Iskusstvo," 1956. 414 p.

     A collection of scholarly essays treating the development of the basic teachings of and problems in Marxist-Leninist aesthetics. For an analysis of architecture within this context, see especially p. 212-217, developing the criteria for realism in Soviet architecture. A lucid work reflecting current reassessments of aesthetic doctrine.

167.   Friche, V. M. *Sotsiologiia iskusstva* [Sociology of Art]. 3d ed. Moscow and Leningrad, Gosizdat, 1930. 203 p. illus.

     Includes analysis of the problems of sociology in art, the origins of art, the social functions of art, and the forms of artistic production. Views modern architecture as an expression of the rising working class and the product of two basic styles, the tectonic and the decorative, after Ginzburg's *Stil' i epokha* (no. 209). Of value for its analysis of the impact of contemporary social problems upon architecture and art within the framework of Marxist dialectic materialism.

168.   Gauzenshtein, Vil'gelm (Hausenstein, Wilhelm).*Iskusstvo i obshchestvo* [Art and Society]. Moscow, "Novaia Moskva," 1923. 336 p.

     Develops a socio-aesthetic of style and form in the arts, including architecture; argues that, since art is form, the sociology of art must be the sociology of form. One of the first major works to attempt to develop Marx's thesis that social existence determines personal consciousness and to apply Marxist dialectics and sociology to the analysis of the various historical phases of art. Useful for understanding the genesis of the Marxist tradition of socio-criticism of art and architecture, which grew out of favor in the thirties. For an illuminating discussion of Hausenstein, see Anatoli V. Lunacharsky, "Vil'gelm Gauzenshtein," *Iskusstvo*, no. 1, 1923: 13-31.

169.   Gegel', F. (Hegel, Georg Wilhelm Friedrich). *Kurs estetiki ili nauka iziashchnogo* [A course of Aesthetics, or the Science of the Elegant). 1st section. Architecture, sculpture, and painting. 2d. ed. Moscow, 1869. 162 p.

       Pages 28-115 devoted to architecture and the analysis of symbolism, classicism, and romanticism in architecture, as well as the theory of its aesthetics and function in society. Useful for suggesting possible Marxist antecedents and determining some aspects of the basis for Soviet aesthetics as applied to art and architecture.

170.   Iezuitsov, Andrei N. *Voprosy realizma v estetike Marksa i Engelsa* [Questions of Realism in the Aesthetics of Marx and Engels]. Moscow and Leningrad, "Iskusstvo," 1963. 321 p.

       Attempts to show that realism is central to the aesthetic system of Marxism and intends, thereby, to validate realism as the theoretical basis of the new socialist art. Useful for its review of the philosophical and aesthetic pronouncements of Marx and Engels.

171.   Ioffe, I. *Kul'tura i stil'* [Culture and Style]. Moscow, "Priboi," 1927, 367 p.

       A comprehensive work which attempts to define a system of social determinants in architecture and art as part of a general study of culture. Argues that there is no art, but that there exist tangible creations whose artistic images vary within different social groups. Thus, the contemporary struggle for an architectural and artistic style is viewed as a struggle among various social groups in Soviet society. Highly illuminating of the motives and underpinnings of the artistic ferment in the twenties.

172.   Lenin, Vladimir I. *V. I. Lenin o literature i iskusstve* [V. I. Lenin on Literature and Art]. 3d ed. Moscow, Khudozhestvennaia Literature, 1967. 822 p.

       A valuable compilation of documents, letters, statements, and speeches by Lenin on various phases and questions of art. Considerably expanded over the second edition. Highly useful for illuminating Lenin's philosophy of and approach to the arts.

173.   Lunacharsky, Anatoli V. *Ob izobrazitelnom iskusstve* [Concerning the Fine Arts]. Moscow, "Sovetskii Khudoznik," 1967. 2 v.

A collection of writings and pronouncements by Lunacharsky on innumerable questions of the Soviet fine arts, including architecture. Valuable for its important, heretofore unpublished, documents that provide an illuminating review of Soviet architecture. See, in particular, "The Socialist Architectural Monument" and "The Theses on the Construction of the Palace of Soviets" (**nos. 740** and **741**), and Le Corbusier's letter of May 13, 1932, to Lunacharsky, expressing dismay at the selection of B. M. Iofan's design for the Palace of Soviets (**no. 753**).

174. ——. *Stat'i ob iskusstve* [Statements about Art].Comp. by I. Satsa. Moscow and Leningrad, "Iskusstvo," 1941. 664 p.

A valuable compilation of statements on the various Soviet arts, including architecture, by Lunacharsky, the first Commissar of Education and a central figure in the evolution of Soviet art and architecture.

175. *Marks i Engels ob iskusstive* [Marx and Engels on Art].M. Lifshits, ed.; commentary by A. Vygodsky and G. Fridlender. Moscow and Leningrad, "Iskusstvo," 1938. 2 v., 764 p. illus.

An important compilation of the voluminous and largely unstudied philosophical, aesthetic, and interpretive pronouncements by Marx and Engels on the various realms of art.

176. Nasimovich, N. F. *K dialektike iskusstva* [To the Dialectic of Art]. Chita, Edition "Dal 'pechat'," 1921. 120 p.

Theoretical polemics discussing realism as one of the creative forms of art. Interesting as one of the earliest works in this period of avant- garde ferment to devote attention to the dialectics of realism in the Soviet arts.

177. Plekhanov, Georgii V. *Iskusstvo i literatura* [Art and Literatura]. Moscow, Goslitizdat, 1948.

Argues that art is an expression of feelings and thoughts, not in an abstract form, but in live images that constitute the central distinguishing features of art. Argues against "pure" art. Of value for helping to establish antecedents of the system of aesthetics that emerged in the 1930s. A reissue of the 19th-century work.

178. *Protiv formalizma i naturalizma v iskusstve* [Against Formalism and Naturalism in Art]. Moscow, Izogiz, 1937. 77 p.

A collection of polemical essays condemning as "formalism" and "naturalism" in art all experiments with new forms in modern art; for essay against formalism in architecture, see p. 56-70.

179.   Schmidt, F. I. *Iskusstvo – ego psikhologiia, ego stilistika, ego evoliutsiia* [Art – Its Psychology, Its Stylistics, Its Evolution]. Kharkov, "Soiuz," 1919. 329 p.
       A comprehensive theoretical work that posits the motives of art as those of arousing emotions, from its beginning through the subsequent ages of man. See p. 158-173 for a general discussion of architecture.

180.   ——. *Iskusstvo. Osnovnye problemy teorii i istorii* [Art. Basic Problems of History and Theory]. Moscow, "Akademiia," 1925. 184 p.
       A succinct abstract of the author's earlier work (**no. 179**), repositing the emotive functions of art and postulating six problems in art and architecture: 1) rhythm, 2) form, 3) composition, 4) movement, 5) space, and 6) light; these have been traced through six historical cycles of development in a manner that reflects the social needs and composition of each of the representative periods.

181.   Trofimov, Pavel S. *Estetika Marksizma-Leninizma. Ocherki istorii i teorii* [Aesthetics of Marxism-Leninism. Essays on History and Theory]. Moscow, "Sovetskii Khudozhnik," 1964. 295 p.
       A concise survey of the major stages in the history and basic theoretical tenets of Marxist-Leninist aesthetics. Though designed to counter "bourgeois ideologues and revisionists," valuable for its analyses of the development of Lenin's theoretical legacy in the realm of aesthetics and of the effect of Stalin's "cult of personality" upon Soviet aesthetics and the arts, including architecture.

182.   ——. *Leninskaia partiinost' i realizm v iskusstve* [Leninist Party Spirit and Realism in Art]. Moscow, "Sovetskii Khudozhnik," 1966. 292 p.
       An analysis of Lenin's ideas and their further development in the work of his colleagues and followers, as well as in the work of the founders and leaders of Communist parties in other countries. Especially useful for its theoretical analysis of actual problems of socialist realism in the soviet arts.

183. Vol'kenshtein, Vladimir. *Opyt sovremennoi estetiki* [Experience of Contemporary Aesthetics]. With an introduction by A. V. Lunacharsky. Moscow and Leningrad, "Akademiia," 1931. 188 p.

A collection of scholarly essays on a series of topics of aesthetic contemplation, reflecting the philosophy of modern art. Introduction by A. V. Lunacharsky, first Commissar of Education, provides an appraisal of the aesthetic legacy of Marx and other socialist theoretists and an evaluation of the current dearth of a Soviet body of aesthetics. A valuable account of Lunacharsky's discussion with the Vesnin brothers and with Peter Behrens, illuminating the commissar's current views on the aesthetics of architecture. Chapter 2 appeared as an article, "Estetika mashin i konstruktivnoi arkhitektury " [The Aesthetics of the Machine and Constructive Architecture], *Iskusstvo*, nos. 3-4, 1929: 141-149.

184. Zetkin, Klara. *Vospominaniia o Lenine* [Recollections of Lenin]. Moscow, Partizdat, 1933. 96 p.

A German communist leader's conversations with Lenin in 1920-22. Includes lengthy passages outlining Lenin's attitudes toward Soviet culture and art and the role he feels they must play in Soviet society. Eng. trans., Klara Zetkin, *Reminiscences of Lenin* (New York, International Publishers, 1934, 64 p.). For the new Soviet ed., see Klara Zetkin, *Vospominaniia o Lenine* Moscow, Gospolitizdat, 1955, 72 p.).

b. Articles

185. Arbatov, B. "Marks o khudozhestvennoi restavratsii" [Marx on Artistic Restoration]. *LEF*, no. 3. 1923: 76-96.

One of the first attempts to apply Marxist system of aesthetics to contemporary artistic activity. Emphasis upon illuminating and attempting preliminarily to resolve contradictions between theory and practice.

186. Denike, Iu. P. "Marks ob iskusstve" [Marx on Art]. *Iskusstvo*, no. 1, 1923: 32-42.

Speaks of the fragmentary state of Marx's views and pronouncements on art but maintains that they are of value to those who aspire to develop or to study historical materialism as a method of social development and a concept of social determinism which must be verified in all spheres of life, including art. Focuses upon Marx's *Einleitung zu einer Kritik der politischen Ökonomie* and *Das Capital* as the sources of the views examined and analyzed.

187.   Fedorov-Davydov, [A?] "Chem dolzhna byt' khudozhestvennaia kritika. Zadachi i metody kritiki v oblasti prostranstvennykh iskusstv" [What Art Criticism Should Be. Problems and Methods of Criticism in the Realm of the Spatial Arts]. *Sovetskoe iskusstvo,* No. 5, 1928: 51-59.

An attempt to apply the general methodology of Marxist art criticism to the development of a methodology for the criticism of the spatial arts. Includes architectural criticism in his postulations and suggestions for improvement. For an insight into the critic's approach, see his "Iskusstvoznanie" [Art Criticism], *Sovetskoe iskusstvo,* no. 5, 1927: 35-44, for a survey of Soviet art criticism during 1917-27, focusing on the Marxist and sociological methods of criticism and analysis. For a critique of Fedorov-Davydov's approach, see R. Pel'she, "O zadachakh i metodakh khudozhestvennoi kritiki" [On the Problems and Methods of Art Criticism], *Sovetskoe iskusstvo,* no. 6, 1928: 5-11.

188.   Kagan, M. S. "Politika kommunisticheskoi partii v oblasti iskusstva v period perekhoda ot kapitalizma k sotsializmu" [Policy of the Communist Party in the Realm of Art in the Period of Transition from Capitalism to Socialism]. In *Istoriia iskusstv* [History of the Arts]. A collection of essays by members of the Zhdanov Leningrad State University. M. K. Karger, ed. Leningrad, Izd-vo Leningradskogo universiteta, 1955. p. 3-66.

Traces the administrative role of the Communist Party in the development of the Soviet arts, including architecture. Not free from the ideological polemic characteristic of works from this period, but of great value in assessing party policy as it related to the various realms of art and determining the considerations which governed the development of policy. A useful barometer of contemporary official thought.

189.   Lunacharsky, Anatoli V. "Arkhitekturnoe oformlenie sotsialisticheskikh gorodov" [Architectural Design of Socialist Cities]. *Revoliutsiia i kul'tura,* no. 1, 1930: 54-61.

Asserts that the majority of classical forms of architecture are superior to any other kind and that they are generally the more appropriate, regardless of epoch.

190.   ——. "Rech o proletarskoi arkhitekture" [Speech on Proletarian Architecture]. *Arkhitektura SSSR,* no. 8, 1934: 4-7.

Speech delivered to VOPRA Plenum on January 14, 1932, at a time when Lunacharsky was a member of the Commission on the Construction of the Palace of Soviets and much concerned

with the problem of determining a new style for Soviet architecture. Scorns functionalism and speaks highly of classicism,
though warning against eclecticism. An important part of the
emerging dialectics on socialist realism in architecture.

191.   Marienbakh, I. A. "V. I. Lenin i pervye gradostroitel'nye meropriatia
sovetskoi vlasti" [V. I. Lenin and the First Measures of City Planning by the Soviet Regime]. *Voprosy sovremennoi arkhitektury*,
no. 1, 1962: 155-181.
       Provides a useful glimpse of the initial attitudes of Lenin and
the Soviet regime on architecture and city planning, especially in
the realm of "monumental propaganda."

192.   Matsa, Ivan L. "Sovetskaia esteticheskaia mysl' v 20-e gody" [Soviet
Aesthetic Thought in the Twenties]. In *Iz istorii sovetskoi
esteticheskoi mysli.* See **no. 163.** p. 18-58.
       A concise critical survey of the development of aesthetic
thought in the twenties. Special attention devoted to the analysis
of aesthetic doctrines developed by the principal architectural
movements of the period. Bibliographical footnotes provide access,
together with the text, to much useful material. A useful and rich
work in an as yet little-worked field.

193.   ——. "Tvorcheskii metod v proletarskom iskusstve" [Creative Method
in Proletarian Art]. *Literatura i iskusstvo*, nos. 3-4, 1930.
       An illuminating exposition of the new "proletarian" ideology
and aesthetics by the president of VOPRA.

194.   Mikhailov, A. I. "Marksistskoe iskusstvoznanie za gody revoliutsii"
[Marxist Art Criticism during the Years of the Revolution]. *Pod
znamenem marksizma*, nos. 10-11, 1927.
       Surveys the principal trends in Soviet art criticism in the first
decade following the 1917 Revolution. Focuses upon the need for
social judgment, rather than simply a social or aesthetic evaluation,
in art.

195.   Milonov, Iu. K. "Vyskazyvanie Marksa i Engelsa ob arkhitekture"
[Statements of Marx and Engels on Architecture]. *Akademiia
arkhitektury*, no. 4, 1936: 3-12.
       Useful for its collection of the numerous random pronounce-
ments by Marx and Engels derived by tracing all their major works
for any reference to architecture. Attempts to deduce from this
collection a consistent view of architecture by Marx and Engels.

196.   Shchekotov, N. "Zametki o soderzhanii i forme v nashem iskusstve" [Comments on the Content and Form of Our Art]. *Iskusstvo,* no. 3, 1941: 77-82.

Provides an illuminating interpretation of contemporary attitudes on the desired form and content in the Soviet arts, including architecture.

197.   Shpet, G. G. "Problemy sovremennoi estetiki" [Problems of Contemporary Aesthetics]. *Iskusstvo,* no. 1, 1923: 43-78.

Deals with the emerging topics of concern in aesthetic debates. An interesting and perceptive account.

198.   Sopotsinsky, O., and V. Tolstoi. "Politika kommunisticheskoi partii v oblasti iskusstva v period 1917-1932 godov" [The Policy of the Communist Party in the Realm of Art in the Period of 1917-1932]. In *Stanovlenie sotsialisticheskogo realizma v sovetskom izobrazitel'nom iskusstve* [The Development of Socialist Realism in the Soviet Fine Arts]. Moscow, "Iskusstvo," 1960. p. 5-38.

Examines Lenin's theoretical works and pronouncements, as well as dicta by the Communist Party and the Soviet government regarding art, in order to identify policy on the arts. Concludes that the basis of this policy was the desire to see art: 1) reflect the interest of the population, 2) help directly in the struggle for socialism, and 3) become an active revolutionary vehicle for mobilizing the population. Though no specific reference is made to architecture, the work provides an excellent overview of key pronouncements and decrees that formed the basis for the official policy affecting all the arts.

199.   Vertsman, I. "Gegel' ob arkhitekture" [Hegel on Architecture]. *Arkhitektura SSSR,* no. 6, 1936: 65-70.

A concise scholarly survey of Hegel's references to architecture useful for determining Hegelian precedents in Soviet aesthetics of architecture.

2.   Non-Soviet Publications

200.   Füllöp-Miller, Rene. *The Mind and Face of Bolshevism.* Trans. from from the German by F. S. Flint and D. F. Tait. New York—London, Knopf, 1928. 433 p., with plates.

Translation of *Geist und Gesicht des Bolschewismus* (Zurich, Amalthea-Verlag, 1926, 490 p.). A broad canvas of cultural and social activity in the Soviet Union during the period of the New

Economic Policy, with particular attention to the arts. Includes a section on Soviet philosophy of aesthetics. For an updated edition, see same title (New York, Harper Torch Books, 1965, 350 p.); contains new epilogue on changes in Soviet life and culture in the last decades.

201. Lehman–Haupt, Hellmut. *Art under a Dictatorship.* New York, Oxford University Press, 1954. 277 p. illus.
Includes a penetrating study of the impact of Socialist Realism on art and artists in the Soviet Union; includes architecture and draws comparisons with Nazi art. Includes also an analysis of Marx's statements on art. A stimulating and interesting study.

202. Philipov, Alexander P. *The Origin and Principles of Soviet Aesthetics (until N. Khrushchev).* New York, Pageant Press, 1967. 161 p.
Argues that the development of Soviet aesthetics has drawn as heavily from Russian nihilists like Bakunin, Nechaev, and Tkachev as from Marx and Engels. A highly useful survey and analysis of both the theoretical and practical applications of Soviet aesthetics and the motivations behind them.

203. Somerville, John P. M. *Soviet Philosophy. A Study of Theory and Practice.* New York, Philosophical Library, 1946. 269 p.
Includes a general survey of Soviet Aesthetics.

B. THEORY OF SOVIET ARCHITECTURE

1. Monographs

204. Burov, Andrei K. *Ob arkhitekture* [About Architecture]. Moscow, Gosstroiizdat, 1960. 147 p. illus.
Written in 1943-44 but published posthumously in 1960. A theoretical postulation of the architect's philosophy of architecture, divided into the following categories: 1) unity in architecture, 2) "academism" and the Old Order, 3) economy, 4) technological progress, 5) illusion and realism in style, and 6) scale, image, material, and form in architecture. Especially illuminating in its speculation about the role of architecture in society, its assessment of the various struggles for tectonic innovation in Soviet architecture, and the analysis of the various trends and stages in its development. Highly recommended.

205. Chernikhov, Iakob G. *Arkhitekturnye fantazii* [Architectural Fantasies]. Leningrad, "Mezhdunarodnaia kniga," 1933. 102 p. 101 color plates.

A richly illustrated work dealing with methods of architectural design, technical and compositional systems, and systems of constructing architectural fantasies.

206. ———. *Konstruktsiia arkhitekturnykh i mashinnykh form* [Construction of Architectural and Machine Forms]. Leningrad, Izd-vo Leningradskogo Obshchestva Arkhitektorov, 1931. 232 p. illus.

Introductory remarks by I. Gollerbakh, "Problemy konstruktivizma v ikh otnoshenii k iskusstvu" [The Problems of Constructivism in Their Relation to Art]. An analysis of the constitution and ideas of constructivism and form-rendering constructions.

207. ———. *Osnovy sovremennoi arkhitektury* [Foundations of Contemporary Architecture]. 2d ed. Leningrad, Izd-vo Leningradskogo Obshchestva Arkhitektorov, 1931. 96 p. illus.

Analyzes architecture in its "analytical" and "graphic" parts. Includes questions of architectural composition, the organization of space, and architectural style. Last chapter deals with philosophical concepts of architecture. Supplemented with plates.

208. Ginzburg, Moisei Ia. *Ritm v arkhitekture* [Rhythm in Architecture]. Moscow, "Sredi Kollektsionerov," 1923. 116 p. illus.

A comprehensive, systematic analysis of a series of historical architectural monuments from the standpoint of their inherent techniques of composition; develops general laws of rhythm and composition that may be applied universally to formulate a sound approach to architectural design. This book provided the basis for the author's lectures for a course on the theory of architectural composition at the VKHUTEMAS and other institutes in Moscow.

209. ———. *Stil'i epokha* [Style and Epoch]. Moscow, Gosizdat, 1924. 238 p. illus.

Basic theses of this work first delivered by author in a speech to the Moscow Architectural Society on May 18, 1923, and one the following year at the Academy of Artistic Sciences. Condemns the old classical order and develops the theoretical bases for constructivism in Soviet architecture. Discussion divided into 1) elements of the old architectural style, 2) the Greco-Italian classical system of thought and its contemporary legacy, 3) the prerequisites of a new style, 4) the influence of the static and dynamic qualities of the machine on contemporary art, 5) constructivism, or structure and form in architecture, 6) industrial and engineering organisms, and 7) architectural projects and designs in the first postrevolutionary years. A vital document for explaining the theory and aims of constructivism in Soviet architecture.

210. ——. *Zhilishche. Opyt piatiletnei raboty nad problemoi zhilishcha* [Housing. The Experience of Five Years' Work on the Problem of Housing]. Moscow, Gosstroiizdat, 1934. 192 p. illus.

Provides a theoretical analysis of the housing problem in the Soviet Union and reviews the author's experience with the design and construction of housing. Emphasizes the work of the Standardization Section of the Construction Committee of the RSFSR (STROIKOM), of which Ginzburg was chief architect. Introductory chapter contains a brief historical overview of the housing problem in various parts of the world. Book completed in 1932, but publication delayed for two years. A valuable source for the author's principal theories of housing and planning.

211. Krinsky, V. F., I. V. Lamtsov, and M. A. Turkus. *Elementy arkhitekturno-prostranstvennoi kompositsii* [Elements of Architectural-Spatial Composition]. Moscow, Gosstroiizdat, 1934. 172 p. illus.

First effort after the disbanding of the architectural movements to amplify the former ASNOVA theory of architectural design and composition within the framework of the new trends in Soviet architecture. Authors formerly members of ASNOVA.

212. Lagutin, K. K. *Arkhitekturnyi obraz sovetskikh obshchestvennykh zdanii. Kluby i teatry* [Architectural Image of Soviet Civic Buildings. Clubs and Theaters.].Moscow, "Iskusstvo," 1953. 236 p. illus.

Analyzes the development of the architectural image in Soviet clubs and theaters. Examines those examples that are most characteristic of each of the respective periods in the development of Soviet architecture. Especially useful for its material on clubs by Konstantin Mel'nikov.

213. Matsa, Ivan L. *Besedy ob arkhitekture* [Discussions about Architecture]. Moscow, Izogiz, 1935. 95 p. illus.

A popular account dealing with the understanding of architecture, its goals and functions in a developing socialist society. Contents divided into 1) what is architecture, 2) how it is distinguished from simple construction and other forms of art, 3) architecture and technology, 4) the development of Soviet architecture and its problems, and 5) supplementary commentary and illustrations. Useful for illuminating an emerging philosophy of a Soviet "socialist" architecture by a prominent contemporary Soviet art historian and former president of VOPRA.

214.   ——. *Za khudozhestvennoe kachestvo sovetskoi arkhitektury* [For an Artistic Quality of Soviet Architecture]. Moscow, Izogiz, 1934. 80 p. illus.

Delivered as a speech by the head of the Historical and Theoretical Department of the Academy of Architecture to the Union of Soviet Architects in 1933. Develops four general conditions as the basis for the development of a socialist architecture: it must 1) be included in an integral plan for the national economy, 2) serve the new mode of life being reconstructed on a socialist basis, 3) be developed on a new technological base, and 4) give singular expression to the attitude of the proletariat. Tectonically, it must utilize decorative surface and volumetric spatial expression, as well as display mastery of architectural form. This provides the first formulation for Soviet architecture following the eclipse of modernism in 1932.

215.   Rozenberg, A. V. *Filosofiia arkhitektury* [Philosophy of Architecture]. Petrograd, "Nachatki znanii," 1923. 53 p. illus.

Develops general bases for the theory of architectural design. Reflects contemporary sensibilities.

216.   ——. *Obshchaia teoriia proektirovania arkhitekturnykh sooruzhenii* [General Theory of Designing Architectural Facilities]. Moscow, Plankhozgiz, 1930. 210 p. illus.

A substantial amplification of the author's previous work (no. 215) reflecting intervening developments among modern movements in Soviet architecture.

217.   Trapeznikov, K., ed. *Problema ansamblia v sovetskoi arkhitekture* [Problem of the Ensemble in Soviet Architecture]. Moscow, Gosstroiizdat, 1952. 103 p. illus.

A collection of essays investigating various theoretical problems of the architectural ensemble in the city and its individual parts, such as streets, residential blocks, squares, and embankments. An attempt to formalize the developing practice of design in preceding years into a viable theory of design. Of interest for reflecting the existing frame of reference dictating the postwar developments in Soviet architecture.

218. Tsires, A. *Iskusstvo arkhitektury* [Art of Architecture]. Moscow, Izd-vo Akademii arkhitektury, 1946. 127 p. illus.

Gives a general view of architecture for the purpose of evaluating aesthetic accomplishments in major periods. Has several chapters on Soviet architecture; useful for its comparison of major stylistic developments.

2. Articles

219. Gabrichesky, A. G. "Prostranstvo i massa v arkhitekture" [Space and Mass in Architecture]. *Iskusstvo*, no. 1, 1923: 292-309.

Analyzes mass and space as the two primary components of the "architectural synthesis." Mass is seen primarily as a development from basic three-dimensional shapes or "unbounded sculptures," such as obelisks; space is seen to emerge from amorphous masses already existing in nature, or "negative architecture."

220. Ginzburg, Moisei Ia. "Voprosy tektoniki i sovremennaia arkhitektura" [Questions of Tectonics and Contemporary Architecture]. *Arkhitektura SSSR*, Part I, no. 9, 1945: 26-31; Part II, no. 10, 1945: 28-32.

A comprehensive theoretical analysis of the major epochs in the history of world architecture for the purpose of articulating the major tectonic achievements of each age of architecture within the given limitations of its technological development. Argues further that Soviet architecture now has, at long last, the opportunity to employ new methods and materials for construction by virtue of the massive destruction brought on by World War II. A revised and updated argument first presented by the author in his *Stil' i epokha* (**no. 209**).

221. Rozenberg, A. V. "Normalizatsiia arkhitekturnykh sooruzhenii" [Normalization of Architectural Structures]. *Stroitel'naia promyshlennost'*, no. 9, 1924: 605-608.

Asserts that there exist three moments by which an architectural structure may be normalized: 1) the structure is always the condition of a certain organizing process, 2) comparable with the means of production, it is an *object* participating in a spatial process in which it is "utilized," and 3) it is itself a *product* of a particular building process.

IV. Histories of Soviet Architecture

A. CHRONOLOGIES

222. "Iz goda v god (illustrirovannaia letopis' sovetskoi arkhitektury)"
[From One Year to the Next (An Illustrated Chronicle of Soviet
Architecture)]. *Sovetskaia arkhitektura*, no. 18, 1968: 14, 18-19,
22-24, 26-28, 30-31, 33-34, 37, 40-41, 43-48, 52-58, 60-61, 66-
67, 70-71, 73-76, 78-79, 84, 90-91, 94, 98-99, 101-102, 106,
108-112, 114, 116-117, 122, 126-132, 134, 136, 142, 146-150,
152-153, 161-168, 172-173, 175, 177, 179-180, 184, 188-189,
191, 194-195, 197, 200-202, 206-207, 211-212, 216, 220-222.
The most comprehensive and richly illustrated chronology yet
assembled, by year, of significant events in the history of Soviet
architecture from 1917 to 1967.

223. "Iz istorii arkhitektury i stroitel'stva v SSSR" [From the History of
Architecture and Construction in the USSR]. *Arkhitektura i
stroitel'stvo*, no. 14, 1947: 4, 6-7, 10-11, 21-23.
A valuable chronicle, by year, of important events in the
development of Soviet architecture, 1917-47.

224. "Iz letopisi sovetskoi arkhitektury" [From the Chronicles of Soviet
Architecture]. *Arkhitektura SSSR*: Part 1, no. 2, 1967: 3-6;
Part 2, no. 3, 1967: 36-40; Part 3, no. 4, 1967: 16-21: Part 4,
no. 5, 1967: 1-5; Part 5, no. 7, 1967: 10-13; Part 6, no. 8, 1967:
25-28; Part 7, no. 9, 1967: 23-24; and Part 8, no. 10, 1967: 11-14.
A concise analytical survey, by year (except for Part 1, which
is by month for 1918), of important developments and events in
the history of Soviet architecture, 1918-60. Part 1 covers April-
October, 1918; Part 2, 1918-23; Part 3, 1923-27; Part 4, 1928-
33; Part 5, 1934-40; Part 6, 1941-49; Part 7, 1950-53; and Part 8,
1954-60. Contains a wealth of information, as well as excellent
plates, many of which were previously unpublished.

225. "Letopis' sovetskoi arkhitektury, 1917-1936" [A Chronicle of Soviet
Architecture, 1917-1936]. *Arkhitektura SSSR*, no. 4, 1936: 62-68.
A valuable chronicle of important events in the development
of Soviet architecture, 1917-36.

226. Petrov, V. "ASNOVA za 8 let" [ASNOVA in 8 Years]. *Sovetskaia arkhitektura*, nos. 1-2, 1931: 48-51.

   A valuable chronology by year of events and work of ASNOVA, 1923-31.

227. "Piat' let S.A." [Five Years of S.A.]. *S.A.*, no. 6, 1930: unnumbered pages, the last three at back of issue.

   An important résumé of the activity of the publication *S.A.* (Contemporary Architecture) and its parent organization, OSA (The Society of Contemporary Architects), by year, 1926-30.

B. GENERAL

1. By Soviet Writers

a. Monographs

228. Academy of Construction and Architecture of the USSR. *Stroitel'stvo v SSSR, 1917-1957* [Building in the USSR, 1917-1957]. N. V. Baranov, et al., eds. Moscow, Gosstroiizdat, 1958. 751 p. illus.

   A collection of essays deliberated at the third session of the Academy. Provides a review and analysis of the Soviet building enterprise by numerous specialists, reflecting contemporary interpretations and official thought. Includes important historical surveys of Soviet architecture, construction, and city planning, as well as authoritative material on the development and mechanization of the Soviet building industry. An important and informative source.

229. Bylinkin, N. P., ed. *Istoriia sovetskoi arkhitektury, 1917-1958* [History of Soviet Architecture, 1917-1958]. Moscow, Gosstroiizdat, 1962. 347 p. illus.

   Authorized by the Ministry of Education of the USSR as a textbook for Soviet schools of architecture. Divides the history of architecture into four periods: 1) 1917-32, civil war, reconstruction, and economic consolidation, 2) 1933-41, completing reconstruction and establishing socialism, 3) 1941-54, World War II, reconstruction, and development of communism, and 4) 1955-58, the historic decision of November 4, 1954, establishing a new direction in Soviet architecture. Pedantic and lacking any scholarly apparatus but useful for providing an overview.

230.   Davidson, B. M. *Arkhitektura i sovremennost'* [Architecture and
        Contemporaneity]. Sverdlovsk, Knizhnoe izd-vo, 1963. 80 p.
        illus.
            A general text for introductory university courses in culture.
        Includes an interpretive survey of developments in Soviet archi-
        tecture. Despite the title, reflects a lingering traditional inter-
        pretation (thirties and forties) of the "Old School" architects as
        the progressives and the modern movements as purveyors of
        decadent formalism.

231.   Kirillova, L. I. et al. *Sovetskaia arkhitektura za 50 let* [Soviet Archi-
        tecture in Fifty Years]. Moscow, Stroiizdat, 1968. 277 p. illus.
            Survey of the history of Soviet architecture, divided by periods :
        1) 1917-32, 2) 1933-41, 3) 1941-54, and 4) 1955-67. Reinforced
        by analysis of works characterizing the basic stages in the develop-
        ment of Soviet architecture. Although a bit general and lacking
        any scholarly apparatus, it is the first Soviet history to deal objec-
        tively with the modern currents in Soviet architecture and thereby
        to provide a sound historical perspective of its development.
        Generous collection of photographs and graphic material, though
        many of only moderate quality.

232.   Riabushin, A. V., and M. V. Fedorov. *Sovremennaia sovetskaia
        arkhitektura* [Contemporary Soviet Architecture]. Moscow:
        "Znanie," 1963. 47 p.
            An introductory text for university cultural courses. Includes a
        useful survey and condensation of contemporary Soviet scholar-
        ship on the history of Soviet architecture. Focuses upon problems
        of city planning and industrial, residential, and civic architecture.
        Includes a discussion of the development of a "socialist" archi-
        tectural style. Provides useful insights into contemporary Soviet
        interpretation of the historical role and place of the modern
        movements in Soviet architecture.

233.   Tsapenko, Mikhail P. *O realisticheskikh osnovakh sovetskoi arkhi-
        tektury* [On the Realistic Foundations of Soviet Architecture].
        Moscow, Gosstroiizdat, 1952. 395 p. illus.
            An analysis of the developments in Soviet architecture from
        the viewpoint of official contemporary Soviet doctrine. The first
        section, on the development of Soviet architecture, cites charac-
        teristics of the development of architecture in a socialist society;
        the second section, on the struggle for realism in Soviet archi-
        tecture, traces the roots of Modernism in Soviet architecture and
        treats the rejection of Modernism and the confirmation of socialist

realism. The final section, devoted to problems of Soviet architecture, deals with the subsequent period of development, including questions of urban and industrial design, housing, and civic architecture. Despite its tendentious ideological polemic, a well-documented source for valuable information relating to the history of Soviet architecture.

234. *Sovetskaia arkhitektura za XXX let. RSFSR* [Sovet Architecture in 30 Years. RSFSR]. 1st ed. V. A. Shkvarikov, ed. Moscow, Izd-vo Akademii arkhitektury, 1950. 21 p., 222 plates.

An album of plates and photographs of Soviet buildings; no commentary. Projects of modern period not included. A good guide to designs deemed acceptable at this time, with the revival of the Zholtovsky school. For Czech edition, see: *Vývoj sovětské arkhitektury* (Prague, Vytvarne nakladatelstvi orbis, 1953, 21 p., 222 plates).

235. Vlasov, Aleksandr V., et al., eds. *Sovetskaia arkhitektura 1917 -1957* [Soviet Architecture 1917-1957]. Moscow, Gosstroiizdat, 1957. Pages unnumbered.

An album of illustrative material depicting examples of the city planning, civic and industrial architecture, and mass construction techniques that have been completed in the course of this period. Organization by cities and regions. Excellent plates.

236. Volodin, P. A. *Put' sovetskoi arkhitektury* [Direction of Soviet Architecture]. Moscow, "Znanie," 1962. 63 p. illus.

Prepared for lecturers on Soviet architecture. A popular survey of the highlights in the development of Soviet architecture. Methodological recommendations not intended for specialists but reflect current historiography. Useful as a synopsis of significant events, pronouncements, buildings, and major personalities within a context of historical continuity.

237. Zhuravlev, A. M., and Selim O. Khan-Magomedov. *Polveka sovetskoi arkhitektury* [Half a Century of Soviet Architecture]. Moscow, "Znanie," 1967. 56 p. illus.

An authoritative condensation of the history of Soviet architecture, 1917-67. Especially useful for Khan-Magomedov's exposition of the progressive aspects of the architecture of the twenties, by way of illuminating unpublished writings and unrealized projects which are seen to have exerted an influence on the architecture of subsequent periods.

b. Articles

238.   Ikonnikov, Andrei V. "Etapy razvitiia sovetskoi arkhitektury" [Stages
        in the Development of Soviet Architecture]. *Arkhitektura   SSSR,*
        no. 11, 1967: 44-50.
           An analysis of economic, technological, and social factors and
        their effect on the development of Soviet architecture. An excellent
        synopsis of the major influences affecting each of the stages in the
        development of Soviet architecture. Especially valuable for charac-
        terizing objectively the circumstances in which the architects of
        the Old School, such as Shchusev, Shchuko, Fomin, Zholtovsky,
        and others, were absorbed into the practice of Soviet architecture.
        An earlier, more comprehensive analysis of architecture, rationaliz-
        ing the return to a contemporary style, is the book by Ikonnikov
        and Georgii P. Stepanov, *K novomu stiliu* [Toward a New Style]
        (Leningrad, "Khudozhnik RSFSR," 1962, 70 p.). See especially
        p. 3-28 for Ikonnikov's essay on the problems of style in archi-
        tecture.

239.   Il'in, Mikhail A. "Nekotorye tendentsii razvitiia sovetskoi arkhitek-
        tury" [Some Tendencies in the Development of Soviet Architec-
        ture]. *Arkhitektura SSSR,* no. 1, 1969: 50-52.
           Compares developments following the decree of November 4,
        1955, banishing superfluous excesses in Soviet architecture with
        those in the modern movements during the twenties. Emphasis on
        contemporary development. Valuable for parallels drawn between
        current demands and the achievements of the modern movement
        in Soviet architecture.

240.   Khiger, R. Ia. "Arkhitektura revoliutsionnykh let" [Architecture
        of Revolutionary Years]. *Arkhitektura SSSR,* nos. 10-11, 1935:
        65-67.
           An illuminating characterization of Soviet architectural practice
        in the fifteen years following the Bolshevik Revolution of 1917;
        evaluates the nature of the work of leading Soviet architects,
        both the modernists, such as Ginzburg and the Vesnins, and the
        classical traditionalists, such as Shchusev, Shchuko, Fomin, and
        Zholtovsky. A valuable historical insight still applicable today.

241.   Kolli, Nikolai Ia. "Letopis' sovetskoi arkhitektury" [A Chronicle of
        Soviet Architecture]. *Arkhitektura SSSR,* nos. 17-18, 1947: 21-45
           A selected record of significant developments and projects
        in Soviet architecture during the period, on the occasion of the

thirtieth anniversary of the October Revolution. Makes no mention of the modern movements but includes useful information framed in the polemics of the day.

242.   Mikhailov, A. I. "Velikoe iskusstvo arkhitektury" [The Great Art of Architecture]. *Arkhitektura SSSR*, no. 1, 1967: 33-42.

A scholarly discourse on the artistic strains in the Soviet architecture of various periods. Includes the aesthetic debates and the official responses to these polemics. A useful, illuminating work.

243.   ——. "Leninskii plan monumental'noi propagandy i arkhitektura" [Lenin Plan for Monumental Propaganda and Architecture] . *Arkhitektura SSSR*, no. 4, 1968: 2-16.

Analyzes the theme of Lenin's program for monumental propaganda and assesses the various phases of its application throughout the fifty years of Soviet architecture. Especially interesting for the parallels drawn between the various periods of Soviet architecture.

244.   Savistky, Iu. "Etapy razvitiia sovetskoi arkhitektury" [Stages in the Development of Soviet Architecture]. *Sovetskaia arkhitektura,* no. 9, 1958: 3-29.

A brief account of the development of Soviet architecture from the first days of the revolution to the fifties. Stresses the acceptable developments, with minor treatment of the modernist movements. Also, discussion about directions in which searches proceeded, their accomplishments and mistakes, and the resolution of these errors. A useful barometer of current attitudes on problems in Soviet Architecture.

245.   Tasalov, V. "Razvitie printsipa narodnosti sovetskoi arkhitektury" [Development of National Character in Soviet Architecture]. In *Iskusstvo i narod* [Art and the People]. A collection of essays. Moscow, "Nauka," 1966. p. 176-209.

A scholarly résumé of architectural thought and development in the Soviet Union. Deals more with the social ramifications and conditions within which Soviet architecture developed. Argues that it was the new social and technological revolution that brought Soviet architecture from the eclectic doldrums of the preceding century to the forefront of the contemporary avant-garde movement. A very thoughtful and illuminating work.

246.   Vesnin, Viktor A. "Tridtsa t' let sovetskoi arkhitektury" [Thirty Years
        of Soviet Architecture]. In *Obshchee sobranie Akademii nauk
        SSSR* [A General Collection of the Academy of Sciences of the
        USSR]. Moscow, Izd-vo Akademii nauk SSSR, 1948. p. 284-294.

        A speech by Vesnin, then president of the Academy of Archi-
        tecture, to a general meeting of the Academy of Sciences devoted
        to a Thirtieth Anniversary of the Bolshevik Revolution. A general
        but authoritative survey of the major stages in the development of
        Soviet architecture. Infused moderately with the polemic required
        at this time but offers insight into the circumstances surrounding
        some of the major developments in Soviet architecture. For same
        article, see *Mastera sovetskoi arkhitektury ob arkhitekture* (no.
        842).

247.   Volodin, P. A. "Znachenie istoricheskogo opyta sovetskoi arkhitek-
        tury" [Significance of the Historical Experience in Soviet Archi-
        ture]. *Voprosy teorii arkhitektury,* v. 5, 1960: 49-63.

        Assesses the characteristic features in the architecture of pre-
        revolutionary Russia and their influence on the development of
        Soviet architecture. Observes that Soviet architecture has under-
        gone essentially two periods of development, 1917-32 and 1933-
        54, and that each of these periods was terminated by directions
        for change imposed by the Communist Party in 1932-33 and
        1954-55, respectively. Valuable for its reevaluation of preceding
        historiographical assessments of the various periods in the develop-
        ment of Soviet architecture, including the modernist period and
        the evaluation of its work during subsequent years.

                          2. By Non-Soviet Writers

                              a. Monographs

248.   Krasceninnicowa, Maria Gibellino. *L'architettura russa nel passato e
        nel presente.* Rome, Fratelli Palombi, 1963. 228 p. illus.

        Primary attention given to prerevolutionary, or Russian, archi-
        tecture. Brief survey of Soviet architecture provided in three short
        chapters.

249.   London, Kurt. *The Seven Soviet Arts.* Trans. Eric S. Bensinger.
        London, Faber and Faber, 1937. 381 p. illus.

        An incisive analysis of all the arts, including architecture. Of
        particular value for descriptions of organizations, systems of
        training, administration of activity, and cultural principles, as well

as interesting accounts of discussions among artists and bureaucrats on socialist realism in the early 1930s.

250. Parkins, Maurice Frank. *City Planning in Soviet Russia; with an Interpretative Bibliography.* Chicago, University of Chicago Press, 1953. 257 p. illus.

Surveys the historical development of city planning in the Soviet Union, 1922-50, and examines decisions affecting city planning made by the Soviet government. Systematic but not comprehensive. Contains useful, documented material relating to Soviet architecture; helpful in assessing political, economic, and social implications. Also contains a useful annotated bibliography (see no. 31).

251. Quilici, Vieri. *Architettura sovietica contemporanea.* Rome, Universale Cappelli, 1965. 215 p. illus.

A concise, well-balanced survey of Soviet architecture, 1917-63 Though not comprehensive in scope, provides a documented access to some important material. A useful reference.

252. *Socialismo, città, architettura URSS 1917-1937. Il contributo degli architetti europi.* Rome: Officina Edizioni, 1971. 342 p. illus.

A collection of essays initially deliberated at a seminar on "socialism, the city, and architecture in the Soviet Union from 1917 to 1937" at the Institute of History at the University Institute of Architecture in Venice on June 16-18, 1970. A number of specialists reexamine the evolution and subsequent decline of modern architecture and planning in the Soviet Union. Focuses upon the participation of Western specialists in the evolution, as well as upon the rise and consolidation of the proletarian ideology. Valuable for presentation of much new rich material, based upon current research, and for the consideration of vital ancillary subjects (economics, etc.) that permit a more complete reconstruction of the period. Papers drawn from unpublished private archival material and from material already published or in the process of being published.

253. Voyce, Arthur. *Russian Architecture.* New York, Philosophical Library, 1948. 296 p. illus.

A cursory survey of the main currents in Soviet architecture. Contains useful information but lacks comprehensiveness and sufficient scholarly apparatus. Many useful illustrations, but of poor quality.

254.   Zevi, Bruno. *Storia dell'architettura moderna.* 2d rev. ed. Torino,
       Giulo Einaudi Editore, 1953. 785 p. illus.
          For discussion of Soviet architecture, see p. 174-193 and 631-
       633. Brief survey of Soviet architecture sets forth six chief argu-
       ments defending the contemporary neoclassical style that emerged
       in the Soviet Union after 1932: modern architecture 1) has no
       roots in Russian history, 2) is formalistic, 3) is not Marxist, 4)is
       individualistic, rather than collective in nature, and is therefore
       counterrevolutionary, 5) is excessively spartan and devoid of
       expression, and 6) is contrary to socialist realism. Proceeds to
       demolish each argument as self-contradictory on the basis of the
       evolution of modern architecture as a whole, but especially of
       that in the Soviet Union. A useful analysis. For an earlier assess-
       ment of the Soviet experience by Zevi, see his *Towards an Organic
       Architecture* (London, Faber & Faber, 1950, 180 p.), especially
       p. 35-52.

b. Articles

255.   "Architecture of the USSR." *RIBA Journal*, 3d ser., v. 55, Feb.
       1948: 149-152.
          A collection of photographs selected to give a general impres-
       sion of Soviet architecture, taken from the RIBA exhibit on
       Russian architecture held March 3-20, 1948. Of general interest;
       Plates of modest quality.

256.   Canella, Guido. "Attesa per l'architettura sovietica." *Casabella con-
       tinuita*, no. 262, April 1962: 4-16.
          A crisp, well-balanced survey, profusely illustrated, of the
       history of Soviet architecture from the roots of modernism to the
       first years of socialist realism in Soviet architecture.

257.   Dal Co, Francesco. "Architettura e piano in Unione Sovietica:
       stalinismo e 'destino dell'avanguardia.' " *Contropiano*, no.3, 1969:
       527-575.
          A stimulating and original discussion of the avant-garde aspect
       of Soviet architecture and planning in the twenties and thirties.
       Seeks to examine the phenomenon as a whole by contrasting its
       internal composition and ideology with the external forces and
       expectations operating in the country; also assesses its long-term
       impact.

258. Hamlin, Talbot. "The Developments of Russian Architecture, II." *Magazine of Art,* v. 38, May 1945: 180-185.

An examination of the historical, cultural, and artistic influences that affected the emergence of modern Soviet architecture, as well as the possible reasons for its eclipse in 1932 and the development of the contemporary neo-classical style. Some useful insights into the historical problem.

259. "Il dibatto sull'architettura in URSS." *Casabella continuita,* no. 262, April 1962: 17-34.

Excerpts from documents, with commentary, organized chronologically, which deal with the development of Soviet architecture. A useful reference.

260. Lubetkin, Berthold. "Soviet Architecture. Notes on Developments from 1917-1932." *Architectural Association Journal*, v. 71, May 1956: 260-264.

A concise analysis of the political, social, economic, and aesthetic factors that affected the evolution of Soviet architecture and the emergence of socialist realism. Useful for characterizing the position of the architects of the "Old School" throughout this period.

261. ——. "Soviet Architecture. Notes on Developments from 1932 to 1955," *Architectural Association Journal*, v. 71, Sept. - Oct., 1956: 85-89.

A reflective account dealing more with abstract analysis of broad ideological concepts governing the disposition of major developments in Soviet architecture during this period. Useful for applying Marxist dialectics to explain official motivations concerning these developments.

262. Rogers, Ernesto N. "Russia, contenuto e forma." *Casabella continuita,* no. 262, April 1962: 3.

A thoughtful introduction to the varied problems in the history of Soviet architecture and to the articles dealing with them that follow in the periodical (**nos. 256 and 264**).

263. Seuphor, Michel, "L'Architecture en URSS." *L'Oeil,* no. 11, 1955: 46-49.

A brief survey, by way of photographs and commentary, largely of postmodern Soviet architecture. An interesting synopsis but of no special value.

264.   Tentori, Francesco. "Mosca, la prima citta dell'URSS." *Casabella continuita,* no. 262, April 1962: 35-62.
       An excellent survey of the development of Soviet architecture in Moscow. Profusely illustrated.

265.   Voyce, Arthur. "Soviet Art and Architecture: Recent Developments," *Russia since Stalin: Old Trends and New Problems.* In *The Annals of the American Academy of Political and Social Sciences,* Jan. 1956: 104-115.
       A general synopsis of major currents in, and antecedents of, Soviet architecture and art. Provides a useful generalization of the historical development.

C. FROM 1917 TO 1932

1. By Soviet Writers

a. Monographs

266.   Khazanova, Vigdariia E. *Sovetskaia arkhitektura pervykh let Oktiabria, 1917-1925 gg.* [Soviet Architecture in the First Years Following October, 1917-1925]. Moscow, Nauka, 1970. 212 p. illus.
       An excellent and important scholarly account of the crucial first years of Soviet architecture. Includes important studies of the emerging trends of architectural thought, as well as experiments with new concepts in architecture, housing, and town planning. Also contains an examination of the "synthesis of the arts" in these first years of architectural activity. An extensive and valuable work based on the author's earlier documentary and archival research (see **nos. 138, 302,** and **303**). Richly illustrated.

267.   Khiger, R. *Puti arkhitekturnoi mysli 1917-1932* [Directions of Architectural Thought 1917-1932]. Moscow, Ogiz-Izogiz, 1933. 144 p. illus.
       A survey of five consecutive stages in the development of Soviet architecture, 1917-32: 1) romanticism and symbolism, 2) formalism, 3) constructivism and functionalism, 4) neoclassicism and eclecticism, and 5) proletarian architecture. Also views approaching problems in the reorientation of Soviet architecture as the need to synthesize both artistic and technological problems. Somewhat biased as a result of author's prior membership in the OSA, although noticeably acquiescent to the new reorganization of Soviet architecture. Provides valuable contemporary insights into the developments of this period.

268.   Lissitzky, Lazar M. (El). *Russland: Architektur für eine Weltere-volution.* Bauwelt Fundamente 14. West Berlin, Verlag Ullstein, 1965. 207 p. illus.

A reprint of Lissitzky's 1930 book (**no. 269**), with additional reprints of articles on Soviet architecture during the period 1928-33. Includes a preface to the new edition by Werner Hebebrant. Photo reproductions of poor quality. English trans.: *Russia: An Architecture for World Revolution,* trans. Eric Dluhosch (Cambridge, Mass., M.I.T. Press, 1970, 239 p., illus.). Plates are better than those in the German issue.

269.   ——. *Russland: die Rekonstruktion der Architectur in der Sowjetunion.* Vienna, A. Scholl, 1930. 103 p. illus.

Manifesto for a new Soviet architecture based on 1) rejection of architecture as merely an emotional, individualistic, and romantic affair, 2) consideration of "objective" work as a work of art, and 3) the use of objective-scientific criteria to achieve consciously goal-directed work in architecture. Also an authoritative and detailed account of modern architecture in the Soviet Union. Valuable photographs of major buildings and projects.

270.   Lukhmanov, N. *Arkhitektura kluba* [Architecture of the Club]. Moscow, Izd-vo "Teakino pechat'," 1930. 118 p. illus.

Assesses the general trends in club design and reviews the principal clubs designed by Soviet architects in the twenties. Greatest emphasis placed on the analysis of the numerous clubs designed by Konstantin Mel'nikov.

271.   Mikhailov, A. I. *Gruppirovki sovetskoi arkhitektury* [Groupings of Soviet Architecture]. Moscow and Leningrad, Ogiz-Izogiz, 1932. 135 p. illus.

Collection of articles previously published by the author in 1930-31. Analyzes the philosophies of the Soviet architectural movements from the point of view of an emerging version of the Marxist-Leninist dialectic as propounded by the All-Union Society of Proletarian Architects, of which the author was a member. Ideological polemics impair objectivity but affirm the character and scope of the growing opposition to constructivism. Contents divided into 1) architectural groupings and the problems of Soviet architects, 2) "restorationism" and national architecture, 3) formalism in Soviet architecture, 4) the ideology of architectural constructivism, 5) VOPRA, ASNOVA, OSA (SASS), and the question of their ideological and methodological differences, and 6) the architectural movements at the competition for the Palace of Soviets.

b. Articles

272.   Afanas'ev, K. N. "Arkhitektura 1917-1920 godov" [Architecture in
        the Years 1917-1920]. In *Istoriia russkogo iskusstva* [History of
        Russian Art]. Igor' Grabar' et al., eds. v. 11. Moscow, Izd-vo
        Akademii nauk SSSR, 1957. p. 135-155.
           A concise survey of the first postrevolutionary years in Soviet
        architecture. Comparative restraint in ideological polemics. Much
        useful data, though little reference to specific activity of the
        modern movements.

273.   Antipov, P. "K voprosu organizatsii arkhitekturnykh konkursov"
        [Concerning the Question of Organizing Architectural Competi-
        tions]. *Stroitel'naia promyshlennost'*, no. 12, 1926: 885-887.
           Reviews what in these years was a very controversial enterprise
        in the Soviet architectural community and the source of much
        heated debate. Suggests two proposals to improve competitions:
        1) establish a central authority to regulate all competitions,
        regardless of sponsoring organization, and 2) develop uniform
        regulations to apply to all competitions.

274.   ——. "Vsesoiuznyi konkurs na proekt Smolenskogo rynka g. Moskvy"
        [All-Union Competition for the Project for the Smolensk Market
        in Moscow] , *Stroitelstvo Moskvy,* no. 4, 1926: 10-11.
           A review of the competition and the prize-winning designs by
        Kondrashev and Parshin (1st prize), I. A. Golosov (2nd prize),
        and M. Ginzburg (3rd prize).

275.   Aranovich, D. "Desiat' let iskusstva" [Ten Years of Art]. *Krasnaia
        nov',* no. 11, 1927: 209-238.
           An interpretive survey of the first decade of Soviet arts. Views
        architecture as being on the bottom of the scale in general
        popularity. For a revealing and perceptive assessment of Soviet
        architectural activity during this period, see p. 210-214.

276.   ——. "Sovremennaia Moskovskaia arkhitektura" [Contemporary Mos-
        cow Architecture]. *Stroitel'naia promyshlennost'*, no. 8, 1927:
        533-538.
           An account of the evolution of Soviet architecture within the
        country's capital city. Provides a revealing analysis of its prob-
        lems with public acceptance, which he views to be the product of
        the modern movements' dogmatic and highly theoretical approach.
        Few plates.

277.   ——. Vystavka sovremennoi arkhitektury [An Exhibit of Modern Architecture]. *Stroitel'naia promyshlennost'*, nos. 6-7, 1927: 451-454.

A review of the exhibit "Modern Architecture," sponsored by "Glavnauka" and held in Moscow in 1927. Laments the concentration of projects by OSA members, causing the exhibit to be very one-sided in its depiction of modern Soviet architecture (ASNOVA refused to participate). Renders an informative critique of the principal projects exhibited, including those by the Vesnins, Ginzburg, the Golosovs, Shchusev, Barkhin, and students from the VKHUTEMAS.

278.   Aranovitz (Aranovich), D. "Baukunst der Gegenwart in Moskau." *Wasmuths Monatshefte für Baukunst,* v. 13, 1929: 112-128.

An excellent summation of the development of Muscovite, though really Soviet, architecture. Includes a wealth of valuable plates; among them, rarely published projects such as Zholtovsky's House of Soviets in Machach-Kala.

279.   Arkin, David E. "Pervye shagi nashei arkhitektury" [First Steps of Our Architecture]. *Krasnaia Niva,* no. 44, 1926: 12-14.

A survey of the first efforts in the development of Soviet architecture. Characterizes modern Soviet architecture as employing 1) simplicity of form, 2) monumentality, 3) rational use of building materials and space. A few photographs of poor quality.

280.   ——. "Segodniashnii den' v arkhitekture i stroitelstve" [Today in Architecture and Construction]. *Izvestiia,* May 13, 1926. See no. 139, p. 37-38.

Published initially under the pseudonym A. Vetrov. Speaks of the emerging new circle of Soviet architects seeking expression in contemporary forms and methods of construction. Discusses the general characteristics and aspirations that bind them to their European counterparts. For a translation of essays by leading Western modern architects, with critical commentary by Arkin, see his *Arkhitektura sovremennogo zapada* [The Architecture of the Contemporary West] (Moscow, Izogiz, 1932, 187 p., illus.).

281.   Babitsky, M. "Klubnoe stroitel'stvo tekstil'shchikov" [Building of a Club for the textile Workers]. *Stroitel'stvo Moskvy,* no. 7, 1928: 5-10.

Examines the emerging field of club design and reviews the designs submitted for the Textile Workers' Club by L. A. Vesnin, V. Shchuko, M. Bibitskii, and Ia. Kornfel'd.

282. Bachinsky, N. M., and M. A. Il'in. "Arkhitektura 1921-34 godov"
      [Architecture in the Years 1921-34]. In *Istoriia russkogo iskusstva*
      [History of Russian Art]. Igor' Grabar' et al., eds. v. 11 Moscow,
      Izd-vo Akademii nauk SSSR, 1957. p. 502-557.
      A concise survey of the period. While comparatively restrained
      in ideological polemics, gives minimal treatment of the activity of
      the modern movements in the forefront of this period of Soviet
      architectural activity. Nevertheless, a marked increase in recogni-
      tion of modernists over that in historical accounts in preceding
      years. Contains much useful data.

283. Brunov, Nikolai I. "Problems of Modern Architecture." *VOKS
      Bulletin*, Nos. 10-12, 1931: 78-82.
      A popularized attempt to characterize the interest in theoreti-
      cal questions of Soviet architecture among the broad Soviet masses
      and to define the theoretical explanation of proletarian architec-
      ture vis-à-vis Marxist dialectics. Suggests the need for Soviet
      architecture to liberate itself from the influence of modern Western
      European architects and to begin giving more expression to the
      Soviet "proletarian" ideology.

284. Cherkassky, I. "Proletarskuiu arkhitekturu na peredovye pozitsii
      stroitel'nogo fronta" [Proletarian Architecture to the Leading
      Position of the Building Front]. *Stroitel'stvo Moskvy*, no. 8,
      1931: 8-9.
      Argues for adequate technical and architectural supervision of
      all projects undergoing construction. Finds that this area has been
      inadequately handled to date. A revealing discussion of a problem
      which became more controversial as the twenties drew to a close.

285. Dmitriew, Alexander. "Zeitgenössische Bestrebungen in der russischen
      Baukunst." *Wasmuths Monatshefte für Baukunst*, v. 10, 1926:
      331-336.
      A concise historical account of the evolution of Soviet archi-
      tecture, especially useful for the early years.

286. "Foreign Architects in the USSR." *Soviet Culture Review*, nos. 10-
      12, 1932: 68-71.
      A summary of the meetings held between French architects,
      whose trip was sponsored by *L'Architecture d'aujourd'hui*, and
      their Soviet counterparts for the purpose of discussing problems
      of Soviet architecture. Three conferences were held, at which
      speeches were given by Soviet architects. The talks by David Arkin

on the basic tendencies of Soviet architecture and by R. Ia. Khiger on formalism and rationalism in modern Soviet architecture are summarized. A good source.

287. Ginzburg, Moisei Ia. *"L'Architecture contemporaine." VOKS Bulletin.* nos. 42-44, Nov. 7, 1927: 26-31.

A concise historical account of the development, aims, and ideals of modern, especially constructivist, architecture in the Soviet Union.

288. ———. "Die Baukunst der Sowjet-Union." *Wasmuths Monatshefte für Baukunst,* v. 11, 1927: 409-412.

An excellent synopsis of modern Soviet architecture of the constructivist idiom in particular. Contains many valuable plates, few of which are readily accessible in other known publications.

289. ———. "Zeitgenössische Architektur in Russland." *Die Baugilde,* Oct. 1928: 1370-1372.

Discusses the state of modern architecture in the Soviet Union Cites factors which he feels have impeded its full development: 1) relatively poor economic situation, 2) low level of Soviet technology in the country's building industry, and 3) the conservatism of older generations of specialists. Factors conducive to modern architecture are seen to be 1) the rapid growth of science, 2) the intrinsic qualities of socialism, 3) the emergence of the proletariat as a new group of "clients," and 4) a growing public interest in architecture. English trans.: "Contemporary Architecture in Russia," in El Lissitzky, *Russia: An Architecture for World Revolution* (no. 268), p. 155-159.

290. Golosov, Il'ia A. "Novye puti v arkhitekture" [New Directions in Architecture]. In *Iz istorii sovetskoi arkhitektury, 1917-1925.* See no. 138. p. 26-31.

Lecture given to the Moscow Architectural Society on December 13, 1922. An illuminating overview of the emerging theoretical searches for new architectural expression. Suggests the motivations for these searches, as well as the possible forms to be employed on the basis of artistic and constructive considerations alike. A perceptive and prophetic account.

291. Il'in, Mikhail A. "L'Architecture moderne en URSS." *L'Architecture d'aujourd'hui,* no. 3, 1931: 126-130.

An elaboration of the author's article for the *VOKS Bulletin* (no. 292); more analytical, with a significant array of plates.

292.   ——. "The Building Season of 1931 in Moscow." *VOKS Bulletin* ,
        nos. 10-12, 1931: 83-87.
        Reviews the work undertaken in 1931 on the Government
        House in Minsk, the Kharkov Theater, and especially the competi-
        tion for the Palace of Soviets and the Palace of Culture in Moscow.
        A number of designs submitted to the last two competitions are
        reviewed, including those by Ladovsky and the ASNOVA groups.

293.   ——. "Dva novykh kluba" [Two New Clubs]. *Stroitel'stvo Moskvy*,
        no. 10, 1931: 15-16.
        Reviews Melnikov's "Svoboda" Factory Club and Pen's "Red
        Proletariat" Club. Interesting commentary.

294.   ——. "Modern Architecture in the Soviet Union." *VOKS Bulletin*,
        nos. 8-10, 1930: 181-185.
        A general historical survey of modern architecture in the Soviet
        Union; with a review of the work performed by the various
        architectural organizations. A useful reference.

295.   ——. "Städtebauliches aus Russland." *Wasmuths Monatshefte für
        Baukunst*, v. 15, 1931: 237-240.
        A cursory survey of modern Soviet urban theory and design,
        focusing upon the new plans for Novosibirsk. Displays the emerg-
        ing Soviet chauvinism. English trans.: "Moscow: Russian Urbanism,"
        in El Lissitzky, *Russia: An Architecture for World Revolution*
        (**No. 268**), p. 179-183.

296.   "K priezdu inostrannykh gostei" [On the Arrival of Foreign Guests] .
        Stroitel'naia promyshlennost', nos. 6-7, 1926: 464.
        Announces the arrival of the German architects Bruno Taut
        and Eric Mendelsohn in Moscow.

297.   Karra, A. Ia. "Dva klubnykh zdaniia" [Two Club Buildings].
        Stroitel'stvo Moskvy, nos. 8-9, 1930: 24-28.
        A critical review of the "Red Textile Workers" Club and
        Mel'nikov's "Burevestnik" Club; the latter evaluated as among the
        least successful of the architect's numerous clubs.

298.   ——, and V. Simbirtsev. "Forpost proletarskoi kul'tury (Konkursy na
        proekt Dvortsa kul'tury Proletarskogo raiona)" [An Outpost of
        Proletarian Culture (Competition for a Project for the Palace of

Culture of the Proletarian Region)] . *Stroitel'stvo Moskvy*, nos. 8-9, 1930: 20-24.

Reviews the designs submitted to the competition by the various architectural societies. Assessment of the various projects framed against a context of generally condemnatory polemics; for amplification, see **no. 299**.

299. ——, and V. C. Smirnov. "Novye kluby Moskvy" [New Clubs of Moscow] . *Stroitel'stvo Moskvy*, no. 11, 1929: 21-27.

Argues that the architecture of clubs must be steeped with proletarian ideas and must therefore be a carrier of proletarian monumental propaganda. Is critical of Melnikov's "Kauchuk" Club of Communication Workers and the Club for the Workers of the Frunze Factory, is somewhat less critical of I. Golosov's Club of Communication Workers on Lesnaia Street, and condemns the Club of the Construction Workers.

300. Khan-Magomedov, Selim O. "Creative Trends, 1917-1932." *Architectural Design*, no. 2, 1970: 71-76.

A detailed summary of the central developments in the evolution of modern Soviet architecture in the twenties. Identifies and discusses the major architects and personalities, clarifies the circumstances that shaped major events, and assesses the major work of the period. An important source for much valuable data, some of which is published for the first time. Profusely illustrated, though with very small plates.

301. ——. "Soviet Architecture and Town Planning of the Twenties." *Art in Revolution: Soviet Art and Design since 1917*. London, Hayward Gallery, 1971. p. 30-46.

An amplified restatement of his article in *Architectural Design* (**no. 300**); prepared for the catalogue of the exhibition "Soviet Art and Design since 1917," held at the Hayward Gallery in London, February 26 to April 18, 1971.

302. Khazanova, Vigdariia E. "K istorii sovetskoi arkhitektury pervykh posle-revoliutsionnykh let" [Toward a History of Soviet Architecture during the First Postrevolutionary Years]. *Voprosy sovremennoi arkhitektury*, no. 1, 1962: 182-226.

A comprehensive analysis of the first crucial postrevolutionary years in Soviet architecture. Argues against the notion long prevalent in the Soviet Union that this phase of architecture was merely one of "paper design" and presents an imposing array of material to develop what she contends was a period that produced a significantly high level of architectural thought and work. A precursor to the author's *Iz istorii sovetskoi arkhitektury* (**no. 139**). An excellent source on the early period.

303.   ——. "Nekotorye voprosy sinteza iskusstv v sovetskoi arkhitekture pervykh poslerevoliutsionnykh let" [Some Questions on the Synthesis of the Arts in the Soviet Architecture of the First Postrevolutionary Years]. *Voprosy sovremennoi arkhitektury*, no. 2, 1963: 97-157.

Examines the most prominent aspects of the problem during this period, such as the creation of monuments within the contemporary city, examples of monumental art in architectural facilities, and the development of new types of architectural facilities on the basis of synthesizing the various forms of art. Notes that all these efforts during this initial period have fundamental points in common: 1) a correlation among all forms of art, 2) a search for a "synthetic" form, and 3) the penetration of all these forms of art actively into the very process of life. Illuminates the work of Soviet architects during the years of heroic communism and monumental propaganda; includes much material from archives and museums that has never before been published, much of which subsequently was included in the author's *Iz istorii sovetskoi arkhitektury* (**no. 139**). An excellent source.

304.   Khomutetsky, N. "Novye materialy o monumental'noi propagande v Petrograde" [New Material Concerning Monumental Propaganda in Petrograd]. *Arkhitektura SSSR*, no. 5, 1968: 43-49.

Analyzes architectural monuments designed in Petrograd for the program of monumental propaganda. Based largely on material recently uncovered in Leningrad archives, especially in the "Leningradskii gosudarstvennyi arkhiv Oktiabr'skoi revoliutsii i sotsialisticheskogo stroitel'stva" [The Leningrad State Archive of the October Revolution and the Building of Socialism]. Valuable for illuminating important aspects of architectural activity in Leningrad during the first postrevolutionary years.

305.   Kosmachevsky G. "Arkhitektura i ratsional'noe stroitel'stvo" [Architecture and Rational Construction]. *Voprosy kommunal'nogo khoziaistva*, no. 8, 1926: 29-32.

Argues that modern rational construction proceeds from an architecture derived from the highest forms of technology, eco-

nomics, and inspired artistic taste. Explains that modern architectural philosophy must be a well-thought-out and scientifically
verifiable system of ideas. For extract of article, see *Iz istorii
sovetskoi arkhitektury, 1926-1932* (**no. 139**), p. 28-30.

306.   Kotyrev, A. "Po Leninskomu planu monumental'noi propagandy"
       [On Lenin's Plan for Monumental Propaganda]. *Arkhitektura
       SSSR*, no. 11, 1969: 34-36.
       A historical vignette on some of the principal participants and
       their work. Helpful in illuminating activity during the crucial first
       years.

307.   Kriukov, M. V. "God bor'by na stroitel'nom fronte" [A Year's
       Struggle on the Construction Front], *Stroitel'stvo Moskvy*, no. 11,
       1930: 9-12.
       A general assessment of current activity. Observes that rapid
       tempos, higher quality, and low cost are the three principal
       characteristics of the current construction campaign. Accuses
       Zholtovsky of a historical eclecticism based upon a literal copy-
       ing of Palladio, as evident in his State Bank, and chides Ginzburg
       for his "contemporary, formalistic" eclecticism in copying Le
       Corbusier in his Narkomfin Apartment House. Concedes that
       Ginzburg's is the more substantive architecture. Views eclecticism,
       formalism (rationalism), constructivism, and proletarianism (VOPRA)
       as constituting the four primary directions in contemporary Soviet
       architecture.

308.   Kroga, Irzhi (Kroha, Jiří). "Razvitie arkhitekturnoi mysli v sovetskom
       zodchestve" [Development of Architectural Thought in
       Architecture]. See **no. 123**.
       An incisive, informative analysis of the aims, ideals, and
       philosophy of the major Soviet architectural movements during
       the twenties by a Czech architect and theoretician who partici-
       pated in numerous activities of the period.

309.   Kukushkin, S. "Zametki o putiakh arkhitektury" [Observations on
       the Directions in Architecture]. *Stroitel'naia promyshlennost'*,
       no. 3, 1923: 10-13.
       A concise review of architectural activity preceding the revolu-
       tion and an assessment of the architecture of the 1923 Agricultural
       Exhibition in Moscow as pointing the way for a new architecture
       in which building materials dictate both construction and archi-
       tectural form. Informative as one of the earliest discussions of the
       new tendencies in Soviet architecture.

310.   Lavrov, F. "Moskovskii krematorii i ego znachenie" [Moscow
       Crematorium and Its Significance]. *Stroitel'stvo Moskvy*, no. 5,
       1926: 5-7.
          Speaks of the crematorium as the new trend of burial. Reviews
       the prize-winning designs for the Moscow crematorium by D.
       Osipov (1st prize), K. Melnikov (2nd prize), and V. Diakonov
       (3rd prize).

311.   Lissitzky, Lazar M. (El). "Architektur der SSSR." *Das Kunstblatt*,
       no. 2, 1925.
          A brief commentary on the evolution of Soviet architecture.
       Especially useful for characterizing the numerous developments
       in the first five postrevolutionary years, a period particularly
       obscured through insufficient availability of material. For English
       trans.: Lissitzky-Küppers, *El Lissitzky* (no. 994), p. 367-369.

312.   ——. "Katastrofa arkhitektury" [Catastrophe of Architecture]. IZO.
       Vestnik otdela izobrazitel'nykh iskusstv [IZO. Annals of the
       Division of Fine Arts], no. 1, March 10, 1921.
          An incisive evaluation of the work being done by the Political-
       Architectural Section within the Department of Fine Arts under
       the Commissariat of People's Education. Assesses the general
       classicizing approach of the "Old School" architects working in
       this section. A valuable reference to this early period. For English
       trans.: Lissitzky-Küppers, *El Lissitzky* (no. 994), p. 365-367.

313.   Liubimova, G. N. "Poiski novykh tipov zhilishcha v sovetskoi
       arkhitekture 20-kh godov" [Searches for New Types of Housing
       in Soviet Architecture during the Twenties]. *Voprosy sovremen-
       noi arkhitektury* no. 1, 1962: 227-263.
          An analytical study of the development of housing design in
       modern Soviet architecture during the twenties, especially by the
       constructivists. Much of the data and plates are taken from the
       periodical *S.A.* and the publications of the Moscow Architectural
       Society. An excellent source.

314.   L-ov. "Novoe zdanie Leninskoi biblioteki, kak monumental'nyi
       pamiatnik epokhi" [New Building for the Lenin Library as a
       Monumental Memorial of the Epoch]. *Stroitel'stvo Moskvy*, no.
       7, 1929: 18-21.
          A review of the second phase of the important competition,
       the participants being D. and V. Friedman, and D. Markov, A. V.
       Shchusev, the Vesnins, and V. A. Shchuko. The latter's design,
       revised from his first submission, was selected by the jury.

315. M. "Krupnye postroiki tekushchego sezona" [Large-scale Construction of the Current Season]. *Stroitel'stvo Moskvy*, no. 9, 1926: 2-5.
Reviews Barkhin's final design for Izvestiia Building and Velikovsky's design for the Gostorg Building. A useful analysis with illustrations.

316. ——. "Krupnye postroiki tekushchego sezona" [Large-scale Construction of the Current Season]. *Stroitel'stvo Moskvy*, no. 10, 1926: 22-25.
Reviews Kokorin's project for the State Research Petroleum Institute and Rerberg's project for the Moscow Central Telegraph, both under construction.

317. ——. "Krupnye postroiki tekushchego sezona" [Large-scale Construction of the Current Season]. *Stroitel'stvo Moskvy*, no. 12, 1926: 6-8.
Reviews Greinert's Anatomical Institute at Moscow State University and the Kozhsindikat Building. Interesting for revealing concurrent traditional trends apart from the mainstream of modern architecture.

318. ——. "Krupnye postroiki tekushchego sezona" [Large-scale Construction of the Current Season]. *Stroitel'stvo Moskvy*, no. 9, 1927: 1-5.
Reviews Zholtovsky's State Bank Building, Tarle's Ambulatory, and Kuznetsov's All-Union Electro-technical Institute.

319. ——. "Krupnye postroiki tekushchego sezona" [Large-scale Construction of the Current Season]. *Stroitel'stvo Moskvy*, no. 11, 1927: 1-7.
A review of Kuznetsov's Wool Laboratory of the Moscow Textile Institute, Melnikov's Club of the Union of Communication Workers, and I. Golosov's Club for the Union of Communication Workers (different clubs). Contains excellent graphic material for the projects.

320. ——. "Novye kluby u khemikov" [New Clubs for the Chemists]. *Stroitel'stvo Moskvy*, no. 1, 1928: 18-21.
Reviews Mel'nikov's "Kauchuk" Club for the Sergievsky Factory. Contains much useful graphic material, though at a small scale.

321.   M., A. "Institut V. I. Lenina" [V. I. Lenin Institute]. *Stroitel'stvo Moskvy*, no. 9, 1926: 1-2.
       Discusses the building designed by S. Chernyshev, nearing completion in Moscow.

322.   ——. "Shablovskaia radiostantsiia" [Shablovsky Radio Station]. *Stroitel'stvo Moskvy*, no. 2, 1927: 10-11.
       A descriptive account of the famous conical wire tower and its construction in Moscow.

323.   Markovnikov, N. "Korbuz'e i ego novye eskizy doma Tsentrosoiuza" [Le Corbusier and His New Plans for the Centrosoiuz Building]. *Stroitel'naia promyshlennost'*, nos. 11-12, 1928: 850-852.
       An analysis of Le Corbusier's latest submission. Critique adapted from the report of the special commission organized to review the project. For a statement by Le Corbusier on the variant, see his "Osnovnye printsipy proekta postroiki doma Tsentrosiuza" [Basic Principles of the Project for Erecting the Centrosoiuz Building]. *Stroitel'naia promyshlennost'*, nos. 11-12, 1928: 849-850.

324.   ——. "Zhiloi dom v traktovke Korbiuz'e" [The House as Interpreted by Le Corbusier]. *Stroitel'naia promyshlennost'*, no. 10, 1926: 732-734.
       A perceptive review and assessment of Le Corbusier's notions on the nature of a house and the manner in which it is best to be designed, as gleaned from his various publications. Includes a discussion of Le Corbusier's notions on the problem of housing.

325.   Mestnov, A. "Konkurs na sostavlenie proekta novogo zdaniia biblioteki im. Lenina" [Competition for Developing a Project for a New Building for the Lenin Library]. *Stroitel'stvo Moskvy*, no. 6, 1928: 3-8.
       Reports on the first round of the competition. Reviews the program and the projects submitted by Shchuko, Shchusev, the Vesnins, Markov and others, Kondrashev and others, Ovsianikov, Serafimov, and P. Golosov and others (the recognition for awards coming in that order).

326.   ——. "Zakliuchitel'nyi konkurs na dom Tsentrosoiuza" [Final Competition for the Centrosoiuz Building]. *Stroitel'stvo Moskvy*, no. 1, 1929:20-24.

A review of projects submitted by the Vesnins, P. M. Nachman, A. A. Ol', Le Corbusier, Peter Behrens, A. Pasternak, et al. (OSA), I. Leonidov (OSA), and A. S. Nikol'sky. Includes commentary by the jury. Le Corbusier's project selected; for additional information of Le Corbusier's involvement, see nos. **323, 325,** and **345.**

327. "Moskovskie arkhitekturnye organizatsii po povodu konkursa na zdanie Leninskoi biblioteki" [Moscow Architectural Organizations on the Competition for the Building of the Lenin Library]. *Stroitel'stvo Moskvy,* no. 7, 1929: 22.

Declarations of protest against the selection of V. A. Shchuko's design from the ARU, the architectural circle at VKHUTEIN, and ASNOVA. The editors of the journal petitioned. A. V. Lunacharsky chairman of the competition commision, to explain why Shchuko's design was selected and why the younger architects were excluded from participation. See no. **336.**

328. "Moskovskie khudozhniki i arkhitektory ob iiun'skom plenume TsK (1931)" [Moscow Artists and Architects on the June Plenum of the Central Committee (1931)]. *Za proletarskoe iskusstvo,* no. 7, 1931: 32.

Reports the unanimous resolution issued at a joint meeting of the Russian Association of Proletarian Artists (RAPKh), the Federation of Artistic Societies, and Izogoz, pledging cooperation with the party's June 1930 decree concerning the rehabilitation of Moscow.

329. "Moskovskoe zhilishchnoe stroitel'stvo v otsenke arkh. Bruno Tauta" [Moscow Housing Construction in the Assessment of Architect Bruno Taut]. *Stroitel'naia promyshlennost',* nos. 6-7, 1926: 466-468.

Summary of a speech delivered to a meeting of the Housing Construction Committee of the Moscow Soviet. Outlines his impressions of the housing enterprise, made as a consultant to the Moscow Soviet. Points out both positive and negative aspects and suggests several concrete measures for improvement. Commentary divided by category into 1) siting of buildings, 2) technological considerations, 3) plans of buildings, and 4) architectural detailing and finishing of buildings.

330. "Nedavnye konkursy" [Recent Competitions]. *Stroitel'naia promyshlennost',* no. 2, 1926: 143-144.

Reviews competitions held in 1925 by the Moscow Architectural Society for the Building of Textile Workers, the Central Telegraph, and the International Radio and Telephone Building.

331.   Nekrasov, Aleksandr I. "Puti arkhitektury (k probleme stilia sovremennoi arkhitektury)" [Directions of Architecture (On the Problem of Style in Modern Architecture)]. *Pechat' i revoliutsiia*, no. 4, 1928: 66-76.

Analyzes rationalist elements prevalent in prerevolutionary Russian architecture and compares them with developments in Soviet architecture. An interesting treatment. For extract, see *Iz istorii sovetskoi arkhitektury 1926-1932* (**no. 139**), p. 14-21.

332.   Novitsky, P. "Stroitel'stvo sotsializma i stil' sovremennoi arkhitektury" [The Building of Socialism and the Style of Contemporary Architecture]. *Pechat' i revoliutsiia*, no. 2, 1928: 54-67.

An article by the director of the VKHUTEIN. Reviews construction, architecture, and "bourgeois art" in the USSR. Focuses upon an analysis of the tectonic components of style in modern Soviet architecture. Underlying the article is an attempt to resolve the controversy between the more profoundly innovative aims of modern Soviet architecture and the superficial interpretation of these aims as the mere copying of certain readily perceivable "modern" forms. A thoughtful, penetrating analysis which brings into sharp focus many of the leading theoretical currents in the architectural activity of the period.

333.   Pasternak, A. "Novye sotsial'nye tipy zhilishcha" [New Social Types of Housing] *Stroitel'stvo Moskvy*, no. 5, 1929: 9-16.

Reviews the experimental work undertaken by Moisei Ia. Ginzburg to develop new prototypes for housing design, what Ginzburg called "social condensers."

334.   "Pervyi otvet" [A First Reply]. *Stroitel'stvo Moskvy*, no. 10, 1929: 21-22.

VOPRA accepts the OSA's call for a conference on housing problems (see **no. 344**). Outlines the framework within which it feels such a conference ought to be conducted.

335.   Popov, N. "Sostoianie zhilishchnogo dela k 10-letii Oktiabria" [State of Housing Affairs on the Tenth Anniversary of October]. *Stroitel'stvo Moskvy*, no. 10, 1927: 2-11.

A highly useful analytical review of a decade of activity in the realm of housing design and construction. Categories under consideration include municipal construction in Moscow, activity during the period of the New Economic Policy (NEP), during the period of reconstruction (1924-27), and new construction. Contains valuable data and statistics.

336. "Protest." *S. A.,*no. 3, 1929: 88.
      Declarations of protest issued by ASNOVA, ARU, OSA, VOPRA, and VKHUTEIN against the selection of V. A. Shchuko's design for the Lenin Library. See also **no. 327.**

337. Rozenberg, A. "Sovremennaia praktika konkursnogo dela v arkhitekture" [Contemporary Practice of Competitions in Architecture]. *Stroitel'naia promyshlennost'*, no. 8, 1926: 564-566.
      A systematic analysis and assessment of competitions in Soviet architecture during the twenties. Reveals serious shortcomings in the manner in which they are conducted. For a comparative study on competitions in prerevolutionary Russian architecture, see author's "Osnovnye polozheniia konkursov v sovremennykh usloviiakh" [Basic Conditions of Competitions in Contemporary Circumstances], *Stroitel'naia promyshlennost'*, no. 2, 1926: 139.

338. Shcherbakov, V, "Arkhitektura zavodskikh sooruzhenii" [Architecture of Factory Complexes]. *Stroitel'stvo Moskvy*, no. 5, 1927: 6-8.
      A review of A. V. Shvidkovsky's design for the Cellulose Paper Factory.

339. ——. "Konkurs na zdaniia tipovykh klubov" [Competition for Buildings for Typical Clubs]. *Stroitel'stvo Moskvy*, no. 5, 1927: 8-13.
      A review of projects submitted to the competition, including P. A. Golosov's prize-winning design.

340. ——. "Vystavka 'Sovremennaia Arkhitektura.' " [The Exhibit "Contemporary Architecture"]. *Stroitel'stvo Moskvy*, no. 7, 1927: 8-11.
      A review of the exhibit sponsored by the Art Department of Glavnauka and the OSA.

341. Shchusev, Aleksei V. "Arkhitektura i gradostroitel'stvo" [Architecture and City Planning]. *Izvestiia,* Oct. 15, 1926.

A general overview of Soviet architecture and city planning, focusing upon the searches for contemporary new directions in Soviet architecture.

342.   ——. "Arkhitektura novaia" [New Architecture]. In *Bol'shaia sovetskaia entsiklopediia* [Great Soviet Encyclopedia]. v. 3. Moscow, izd-vo Bol'shaia sovetskaia entsiklopediia, 1926, p. 569-570.
        Describes the scope and intent of the activity of modern Soviet architecture. Interestingly, assumes a distinct tone of advocacy.

343.   Simbirtsev, V. N. "Itogi goda (arkhitekturnyi obzor)" [Results of the Year (An architectural Review)]. *Stroitel'stvo Moskvy*, no. 11, 1929: 2-5.
        An informative and revealing review of architectural practice. Notes two concurrent trends of eclectical revival and contemporary innovation in Soviet architecture. A useful analysis.

344.   "Sotsialisticheskoe sorevnovanie. OSA vyzyvaet." [A Socialist Competition. The OSA Issues a Challenge]. *Stroitel'stvo Moskvy*, no. 10, 1929: 21.
        A call to ASNOVA, MAO, VOPRA, VOGI, ARU, and other organizations to participate in a conference and competition on the problem of housing. See no. 334.

345.   Tatarinov, E. "Dva konkursa na dom Tsentrosoiuza" [Two Competitions for the Centrosoiuz Building]. *Stroitel'stvo Moskvy*, no. 11, 1928: 2-6.
        Reviews the initial designs submitted to the competition in which B. M. Velikovskii was awarded first prize, although Le Corbusier's project was recommended for further development and resubmission. Discussion supplemented by extracts from the responses of the jury to the projects cited. For information on further phases of the competition, see nos. 323, 325, and 326.

346.   Turkenidze, A. "Vnimanie arkhitekturnym kadram" [Attention Architectural Cadres]. *Stroitel'stvo Moskvy*, no. 11, 1929: 35-36.
        Admonishes Soviet architects to be mindful of the task besetting the country in the fulfillment of the First Five Year Plan.

347.   Velikovsky, G. "Arkhitekturnye konkursy v zhil'stroitel'stve" [Architectural Competitions in Housing Construction]. *Stroitel'naia promyshlennost'*, no. 1, 1925: 3-4.

Argues for intensifying competitions by establishing the following conditions: 1) establish new practical criteria related to realistic, and especially economic, conditions, 2) diminish the influence of the "graphic factor" or mere outward artistic effect of the presentation in favor of judging the essence and feasibility of the solution, 3) pay attention to the make-up of the jury, making sure that it is aware of the program, and 4) introduce a wide spectrum of specialists into the jury.

348.   Venderov, V. "Arkhitektura staroi i novoi Moskvy" [Architecture of Old and New Moscow]. *Stroitel'stvo Moskvy*, no. 10, 1927: 37-45 .

A comprehensive review of principal buildings recently erected in Moscow, including Chernyshev's Lenin Institute and his Export-Bread Building, V. Vesnin's Mineral Institute, Barkhin's Izvestiia Building, Velikovsky's Gostorg Building, and Rerberg's Moscow Central Telegraph Building. A useful analytical overview.

349.   ——. "Istochniki sovremennykh arkhitekturnykh form" [Sources of Contemporary Architectural Forms]. *Stroitel'naia promyshlennost'*, no. 3, 1926: 217-218.

An interpretive survey of recent architectural work, focusing upon the basis of their designs.

350.   ——. "Tsentral'nyi telegraf v Moskve" [Central Telegraph Building in Moscow]. *Stroitel'stvo Moskvy*, no. 2, 1926: 6-8.

Reviews the competition for the building and comments on the growing trend toward the glass, concrete, and steel expression of the constructivist style. Paradoxically, article was written prior to the announcement of Rerberg's as the winning design.

351.   Vesnin, Viktor, and Moisei Ia. Ginzburg. "Dostizheniia sovremennoi arkhitektury" [Accomplishments of Modern Architecture]. In *Nauka i tekhnika SSSR 1917-1927* [Science and Technology in the USSR, 1917-1927]. v. 3. Moscow, 1928, p. 405-453.

A comprehensive survey of the development of modern Soviet architecture and the aims, ideals, and accomplishments of the various movements and organizations, with emphasis placed on the OSA and the functionalists. Cites technological developments as providing the basis for the achievements of modern architecture both in the Soviet Union and elsewhere.

352.   Vygodsky, L. "Sovremennaia arkhitektura na Zapade" [Contemporary
        Architecture in the West]. *Stroitel'stvo Moskvy*: Part I, No. 4,
        1927: 24-26; Part II, no. 5, 1927: 24-27; Part III, no. 6, 1927:
        25-26.

        A receptive review of the work of Wright, Gropius, Mies van der
        Rohe, Mendelsohn, Perret, Le Corbusier, Wagner, Berlage, and
        Oud, with commentary relating their work to developments in the
        Soviet Union. An interesting comparative commentary.

2. By Non-Soviet Writers

a. Monographs

352a.   Bliznakov, Milka T. "The Search for a Style: Modern Architecture in
        the U.S.S.R., 1917-1932." Ph.D. dissertation. Columbia University,
        1971. 242 p.

        An examination of the growth of Soviet architectural thought
        and its relation to the theory in the Soviet arts. Emphasis on the
        first half of the period. Includes an account of the basic historical
        sources for aesthetic ideas in the first decade of the twentieth
        century. Provides access to much useful material.

353.   De Feo, Vittorio. *URSS: Architettura 1917-1936.* Rome, Editori
        Riuniti, 1963. 194 p. illus.

        One of the best available surveys of Soviet architecture, 1917-
        36, based largely on a synthesis of published sources. Begins with
        an analysis of prerevolutionary activity to investigate the antece-
        dents of Soviet architecture, discusses the activities and work of
        the architectural movements and their exchange with European
        architects, and investigates city planning which, it is argued, binds
        the various movements more directly to political considerations.
        Concludes that the monumental neoclassical revival was launched
        by the competitions for the Palace of Soviets and the Kharkov
        Theater. Amply supplemented with pictorial and supporting
        material, though with lax format of footnote and bibliographical
        entries. Useful for its attempt to place the developments in Soviet
        architecture, as well as their precedents, in a historical context of
        continuity and interrelationships.

354.   Freeman, Joseph, Joshua Kunitz, and Louis Lozowick. *Voices of
        October. Art and Literature in Soviet Russia.* New York, Vanguard
        Press, 1930. 317 p., with front plates.

        A penetrating, useful investigation of the political, ideological,
        and aesthetic roots of the emerging Soviet traditions in art and
        architecture, with a general appraisal of architectural activity.
        Bibliography, p. 315-317.

355.   Kopp, Anatole. *Ville et révolution. Architecture et urbanisme soviétiques des années vingt.* Paris, Editions Anthropos, 1967. 278 p. illus.

The first interpretive survey of developments in modern Soviet architecture and city planning in the twenties based largely upon primary sources and supplemented by a wealth of illustrations and documented material. Romanticized account provides an introduction to the social, political, and economic circumstances of the country and a survey of prerevolutionary architecture as a background for the discussion of the development of modern architecture and planning. Appendixes provide translated excerpts from important theoretical texts, manifestos, and official documents. Of greatest value for making available a wealth of material published heretofore only in the Russian language; ineffective organization of material and laxity of format detract somewhat from the effectiveness of the work. For bibliography, see **no. 30.** For English trans.: *Town and Revolution. Soviet Architecture and City Planning, 1917-1935,* trans. Thomas E. Burton (New York, G. Braziller, 1970, 274 p., illus.).

356.   Mendelsohn, Erich. *Russland, Europa, Amerika, ein architektonischer Querschnitt.* Berlin. R. Mosse, 1929. 214 p. illus.

An overview of architecture in the Soviet Union from medieval times to the date of publication, through a random selection of plates with brief commentary. A number of valuable plates on modern Soviet architecture, though of modest quality.

357.   Miliukov, Paul N. *Architecture, Painting, and Music in Russia.* v. 3 of his *Outlines of Russian Culture.* Michael Karpovich, ed. Trans Valentine Ughet and Eleanor Davis. Philadelphia, University of Pennsylvania Press, 1942.

A translated abridgment of Miliukov's *Ocherki po istorii russkoi kul'tury* [Essays on the History of Russian Culture]. (Paris, 1930-37, 3 v.). Includes an informed essay on Soviet architecture through the early thirties, "Art in Soviet Russia," see especially p. 96-100. Especially useful for a perceptive analysis of the factors operating behind the negation of modernism in favor of the classical reincarnation.

358.   Quilici, Vieri. *L'architettura del Construttivizmo.* Bari, Laterza, 1969. 217 p. illus.

A comprehensive account of the entire modern movement in Soviet architecture, rather than only of constructivism, during the 15 years following the Revolution. Divided into two sections:

1) essay treating the various currents and countercurrents, the official reactions, and the personal feuds among the leading personalities, and 2) an anthology of writings, manifestos, programs, and official decrees. Among the best attempts to date to place developments in their historical perspective and to provide effective access to much useful Soviet source material.

359.   Senkevitch, Anatole Jr. *Soviet Architecture: The Evolution of the Contemporary Idiom.* Brownsville, privately printed, 1967. 97 p.
Examines the roots and development of modern Soviet architecture and the factors of long-range change that accounted for the ultimate denial of modernism in favor of socialist realism in 1932.

360.   Willen, Paul. "Soviet Architecture in Transformation: A Study in Ideological Manipulation." Master's thesis. Columbia University, 1953. 239 p.
Submitted to the Graduate Faculty of Political Science at Columbia University. An analysis of Soviet architecture, 1917-36, with concentration on ideological considerations consistent with the general goals set for the work. Discusses major developments and architectural movements, summarizes some crucial debates and key governmental decisions and decrees, and notes important personalities. Of great value for providing access to much important documented material. The author published an article generally adapted from his thesis in *Problems of Communism* (**no. 407**) in 1954.

b. Articles

361.   Agache, Alfred. "L'Urbanisme et l'architecture chez les Soviets." *L'Architecture d'aujourd'hui,* v. 2, no. 8, 1932: 59-60.
A brief review, with photographs, of current work in the Soviet Union.

362.   "Architecture moderne et le problème de l'habitation en URSS." *L'Architecture d'aujourd'hui,* v. 1, no. 8, 1931: 11-16.
An illustrated account of housing and modern architecture in the Soviet Union. Contains many useful plates.

363.   "Architektur Russlands." *ABC,* nos. 3-4, 1925: 1-2.
A summary of the highlights in Soviet architectural activity. Focuses upon the campaign for modern architecture.

364.   Auffray, Pierre. "Architecture soviétique." *Cahiers d'art,* v. 1,
       June 1926: 103-108.
           A concise analysis of the emergence of modern Soviet archi-
       tecture, including excellent plates of early designs. A useful source.

365.   Badovici, Jean. "Le Moment architectural en URSS." *L'Architecture
       vivante,* Fall and Winter, 1930: 5-10, with accompanying plates,
       p. 11-50.
           A general account of the development of modern architecture
       in the Soviet Union from its beginnings to 1930. Provides an
       excellent synopsis. Most valuable for its extensive assortment of
       excellent photographs and drawings of projects.

366.   ——. "Le Moment héroique de l'architecture moderne en URSS."
       L'Architecture vivante, Spring-Summer, 1933: 5-6.
           Speaks of the initial hope for modern architecture created by
       the Bolshevik Revolution and the overthrow of the *ancien régime*
       and notes the gradual rise of the older generation of architects
       schooled in the classical idiom of the academy over the younger
       modernists, as seen in the competition for the Palace of Soviets.
       Refers to the competition for a theater in Kharkov as modern
       architecture's heroic last stand in the Soviet Union.

367.   Bardi, P. M. "La Soi-disant Architecture russe." *L'Architecture
       d'aujourd'hui,* v. 2, no. 8, 1932: 73-74.
           An interesting appraisal of recent developments in Soviet
       architecture vis-à-vis the competition for the Palace of Soviets.

368.   Barr, Alfred. "Notes on Russian Architecture." *The Arts,* v. 15,
       Feb. 1929: 99-105.
           An interesting and useful survey of the development of modern
       Soviet architecture, with accounts of work and personalities of
       the OSA and ASNOVA. Based on personal travel to the USSR.

369.   Bueckschmitt, Justus. "Städtplanung in der Sowjetunion." In his *Ernst
       May.* Stuttgart, Alexander Koch, 1963. p. 59-77.
           An account of Ernst May's work in the Soviet Union in 1930-
       34. Includes useful observations and assessments of developments
       in Soviet architecture and planning during the period.

370.   Byron, Robert. "The Russian Scene, I: The Foundations." *Architectural Review,* v. 71, May 1932: 173-195.
         Attempts to deal comprehensively with the substance not only of Soviet architecture but also of Soviet life from a position of ostentatious and highly superficial assumptions. Based upon a brief period of travel and observation in the country.

371.   "Les Dernières Réalisations architecturales en Russie." *Cahiers d'art,* v. 4, no. 1, 1929: 46-50.
         A survey of current work by Soviet architects; includes excellent photographs of Zholtovsky's Moscow Hydroelectric Station, The Vesnins' "Mostorg" Department Store, Velikovsky's "Gostorg" Building, Barkhin's Izvestiia Building, and Ginzburg's "Gostrakh" Building.

372.   Drubkin, A. L. "American Architects and Engineers in Russia." *Pencil Points,* v. 11, June 1930: 435-440.
         A survey of American personnel and their work in the Soviet Union.

373.   Elderfield, John. "Constructivism and the Objective World: An Essay on Production Art and Proletarian Culture." *Studio International,* v. 180, Sept. 1970: 73-80.
         Surveys the evolution of the modern movement in the Soviet arts. Includes an impressionistic assessment of the positions of the principal currents in modern Soviet architecture: the constructivists (OSA), the rationalists (ASNOVA), and the proletarians (VOPRA).

374.   ——. "The Line of Free Men: Tatlin's 'Tower' and the Age of Invention." *Studio International,* v.178, Nov. 1969: 162-167.
         Maintains that the political connection of art is an important aspect of an avant-garde consciousness and suggests that the great period of Russian art after the Revolution is perhaps its most significant demonstration. Views Tatlin's Monument for the Third International as a unique achievement in twentieth-century art and architecture and as the genesis of much work in the period. An absorbing analysis and appraisal.

375.   Frampton, Kenneth. "Notes on a Lost Avant-Garde: Architecture USSR, 1920-30." In *The Avant-Garde,* v. 34 of *Art News Annual.* New York, Macmillan, 1968.

A perceptive characterization and overview of the modern movement in Soviet architecture during the twenties. Reproduced in *Avant-Garde Art,* Thomas B. Hess and John Ashbery, eds. (London, Collier, 1968), p. 107-124. For a more recent version of the essay, see his "Notes on a Lost Avant-Garde," *Art in Revolution. Soviet Art and Design since 1917* (London, Hayward Gallery, 1971), p. 21-29.

376.   ——. "Notes on Soviet Urbanism, 1917-32." *Architect's Yearbook 12.* London, Elek Books, 1968. p. 246-252.

An account of planning activity in the Soviet Union during the twenties, summarizing the work of leading Soviet and Western architects during this period. Useful as a good synopsis of material readily available in the West.

377.   "Gutachten der Jury auf Architektursusstellung in Moskau. Mai 1926." *Wasmuths Monatshefte für Baukunst,* v. 10, 1926: 337-339.

Contains the results of the architectural competition organized by the Moscow Architectural Society in May 1926. Plates of A. Dmitriev's design for the Administrative Building and a factory in Kharkov.

378.   Hegman, Werner. "Lenin-ehrung: Auditorium, Glühbirne oder Luft-balloon?" *Wasmuths Monatshefte für Baukunst,* v. 13, 1929: 129-132.

A thoughtful analysis of the ideals behind the works of modern Soviet architecture, as well as the tectonic translation of these ideals into architectural form.

379.   Hoog, Michel. "Situation de l'avant-garde russe/The Situation of the Avant-Garde in Russia." *Cimaise,* nos. 85-86, 1968: 11-22.

Article in both French and English. Characterizes the general ambiance of the period 1917-30 within both a national and an international context.

380.   "In che consiste l'avanguardia russa?" *Stile,* no. 10, 1946: 4-8.

An interesting survey of the avant-garde in Soviet art, including the roots of modern Soviet architecture.

381.   Junghanns, Kurt. "Die Beziehungen zwischen und sowjetischen
       Architekten in den Jahren 1917 bis 1933." *Wissenschaftliche
       Zeitschrift der Humbolt Universität*, v. 16, no. 3, 1967: 369-381.
       Illuminates the contacts established between Soviet and Western
       architects during the given period. Contains much useful informa-
       tion, the result of recent research.

382.   Kopp, Anatole. "Architecture in the Soviet Union of the Twenties"
       International Asbestos Cement Review, no. 44, 1966: 12-15.
       A general review. Focuses on the work of the architects Moisei
       Ginzburg, Ivan Leonidov, and the Vesnin brothers. A precursor to
       the author's book on the subject (**no. 355**).

383.   ——. "Zux sources de l'architecture contemporaine: L'URSS des
       années vingt." *La pensée*, no. 127, May-June 1966: 44-69.
       A general account of modern Soviet architecture in the twenties
       with emphasis upon its theoretical genesis and its principal move-
       ments. Preceded the author's book on the subject. (**no. 355**).

384.   Lubetkin, Berthold. "Recent Developments of Town Planning in the
       USSR." *Architectural Review*, v. 71, May 1932: 209-214.
       A review of the theories and organizations in Soviet city
       planning, with the struggle to receive official approval in line with
       Marxian dialectics. Highly useful for clarifying theories and aspects
       of work of major Soviet architects.

385.   ——. "The Russian Scene, II: The Builders." *Architectural Review*,
       v. 71, May 1932: 201-208.
       A comprehensive review of the aims and ideals of the major
       architectural organizations and movements in Soviet architecture
       by a Soviet architect who participated in the very activities
       he describes. Of great value for illuminating the historical relation-
       ships of these movements and their struggle for official recognition.

386.   ——. "Town and Landscape Planning in Soviet Russia." *Journal of the
       Town Planning Institute*, v. 19, Feb. 1933: 69-75.
       One of the best analytical descriptions of Soviet city planning
       principles and practices of the period. Especially interesting for its
       comparison of the architectural ideologies of the twenties and the
       emerging official concept of architecture and aesthetics.

387. May, Ernst. "Neue Bauen in der Sowjetunion" *Das neue Russland,*
v. 8-9, Aug.-Sept. 1931: 50-52.
A comprehensive survey of the various aspects of contemporary
Soviet urban design. A useful reference. English Trans.: "Moscow:
City Building in the USSR," in El Lissitizky, *Russia:An Architecture for World Revolution* (no. 268), p. 188-203.

388. ——. "Von Frankfurt nach dem neun Russland." *Frankfurt Zeitung,*
no. 892, 1930.
Report of the architect's initial impressions of the Soviet Union
and of his work there. English trans.: "From Frankfurt to the
New Russia," in El Lissitzky, *Russia: An Architecture for World
Revolution* (no. 268), p. 175-179.

389. Meyer, Hannes. "Bauen, Bauarbeiter und Techniker in der Sowjetunion." *Das Neue Russland,* v. 8-9, 1931.
A highly sympathetic account of the Soviet experience by the
third Bauhaus director, then practicing in Moscow. Contains some
interesting insights into emerging trends and especially of the
general VOPRA mentality, Meyer having been a member of the
group. English trans.: "Moscow: Construction, Construction
Workers, and Technicians in the Soviet Union," in El Lissitzky,
Russia: An Architecture for World Revolution (no. 268), p. 213-
217.

390. Midana, Arturo. "Nota sull'architettura e l'edilizia del l'URSS."
L'architettura italiana, Oct. 1935: 344-353.
An analysis of Soviet architecture and of the transition from
modernism to a revival of classicism.

391. "Nouvelles architectures soviétiques." *Cahiers d'art,* v. 2, no. 1,
1927: 40-44; v. 2, no. 2, 1927: 79-84.
Both installments provide a review of current projects; the
first contains brief introductory comments, while the second
presents statements by I. N. Sobolev on his design for the Palace
of Labor and by M. Barshch and M. Siniavsky on their design for
the Central Hall. Excellent plates.

392. Pasternak, A. "Pis'mo v redaktsiiu" [Letter to the Editor]. *S.A.,*
no. 3, 1927: 107-108.
An account of the invitation extended to Eric Mendelsohn,
Berlin architect, to design the "Krasnaia Znamia" Factory for the

Leningrad Textile Trust and the subsequent attacks upon the architect's design, to which Mendelsohn's letter (p. 108) is responding. Letter outlines the work which Mendelsohn completed for the realization of the project, establishing the extent of technical work developed for the project after being accused of having employed little technical expertise in the project. For extracts from his personal letters containing additional background on Mendelsohn's design, see *Eric Mendelsohn: Letters of an Architect*, trans. Geoffrey Strachan, Oskar Beyer, ed. (London, New York, Toronto, Abelard-Schuman, 1967), p. 86-88, 90, 92-92, 96-97.

393.   Ragon, Michel. "La Revolution architecturale en URSS de 1921 a 1932/The Architectural Revolution in USSR from 1921 to 1932." *Cimaise,* nos. 85-86, 1968: 46-57.

Article in both French and English. A brisk characterization of the highlights of the period, both theory and practice. Laments the Soviet episode's having been ignored, until just recently, in the consideration of modern architecture.

394.   Schmidt, Hans. "Die Sowjetunion und das neue Bauen." *Die neue Stadt*, v. 6-7, 1932: 146-148.

Commentary on the outcome of the competition for the Palace of Soviets. Provides a cogent assessment of the emerging turn away from modern architecture. English trans.: "The Soviet Union and Modern Architecture," in El Lissitzky, *Russia: An Architecture for World Revolution* (**no. 268**), p. 218-222.

395.   Seidenberg, Roderick. "Symmetry and Ornament Discarded as Russia Cast Off the Past." *American Architect*, v. 137, Dec. 1930: 48-49, 72, 74.

A thoughtful, concise analysis of the modern developments in Soviet architecture by an American who acted as consulting architect on a number of building projects in the Soviet Union. Discusses the salient characteristics of modern Soviet architecture as 1) functional, 2) stark and barren, the product of an economy of means, 3) devoid of superficial ornamentation, with expressiveness achieved by manipulation of form alone, 4) rejection of symmetry, 5) use of circular and semicircular forms in conjunction with rectangular masses, and 6) communal in nature, expressive of the mass functions it is designed to serve.

396. Seuphor, Michel. "Au temps de l'avant-garde." *L'Oeil*, no. 11, 1955: 24-39.

An excellent survey of avant-garde art in Russia and the Soviet Union, including the roots of modern architecture. Profusely illustrated with good plates.

397. Stein, Wilm. "Versuch sozialistischer Städte." *Bauwelte*, v. 21, 1931: 703-704.

An assessment of the construction of socialist cities and communal facilities, as well as of the changing concepts in their design. English trans.: "Experiment: 'Socialist Cities,' " in El Lissitsky, *Russia: An Architecture for World Revolution* (**no. 268**), p. 184-187.

398. Stern, Serge. "Les Intellectuels en Russie sovietique: Les architectes." *Cahiers bleus,* no. 1, 1924: 230-238.

An illuminating interpretive account of the nucleus of Soviet architects involved in seeking new contemporary architectural forms.

399. Taut, Bruno. "Arkhitektura kak vyrazitel' vlasti" [Architecture As an Expression of Power]. *Stroitel'naia promyshlennost'*, nos. 6-7, 1926: 465-466.

Article by Taut, in Moscow as a consultant to the housing division of the Moscow Soviet (city council). Lauds the rise of the proletariat as an important historical event. Maintains that its forms of art must not be the product of blind repetitions of the forms and methods of the vanquished epoch. Outlines the general revolutionary character which he feels Soviet architecture ought to assume. For a summary of Taut's speech to the Moscow Architectural Society, the first portion of which repeated this article, see O. Vutke, "Na Doklade B. Tauta v Moskovskom Arkhitekturnom Ob-ve" [Bruno Taut's Speech at the Moscow Architectural Society], *Stroitel'naia promyshlennost'*, nos. 6-7, 1926: 466.

400. ——. "Novaia arkhitektura v SSSR (vpechatleniia inostrannogo arkhitektora ot prebyvaniia v Moskve i Leningrade)" [New Architecture in the USSR (Impressions of a Foreign Architect as the Result of His Stay in Moscow and Leningrad)] *Stroitel'naia promyshlennost'*, no. 8, 1926: 562-564.

Observes that in the Soviet Union, more than anywhere else, there exists a divergence between theory and practice in architecture. Chides Soviet architects for emulating their Western counterparts.

401.   ——. "Russlands architektonische Situation." In El Lissitzky, *Russland: Architektur für eine Welterevolution.* See **no. 268**, p. 147-153.

Apparently an unpublished manuscript, dated Berlin, November 2, 1929. Summarizes Taut's impressions of Soviet architecture following his visit to Moscow and Leningrad. More than any other of his known published accounts, reveals Taut's true inner feelings about developments in Soviet architecture. Provides useful interpretive insight into the conflicts between the principal modern Soviet architectural movements. For English trans.: "Russia's Architectural Situation," in El Lissitzky, *Russia: An Architecture for World Revolution* (**no. 268**), p. 167-173.

402.   ——. "Sovremennaia arkhitektura i ee osnovaniia" [Contemporary Architecture and Its Foundations]. *Stroitel'naia promyshlennost'*, no. 3, 1929: 272-275.

Speech delivered in Moscow during the week of January 7-15, 1929; trans O. Vutke. Argues for limits of narrow specialization and introduces broader cultural implication into the function of contemporary architecture. Compares his own theses and those of Karl Friedrich Schinkel, Theophile Gautier, and Le Corbusier. A perceptive and illuminating analysis. For a similar account, see his "Sovremennaia arkhitektura i ee printsipy" [Contemporary Architecture and Its Principles], *Stroitel'stvo Moskvy*, no. 2, 1929: 17-18.

403.   ——. "Stroitel'stvo i arkhitektura Novoi Moskvy" [Construction and Architecture of New Moscow]. *Stroitel'stvo Moskvy*, no. 4, 1929: 11-12.

Outlines his impressions of modern architecture in Moscow. Observes that the rationalists are preoccupied with form and "play" with construction, while the functionalists consider that architecture consists only of the correct constructional solution.

404.   Tschichold, Iwan. "Die neue Gestaltung." *ABC*, no. 2, 1926: 1-3.

A brief survey of modern movements of art; includes suprematism, constructivism, and the VKHUTEMAS, which is likened to the Bauhaus.

405.   Voyce, Arthur. "Contemporary Soviet Architecture." *American Magazine of Art,* v. 28, Sept. 1935: 527-535.

A good overview of the historical and cultural context in which modern architecture first emerged and was subsequently eclipsed in the Soviet Union. A simplified analysis of Soviet theory and practice.

406. Weidle, Vladimir "Pis'ma o sovremennom iskusstve; pis'mo vtoroe, o razryve s proshlym v nachale veka. Otkaz ot ukrasheniia. Funktsional'naia arkhitektura" [Letters on Contemporary Art, Second Letter, On the Break with the Past at the Beginning of the Century. Rejection of Ornamentation. Functional Architecture]. *Mosty*, no. 4, 1960: 95-105.

   A reflective analysis of the emergence of modern architecture in the Soviet Union, focusing on the new criteria upon which it was based.

407. Willen, Paul. "Soviet Architecture: Progress and Reaction." *Problems of Communism*, v. 3, no. 1, 1954: 24-33.

   Adapted from the author's master's thesis (no. 360), but architectural analysis here is less hampered by analysis of political ideology. A good, well-documented account of the development of Soviet architecture through the declaration of socialist realism interspersed with quotations from key personalities and published criticisms.

408. Woznicki, S. T. "USSR—On the Problems of Architecture." *T-Square*, v. 2, Nov. 1932: 80-83.

   Translated from the article that appeared in the July 1932 issue of *Architekture i Budownictwo*. Attempts to assess, on the basis of the published report of the Commission for the Competition for the Palace of Soviets, the shift in official opinion on architectural problems, from modernism back to classicism, as evidenced by the results of the competition. Valuable for its quotations from this report, especially the critical essay by Aleksei Tolstoi (no. 748).

409. Zimmer, W. "Geistiges, Allzugeistiges in der russischen Architektur." *Wasmuths Monatshefte für Baukunst*, v. 13, 1929: 132-134.

   Treats the work of pure theoreticians, such as Tatlin, whose visionary designs could not be translated into reality, as well as the romantics in Soviet architecture. An interesting analysis.

D. FROM 1932 TO 1941

1. By Soviet Writers

a. Monographs

410.   Academy of Architecture of the USSR. *Tvorcheskie voprosy sovet-skoi arkhitektury* [Creative Questions of Soviet Architecture]. I. G. Sushkevich, ed. Moscow, Izd-vo Akademii Arkhitektury SSSR, 1940. 179 p.

An abridged stenographic account of the meeting held in Moscow on April 22-24, 1940, of Moscow and Leningrad architects and organized by the Union of Soviet Architects. Introductory and concluding remarks by K. S. Alabian, review of work of Moscow architects by A. V. Vlasov, and review of work of Leningrad architects by L. A. Il'in. An important summary of contemporary interpretations of acceptable architectural aesthetics and ideology. Zholtovsky condemned for copying Renaissance forms without attempting to solve the problems placed before Soviet architecture; arguments heard for innovative searches in contemporary Soviet architecture.

411.   Alabian, Karo S. *Zadachi sovetskoi arkhitektury* [Problems of Soviet Architecture]. Moscow, Izd-vo Akademii arkhitektury, 1937. 32 p.

Speech delivered to the first All-Union Congress of Soviet Architects, June 1936. Develops criteria for the social function and forms of the new architecture to be an embodiment of the new socialist epoch and society. Attacks the formalists like Mel'nikov as indifferent to living reality, criticizes the constructivists like the Vesnins as having turned their backs completely on the rich architectural heritage of the past and particularly that of Russia and the affiliated national republics, and castigates eclecticists, such as Zholtovsky, for copying too mechanically the old masters without due regard for solving contemporary problems.

412.   Kolli, Nikolai Ia. *Zadachi sovetskoi arkhitektury* [Problems of Soviet Architecture]. Moscow, Izd-vo Akademii arkhitektury, 1937. 54 p.

Speech delivered to the first All-Union Conference of Soviet Architects in Moscow, 1937, assessing the basic stages in the development of Soviet architecture: 1) Russian architecture prior to 1917, 2) the early revolutionary years, 3) the period of reconstruction, 4) formalism and constructivism, and 5) the new directions in Soviet architecture. An informative synopsis of contemporary attitudes in Soviet architecture, framed against a general condemnation of the modern movements.

413. Union of Soviet Architects. *Arkhitekturnye voprosy rekonstruktsii Moskvy* [Architectural Questions Concerning the Reconstruction of Moscow]. Moscow, Izd-vo Akademii arkhitektury SSSR, 1940. 158 p.

An abridged stenographic account of the 7th plenary meeting of the administration of the Union of Soviet Architects. Provides an assessment of implementation and execution of the five year plan for the reconstruction of Moscow and an analysis of the architectural problems confronting the effort. A useful source.

b. Articles

414. Alabian, Karo S. "The Soviet Approach to Architecture." *American Quarterly on the Soviet Union*, v. 2, July-Oct. 1939: 76-80.

Speech delivered at the Soviet pavilion of the New York World's Fair on August 14, 1939. Outlines the basic principles that are seen to form the basis for Soviet architecture: 1) architecture as the synthesis of art and technical knowledge, 2) progress in architecture, based on what is positive and valuable in the past, 3) architecture national in form and socialist in content, 4) the synthesis of the other arts with architecture, and 5) multiformity. Characterizes the Soviet pavilion as the synthesis of these five principles.

415. ——. "Tricet let architektury v sovetskom svazu" [Thirty Years of Architecture in the Soviet State]. *Architektura CSR*, no. 10, 1947: 293-294.

A synopsis of the development of Soviet architecture, with special emphasis on events and achievements following the eclipse of modern architecture in 1932.

416. Arkin, David E. "Architecture." *Art in the USSR*, special Autumn 1935 issue of *The Studio*. C. G. Holme, ed. p. 12-26.

A survey of the development of Soviet architecture. Suggests two basic characteristics of Soviet architecture: 1) basic subjects of architectural work in the USSR are buildings of a mass character, such as public buildings, workers' clubs, "palaces of culture," etc., and 2) all architectural work in the USSR is bound up indissolubly with a unified general plan which determines the economic and cultural development of the country. Discusses the problems of Soviet architecture, including the recent postulation of Socialist Realism.

417. Bunin, A. V., and O. A. Shvidkovsky. "Arkhitektura 1934-1941
      godov" [Architecture in the Years 1934-1941]. In *Istoriia russkogo
      iskusstva* [History of Russian Art]. Igor' Grabar' et al., eds. v. 12.
      Moscow, Izd-vo Akademii nauk SSSR, 1961. p. 20-147.
          A concise survey of the architectural developments of the
      period, including the planning and reconstruction of Moscow.
      Provides access to some useful material.

418. Dediukhin, V. A. "God raboty" [One Year of Work]. *Arkhitektura
      SSSR*, no. 9, 1934: 3-7.
          Provides an illuminating synopsis of events following the re-
      organization of Soviet architectural practice after the decree of
      April 1932 and discusses the role of L. M. Kaganovich and the
      Moscow Soviet in bringing this about.

419. Gai, M. "Teatr krasnoi armii v Moskve" [The Red Army Theater in
      Moscow]. *Stroitel'stvo Moskvy,* no. 8, 1933: 27-32.
          Reviews the initial phase of the designs submitted, including
      those by Friedman and Glushchenko, I. A. Fomin, L. V. Rudnev,
      and V. O. Munts.

420. Ginzburg, Moisei Ia., Viktor A. and Aleksandr A. Vesnin. "Tvorches-
      kaia tribuna: problemy sovremennoi arkhitektury" [Creative
      Tribune: Problems of Contemporary Architecture]. *Arkhitektura
      SSSR*, no. 2, 1934: 63-69.
          Response to the continuing criticism of modern architecture
      and constructivism following the reorientation established in 1932
      for Soviet architecture. Presents what the authors feel still to be
      the fundamental problems of architecture and proceeds to formu-
      late them for the problems currently before Soviet architecture
      in the official search for a new idiom. Important.

421. Il'in, Lev A. "Arkhitektura Leningrada za dvadtsat' let" [Architecture
      of Leningrad in Twenty Years]. *Arkhitektura Leningrada*, Feb.
      1937: 14-23.
          A highly useful survey of the architecture of Leningrad for the
      period 1917-37. Illustrated.

422. Mikhailov, A. I. "Smotr sovetskoi arkhitektury" [Review of Soviet
      Architecture]. *Novyi mir,* no. 7, 1937: 263-280.

A comprehensive review of Soviet architecture on the basis of newly evolved criteria. Negates the modernists, especially Melnikov and Ladovsky. Valuable for illuminating in a cogent manner the new official attitudes stemming from the First All-Union Congress of Soviet Architects, held in Moscow in 1937.

423. "Ob organizatsii dela proektirovaniia zdanii, planirovki goroda i otvoda zemlenykh uchastkov v g. Moskve" [On the Organization of the Design Enterprise, the Planning of Towns, and the Assignment of Land Plots in Moscow]. *Stroitel'stvo Moskvy*, no. 9, 1933: 5-7.

A detailed outline of the new organization of architectural studios under the Moscow Soviet. Includes the general program of activity issued for these studios by the Soviet.

424. Shchusev, Aleksei V. "Protiv asketicheskoi arkhitektury" [Against an Ascetic Architecture]. *Stroitel'stvo Moskvy*, nos. 2-3, 1933: 17.

Criticizes the designs for the Meyerhold Theater. Finds Golts's classical design to be artistic, Vlasov's and Burov's to be original and appropriate, and Barkhin's—designed in a modern vein—to be superficial and ill-conceived.

425. "Tri raboty Mosproekta" [Three Projects of Mosproekt]. *Stroitel'stvo Moskvy*, nos. 2-3, 1933: 16.

A discussion of the three projects for the Meyerhold Theater by Golts and Parusnikov, Vlasov and Burov, and I. Golosov. For plates of the projects, see p. 14-15 preceding the article.

426. Vesnin, Viktor A. "Men'she 'akademizma'!" [Less "Academism"!] . *Arkhitekturnaia gazeta*, Jan. 12, 1937.

Condemns the revival of academic classical designs as the result of the official proclamation reviving the classical heritage. Argues that designs in the classical idiom need not be sterile copies but can be innovative and reflective of contemporary conditions and demands.

427. ——. "Za iasnost' arkhitekturnoi mysli" [For a Clarity of Architectural Thought]. *Stroitel'naia gazeta*, April 28, 1940.

Argues for a clarity of thought as the result of observing a lack of substantive work, creativity, and inventiveness in the current architectural solutions to the problems at hand.

428. Vlasov, Aleksandr V. "Nash put'. Vsesoiuznoe soveshchanie sovet-skikh arkhitektorov" [Our Course. The All-Union Conference of Soviet Architects]. *Arkhitektura SSSR*, no. 6, 1937: 23-25.

Summarizes what are seen to be the principal achievements thus far in Soviet architecture: the competition for the Palace of Soviets and the erection of the Moscow Metro. Highlights what are seen to be the affirmative aspects in the work of I. V. Zholtovsky, A. V. Shchusev, M. Ia. Ginzburg, and the Vesnins.

429. Zapletin, N. P. "Magnitostroi arkhitektury" [Magnitostroi Architecture]. *Stroitel'stvo Moskvy*, nos. 5-6, 1933: 10-32.

A comprehensive review of the competition and the principal projects submitted. A wealth of graphic material.

2. By Non-Soviet Writers

a. Monographs

430. Meyer, Hannes. *La realidad soviética, los arquitectos; el espacio de vida, criterio económico herencia y folklore, arte arquitectural.* Mexico, D.F., *Arquitectura*, 1942. 20 p. illus.

First published as a special issue of the periodical *Arquitectura* (no. 9, 1942). A collection of previously published articles and new material by the German architect who worked in the Soviet Union in the thirties. Provides a favorable survey of Soviet architecture, art, and culture and an analysis of the position of the architect in a planned economy.

b. Articles

431. "Architecture in the U.S.S.R." *RIBA Journal*, 3d ser., v. 48, July 1941: 155-158.

Provides a thoughtful analysis of the possible reasons for the eclipse of modern architecture in the Soviet Union and attempts to understand the prime motivations and circumstances surrounding this change. Emphasis placed on explaining the lack of popular support for modern architecture in the Soviet Union.

432. "Berichte aus Moskau." *Bauwelt*, v. 7, 1933: 72.

Assesses the growing symptoms of the turn away from modern architecture.

433.   Breines, Simon. "First Congress of Soviet Architects." *Architectural Record*, v. 82, Oct. 1937: 63-65, 94, 96.

A report on the sessions of the First All-Union Congress of Soviet Architects, held in Moscow on June 15-25, 1936. Interesting for its interpretation of the proceedings and major points discussed during this crucial congress in which the newly emerging ideals of socialist realism in Soviet architecture were substantially postulated.

434.   Carter, Edward. "Soviet Architecture Today." *Architectural Review*, v. 92, Nov. 1942: 107-114.

One of the first sympathetic, though objective, attempts in the West to understand both recent Soviet architecture and its motives, by the librarian of the Royal Institute of British Architects. Argues that the new style 1) proceeds from strong national tradition, 2) expresses the architectural ambitions of the masses, and 3) has the vitality that marks recent Soviet achievements in other fields. An excellent, thoughtful analysis. For a later reprint, see same title, *Task,* no. 6, 1944: 37-45.

435.   Hamlin, Talbot. "Style Developments in Soviet Russia." *American Quarterly on the Soviet Union*, v. 1, April 1938: 15-20.

Posits constructivism, formalism (expressionism), and functionalism as the three basic theories of Soviet architecture, unaware that constructivism and functionalism stemmed from the same movement. Refers to report of the Commission of the Competition for the Palace of Soviets and A. Tolstoi's article to speculate on the motives behind the purging of modern architecture in favor of the classical formula of socialist realism.

436.   Ling, Arthur. "Soviet Architecture: the Present Phase." *Architect and Building News*, Part 1, v. 160, Oct. 6, 1939: 11-13; Part 2, v. 160, Oct. 13, 1939; 42-44; Part 3, v. 160, Oct. 20, 1939: 64-66.

Three articles prepared as the result of a brief visit to Russia. An attempt to convey the theory and practice of Soviet architecture as gleaned through conferences with Soviet architects. Somewhat naive but contains useful information and interesting analyses of the transitional period from modernism to the new classicism, planning and housing within the current context, and building technology. Analysis generally sympathetic with Soviet view. Plates of no particular value.

437.   Lurcat, Andre. "L'Architecture en URSS." *Art vivante*, April 1934: 161-167.

An account of Soviet architecture by a French architect who spent some one and one-half months in the Soviet Union. Distinguishes two periods in Soviet architecture: 1) 1917-32, when problems of construction, and therefore constructivism, prevailed over problems of aesthetics, and 2) post-1932, which negates functionalism in favor of expressing the ideology of the Soviet government. Somewhat sympathetic to Soviet view. For Soviet reaction to article, see "Andrei Lursa o sovetskoi arkhitekture" [Andre Lurcat on Soviet Architecture], *Arkhitektura SSSR*, no. 6, 1934: 63.

438.   Maigrot, Emile. "L'Urbanisme et l'architecture en URSS." *L'Architecture*,v. 48, Dec. 15, 1935: 449-462.
        A penetrating, though brief, analysis of Soviet architecture since the untimely eclipse of modernism. Based on a discussion between author and a group of leading Soviet architects. A good collection of plates.

439.   Meyer, Hannes. "El arquitecto soviético." *Arquitectura*, no. 9, Jan. 1942: 5-19.
        A comprehensive survey of Soviet architecture by a German architect who spent several years in the thirties working in the Soviet Union. Deals with the Soviet concept of architecture; the economic indices and development affecting Soviet architecture, the organization of architectural societies, and the status of the Soviet architect; and the historical development of Soviet architecture, analyzed in parallel with the economic stages of the country's development. Sympathetic with the Soviet view but contains much useful information. English trans.: "The Soviet Architect," *Task*, no. 5, 1942: 24-32.

440.   Percival, David. "The Developments of Soviet Architecture." *Anglo-Soviet Journal*,v. 2, Nov. 1, 1941: 30-31.
        A concise analysis of the official Soviet style and the reasons for the eclipse of modernism.

441.   Rocco, Giovanni. "Architettura dell'URSS." *Rassegna di architetura*, Sept. 1935: 313-324.
        Views the competition for the Palace of Soviets as a central force in the eclipse of modern architecture in the Soviet Union and surveys recent work in Soviet architecture. Good plates.

442. Schmidt, Hans. "Das neue Bauen und die Sowjetunion, 1930-1937." Part II of his *Beiträge zur Architektur 1924-1964*. Berlin, VEB Verlag für Bauwesen, 1965. p. 81-136.

   A collection of his essays, some previously published and others published for the first time, dealing perceptively with various problems of the period.

443. ——. "Die Tätigkeit deutscher Architekten und Spezialisten des Bauwesens in der Sowjetunion in den Jahren 1930 bis 1937." *Wissenschafliche Zeitschrift der Humbolt Universität*, v. 16, no. 3, 1967.

   Illuminates the activity of German specialists in the Soviet Union during the given period. Contains much useful information.

444. Wright, Frank Lloyd. "Architecture and Life in the USSR." *Architectural Record*, v. 82, Oct. 1937: 58-63.

   A highly impressionistic account of Soviet architecture based upon personal observations made as a delegate to the First All-Union Congress of Soviet Architects held in Moscow June 15-25, 1936. Useful for accounts of conversations with major Soviet architects and personalities.

445. "Zu den Auseinandersetzungen über Russland." *Die neue Stadt,* v. 12, 1933: 270-271.

   Assesses the declining position of modern architecture in the Soviet Union and examines some of the theoretical guidelines and ideological devices used by Soviet architects to justify and explain their current work. A useful source. English trans.: "On the Subject of Discussions Concerning Russian Architecture," in El Lissitzky, *Russia: An Architecture for World Revolution* (**no. 268**), p. 225-229.

E. FROM 1941 TO 1954

1. By Soviet Writers

a. Monographs

446. Academy of Architecture of the USSR. *Materialy VI sessii Akademii arkhitektury SSSR.   Voprosy vosstanovitel'nogo stroitel'stva* [Material of the Sixth Session of the Academy of Architecture of the USSR. Questions of Construction in the Period of Reconstruction]. Moscow, Izd-vo Akademii arkhitektury, 1945.

Outlines the specific approach by which entire architectural ensembles in cities destroyed during the war would be redesigned and rebuilt, generated by an integral architectural concept.

447.   Arkin, David E., ed. *Arkhitektura* [Architecture]. *VOKS Bulletin*, no. 1, 1947.
        The entire issue is devoted to essays on the post-World War II Five Year Plan and its effects on Soviet architecture, urban development, new construction, and housing. Reviews current projects. Bibliography.

448.   Bylinkin, N. P., and N. N. Stoianov. *Vysotnye zdaniia v Moskve* [Tall Buildings in Moscow]. Moscow, Gosstroiizdat, 1951. 36 p. 126 illus.
        An illustrated analysis of the eight Moscow skyscrapers then under construction. Important source for a comparison of all eight complexes through good graphics and illustrations.

449.   Union of Soviet Architects. *Tvorcheskie zadachi sovetskikh arkhitektorov v piatiletnem plane vosstanovleniia i razvitiia narodnogo khoziaistva* [Creative Problems of Soviet Architects in the Five Year Plan of Rehabilitating and Developing the National Economy]. Moscow, Izd-vo Akademii arkhitektury, 1948. 69 p.
        An abridged stenographic account of the 12th Plenary meeting of the Union of Soviet Architects in Moscow July 30-August 2, 1947. Keynote speech by Karo S. Alabian, executive secretary of the Union. Valuable for its self-critique of ideological deviations from acceptable architectural design, the prevalence of "formalism" in Soviet architecture and the need to eliminate it, as well as a review of the contemporary problems of Soviet architecture.

450.   ——. *Zadachi arkhitektorov v dni Velikoi Otechestvenoi voiny* [Problems of the Architects in the Days of the Great Patriotic War]. Moscow, Izd-vo Akademii arkhitektury SSSR, 1942. 65 p.
        An abridged stenographic account of the 5th Plenary meeting of the Union of Soviet Architects, held in Moscow April 22-25, 1942. A review of the problems brought about by the war and an outline of mobilizing the architectural forces of the country to respond to the extraordinary circumstances and developments of wartime.

b. Articles

451. Alabian, Karo S. "Arkhitekturnaia praktika v svete reshenii TsK VKP(b) o literature i iskusstve" [Architectural Practice in Light of the Decision of the Central Committee of the All-Union Communist Party (Bolsheviks) on Literature and Art]. *Arkhitektura SSSR*, no. 14, 1947: 1-4.

A blistering self-critique of contemporary Soviet architectural practice following the criticism made by the Central Committee of the Communist Party of the magazines *Zvezda* [Star] and *Leningrad,* the present repertoire of Soviet theaters, and the film *Velikaia zhizn'* [Great Life]. Cites many errors, more nearly ideological than technical, in the current practice of Soviet architecture; argues that every architect must be a city planner, regardless of the size of the building being designed.

452. ——. "Po arkhitekture i gradostroitel'stve" [On Architecture and City Planning]. *Sovetskoe iskusstvo*. Oct. 25, 1946.

A survey of the development of Soviet architecture and city planning, from functionalism and constructivism to a formalism of style and building technology in contemporary times. Criticizes the contemporary trend of pomposity and facadism in design, with a lack of attention to the development of the plan. Blames the Academy of Architecture and the Union of Soviet Architects for failure to indoctrinate architects with a viable theory of architecture, as well as for the current lack of interest in practical problems.

453. "Arkhitektura strany sotsializma" [Architecture of the Country of Socialism]. *Arkhitektura SSSR*, nos. 17-18, 1947: 3-6.

A highly charged editorial synopsis of what were viewed as major events in the development of Soviet architecture on the occasion of the 30th anniversary of the Bolshevik Revolution. Significant both for omitting any mention of modernism and for characterizing the nature of administrative control in Soviet architecture during the various stages of its development.

454. Arkin, David E. "Some Thoughts on Reconstruction." *Architectural Review*, v. 101, May 1947: 178-179.

A brief review of postwar efforts of reconstruction, explaining and defending present trends in Soviet architecture. For impact of this and its companion articles, see **nos. 455 and 492.**

455.   Arkin, David E., AV. Bunin, and N.P. Bylinkin. "A Letter from the USSR." *Architectural Review*, v. 103, March 1948: 75-81.

A letter from the authors of three articles published in the May 1947 issue of the *Architectural Review*. Protests the preface accompanying the articles, which the authors feel was slanderous to Soviet architecture. The letter led the *Review* to attach an article attempting to assess the context and significance of these unforeseen developments. Simultaneously with the publication of this letter in the *Review*, Arkin was being censured in the USSR for his cosmopolitan attitude toward architecture in the West, and his *Review* article was among the works cited to indict him (see no. 128).

456.   Borisovsky, G. "Narodnoe tvorchestvo, klassicheskii order, i sovremennyi standart" [Popular Creativity, the Classical Order, and the Contemporary Standard]. *Arkhitektura SSSR*, no. 13, 1946: 30-33.

A brief but thoughtful essay which, despite its apparent superficiality, attempts to argue for overcoming the blandness of standardized design by suggesting greater variety. Argues also for the use of the classical order and folk motifs, though not simply as predetermined systems but rather as sources for the desired variety.

457.   Bunin, A. V. "The Reconstruction of Urban Centers." *Architectural Review*, v. 101, May 1947: 179-182.

One of three articles submitted on request to this issue. A general survey of recent Soviet attempts.

458.   Burov, Andrei K. "Na putiakh k novoi russkoi arkhitekture" [On the Way to a New Russian Architecture]. *Arkhitektura SSSR*, no. 4, 1943: 30-36.

Denounces the superficial classicizing predilections which had impeded the progress of Soviet architecture prior to the Second World War. Advocates a new approach to architecture, utilizing the achievements of American technology and the commensurate accomplishments of Soviet architecture in the twenties. One of the important pronouncements of the wartime period seeking a renewal of Soviet architecture.

459.   ——. "The War and Architecture." *VOKS Bulletin*, nos. 1-2, 1946: 53-62.

A good discussion of Soviet architecture and city planning during the period of reconstruction.

460. Bylinkin, N.P. "Reconstruction and Housing." *Architectural Review,* v. 101, May 1947: 182-184.

A general review of efforts and accomplishments in mass housing and the reconstruction of major urban centers.

461. Chernishev, S. "Arkhitektura Stalinskoi epokhi" [Architecture of the Stalin Epoch]. *Arkhitektura SSSR,* no. 11, 1952: 3-12.

A review of the accomplishments during the height of the postwar period. Emphasis is on the Moscow skyscrapers and corresponding complexes.

462. ——. "Sovetskaia arkhitektura na sluzhbe naroda" [Soviet Architecture in Service to the People]. *Bol'shevik,* no. 24, 1950: 22-31.

A popular ideological polemic that examines the basic problems facing Soviet architects and argues for an improvement in the attempt of Soviet architecture to give expression to the will of the masses.

463. Ginzburg, Moisei Ia. "Mass-Production Housing Proposals in the USSR." *Architectural Association Journal,* v. 59, Nov.-Dec. 1944: 114-116.

An authoritative review of current proposals for mass production of Soviet housing. Provides also a useful outline of considerations then formulated both by the Soviet architectural profession and by the Academy of Architecture for solving the housing problem.

464. Iofan, Boris M. "L'Architecture en URSS." *L'Architecture d'aujourd' hui,* v. 18, July 1947: 2 p., unnumbered.

A brief review of current work in Soviet architecture, with photographs.

465. Kalinin, Mikhail I. "Bol'shaia obshchenarodnaia zadacha" [Great National Problem]. *Izvestiia,* Dec. 10, 1943.

Characterizes the official view of the problems facing Soviet architecture during the postwar period of construction. Argues against restoring the plan of cities almost entirely demolished and for rebuilding them according to newly developed plans. Urges that all Soviet architects be mobilized for this purpose.

466. ——. "Pis'mo Predsedatelia Prezidiuma Verkhovnogo Soveta SSSR Predsedateliu Komiteta po delam arkhitektury pri SNK SSSR"

[Letter from the President of the Supreme Soviet to the President of the Committee on Architectural Affairs under the Council of People's Commissars of the USSR). *Arkhitektura SSSR*, no. 6 , 1943: 1.

A letter from Kalinin to Arkadii G. Mordvinov, formulating a series of important principles for Soviet architects in their post-war reconstruction efforts. Suggests that the cities which were substantially destroyed during the war may well be subjected to an entire replanning, thereby providing an opportunity for creating entirely new Socialist cities answering to the new needs of Soviet society.

467.   Lebedev, V., and P. Shteller. "Vysotnye zdaniia i novye ansambli Moskvy"[Skyscrapers and New Ensembles of Moscow] . *Arkhitektura SSSR*, no. 8, 1952: 6-14.

An analysis and review of the skyscrapers and complexes by two of the architects involved. Contains excellent plates.

468.   Matsa, Ivan L. "Demokraticheskie vsenarodnye osnovy sovetskoi arkhitektury" [Democratic and National Bases of Soviet Architecture] . *Arkhitektura SSSR*, no. 3, 1943: 3-7.

A commemorative survey on the occasion of the 25th anniversary of Soviet architecture. Discusses the characteristics that give Soviet architecture its own distinctive style and assesses its basic accomplishments in 25 years. Somewhat polemical but still a useful study for illuminating fundamental assumptions operating within Soviet architecture during the current period.

469.   ——. "Sovetskaia arkhitektura—novyi etap v razvitii mirovoi arkhitektury" [Soviet Architecture—A New Stage in the Development of World Architecture].*Arkhitektura SSSR*, nos. 17-18, 1947: 11-14.

A highly polemicized characterization of the achievements and characteristics of Soviet architecture on the occasion of the 30th anniversary of the Revolution. However, provides a useful citation of a few valid characteristics.

470.   "Na sobranii aktiva Moskovskikh arkhitektorov" [At the Meeting of the Active Moscow Architects] . *Arkhitektura i stroitel'stvo*, no. 4, 1948: 13-16.

An account of the four-day conference held as a result of the issuance of the decree by the Central Committee of the Communist Party on V. Muradeli's opera, *Velikaia druzhba* [The Great Friendship] , and the need the architects felt to reexamine their own field in light of this criticism. Discusses the prevalence of "formalism" in Soviet architecture and the need to combat it.

471. "O reorganizatsii Soiuza sovetskikh arkhitektorov" [On the Reorganization of the Union of Soviet Architects]. *Sovetskoe iskusstvo,* Aug. 14, 1948.

Account of the ineffectual results of a special closed two-day session of the Union of Soviet Architects. Acting President Karo S. Alabian criticized the Union for failing to resist foreign influences and tendencies in Soviet architecture, to educate young architects in ideology and architectural theory, and to organize architectural and planning cadres. Architect L. Rudnev expressed resentment at criticism by those not in the profession. See **no. 451** for comparison with the nature of Alabian's earlier criticism and the criticism apparently being imposed from above on the directions in Soviet architecture.

472. "Ob obrazovanii komiteta po delam arkhitektury pri Sovnarkome SSSR" [Concerning the Organization of the Committee on Architectural Affairs under the Council of People's Commissars of the USSR]. *Arkhitektura SSSR,* no. 5, 1944: 1-2.

The decree by the Council creating a Committee on Architectural Affairs to facilitate governmental supervision of planning and reconstruction of towns and urban centers destroyed during World War II. Arkadii G. Mordvinov named president of the Committee.

473. Shvidkovsky, Oleg A. "Arkhitektura." In *Istoriia russkogo iskusstva* [History of Russian Art]. R. S. Kaufman, et al., eds. v. 13 Moscow, Izd-vo "Nauka," 1964. p. 284-346.

A history of the developments in Soviet architecture 1941-45. A survey of architectural activity during World War II and the initial efforts at reconstruction.

474. Stupin, V. "Ob arkhitekture Vsesoiuznoi sel'skokhoziaistvennoi vystavki" [Concerning the Architecture of the All-Union Agricultural Exhibit]. *Arkhitektura SSSR,* no. 9, 1954: 1-17.

A general survey of the 1954 Agricultural Exhibit in Moscow. Profusely illustrated with good plates.

475. Vlasov, Aleksandr V. "Vital Problems of Soviet Architecture." *Architect and Building News,* v. 194, Nov. 12, 1948: 403-405.

A review of Soviet reconstruction efforts in major cities and efforts to solve the problems of mass housing.

2. By Non-Soviet Writers

a. Monographs

476. Architect's Committee of the National Council of American-Soviet Friendship. *Proceedings, American-Soviet Building Conference.* Louise Cooper and James Fitch, Jr., eds. New York, Architectural Forum, 1945. 206 p.

Condensed version of the transcript taken at the four panel sessions held on May 5, 1945, on building industry organization, prefabrication, industrial buildings, and mechanical systems and utilities. Contains some useful information on the current Soviet experience.

b. Articles

477. Adams, K. G. "Architecture of the USSR." *The Builder,* Feb. 27, 1948: 248-252.

A general review of recent work, with a random selection of plates.

478. "The Architecture of the USSR Exhibition at the RIBA." *RIBA Journal,* 3d. ser., v. 55, March 1948: 218-221.

Another brief review of the RIBA Exhibit on Soviet architecture, held March 3-20, 1948 (see **no. 486**).

479. Blake, Peter. "The Soviet Architectural Purge." *Architectural Record,* v. 106, Sept. 1949: 127-129.

An assessment of the purge of the Academy of Architecture by the Soviet government in 1948 because of the allegedly pro-Western, pro-American, and generally "cosmopolitan" outlook of its leading members. A useful reference.

480. "How Building and Planning Are Organized in the USSR." *Architects' Journal,* v. 104, Aug. 1, 1946: 79-86.

A useful analysis of the professional Soviet architectural hierarchy, with general references to current developments in Soviet architecture.

481. Jones, A. D. "Visit to Russia." *Architect and Building News,* v. 204, Dec. 3, 1953: 682-688.

An interesting account of impressions and analysis of problems of Soviet architecture. Of general value.

482. Ling, Arthur. "Soviet Architecture." *Soviet Cultural Relations Journal*, Spring 1949: 31-32.

A brief interpretive analysis of the postwar developments in Soviet architecture, sympathetic with the Soviet interpretation and point of view.

483. Meek, H. A. "Retreat to Moscow. Architecture in the Soviet Satellites." *Architectural Review*, v. 113, March 1953: 143-151.

Examines the subjugation of modern Eastern European architecture to Soviet formula of socialist realism following occupation by the Soviets after World War II. Of interest in illuminating the tenacity of the Soviet formula.

484. "Neues von der sowjetischen Architektur." *Deutsche Architektur*, no. 2, 1952: 76-82.

Translations of three articles by S. Kolesnikov, G. Ostchepkov, and B. Rubanenkov, respectively, that appeared in *Arkhitektura SSSR*. Deals with the latest developments of Soviet architecture under the influence of the classical Zholtovsky school. Useful plates.

485. Noviant, Louis G. "Architecture en URSS. Urbanisme et habitation." *L'Architecture française*, v. 8, nos. 73-74, 1947: 68-75.

Surveys contemporary efforts of reconstruction and mass design in Soviet architecture and city planning. Good photographs.

486. Pierce, S. Rowland. "The Architecture of the USSR." *Architect and Building News*, v. 193, March 12, 1948: 237-239.

An impression of the RIBA Exhibit on Soviet architecture organized by VOKS. Contains an interesting interpretation of exhibit commentary explaining the bases for the evolution of Soviet architecture. Plates of no particular value.

487. Plojhar, Ernst. "Neue Wege in Sowjetischen Bauwesen." *Der Aufbau*, v. 6, April 1951: 153-160.

A general description and analysis of the recent monumental Soviet architecture, including the seven skyscrapers. A few useful plates.

488. ——. "Sowjetunion: Umstellung in Bauwesen." *Der Aufbau*, v. 10, Sept. 1955: 351-357.

Description of Moscow's skyscrapers and a discussion of mass construction. Few plates.

489.   "Reconstruction in the USSR." *Architectural Review*, v. 101, May
           1947: 177-178.
           An editorial preface to three articles by Soviet writers (**nos.
           455, 457, and 460**), to which the Soviet writers responded with a
           letter of protest (**no. 455**) against what they termed unjustified
           attack and criticism of Soviet architecture.

490.   Rogers, Ernesto N. "Politica e architettura." *Casabella*, no. 208,
           1955: 1-5.
           A thoughtful study of Soviet architecture in light of the
           Communist Party decree of December 5, 1954, condemning
           architectural and economic excesses in Soviet architecture. In-
           cludes a translation in its entirety of this decree.

491.   Schmidt, Hans. "La arquitectura en Rusia." *Nuestra arquitectura*,
           September 1948: 319-324.
           A review of Soviet architecture in the post-Second World War
           period, with an explanation of the motivations behind the latest
           developments.

492.   Shankland, Graeme. "Architecture in Soviet Democracy." *Architec-
           tural Review*, v. 104, Dec. 1948: 299-300.
           A continuation of the discussion of current Soviet architecture
           initiated by the letter from the Soviet architects, D. Arkin, A.
           Bunin, and N. Bylinkin, which was published, together with the
           editor's reply in the *Review* issue for March 1948 (**no. 455**).

493.   "The Wide Gulf: Western Architects Find Russian Notion of Beauty
           Hard to Understand." *Architectural Forum*, v. 88, May1948: 15-16.
           An illuminating revelation of Western attitudes and responses
           to recent Soviet architecture. In response to the letter which ap-
           peared in the March 1948 issue of *Architectural Review* (**no. 455**).

F. POST-1954

1. By Soviet Writers

a. Monographs

494.   Tsapenko, M. P. *Nekotorye voprosy sovetskoi arkhitektury* [Some
           Questions on Soviet Architecture] . Kiev, Ukrainskaia Akademiia
           arkhitektury, 1955. 42 p.

A pamphlet projecting the author's earlier vilification of modernism in Soviet architecture, developed in his *O realisticheskikh osnovakh sovetskoi arkhitektury* (**no. 233**), into a program for contemporary Soviet architecture.

495. ——. *Sovetskaia arkhitektura na novom etape* [Soviet Architecture at a New Level]. Kiev, Gosstroiizdat, 1957. 119 p.

A supplement and elaboration of the author's earlier pamphlet, *Nekotorye voprosy* . . . (**no. 494**). However, in response to the Party decree of November 4, 1955, regarding the elimination of excesses in design, attempts to superimpose at once a "contemporary" evaluation upon the monumental classical idiom of Soviet socialism realism in order to align its methods with current demands. Interesting for its transparent attempt to vindicate the classicizing theses of the author's two earlier works (**nos. 233** and **494**).

b. Articles

496. Abrosimov, P. "Tvorcheskie zadachi sovetskoi arkhitektury" [Creative Problems of Soviet Architecture]. *Arkhitektura SSSR*, no. 12, 1955: 2-6.

An excellent synopsis of the latest developments in Soviet architecture as the result of recent decrees by the Communist Party and the Council of Ministers (see **no. 155**). Cites the problems, achievements, and projected plans for the professional and scholarly aspects of architectural activity as presently envisioned in light of the referenced decrees. An important source.

497. "Dvadtsatyi s'ezd kommunisticheskoi partii i zadachi arkhitektorov" [Twentieth Congress of the Communist Party and the Problems of the Architects]. *Arkhitektura SSSR*, no. 3, 1956: 2-3.

Reviews the directives of the Congress concerning the fulfillment of the Sixth Five Year Plan and especially the industrialization of the building industry in the realms of precast concrete construction and the standardization of building components. Reasserts Khrushchev's admonitions to improve the quality of construction by eliminating decorative excesses in architectural design (see **no. 150**).

498. Gradov, G. "Sovetskuiu arkhitekturu na uroven' novykh zadach" [Bringing Soviet Architecture on a Level with the New Problems]. *Arkhitektura SSSR*, no. 2, 1955: 4-8.

Argues that socialist realism can be viewed as the method for solving problems of design only insofar as it provides for the depiction of reality in artistic creations. However, it cannot, by its very nature, provide for all aspects of architectural production and must therefore be defined as affecting more the artistic image of Soviet architecture rather than its technological basis of production. Deplores the aesthetics by which buildings are designed in archaic forms and argues that new building materials demand a new engineering aesthetic. Includes a comprehensive critical analysis of existing work within the newly defined criteria. Valuable for revealing new interpretations and evaluations of leading architects and their work.

499.   "K novomu pod'emu arkhitekturnogo tvorchestva" [For New Improvements in Architectural Creativity]. *Arkhitektura SSSR*, no. 7, 1955: 1-3.

Editorial which speaks of the primary importance of economic criteria in design and construction, as well as of the need for considering simultaneously both economic and technological advances. Castigates rhetorically and without specifying by name those architects who have failed previously to take these factors into account.

500.   Mikhailov, A. I. "O nekotorykh tvorcheskikh zadachakh na novom etape sovetskoi arkhitektury" [Concerning a Few Creative Problems at the New Stage of Soviet Architecture]. *Arkhitektura SSSR*, no. 12, 1955: 43-47.

States that recent demands made through official decrees and pronouncements are not new but have been made by Party and government officials consistently since the thirties, citing the various decrees and drawing parallels. Thus, argues that Soviet architecture was provided a viable course of development, from which it diverged toward extravagance of design through "ideological" and "technological" fetishisms, i.e., "art for art's sake" and "technological determinism" in architecture. Of significance for its transparent attempt to assert the essential integrity of Soviet architecture by placing blame on individuals rather than on official policy and for its effort to support a new unity between "aesthetic" and "constructional" prerequisites, as called for in the decree of November 4, 1955.

501.   "Na puti reshitel'noi tvorcheskoi perestroiki" [On the Way to a Decisive Creative Reorganization]. *Arkhitektura SSSR*, no. 5, 1955: 1-2.

An editorial on the recent conference in December 1954 of builders and architects and the 17th plenary meeting of the administration of the Union of Soviet Architects, both of which indicated the necessity of decreasing the cost of construction, reorganizing technological methods of construction, developing standardized design, and implementing these changes through new, innovative methods of design.

502.   "Nash schet i pozhelaniia arkhitektoram" [Our Evaluation and Advice for the Architects]. *Arkhitektura SSSR*, no. 11, 1955:12-25.

An interesting collection of 25 vignettes by assorted professionals, each of whom cites a particular area in which he feels Soviet architecture should be improved. No basis given for what seems to be a random sample of individual sentiments but interesting as a barometer of a segment of Soviet public opinion on architectural affairs.

503.   "Obobshchat' i propagandirovat' peredovoi opyt arkhitekturno-stroitel'noi praktiki" [To Generalize and Propagandize Advanced Experience in Architectural and Building Practice]. *Arkhitektura SSSR*, no. 8, 1955: 1-4.

An editorial that argues for the active and effective dissemination among all professional and theoretical architectural institutions of positive experience in the realms of planning and, especially, the industrialization and standardization of mass construction. Specifies those areas with both the greatest achievements and the greatest deficiencies.

504.   Parusnikov, M. "Aktual'nye voprosy razvitiia arkhitektury" [Actual Questions in the Development of Architecture]. *Arkhitektura SSSR*, No. 10, 1955: 21-22.

States that the primary problem of Soviet architects is to reduce the cost of construction while learning to create beauty with an economy of means. Argues that the most effective means of improving standardized design is to create a research institute specifically for that purpose, noting that the Academy of Architecture has been derelict in developing such work.

505.   "Protiv formalizma v arkhitekturnoi praktike i nauke" [Against Formalism in Architectural Practice and Scholarship]. See no. 129.

Proceedings and abstracts of speeches and discussions at a meeting of the Academy of Architecture. In his keynote speech,

Arkadi G. Mordvinov, president of the Academy, asserts that Soviet architects in the past incorrectly interpreted the Party's admonitions to assimilate the architectural heritage, succumbing to a "decorativism." States that the present problem is one of appropriating contemporary technology. Most comments support the general theme that Soviet architecture had heretofore been preoccupied with decorative excesses at the expense of technical considerations. Some (Mordvinov, A. Mikhailov) cautioned against returning to a "constructivist decadence," while others (N. Shchetinin, K. Ivanov) faulted the Academy in general and Mordvinov in particular for the present preoccupation with decorative excesses. An illuminating record, providing much valuable insight into the current trends in, and interpretations of, architectural and aesthetic thought in Soviet architecture.

506.   "Puti korennogo uludsheniia stroitel'nogo dela" [Directions for the Fundamental Improvement of Construction Affairs]. *Arkhitektura SSSR*, no. 11, 1955: 1-4.
        An editorial that cites recent official decrees in order to define the direction in which mass construction with prefabricated elements and the standardization of design and construction are to proceed. A useful source for establishing the relationship and continuity of these decrees.

507.   "Razvivat' tvorcheskuiu kritiku i samokritiku" [To Develop a Creative Criticism and Self-criticism]. *Arkhitektura SSSR*, no. 6, 1955: 1-3.
        An editorial appealing for an intensification of architectural criticism and self-criticism in the Union of Soviet Architects, the Academy of Architecture, and other architectural organizations to facilitate the current transition directed by recent official pronouncements and decrees.

508.   "Reshitel'no pokonchit' s rastochitel'stvom v arkhitekture i gradostroitel'stve" [Putting a Decisive End to Extravagance in Architecture and City Planning]. *Arkhitektura SSSR*, no. 9, 1955: 1-3.
        An editorial that renews the plea for developing mass-housing and standardized design as directed in recent official decrees and pronouncements.

509.   Shvidkovsky, Oleg A. "Teoriia i praktika sovetskoi arkhitektury" [Theory and Practice in Soviet Architecture]. *Voprosy sovremennoi arkhitektury*, no. 1, 1962: 3-30.

Useful for its analysis of the nature and impact of the transition in Soviet architecture brought about by the official decrees and pronouncements in 1954-55.

510. Vlasov, Aleksandr V. "Architecture in the USSR: a Report from Within." *Architectural Record*, v. 122, Sept. 1957: 16B, 338, 342, 346.

One of the first published reports, by the vice-president of the Academy of Construction and Architecture of the USSR, on the architectural profession and building industry in the Soviet Union following the reorganizations in those fields as ordered by the decree on November 4, 1955. Submitted in response to the *Record's* request.

511. ——."Napravlennost' sovetskoi arkhitektury v usloviakh dal'neishego razvitiia industrializatii stroitel'stva" [Direction of Soviet Architecture in Conditions of the Further Development of the Industrialization of Construction]. *Arkhitektura SSSR*, no. 1, 1960: 1-8.

A review of the emergence of the socialist architectural style and its current state of development. Of great significance for postulating formally the new aesthetic basis for Soviet architecture following the decree of November 4, 1955. Where the architecture of the preceding decades was based on a superficial attention to the outward appearance of the building, the primary considerations for contemporary Soviet architecture are to be man's needs and comforts and the optimum provision for his work and rest; these requirements are to be synthesized with aesthetic considerations. Finally, newly emerging building materials and a constantly progressing building technology should permit a great diversity of idioms and preclude the promulgation of any single style. Of great significance both as a new manifesto for Soviet architecture and an indication of the cycle through which Soviet architecture has developed since 1917.

512. Volodin, P. A. "O napravlennosti sovetskogo zodchestva" [Concerning the Direction of Soviet Architecture]. *Voprosy teorii arkhitektury*, no. 1, 1955: 48-74.

A polemical criticism of the directions in the architectural practice of the great masters of the Old School. Argues for the implementation of modern techniques in design and construction. Of value for its particular evaluation of the old classical school in Soviet architecture, in view of Khrushchev's speech of December 7, 1954, first condemning excesses in design and construction.

513.   ——, N. A. Pekareva, and V. I. Pavlichenkov. "O napravlennosti tvorcheskoi raboty sovetskikh arkhitektorov na sovremennom etape" [Concerning the Direction in the Creative Work of Soviet Architects at the Current Stage]. *Voprosy teorii arkhitektury*, v. 3, 1958: 3-92.

A comprehensive analysis of the directions in the work of Soviet architects in view of current developments brought about by the official decrees and pronouncements in 1954-55. Assesses the errors of preceding periods and outlines the problems to be resolved by Soviet architects. Of special value for its historical survey of Soviet architecture in order to support the argument that the requirements and demands imposed by the current decrees had their roots in the official decrees and pronouncements of the thirties.

2. By Non-Soviet Writers

514.   Forshaw, J. H. "Russian Architecture and Building 1955." *RIBA Journal*, 3d ser., v. 63, March 1956: 182-189.

A review based on a tour of the country by a small group of British officials. Travelogue format, but conveys generally useful information, including an analysis of current problems in Soviet architecture.

515.   Kopp, Anatole. "Impressions de voyage d'un architecte en URSS." *La Construction moderne,* Nov. 1956: 382-388.

A record of an architect's response to Soviet architecture. See No. 355 for author's recent book on modern architecture in the Soviet Union.

516.   "Nouvelles tendances de l'architecture en URSS." *L'Architecture d'aujourd'hui*, v. 27, July 1956: 96-97.

A brief view of new developments in Soviet architecture following the 1955 decree to eliminate excesses in architecture and construction. Of general interest.

517.   Willen, Paul. "New Era in Soviet Architecture." *Problems of Communism*, v. 5, no. 4, 1956: 29-33.

A concise investigation of recent trends in Soviet architecture since Khrushchev's speech of December 7, 1954 (see **no. 150**), condemning architectural and decorative excesses, the subsequent decree of November 4, 1955 (see **no. 155**), and the circumstances in which this change in trends away from the Stalinist classical monumentality evolved.

V. Works about Architectural Institutions and Movements

A. GENERAL

518. Khazanova, Vigdariia E. "Soviet Architectural Associations." *Architectural Design*, no. 2, 1970: 76-78.

A summary of the history, aims, ideals, and activity of architectural organizations prior to 1932. Includes an appended comprehensive list of these associations, including their officers and principal members. An important source.

519. Piliavsky, V. "Arkhitekturnye obshchestva Peterburga-Petrograda" [Architectural Societies of Petersburg-Petrograd]. *Arkhitektura SSSR*, no. 12, 1967: 17-18.

A brief historical account of the founding and activities of the principal architectural societies in the city, both during pre-revolutionary and in Soviet times. A good source.

B. SCHOOLS AND INSTITUTIONS

1. INKHUK — Institut khudozhestvennoi kul'tury
[Institute of Artistic Culture]

520. "Inkhuk." In *Sovetskoe iskusstvo za 15 let. Materialy i dokumentatsiia.* See **no. 140.** p. 126-137.

A collection of documentary and archival material relating to the Institute, as well as summary articles of its activity.

2. MVKHTI — Moskovskii vysshii khudozhestvenno-tekhicheskii Institut
[Moscow Higher Artistic-Technical Institute]

521. L. "Iz rabot arkhitekturnogo fakul'teta MVKHTI" [From the Work of the Architectural Faculty of the MVKHTI]. *Stroitel'stvo Moskvy*, no. 8, 1929: 18-21.

A review of student work at the Institute.

522.   Krutikov, G. "Arkhitekturnaia Nauchno-issledovatel'skaia Laboratoriia
pri arkhitekturnom fakul'tete Moskovskogo Vysshego Khud.
Tekhnich. Instituta" [Architectural Scientific Research Laboratory
in the Architectural Faculty of the Moscow Higher Artistic-
Technical Institute]. *Stroitel'naia promyshlennost'*, no. 5, 1928:
372-375.
An outline of Ladovsky's experiments at the Institute. For
more information, see **no. 971**.

3. MVTU — Moskovskoe vysshee tekhnicheskoe uchilishche
[Moscow Higher Technical Institute]

523.   "Arkhitekturnoe otdelenie Moskovskogo Vysshego Tekhnicheskogo
Uchilishcha" [Architectural Department of the Moscow Higher
Technical Institute]. *Stroitel'stvo Moskvy*, no. 6, 1927: 14-16.
A brief history of the Department and a review of representa-
tive student work.

524.   M., N. "Nauchno-issledovatel'skaia rabota v oblasti arkhitektury"
[Scientific Research in the Realm of Architecture]. *Stroitel'naia
promyshlennost'*, no. 1, 1929: 75-77.
A discussion of the new Institute of Architectural Research
within the MVTU. Includes extracts from its program. A good
source of material about the Institute.

4. UNOVIS—Utverditeli novogo iskusstva
[Affirmants of the New Art]

525.   Rakitin, V. "Unovis." *Architectural Design*, no. 2, 1970: 78-79.
A concise history of the founding and activities of the Unovis
School at Vitebsk. States that the school was founded by Malevich
not by Chagal, in 1919, that Lissitzky was an active member and
propagandizer of its activities, and that Unovis strongly influenced
A. S. Nikol'sky's architectural work in Leningrad and, to some
extent, the work of I. I. Leonidov. Mentions also that the
influence of the school was felt in the architecture of the Ukraine
during the twenties.

5. VKHUTEMAS–vysshie gosudarstvennye khudozhestvenno-tekhnicheskie masterskie [Higher State Artistic-Technical Studios]

a. Monographs

526. *Arkhitektura VKHUTEMAS. Raboty arkhitekturnogo fakul'teta VKHUTEMASa, 1920-1927* [Architecture of VKHUTEMAS. The Work of the Architectural Faculty at the VKHUTEMAS, 1920-1927]. Moscow, Izd-vo VKHUTEMASa, 1927.

An excellent review of the architectural projects undertaken in the school. Profusely illustrated. Introduction by Pavel Novitsky, rector of the school. See especially the account of the curriculum and methods of instruction by N. V. Dokuchaev, "Arkhitekturnyi fakul'tet VKHUTEMASa" [The Architectural Faculty of VKHUTEMAS], p. v-xiv.

b. Articles

527. K., V. "Otchetnaia vystavka arkhitekturnogo fakul'teta VKHUTEMAS" [Current Exhibit of the VKHUTEMAS Architectural Faculty]. *Stroitel'naia promyshlennost'*, nos. 6-7, 1926: 470-472.

An analytical review of student projects exhibited on May 19-June 1, 1925. Includes projects by M. P. Korzhev, M. E. Barshch, and S. N. Kozhin.

528. —."Rabota diplomatov na Arkhitekturnom fakul'teta VKHUTEMASa" [Projects of the Diploma Students in the VKHUTEMAS Architectural faculty]. *Stroitel'stvo Moskvy*, no. 6, 1927: 9-13.

An analytical review of the projects, including those by P. N. Blokhin, A. Ia. Karra, I. I. Komarov, P. M. Panin, F. I. Mikhailovsky, N. P. Rakcheev, L. I. Kuznetsov, and N. P. Il'insky.

529. Khazanova, Vigdariia E. "VKHUTEMAS-VKHUTEIN." *Architectural Design*, no. 2, 1970: 80-81.

A brief history of the development and activity of the first established Soviet art schools, with emphasis on the architects who formed the various studios within the institutes. An important source for illuminating the particular activities of the principal Soviet architects during these early years both within and outside the VKHUTEMAS.

530. Lavrov, V. "Arkhitektura VKHUTEMAS" [Architecture of VKHUTEMAS]. *Stroitel'naia promyshlennost'*, no. 10, 1927: 701-702.

A review and synopsis of the book *Arkhitektura VKHUTEMAS* (no. 526). Provides a useful supplement and abstract. See also his article, "Arkhitektura VKHUTEMASa (rabota arkhit. fakul'teta za 1920-1927 gg.)" [Architecture of **VKHUTEMAS** (the Work of the Architectural Faculty during 1920-1927)], *Stroitel'stvo Moskvy,* no. 11, 1927: 15-17.

531.   ——. "O novom zdanii Vysshei Khudozhestvennoi shkoly v Moskve" [On the New Building of the Higher Artistic School in Moscow]. *Stroitel'stvo Moskvy.* no. 4, 1927: 8-10.

        Includes a review of the work of the architectural faculty at VKHUTEMAS. Includes projects by Travin, Glushchenko, and Lavrov.

531a.   Zhadova, L. "VKHUTEMAS–VKHUTEIN." *Dekorativnoe iskusstvo SSSR,* no. 11, 1970: 36-43.

        A documented account of the institution, with emphasis upon curricular and administrative developments. Provides much new insight into its workings.

6. VKHUTEIN–Vysshii gosudarstvennyi
khudozhestvenno-tekhnicheskii institut
[Higher State Artistic-Technical Institute]

a. Monographs

532.   *Arkhitektura i VKHUTEIN.* See **no. 65.**

        A comprehensive review of work undertaken by students and faculty at the Institute, including Ladovsky's laboratory experiments.

b. Articles

533.   Khazanova, Vigdariia E. "VKHUTEMAS-VKHUTEIN." See **no. 529.**

        Includes a brief discussion of the evolution of VKHUTEIN.

534.   Krasil'nikov, N., and L. Nappel'baum. "Eshche iz diplomnykh rabot arkhitekturnogo fakul'teta VKHUTEINa" [More Diploma Projects of the Architectural Faculty at VKHUTEIN]. *Stroitel'stvo Moskvy,* no. 2, 1929: 11-13.

        A review of the projects by the authors and by V. Semenov.

535.   Krasin, G. "Ob uchastii VKHUTEINa v proizvoditel'nnykh rabotakh (po opytu zhilishchno-stroitel'nogo komiteta Mossoveta)" [On the Participation of VKHUTEIN in Manufacturing Projects (in the

Experience of the Housing Construction Committee of the Moscow Soviet)]. *Stroitel'stvo Moskvy,* no. 11, 1928: 16-17.

Reports on the results of the collaboration with the Committee in an academic exercise. Provides much useful insight into the VKHUTEIN approach employed by Ladovsky and Lavrov.

536. L. "Proekty 'Doma promyshlennosti i torgovli' i 'Dom s'ezdov' " [Projects for the "House of Industry and Trade" and for the "House of Congresses"]. *Stroitel'stvo Moskvy,* no. 1, 1929: 12-16.

Reviews the projects developed by the VKHUTEIN diploma students in 1928. Includes projects by I. Volodko, A. Silchenko, R. Smolenskaia, S. Gel'fel'd, and G. Glushchenko.

537. Lavrov, V. "Iz poslednikh rabot Arkhitekturnogo fakul'teta VKHU-TEINa" [From the Most Recent Work of the VKHUTEIN Architectural Faculty]. *Stroitel'stvo Moskvy,* no. 10, 1928: 14-18.

Discusses the problem of the new city as defined by VKHUTEIN, as well as reviewing the most recent research conducted by Ladovsky on "psycho-technical" perception.

538. ——. "Proektirovanie rabochego poselka u Izmailovskogo shose" [Design of a Workers' Settlement near the Izmailovsky Highway]. *Stroitel'stvo Moskvy,* no. 8, 1928: 9-12.

Expounds the aims and program of the newly established VKHUTEIN method of instruction. Focuses on the workers' settlement project to illustrate the new approach.

539. ——. "Teoriia i praktika kommunal'nogo zhilishcha" [Theory and Practice of Communal Housing]. *Stroitel'stvo Moskvy,* no. 12, 1929: 3-5.

Outlines the planning principles for the design of communal housing, as developed in the VKHUTEIN.

C. ARCHITECTURAL MOVEMENTS AND SOCIETIES BEFORE 1932

1. ARU – Ob'edinenie arkhitektorov-urbanistov
[Society of Architects-Urbanists]

540. "ARU–Ob'edinenie arkhitektorov-urbanistov" [ARU–Society of Architects-Urbanists]. *Sovetskaia arkhitektura,* nos. 1-2, 1931: 19-43.

The new ARU declaration and samples of the organization's work. Includes self-criticism of having formerly been nonideologically oriented and subjective.

541.   Barutchev, A. "ARU v Leningrade" [ARU in Leningrad] . *Sovetskaia arkhitektura*, no. 18, 1969: 35-37.
       A brief but informative account of the Leningrad branch of the organization. Provides a revealing study of the four members and their active collaboration in practice.

542.   "Deklaratsiia arkhitektorov-urbanistov" [Declaration of the Architects-Urbanists] . In *Sovetskoe iskusstvo za 15 let. Materialy i dokumentatsiia.* See **no. 140.** p. 529-531.
       The first declaration of the group upon its formation on November 7, 1928. Declares dissatisfaction with the meager activity of architects in the realm of city planning and proposes a program by which all interested specialists can intensify their participation and assist state agencies in developing and coordinating efforts of city planning. Declaration reproduced also in *Iz istorii sovetskoi arkhitektury 1926-1932* (**no. 125**), p. 125.

543.   Khazanova, Vigdariia E. "Ob'edinenie arkhitektorov-urbanistov (ARU)" [Society of Architects-Urbanists (ARU)] . In her *Iz istorii sovetskoi arkhitektury 1926-1932.* See **no. 139,** p. 123-124.
       A concise summary of the development and the principal participants and philosophies of the organization. A source of important material.

544.   Ladovsky, N. "Pis'mo v redaktsiu" [Letter to the Editor] . *Sovetskaia arkhitektura*, no. 4, 1931: 64.
       A response to Petrov's article, "ASNOVA za 8 let" (**no. 565**). Clarifies the circumstances in which Ladovsky and his followers broke away from ASNOVA and formed ARU. An important source.

545.   Lavrov, V. "Ob'edinenie arkhitektorov-urbanistov (ARU)" [Society of Architects-Urbanists (ARU)] . *Sovetskaia arkhitektura*, no. 18, 1969: 29-34.
       An authoritative review of the organization and its activity by one of its founding members. Contains much useful material; however, formality of presentation precludes gaining added valuable insight into the background circumstances of the organization.

2. ASNOVA – Assotsiatsiia novykh arkhitektorov
[Association of New Architects]

a. Monographs

546. *Izvestiia ASNOVA.* See **no. 70.**

Provides a record of the organization's theoretical positions
and its activities and surveys the work of its members and
followers. Though intended as a journal, only one issue ever
published.

b. Articles

(1) *General and Theoretical Works*

547. ["ASNOVA's Platform"]. *Izvestiia ASNOVA*, no. 1, 1926: 1.

Announces the Association's intention to implement in architecture the principles of the USSR, to imbue architecture with
modern scientific principles, to liberate architecture from atro-
phied forms, and to create precise, scholarly nomenclature in
modern architecture. For extract, see *Iz istorii sovetskoi arkhitektury, 1926-1932* (**no. 139**), p. 41.

548. Bunin, A., and M. Turkus. "Rabota sektora ASNOVA" [Work of
the Sector ASNOVA]. *Sovetskaia arkhitektura*, nos. 1-2, 1931:
53.

A brief review of ASNOVA's work, outlining the organization's
methodology of design and suggesting improvement in synthesis
of the arts in its work.

549. Dokuchaev, N. V. "Arkhitektura rabochego zhilishcha i byt" [Archi-
tecture of Workers' Housing and Life]. *Sovetskoe iskusstvo*, no.
3, 1926: 20-24.

Asserts that the problem of designing adequate workers'
housing should not be one of fomenting aspirations toward
"bourgeois individualism" among the working classes. Maintains
that the solution lies in solving narrowly utilitarian conditions
(comfort, hygiene, lighting, ventilation, etc.) and resolving ideological, formal, and social considerations (architectural design, planning policy, etc.). The latter considerations are cardinal, for a
viable planning policy can arise only from their successful solution.

550. ——. "Arkhitektura i planirovka gorodov" [Architecture and Planning
of Cities]. *Sovetskoe iskusstvo*, no. 6, 1926: 8-17.

Maintains, with Ladovsky, that architecture is an indispensable tool for synthesizing the social, economic, technical, and functional considerations in the effective planning of the physical aspects of the city.

551. ——. "Arkhitektura i tekhnika" [Architecture and Technology]. *Sovetskoe iskusstvo*, nos. 8-9, 1926: 3-9.

Examines the nature of art and technology to determine the nature of their synthesis in modern architecture. Deplores the superficiality of the constructivist method of deriving forms simply from advanced technological methods of construction. Views this method as an exercise concerned less with the logical, formal, or constructive sensibilities of the viewer than with mere superficial graphics, ignoring the primary formal problems of architecture (architectural form, construction, and space). For extract of article, see *Iz istorii sovetskoi arkhitektury, 1926-1932* **(no. 139)**, p. 43-44.

552. ——. "Korbiuz'e-Son'e" [Le Corbusier-Sonniet]. *Iskusstvo*, nos. 3-4, 1929: 128-140.

Uses the occasion of commenting on Le Corbusier's Centrosoiuz Building in Moscow to chide his emulation by Soviet constructivists, who are accused of not seeing the difference between the aesthetics of Le Corbusier's "purism" and the utilitarianism of their own position. An illuminating and provocative article.

553. ——. "Po povodu vystavki 'iskusstvo narodov SSSR' arkhitekturnyi otdel" [Concerning the Exhibit "Art of the Peoples of the USSR," the Architectural Section]. *Sovetskoe iskusstvo*, no. 1, 1927: 35-41.

Laments the lack of attention paid to architecture at the exhibit. Uses this occasion to argue that the cause of a national architecture cannot be served by indiscriminately reviving styles of the past which are incapable of responding to the unique circumstances and requirements of the present day.

554. ——. "Sovremennaia russkaia arkhitektura" [Contemporary Russian Architecture]. *Krasnaia niva*, no. 14, 1925: 330-331.

Assesses the current state of Soviet architecture and asserts that, in the future, it will once again proceed from art and become an organizing and socially necessary force in the life of the country.

555.   —. "Sovremennaia russkaia arkhitektura i zapadnye paralleli" [Contemporary Russian Architecture and Western Parallels]. *Sovetskoe iskusstvo:* Part 1, no. 1., 1927: 5-12; Part 2, no. 2, 1927: 5-15.

Part 1 discusses three tendencies in Soviet architecture operating in 1920-23 which continued to 1927: 1) academic eclecticism, 2) the romanticism of modern technology, or constructivism, later evolving into functionalism, and 3) rationalism, professing the psychoanalytical method of architectural organization and design. Part 2 elaborates the principal tenets and arguments of the rationalist doctrine. The "Western parallels" are seen to apply more to the eclectic and constructivist phases of activity. For extract of Part 2, see *Iz istorii sovetskoi arkhitektury, 1926-1932* (**no. 139**), p. 45-50.

556.   —. "Zhilishchnoe stroitel'stvo i arkhitektura" [Housing Construction and Architecture]. *Sovetskoe iskusstvo*, no. 3, 1928: 48-58.

Surveys the housing problem and maintains that its solution is dependent upon a positive intervention by governmental agencies to prompt and administer policy, the participation of innovative architectural and technical talent in the task, and increasing flexibility in dealing with the problem.

557.   Il'in, Mikhail A. "L'Expressionisme en architecture." *L'Architecture d'aujourd'hui*, v. 1, no. 2, 1930: 29-34.

Includes an incisive account of the activities of ASNOVA, its members and followers, with a series of good plates. A good résumé.

558.   Khazanova, Vigdariia E. "Assotsiatsiia novykh arkhitektorov(ASNOVA)" [Association of New Architects (ASNOVA)]. In her *Iz istorii sovetskoi arkhitektury, 1926-1932.* See **no. 139**. p. 39-41.

A concise history of the Association, its members, aims, and activities. Contains much useful information and references.

559.   Kortev, M., and N. V. Markovnikov. "Pis'mo v redaktsiiu" [Letter to the Editor]. *Stroitel'naia promyshlennost'*, nos, 6-7, 1927: 454.

Protests the preferential treatment given the OSA in the exhibit "Modern Architecture," explaining ASNOVA's refusal to participate. Kortev is the president of ASNOVA; Markovnikov, vice-president of the "Moscow Circle of Architects-Artists."

560. Krinsky, Vladimir F. "Vozniknovenie i zhizn' Assotsiatsii novykh arkhitektorov (ASNOVA)" [Emergence and Life of the Association of New Architects (ASNOVA)]. *Sovetskaia arkhitektura,* no. 18, 1969: 20-28.

Recollections on the evolution of ASNOVA by one of its founding members. Provides much valuable insight into the motivations and personalities of its leading members and illuminates numerous important highlights in the organization's activity. An important source.

561. Ladovsky, Nikolai A. "Osnovy postroeniia teorii arkhitektury" [Bases for the Construction of a Theory of Architecture]. *Izvestiia ASNOVA.* no. 1, 1926: 3-5.

Analyzes the dynamics of composition, construction, color, and material, outlining a theoretical program for ASNOVA. For extract, see *Iz istorii sovetskoi arkhitektury, 1926-1932* (no. 139), p. 41-43.

561a. ——. Psikho-tekhnicheskaia laboratoriia arkhitektury (V poriadke postanovki voprosa)" [A Psycho-Technical Architectural Laboratory (By Way of Posing the Question)]. *Izvestiia ASNOVA,* no. 1, 1926: [7].

A proposal to establish a psycho-technical laboratory for investigating various perceptual phenomena in architecture; modeled after the Harvard Psychological Laboratory established by Hugo Münsterberg in the 1890s. Ladovsky's laboratory was established the following year at VKHUTEIN.

562. Lavrov, V. "Uchastie ASNOVA v zhilishchnom stroitel'stve Mossoveta" [Participation of ASNOVA in the Housing Construction Undertaken by the Moscow Soviet]. *Stroitel'stvo Moskvy,* no. 1, 1928: 14-16.

Reviews the work undertaken by members of ASNOVA in a closed competition sponsored by the Moscow Soviet.

563. Lissitzky, El. "Moskau." *ABC,* no. 1, 1924: 1.

A brief announcement of the founding of ASNOVA in Moscow in the summer of 1923. Contains a brief description of the organization's aims.

564. Myslin, Vladimir. "Chem i kak zhivet ASNOVA" [How ASNOVA Operates]. *Sovetskaia arkhitektura,* nos. 1-2, 1931: 52-53.

Analyzes ASNOVA's work and motives both earlier as an independent organization and presently as a sector within MOVANO, which it joined along with other architectural organizations to consolidate the architectural forces in the country. Views a change from a collective effort in earlier years to an increasing trend toward individual efforts in competitions and suggests that ASNOVA, like OSA (SASS), does not really reflect proletarian architecture.

565. Petrov, V. "ASNOVA za 8 let" [ASNOVA in 8 Years]. See **no. 226.**
       A chronology of events and work of ASNOVA, 1923-31.

566. "Programno-ideologicheskaia ustanovka sektora ASNOVA" [Program and Ideological Purpose of the Sector ASNOVA]. *Sovetskaia arkhitektura*, nos. 1-2, 1931: 46-47.
       An outline of ASNOVA's platform, including sections on 1) the definition of the social functions of proletarian architecture, 2) the dialectic nature of proletarian architecture, 3) the characteristics of proletarian architecture, and 4) programmatic and organizational conclusions. ASNOVA then a sector of VANO.

567. Rukhliadev, A., and Krinsky, V. "Ob ideologicheskoi vyrazitel'nosti v arkhitekture" [Concerning Ideological Expressiveness in Architecture]. *Sovetskaia arkhitektura*, nos. 1-2, 1931: 54-58.
       A critique of ASNOVA's work, tectonic formulation, and ideological expressiveness as based on the designs submitted to the competition for a Palace of Culture on the site of the former Simonov Monastery in Moscow. Includes suggestions for improving both the design and the general approach of the group. Interesting for illuminating the emerging basis of the new architectural criticism.

(2) *Criticisms*

568. "ASNOVA." *S.A.*, no. 2, 1926: 59.
       An article welcoming ASNOVA into existence. Points out differences between ASNOVA and OSA, in an item by item commentary in response to the article by its founder, Prof. Ladovsky, "Osnovy postroenniia teorii arkhitektury" (**no. 561**).

569. Khiger, R. "Formalizm: ideologiia upadochnichestva v sovetskoi arkhitekture" [Formalism: Ideology of Decadence in Soviet Architecture]. *S.A.*, no. 4, 1929: 142-146.

Speech given at the First Congress of the Society of Contemporary Architects in May 1929. Analyzes formalism (ASNOVA) as the one current movement that has succeeded in countering constructivism. Argues that it stems from prerevolutionary, and not Soviet, times. Analysis divided into: 1) formalism as a world outlook, 2) the theory of formalism in architecture, 3) the pedagogical system of formalism, 4) formalism and "psychotechnology," and 5) conclusions. A biased but comprehensive account. Important.

570.   M., N. "Po povodu No. 1 *Izvestiia assotsiassii novykh arkhitektorov"* [On the First Issue of the *News of the Association of New Architects*] . *Stroitel'naia promyshlennost'*, no. 8, 1926: 566-568.
       A critique of the publication and a review of its principal articles, including those by Ladovsky, Dokuchaev, and Lissitzky. Reviewer displays mixed reaction.

571.   Mikhailov, A. "VOPRA, ASNOVA, SASS: K voprosu ob ideino-metodologicheskikh raznoglasiakh" [VOPRA, ASNOVA, SASS: Concerning the Question of Ideological-Methodological Differences]. *Sovetskaia arkhitektura,* Part 1, no. 1-2, 1931: 73-77; Part 2, no. 3, 1931: 48-54.
       Includes comprehensive analysis of ASNOVA, based on their work and published statements. A useful study for articulating the emerging "Marxist proletarian" point of view. See author's *Gruppirovki sovetskoi arkhitektury* (no. 271) for an adaptation of this and other articles.

3. LAO — Leningradskoe obshchestvo arkhitektorov
[Leningrad Society of Architects] and
OAKH — Obshchestvo arkhitektorov-khudozhnikov
[Society of Architects-Artists]

a. Monographs

572.   *Obshchestvo arkhitektorov-khudozhnikov; Ezhegodnik* [Society of Architects-Artists; Yearbook] . See **no. 71.**
       Provides a review of work by members and area architects.

573.   *Zodchii* [The Architect]. Organ of the Leningrad Society of Architects. Only one issue published in 1924.
       A useful review of the Society's activity.

b. Articles

574. "Iz ustava Leningradskogo obshchestva arkhitektorov" [From the
      Charter of the Leningrad Society of Architects]. In *Iz istorii
      sovetskoi arkhitektury, 1926-1932.* See no. **139**. p. 28.
      The Charter of the Society, registered with the Leningrad
      Gubispolkom on August 28, 1926.

575. Karpovich, V. "Arkhitekturnaia zhizn' v Leningrade" [Architectural
      Life in Leningrad]. *Stroitel'naia promyshlennost'*, no. 4, 1927:
      286-287.
      Focuses upon the activity of the Leningrad Society of Archi-
      tects and the Society of Architects-Artists.

576. Khazanova, Vigdariia E. "Leningradskoe Obshchestvo Arkhitektorov
      (LOA); Obshchestvo arkhitektorov-khudozhnikov (OAKH)" [Len-
      ingrad Society of Architects (LOA); Society of Architects-Artists
      (OAKH)]. In her *Iz istorii sovetskoi arkhitektury, 1926-1932.*
      A succinct review of the history and activities of these two
      Leningrad architectural societies. Provides much useful material
      on membership.

577. Kosmachevsky, G. "Arkhitektura i ratsional'noe stroitel'stvo" [Archi-
      tecture and Rational Construction]. See no. **305**.
      Argues that the change in economic conditions calls for drastic
      changes in the character of housing and urban design and that the
      ideological principles of contemporary architecture (new archi-
      tectonics and construction) must begin serving the working
      classes. Outlines steps for implementing these goals.

578. ——. "Sovremennaia arkhitektura" [Contemporary Architecture].
      Stroitel'naia promyshlennost', no. 9, 1926: 655-657.
      An analytical assessment of modern architecture. Provides a
      rationalist framework for defining the nature both of architec-
      tural production and of the artistic aspect of contemporary
      architecture.

579. Piliavsky, V. "Arkhitekturnye obshchestva Peterburga-Petrograda"
      [Architectural Societies of Petersburg-Petrograd.] See no. **519**.
      Includes an account of the founding and activities of the
      Society of Architects-Artists and the Leningrad Society of Archi-
      tects.

4. MAO — Moskovskoe arkhitekturnoe obshchestvo
[Moscow Architectural Society]

a. Monographs and Publications

580.   *Arkhitektura* [Architecture]. Publication of the Moscow Architectural Society. See **no. 63**.
Edited by Moisei Ia. Ginzburg, later a founder of the OSA and an editor of its journal, *S.A.* Contains valuable material reflecting the work and polemic of the period.

581.   *Ezhegodnik MAO* [Yearbook of MAO]. Publication of the Moscow Architectural Society. See **no. 69**.
Includes some data on the activities of the Society, including the programs and winning entries for the competitions that it sponsored.

582.   *Konkursy Moskovskogo arkhitekturnogo obshchestva, 1923-1926* [Competitions of the Moscow Architectural Society, 1923-1926]. Moscow, Izd-vo MAO, 1927.
A review of winning designs submitted to competitions sponsored by the Society. An excellent review of representative work of the period.

b. Articles

583.   Khazanova, Vigdariia E. "Moskovskoe arkhitekturnoe obshchestvo (MAO)" [Moscow Architectural Society (MAO)]. In her *Iz istorii sovetskoi arkhitektury, 1926-1932.* See **no. 139**. p. 7-9.
A concise historical review of the Society's activities from its founding in 1867 to its incorporation into MOVANO in May 1930. Contains much useful information.

584.   "MAO." *Arkhitektura SSSR*, no. 12, 1967: 14-16.
A concise history of the Society's activities from its founding in 1867 to 1932, when it was disbanded along with the other architectural organizations by decree to form the Union of Soviet Architects.

585.   "Shest'desiat let Moskovskogo arkhitekturnogo obshchestva" [Sixty Years of the Moscow Architectural Society]. *Stroitel'stvo Moskvy*, no. 3, 1928: 32.

A commemorative article on the occasion of the Society's 60-year jubilee, celebrated on April 29 and 30, 1928. Includes a brief history of the Society's activities during prerevolutionary years and, especially, during the Soviet period.

5. "OKTIABR'" [October] —Vserossiiskoe ob'edinenie
rabotnikov novykh vidov khudozhestvennogo truda
[All-Russian Society of Workers in New Areas of Artistic Labor]

586.   "Deklaratsiia natsional'nogo sektora ob'edineniia 'Oktiabr'' " [Declaration of the National Sector of October"]. In *Sovetskoe iskusstvo za 15 let.* See **no. 140.** p. 611-614.

Calls for the development of an integral front of culture and art, uniting the proletarian artistic strains of every nationality in the country to assure the "hegemony of the proletariat." Declaration reproduced also in *Iz istorii sovetskoi arkhitektury, 1926-1932* (**no. 139**), p. 121-122.

587.   [Editorial] . *S.A.,* no. 3, 1928: 73-74.

Announces the creation of "Oktiabr'" and summarizes its declaration and theoretical position. Includes an open letter from Moisei Ginzburg, Aleksandr and Viktor Vesnin, and Aleksei Gan explaining that they are not deserting the ranks of the OSA, which is described here as only a scientific body rather than an "artistic grouping" of new aesthetic currents.

588.   Khazanova, Vigdariia E. "Vserossiiskoe ob'edinenie rabotnikov novykh vidov khudozhestvennogo truda 'Oktiabr'' " [All-Russian Society of Workers in New Areas of Artistic Labor, "October"]. In her *Iz istorii sovetskoi arkhitektury, 1926-1932.* See **no. 139.** p. 115-117.

Examines the evolution of the organization, its aims and members. Though brief, the only known competent published account of this little-known organization.

589.   "Ob'edinenie 'Oktiabr'.' Deklaratsiia." In *Sovetskoe iskusstvo za 15 let.* See **no. 140.** p. 608-611.

Asserts that the spatial arts can escape their present crisis only when they begin to serve the concrete needs of the proletariat and to participate consciously in the ideological class struggle. This is to be achieved in the realms of ideological propaganda and of the production and organization of the collective conditions of life.

590. "Predvaritel'naia skhema pokaza rabot ob'edineniia 'Oktiabr',' sos-
      tavlennaia pravleniem" [Preliminary Scheme for the Display of
      the Work of the Organization "October," Organized by the
      Administration]. In *Iz istorii sovetskoi arkhitektury, 1926-1932.*
      See **no. 139.** p. 119-121.
          Outlines the program and discusses the participants. Contains
      much valuable material clarifying the composition and ideological
      aims of the group.

6. OSA – Ob'edinenie sovremennykh arkhitektorov
[Society of Contemporary Architects], later known as
SASS – Sektor arkhitektorov sotsialisticheskogo stroitel'stva
[Sector of Architects of Socialist Construction]
(Constructivists-Functionalists)

a. General and Theoretical Works

(1) *Soviet Writers*

(a) *Monographs and Publications*

591. Gan, Aleksei. *Konstruktivizm* [Constructivism]. Tver, Tverskoe izd-
      vo, 1922. 70 p.
          The first postulation of the constructivist philosophy in the
      Soviet arts. Highly charged polemic negates art and emphasizes a
      purely technical mastery and organization of materials based on
      the principles of 1) the tectonic, or the system of creation, 2)
      factura, the process of working the material, and 3) construction
      as the product of an industrial order. For brief excerpts in Eng-
      lish, see Camilla Gray, *The Great Experiment in Russian Art,
      1863-1922* (New York, Abrams, 1962), p. 284-287.

592. Ginzburg, Moisei Ia. *Ritm v arkhitekture* [Rhythm in Architecture].
      See **no. 208.**
          Provides an insight into the author's approach to basic design
      and to the emerging techniques of composition implicit in his
      formualtions of the constructivist method.

593. ——. *Stil' i epokha* [Style and Epoch]. See **no. 209.**
          The first postulation of constructivist philosophy in architecture.
      Essential for understanding the constructivist method and philo-
      sophy in Soviet architecture.

594. ——. *Zhilishche. Opyt piatiletnei raboty nad problemoi zhilishcha* [Housing. The Experience of Five Year's Work on the Problem of Housing]. See **no. 210**.

Valuable for illuminating both Ginzburg's experience and theory in the field of housing design.

595. *S.A.* See **no. 73**.

Publication of the OSA, propagandizing its work and theoretical postulations.

b. *Articles*

596. Gan, Aleksei. "Chto takoe konstruktivizm" [What Is Constructivism]. *S.A.*, no. 3, 1928: 79-80.

A theoretical essay reformulating principles established earlier in his book **(no. 591)** and outlining their application to architecture. See also his "Fakty za nas" [The Facts Are on Our Side], *S.A.*, no. 2, 1926: 39.

597. Ginzburg, Moisei Ia. "L'Architecture contemporaine." See **no. 287**.

A general historical synthesis of the development of constructivist architecture in the Soviet Union.

598. ——. "Arkhitekturnye vozmozhnosti sovremennoi industrii" [Architectural Possibilities of Modern Industry]. *Arkhitektura SSSR*, no. 3, 1934: 30-31.

Speaks of the fact that Soviet architecture has not exploited the possibilities afforded by the newly developing building technology and refers to the constructivists' efforts in this regard and the need to benefit from this experience. A general but useful statement.

599. ——. "Funktsional'nyi metod i forma" [Functional Method and Form]. *S.A.*, no. 4, 1926: 89-92.

Postulates the primary circumstances which permitted the modern architect to break with the architectural styles of the past: the technological and industrial revolution in Western Europe and America and the social revolution in the Soviet Union. Explains the evolution of functionalism in modern architecture and develops a framework for its systematic application in all phases of architectural work. For extract, see *Iz istorii sovetskoi arkhitektury, 1926-1932* **(no. 139)**, 72-73.

600. ——. "Itogi i perspektivy" [Results and Perspectives]. *S.A.*, nos. 4-5, 1927: 112-118.

An important review of the development of constructivism in Soviet architecture, from the first attempt by Gan in his book *Konstruktivizm* to formulate and propagandize constructivism, through its moment in the Soviet theater, to the Vesnins' design for the Palace of Labor and the subsequent organization of the Society of Contemporary Architects. Discusses constructivist philosophy, notes beginning of exchange with Western architects in 1924-25, and subsequent Soviet influence on the West, discusses the activity and accomplishments of the OSA, and postulates a formula for its continued work: 1) solve social problems, 2) popularize constructivism, and 3) improve quality of architectural design. For extract, see *Iz istorii sovetskoi arkhitektury, 1926-1932* (no. 139), p. 82-85.

601. ——. "Konstruktivizm kak metod laboratornoi i pedagogicheskoi raboty" [Constructivism as a Laboratory and Pedagogical Method of Work]. *S.A.*, no. 6, 1927: 160-166.

A schematic, preliminary plan for a course on the theory of architecture. First presented in a speech by the author to the architectural faculty of VKHUTEMAS and at the M.V.T.U. For extract, see *Iz istorii sovetskoi arkhitektury, 1926-1932* (no. 139), p. 86-87.

602. ——. "Konstruktivizm v arkhitekture" [Constructivism in Architecture]. *S.A.*, no. 5, 1928: 143-145.

Speech delivered to the First Conference of the OSA (Society of Contemporary Architects). Presents a survey and comparison of modern architecture in the West and in the Soviet Union, followed by an analytical review of the development of constructivism in Soviet architecture. An important analytical document. For extract, see *Iz istorii sovetskoi arkhitektury, 1926-1932* (no. 139), p. 94-95.

603. ——. "Mezhdunarodnyi front sovremennoi arkhitektury" [The International Front of Contemporary Architecture]. *S.A.*, no. 2, 1926: 41-46.

Provides a synopsis of developments in modern architecture of Germany, France, Holland, America, and argues for a corresponding intensity of development in the Soviet Union, in view of the advantages wrought both by the Revolution and by the technological developments of the times.

604. ———. "Natsional'naia arkhitektura narodov SSSR" [The National Architecture of the Peoples of the USSR]. *S.A.*, nos. 5-6, 1926: 113-114.

Outlines the criteria for applying functionalism to derive a "national" architecture: 1) prerequisites of the particular climate and physical life style of given region, 2) prerequisites of its new social structure, and 3) the development of its technology. Negates outward concern for maintaining national forms in modern architecture. For extract, see *Iz istorii sovetskoi arkhitektury, 1926-1932* (no. 139), p. 74.

605. ———. "Novye metody arkhitekturnogo myshleniia" [New Methods of Architectural Thought]. *S.A.*, no. 1, 1926: 1-4.

In the first issue of this magazine, a general introduction to the functional method of architectural production and design, citing its many advantages over the architecture of preceding years, especially prior to the Revolution. For extract, see *Iz istorii sovetskoi arkhitektury, 1926-1932* (no. 139), p. 70-71.

606. ———. "Tselevaia ustanovka v sovremennoi arkhitekture" [Special Aim of Contemporary Architecture]. *S.A.*, no. 1, 1927: 4-10.

Contends that a functional architecture is impossible without a concrete, utilitarian goal, made more complicated by the material and cultural progress of modern man. Proceeds to examine the basis for the functional method and its application in solving architectural problems. For extract, see *Iz istorii sovetskoi arkhitektury, 1926-1932* (no. 139), p. 74-76.

607. ———. "Tvorcheskaia diskussiia soiuza sovetskikh arkhitektorov" [Creative Discussion at the Union of Soviet Architects]. *Arkhitektura SSSR*, nos. 3-4, 1934: 12.

An attempt to redefine the viable implications of functionalism within the new framework of socialist realism.

608. ———, and Viktor A. and Aleksandr A. Vesnin. "Tvorcheskaia tribuna: problemy sovremennoi arkhitektury" [Creative Tribune: Problems of Contemporary Architecture]. . See **no. 420.**

A response to continuing criticism of modern architecture and constructivism following the eclipse of modernism in 1932 and a presentation of what authors feel still to be fundamental problems of architecture. Treats general theoretical presuppositions and creative limits of architecture and applies them to the problems currently before Soviet architecture in the official search for a new idiom.

608a. Khan-Magomedov, Selim O. "Traditsii i uroki konstruktivizma" [Traditions and Lessons of Constructivism]. *Dekorativnoe iskusstvo SSSR*, no. 9, 1964: 25-29.

An address delivered to a conference convened by the Union of Soviet Architects in the summer of 1964 to deliberate the controversial aspects of constructivism and to ascertain its place in the history of Soviet architecture. Khan-Magomedov's is one of the more penetrating summaries of the salient elements operating in the movement, providing much useful insight into its *modus operandi*. Highly recommended.

609. Khazanova, Vigdariia E. "Ob'edinenie sovremennykh arkhitektorov (OSA)" [Society of Contemporary Architects (OSA)]. In her *Iz istorii sovetskoi arkhitektury, 1926-1932*. See no. **139**. p. 65-68.

A concise historical essay on the evolution of the constructivist movement in the early twenties and its subsequent organization into the OSA in 1926. Provides an abundance of important data concerning participants, activities, and major pronouncements.

610. ——. "Sektor arkhitektorov sotsialisticheskogo stroitel'stva (SASS) pri VANO" [Sector of Architects for Socialist Construction (SASS) under VANO]. In her *Iz istorii sovetskoi arkhitektury, 1926-1932*. See no. **139**. p. 149.

A brief account of the transformation of the OSA into the SASS.

611. Khiger, R. Ia. "K voprosu ob ideologii konstruktivizma v sovremennoi arkhitekture" [On the Question of the Ideology of Constructivism in Contemporary Architecture]. *S.A.*, no. 3, 1928: 92-102 .

A comprehensive postulation and analysis of the theory and application of the constructivist-functionalist doctrine. For extract, see *Iz istorii sovetskoi arkhitektury, 1926-1932* (**no. 139**), p. 90-91.

612. ——. "Konstruktivizm v arkhitekture" [Constructivism in Architecture]. *Revoliutsiia i kul'tura*, nos. 19-20, 1929: 28-31.

Argues that the artistic manifestations (beauty) of constructivist architecture derive from the extent to which it is logical and functionally expressive.

613.   ——. "O sotsiologii iskusstva" [On the Sociology of Art]. *S.A.*, No. 3, 1929: 114-120.

A penetrating review of Hausenstein's *Iskusstvo i obshchestvo* (no. 168), Friche's *Sotsiologiia iskusstva* (no. 167), Schmidt's *Iskusstvo: Osnovnye problemy teorii i istorii* (no. 180), and Ioffe's *Kul'tura i stil'* (no. 171). Argues that a thorough knowledge of sociology is as essential to the architect as is expertise in the techno–building disciplines.

614.   ——. "Obshchestvo sovremennykh arkhitektorov (OSA)" [Society of Contemporary Architects (OSA)]. *Sovetskaia arkhitektura*, no. 18, 1969: 13-19.

An introspective review of the constructivist movement and the activity of the OSA by one of its former members. Provides valuable insight into the various currents operating among its members.

615.   ——. "SASS – Zametki ob arkhitekturnom dvizhenii posle Oktiabria" [SASS – Comments about the Architectural Movement after October]. *Sovetskaia arkhitektura*, no. 3, 1931: 60-67.

An excellent résumé of the development of constructivism. Valuable for its account of the process of formulation during the initial periods of romanticism and symbolism.

616.   Kornfel'd, Ia. "Arkhitektura na pervom vsesoiuznom s'ezde po grazhdanskomu i inzhenernomu stroitel'stvu" [Architecture of the First All-Union Congress of Civic and Engineering Construction]. *S.A.*, no. 2, 1926: 58-60.

A review of the projects exhibited at the Congress, held in May 1926. Includes an assessment of the implications which the projects exhibited have for contemporary Soviet architecture.

617.   Miliutin, Nikolai A. "Konstruktivizm i Funktsionalizm: k kharakteristike arkhitekturnykh techenii XX veka" [Constructivism and Functionalism: Characteristics of the Architectural Movements of the 20th Century]. *Arkhitektura SSSR*, no. 8, 1935: 5-10.

A comprehensive survey of the evolution and aesthetics of constructivism, the social basis and method of functionalism, and the achievements that should be appropriated from its work. Though essentially oriented toward postmodernist dialectics, valuable for its illuminating assessment of the problems that beset constructivism.

618. "Nasha deistvitel'nost" " [Our Reality]. *S.A.*, no. 2, 1927: 47-50.

An editorial attacking classical eclecticism as practiced by Zholtovsky and his followers. Contains illustrations of his recent buildings and their direct Palladian antecedents.

619. "Rezoliutsiia obshchego sobraniia sektora arkhitektorov sotsialistiches-kogo stroitel'stva pri VANO po dokladu o tak nazyvaemoi 'Leonidovshchine'" [Resolution of the General Meeting of the Sector of Architects of Socialist Construction under VANO Concerning the So-called "Leonidovism"]. *Sovetskaia arkhitektura,* nos. 1-2, 1931: 102.

In response to recent speeches and articles attacking "Leonido-vism" as an extreme leftist tendency within SASS (OSA) with its own methodology. Characterizes such charges as products of the critics' imaginations and defends the architect Leonidov and the SASS. Points up deficiencies in Leonidov's work but observes that they are not peculiar to Leonidov but characteristic of Soviet architectural practice as a whole. Suggests that the problem can be remedied only through the creation of a truly proletarian architecture on the basis of close contact with the working masses and a reliance on Marxist political competence. The resolution reflects the growing tide of the "proletarian" movement in Soviet culture.

620. "Rezoliutsiia po dokladam ideologicheskoi sektsii OSA" [Resolution on the Speeches in the Ideological Section of OSA]. *S.A.*, No. 3, 1928: 78.

Enacted at the First Conference of the Society of Contemporary Architects, held in Moscow on April 25, 1928. A platform out-lining the Society's philosophy, negating eclecticism, expres-sionism, and superficial decoration, while arguing for the maximum quality of components, use of all the intrinsic elements of basic architectural design, and the consideration of the social, economic, climatic, and technological circumstances of respective localities.

621. "Rezoliutsiia po dokladu zhilishchno-planirovochnoi sektsii OSA" [Resolution on the Speech by the Housing-Planning Section of OSA]. *S.A.*, no. 4, 1928: 123.

Enacted at the first conference of the OSA held in April 1928. Declares the necessity of shifting emphasis in housing design from a single family dwelling unit to a multifamily unit, based on a thorough study of the functions to be contained and the optimum provision for social needs. Also specifies the bases for planning as the result of considering all factors that determine the character and role of the city in the conditions of the socialist reorganization of the country and the search for those materials and methods of construction that can assure the optimum flexibility both of the entire city and of its component parts.

622. "SASS − na novom etape" [SASS − On a New Plateau] . *Sovetskaia arkhitektura*, nos. 1-2, 1931: 96-102.

An explanation of the name change of the organization from OSA to SASS. Outlines 55 theses constituting the platform of SASS.

623. Vesnin, Aleksandr A. and Viktor A. "Forma i soderzhanie" [Form and Content] . *Arkhitekturnaia gazeta*, April 8, 1935.

Argues for developing designs with integrally related form and content rather than copying blindly designs of preceding epochs and forcing them to conform to incompatible functions. Functionalist intentions evident throughout.

624. Vesnin, Aleksandr A. and Viktor A., and Moisei Ia. Ginzburg. "Problemy arkhitektury:: [Problems of Architecture]. *Front nauki i tekhniki* [Front of Science and Technology] , no. 1, 1934: 115-117.

A succinct restatement of the arguments authors developed in their article "Problemy sovremennoi arkhitektury" (no. 420).

625. Vesnin, Viktor A., and Moisei Ia. Ginzburg. "Dostizheniia sovremennoi arkhitektury"[Accomplishments of Modern Architecture] . See no. 351.

Cites technological developments as providing the bases for modern architecture and reviews especially the efforts by constructivists to exploit these developments to maximum advantage.

626. "Zaiavlenie Ob'edineniia sovremennykh arkhitektorov 'OSA' v Khudozhestvennyi otdel Narkomprosa" [Application of the Society of Contemporary Architects "OSA" to the Artistic Department of the Central Administration for Scientific, Scientific-Artistic, Museum and Conservation Organizations in the People's Commissariat for Education] . In *Iz istorii sovetskoi arkhitektury, 1926-1932*. See No. 139. p. 69.

The Moscow Soviet Administrative Department turned down OSA's initial petition (see **no. 627**) on February 26, 1926, for the reason that similar groups (ASNOVA, MAO) were already in existence. The OSA next petitioned the Commissariat of Education, explaining that their aims were in no way similar to those of any other existing organization. The petition outlines this argument.

627.   "Zaiavlenie po upolnomochiiu gruppy OSA v Administrativnyi otdel Mossoveta" [Application for Registering the OSA Group by the Administrative Department of the Moscow Soviet]. In *Iz istorii sovetskoi arkhitektury, 1926-1932.* See **no. 139.** p. 68.
Dated February 1926, summarizes the aims of the organization.

(2) *Non-Soviet Writers*

628.   Badovici, Jean. "Le Mouvement constructif russe." *L'Architecture vivante,* Spring-Summer 1926: 7-11; accompanying plates and commentary, p. 12-14, 16, 18, and plates 1-13.
A succinct analysis of the circumstances surrounding the emergence of constructivism and its companion modern movements in Soviet architecture. Excellent plates. See *L'Architecture vivante,* Autumn-Winter 1928, plates 16-50, for additional excellent photographs and drawings.

629.   Bourgeois, Victor. "Salut au constructivisme." *Zodiac,* no. 1, 1957: 193-195.
A brief review with illustrations of the work of constructivist architects in the Soviet Union in the early twenties. Very general. Classifies Konstantin Mel'nikov as a constructivist.

630.   Martienssen, Rex. "Constructivism and Architecture: A New Chapter in the History of Formal Building." *South African Architectural Record,* v. 26, no. 7, 1941: 241-272.
Adapted from the author's master of architecture thesis in 1939. An analysis of the constructivist tradition in modern architecture, illuminating its roots in the revolutionary designs of Russian artists and architects for the Meyerhold and other theaters. Extremely interesting and thought-provoking.

630a. Sharp, Dennis, ed. "Constructivism." *Journal of the Royal Institute of British Architects,* v. 78, no. 9, 1971: 383-392.

Proceedings of a forum on Russian constructivism held at the RIBA on March 9, 1971. Papers presented include Michael Scammell, "From Realism to Constructivism" (p. 383-385), considering the literary situation in prerevolutionary Russia as a springboard for Futurism and Constructivism; Anatole Kopp, "Architecture and Social Transformation" (p. 385-387), emphasizing the social problems of concern to the constructivists and underscoring the importance they placed on the "social project"; Gerritt Oorthuys, "European Responses to Constructivism" (p. 387-389), examining the response of Dutch and other European architects to the atmosphere generated by the revolution; Charles Jencks, "Libertarian and Authoritarian Views of the Revolution" (p. 389-391); and Dennis Sharp, "The Revolution That Failed" (p. 391-392), summarizing the proceedings. An interesting and provocative assemblage of interpretations, exemplifying the scope and caliber of interest in Russian modernism that has recently been unleashed by the West.

b. Criticisms

631. Brunov, N. I. "Sovremennaia arkhitektura. Zhurnal OSA" [Contemporary Architecture. The Journal of the OSA]. *Pechat' i revoliutsiia,* no. 3, 1927: 222-224.

An assessment of the Society of Contemporary Architects and their journal, *S.A.* Views the strength of the new architectural doctrine espoused by the OSA to be its freedom from dogma, its search for innovation, and its orientation toward the future. Observes, however, that the leaders of the movement have a tendency to be too self-assured about the correctness of their positions. Sees the principal issue of contemporary architecture to be the question of what distinguishes architecture-art from architecture technology and observes that contemporary life is much more than simply industrialism. For extract, see *Iz istorii sovetskoi arkhitektury, 1926-1932* (**no. 139**), p. 87.

632. "Kak ne nado stroit'" [How Not to Build]. *S.A.,* no. 2, 1928: 41-47.

Criticizes the Central Telegraph Building by I. I. Rerberg for its nonsolution of the plan, naive structural solution, and total lack of correspondence between elements of volume, space, and the concept of design. Also criticizes Zholtovsky's State Bank Building in Moscow as eclectic and neither reflecting nor responding to the new conditions of life.

633.   Khiger, R. Ia. "Nekotorye raziasneniia kritikam" [Some Explanations
        to the Critics] . *S.A.*, no. 4, 1930: 11-12.
            Deals with the criticism by **VOPRA** sympathizers in response
        to author's earlier article, "K voprosu ob ideologii konstruktivizma
        . . ." **(no. 611)**; two articles specifically, by Shalavin and Lamtsov
        (no. 642) and by Roshchin **(no. 641)**. Essay divided into 1)
        dialectic development of culture, 2) contradictions in architecture,
        3) "objective" and "subjective" architecture, 4) "mechanism"
        in architecture, and 5) architecture as an "image art." A compre-
        hensive discussion of the two criticisms with carefully formulated
        rebuttals.

634.   ——. "Protiv vulgarizatorov" [Against Vulgarizers]. *S.A.*, no. 4, 1930:
        20-23.
            A general response to recent criticisms of the OSA, organized
        in the following categories: 1) dialectic development of art, 2) con-
        tradictions in architecture, 3) "subjective" and "objective"
        architecture, 4) "the sense of the mechanical," and 5) architecture
        as an example of art.

635.   "Kritika konstruktivizma" [Criticism of Constructivism] . *S.A.*, no. 1,
        1928: 1-4.
            An editorial giving a systematic rebuttal to current criticism of
        the OSA and constructivism. Argues that 1) the problem of the
        architect is to create new social condensers as a new type of
        architecture, 2) exploiting achievements of technology is but the
        means, not the *goal* of constructivism, 3) the artistic content of
        architecture is *interdependent* upon the synthesis of its functional
        and structural elements, 4) the working method of constructivism
        first posits the problems of creating architectural condensers in
        response to social needs, and 5) because industrializing the USSR
        is a pressing problem, there is nothing wrong with publicizing
        the latest American achievements. Views criticisms as petty and
        shallow.

636.   Kuz'm, A. "Protiv bezotvetstvennoi kritiki. K napadkam na proektu
        I. Leonidova" [Against Irresponsible Criticism. Regarding the
        Attacks on the Project of I. Leonidov] . *S.A.*, no. 4, 1930: [17] .
            Rebuttal to recent criticism of Leonidov. Cites three categories
        in which Leonidov's work is generally criticized: 1) it is too
        schematic and not fully developed, 2) it is incomprehensible to
        the masses, and 3) all modern architecture is reprehensible. Finds
        most such criticism to be highly irrational.

637. Markovnikov, N. "Novyi arkhitekturnyi zhurnal 'Sovremennaia arkhitektura' " [New Architectural Journal, "Contemporary Architecture"]. *Stroitel'naia promyshlennost'*, no. 9, 1926: 653-655.

A review of the second number for 1926. Provides an interpretive assessment of the Society and its aims. For a response, see *S.A.* editorial, *"Stroitel'naia promyshlennost' kritikuet S.A."* [*Stroitel'naia promyshlennost'* Criticizes *S.A.*], *S.A.*, no. 4, 1926: 105-106.

638. Mikhailov, A. "VOPRA, ASNOVA, SASS: K voprosu ob ideino-metodologicheskikh raznoglasiakh" [VOPRA, ASNOVA, SASS: Concerning the Question of Ideological-Methodological Differences]. See **no. 571.**

Includes a comprehensive analysis of OSA (later SASS), based on its work, philosophy, and published statements. A member of VOPRA, the author assumes a highly critical point of view, articulating the emerging "Marxist proletarian" point of view. See also his *Gruppirovki sovetskoi arkhitektury* (**no. 271**) for this and other articles.

639. Mordvinov, Arkadi G. "Leonidovshchina i ee vred" [Leonidovism and Its Dangers]. *Iskusstvo v massy*, no. 12, 1930: 12-15.

A heated criticism by a member of VOPRA. Views Leonidov's abstract approach to design as incomprehensible to the masses and taxing the technological capacity of the country's building industry, as a radical style incapable of embodying the ideals of proletarian architecture, and expressing increasingly Western aspirations rather than the revolutionary ideals of the new Soviet society.

640. Popov, V., and A. Lavrov. "Protiv nekriticheskogo otnoshenniia k eksperimentam zapadnykh arkhitektorov" [Against the Uncritical Attitude toward the Experiments of Western Architects]. *Stroitel'stvo Moskvy*, no. 10, 1930: 8-12.

A criticism of OSA's publicizing the latest technological and aesthetic experiments and achievements of Western architects. Condemns Ginzburg's and Milinis's design for the "Narkomfin" Apartment Building as an indiscriminate adaptation of Le Corbusier's "Five Theses." Asserts that constructivism stems from an idealism which is the product not of the dynamics of the Soviet socialist society, but rather of the incompatible capitalism of Western Europe and America.

641.   Roshchin, L. "Funktsionalizm – ne nash stil'" " [Functionalism –Not
Our Style] . *Iskusstvo v massy*, no. 6, 1930: 14-17.

Attacks functionalism, the Society of Contemporary Architects
(OSA), and its journal, *S.A.*, for promulgating a style that is life-
less, unattractive, and incapable of satisfying the need, desires,
and tastes of the proletarian masses. One of the first prominent
published criticisms of the OSA and its work.

642.   Shalavin, F. and I. Lamtsov. "O levoi fraze v arkhitekture (k voprosu
ob ideologii konstruktivizma)" [Concerning the Left Phrase in
Architecture (On the Question of the Ideology of Constructivism)] .
Krasnaia nov' [Red Virgin Soil] , no. 8, 1927: 226-239.

Condemns OSA's architectural platform and functional method
as outlined by M. Ia. Ginzburg in *S.A.* (see **no. 599**). Argues that
Soviet architecture should be less preoccupied with giving expression to technology and the machine and more concerned with
giving expression to the ideological class aspirations of the
proletariat. Important as a precedent for further criticism.

643.   ——. "O putiakh razvitiia sovremennoi arkhitekturnoi mysli" [Concerning the Directions in the Development of Contemporary
Architectural Thought] . *Pechat' i revoliutsiia*, no. 9, 1929: 49-69.

Challenges Khiger's use of term "dialectic method" as applied
to functionalist architecture in his article in *S.A.* (**no. 611**) and
develops a protracted rebuttal to the OSA and the above article
on the basis that neither takes into account the spirit of Marxism-
Leninism. Important as one of the first attempts by ASNOVA
members to adapt VOPRA'S rhetoric for the purpose of condemning Constructivist architecture.

644.   ——. "Otkrytoe pis'mo" [An Open Letter] . *S.A.*, no. 3, 1928: 92-93.

A rebuttal to the editorial in *S.A.*, "Kritika konstruktivizma"
(**no. 635**). Clarifies the author's original criticism of *S.A.* : 1) *S.A.*
does not distinguish between the roles of the inventor and the
architect, 2) *S.A.* identifies engineering with architecture without
recognizing the monistic nature of architecture as art, and is
therefore incapable of solving architectural problems, 3) the
functional method is essentially a "techno-formal" method,
4) possessed with "subjective idealism," functionalism is unable
to imbue architecture with ideological content and influence, and
5) Constructivism is pure idealism masked by materialist and
leftist phrases.

645.   Yalovkin, F. "VOPRA i OSA" [VOPRA and the OSA] . *S.A.*, no. 5, 1929: 171.
       A rebuttal to the VOPRA platform which condemns constructivism as having emerged strictly on the basis of capital and its attendant bourgeois influences. A useful document providing a decidedly biased, yet systematic comparison of the principal doctrines of the two organizations.

7. VANO — Vsesoiuznoe arkhitekturno-nauchnoe obshchestvo [All-Union Architectural-Scientific Society]

646.   "Deklaratsiia VANO pri profsoiuze stroitel'ei" [Declaration of VANO under the Professional Union of Builders] . *S.A.*, no. 3, 1930: inside front cover.
       Condemns neutrality in political thought, urges the consolidation of architectural organizations for the purpose of improving Soviet society. Declares architecture to be one of the spatial arts determined both by economic and by technological developments of a given age. Further declares the task of architecture to be that of inspiring the proletariat to greater achievements; only through collective work of a united architectural front, exploiting the cultural heritage of the past and providing for the active participation of the proletarian masses, can there be created an architecture for the dictatorship of the proletariat. From this ideological preamble, there follow 13 planks that form the basis upon which the autonomous constituent sectors (such as ASNOVA, OSA, or SASS, and others), who have united to form VANO, will continue their work. Declaration also published: "Iz deklaratsii VANO"[From the Declaration of VANO] , *Stroitel'stvo Moskvy*, no. 7, 1930:24; also published in *Iz istorii sovetskoi arkhitektury 1926-1932* (**no. 139**), p. 148. For discussions on forming a federation that preceded the formation of VANO, see **nos. 664-671**.

647.   Khazanova, Vigdariia E."Vsesoiuznoe arkhitekturno-nauchnoe obshchestvo (VANO)" [All-Union Architectural-Scientific Society (VANO)] . In her *Iz istorii sovetskoi arkhitektury 1926-1932*. See **no. 139**, p. 147.
       A succinct treatment of the organization.

648.   Lapinsky, Ia. "Za massovuiu arkhitekturnuiu organizatsiiu" [For a Mass Architectural Organization] . *Stroitel'stvo Moskvy*, no. 7, 1930: 23.

Reviews the initial organizing activity of VANO, noting the persisting autonomy of its sector members. Urges the federation to become a truly *mass* scientific organization in order the better to promulgate proletarian values and to participate actively in the building of socialism in the Soviet Union.

8. VOPRA — Vsesoiuznoe ob'edinenie Proletarskikh arkhitektorov
[All-Union Society of Proletarian Architects]

a. General and Theoretical Works

(1) *Monographs*

649.   Mikhailov, A. *Gruppirovki sovetskoi arkhitektury.* See **no. 271.**
Includes the article-chapter, "Gruppirovki arkhitekturnogo fronta i zadachi proletarskikh arkhitektorov" [Groupings in the Architectural Front and the Problems of Proletarian Architects], which is an assessment of VOPRA's aims, ideals, and work.

(2) *Articles*

650.   Alabian, Karo S. "O rabote OPRA Armenii" [On the Work of the Armenian OPRA]. *Sovetskaia arkhitektura,* nos. 1-2, 1931: 67.
Reviews the evolution of the organization, its work and struggle with eclecticism, and its disclosure of the "reactionary" essence of the "Un-Armenian" style. Contains much useful material concerning the movement's activity in Armenia.

651.   "Deklaratsiia VOPRA" [Declaration of VOPRA]. *Pechat' i revoliutsiia,* no. 6, 1929: 125-128.
Outlines elaborate arguments condemning formalism (ASNOVA), constructivism (OSA), and eclecticism (the Old School of architects), and declares these organizations to be "bourgeois." Further declares that a proletarian architecture must be developed on the basis of applying dialectic materialism to architectural theory and practice, considering the realistic demands of the new order, and synthesizing organizationally the social, economic, ideological, tectonic, and structural determinants of architecture. This declaration also appeared as follows: "Deklaratsiia ob'edineniia proletarskikh arkhitektorov" [Declaration of the Society of Proletarian Architects], *Stroitel'stvo Moskvy,* no. 8, 1929: 25; also reproduced in *Iz istorii sovetskoi arkhitektury 1926-1932* (**no. 139**), p. 138-139.

652. Khazanova, Vigdariia E. "Vsesoiuznoe ob'edinenie proletarskikh arkhitektorov (VOPRA)" [All-Union Society of Proletarian Architects (VOPRA)]. In her *Iz istorii sovetskoi arkhitektury,1926-1932.* See **no. 139.** p. 134-135.

A succinct history of the evolution and aims of the Society, founded in August 1929.

653. Kriukov, M. V. "Sotsialisticheskomu stroitel'stvu—novyi arkhitektor" [A New Architect for Socialist Construction]. *Stroitel'stvo Moskvy,* no. 6, 1930: 22-24.

Posits the proletarian argument of the class struggle and the need for architecture to fulfill its demands.

654. Matsa, Ivan L. "Puti razvitiia prostranstvennykh iskusstv. Arkhitektura" [Directions in the Development of the Spatial Arts. Architecture]. In *Ezhegodnik literatury i iskusstva za 1929 god* [Annual of Literature and Art for 1929]. Moscow, 1929. p. 424-426; for entire article, see pp. 391-427.

Speaks of the emerging architectural organization (VOPRA) and elaborates its aims. One of the better expositions of the Society's doctrine, by its president.

655. Mikhailov, A. "Eklektika i restavratory. Voprosy razvitiia sovetskoi arkhitektury" [Eclecticism and Restorationists. Questions on the Development of Soviet Architecture]. *Molodaia gvardiia,* no. 18, 1929: 82-86.

Observes that the Soviet architectural community is composed of right reactionary movements (eclectics and restorationists) and the comparatively progressive movements on the left, such as ASNOVA, OSA, and VOPRA. Discusses the eclectic segment and what is seen to be its negative influence upon the progress of Soviet architecture. This article adapted in the author's book, *Gruppirovki . . .* (**no. 271**).

656. ——. "VOPRA, ASNOVA, SASS: K voprosu ob ideino-metodologicheskikh raznoglasiakh" [VOPRA, ASNOVA, SASS: Concerncerning the Question of Ideological-Methodological Differences]. See **no. 571.**

A comprehensive assessment of the philosophy and work of the three organizations by a member of VOPRA, concluding in favor of VOPRA as the only movement capable of embodying the spirit of the proletarian revolution and masses. For this and other related articles, see author's book, *Gruppirovki . . .* (**no. 271**).

657.   Mordvinov, Arkadi G. "Leonidovshchina i ee vred" [Leonidovism
        and Its Harm] . See no. 639.
        An attack on OSA architect Ivan Leonidov.

658.   —. "Nashi zadachi [Our Problems]. *Sovetskaia arkhitektura,*nos. 1-
        2, 1931: 65-66.
        Speaks of VOPRA's struggle with eclecticism, constructivism,
        and formalism. Posits the primary problem facing the organization
        as the mobilization of all architectural forces for the fulfillment of
        the Five Year Plan. This is to be accomplished by developing
        techniques for inexpensive, speedy, and substantial construction.

659.   "Rezoliutsiia sektsii IZO instituta LIIa Komakademii po dokladu
        t. Mordvinova o 'Melkoburzhuaznom napravlenii v arkhitekture
        (Leonidovshchina)' priniata 20, XII 1930 g." [Resolution of the
        Section of the Fine Arts Department Institute of Literature, Art,
        and Language of the Communist Academy on the Speech by
        Comrade Mordvinov, "Concerning the Petit-bourgeois Direction
        in Architecture (Leonidovism)," passed on December 20, 1930].
        Sovetskaia arkhitektura, nos. 1-2, 1931: 18.
        Condemns the work of the constructivist architect Leonidov as
        exemplifying everything that is negative in constructivism and
        formalism: the negation of architecture as art and the fetishism
        for abstract architectural forms. It further condemns Leonidov's
        method as totally contradicting the method of dialectic materialism
        and thereby exerting a harmful influence upon the cadres of
        rising young architects. For the article by Mordvinov on this sub-
        ject, see no. 657. Resolution reproduced in *Iz istorii sovetskoi
        arkhitektury, 1926-1932* (no. 139), p. 142-143.

660.   Roshchin, L. "Funktsionalizm—ne nash stil'" [Functionalism—Not
        Our Style] . See no. 641.
        A pervasive attack on the OSA, employing the rhetoric and
        argumentation typical of the VOPRA polemics.

661.   Simbirtsev, V. "Vserossiiskoe obshchestvo proletarskikh arkhitek-
        torov (VOPRA)" [All-Russian Society of Proletarian Architects
        (VOPRA)] . *Sovetskaia arkhitektura,* no. 18, 1969: 38-41.
        A cursory overview of the evolution of the organization by
        one of its founding members. Provides useful insight and infor-
        mation on activities undertaken by various members.

662. "VOPRA—Vsesoiuznoe ob'edinenie proletarskikh arkhitektorov" [VOPRA—All-Union Society of Proletarian Architects]. *Sovetskaia arkhitektura*, nos. 1-2, 1931: 65-71.

An informative account of the organization's activity and its struggle against constructivism, formalism, and eclecticism.

b. Criticisms

663. Yalovkin, F. "VOPRA i OSA" [VOPRA and the OSA]. See **no. 645.**

Responds to VOPRA's condemnation of constructivism in its platform, defending and clarifying the controversial phrase "negation of art," initially formulated by the constructivists.

D. PROPOSALS FOR A FEDERATION OF SOVIET ARCHITECTS

664. Cherkassky, I. "Arkhitekture reshaiushchuiu rol' (novoe stroitel'stvo Moskvy)" [Decisive Role for Architecture (the New Construction of Moscow)]. *Stroitel'stvo Moskvy*, no. 5, 1932: 2-5.

Argues for establishing a single architectural organization in order to eliminate individualism as an approach to solving architectural problems.

665. "Federatsiia revoliutsionnykh arkhitektorov" [Federation of Revolutionary Architects]. *Stroitel'stvo Moskvy*, no. 10, 1929: 22.

Reprints the proposal published by the *S.A.* (**670**), calling for the union of all existing architectural organizations into a federation. Commentary following the proposal includes a favorable response by the editors of *Stroitel'stvo Moskvy*.

666. Karra, A. Ia. "Za sotsialisticheskuiu ratsionalizatsiiu proektnykh kontor" [For a Socialistic Rationalization of Design Studios]. *Stroitel'stvo Moskvy*, no. 4, 1930: 2-4.

Argues that the existing studios have failed to take new conditions into account and that a conscious planning organization to provides the basis for a socialist practice is totally lacking. Asserts that conventional notions of practice must be overcome in favor of establishing a new collective approach to design and that the design studios must be the prime movers of this necessary reform. Seems to augur the reorganization of the design studios under the Moscow Soviet in 1933.

667.   Lapinsky, Ia. "Za massovuiu arkhitekturnuiu organizatsiiu" [For a
        Mass Architectural Organization]. See **No. 648.**
        While seeking a reorientation of VANO, seems clearly to call
        for a single mass-oriented organization—a VOPRA argument.

668.   Matveev, I. "O sotsialisticheskoi ratsionalizatsii proektnykh kontor"
        [On the Socialistic Rationalization of Design Studios]. *Stroitel'-
        stvo Moskvy,* no. 7, 1930: 17.
        Accedes to the arguments developed by A. Karra (see **no. 666**)
        but maintains that implementing his detailed suggestions for re-
        organization at the present time would be unfeasible.

669.   "Postanovlenie ob'edinennogo sobraniia aktiva arkhitekturnykh
        obshchestv Moskvy—ARU, ASNOVA, VOPRA, SASS—ot 28 iiulia
        1931 g." [Resolution by the Organizational Meeting of the Active
        Members of the Moscow Architectural Societies—ARU, ASNOVA,
        VOPRA, and SASS—dated July 28, 1931]. *Sovetskaia arkhitektura,*
        no. 3, 1931: 7.
        Calls for merging the referenced societies for the purpose of
        supervising the open competition for the Palace of Soviets. Signed
        by K. S. Alabian, member of VOPRA.

670.   "Sozdadim Federatsiiu revoliutsionnykh arkhitektorov" [Let Us
        Create a Federation of Revolutionary Architects]. *S.A.,* no. 3,
        1929: 89.
        An editorial that calls for the organization of a Federation of
        Revolutionary Architects in order to facilitate the proper super-
        vision of the country's expanding architectural activity. Views the
        basic tasks of such a federation to be to resist eclecticism,
        reorganize the system of competitions, reduce construction costs,
        elevate the quality of construction, and attract the Soviet
        society's attention to architecture.

671.   Zaslavsky, A. "Za federatsiiu sovetskikh arkhitektorov" [For a
        Federation of Soviet Architects]. *Sovetskaia arkhitektura,* nos. 1-
        2, 1931: 94-95.
        Speaks of the dissolution of VANO, whose autonomous sectors
        lacked sufficient awareness that the proletarian class struggle has
        a central place in the conduct of Soviet architecture. Interesting
        for its similarity to propaganda waged by VOPRA, the only
        movement in Soviet architecture *not* to join VANO, citing the
        need for a federation in order to unite all architectural organiza-
        tions for the building of socialism.

E. SSA – SOIUZ SOVETSKIKH ARKHITEKTOROV
[UNION OF SOVIET ARCHITECTS]

1. General Works

672. "Edinyi tvorcheskii" [A Single Creative Entity]. *Sovetskaia arkhitektura*, no. 18, 1969: 42-48.
Outlines the emergence of the Union of Soviet Architects and summarizes the resolutions of the first three Congresses of Soviet Architects. Contains useful material.

673. "O perestroke literaturno-khudozhestvennykh organizatsii" [Concerning the Reorganization of Literary-Artistic Organizations]. See **no. 152.**
Decree which disbanded all previous artistic organizations, including those in architecture, and paved the way for the creation of the Union of Soviet Architects.

674. "Sozdanie Soiuza sovetskikh arkhitektorov" [Creation of the Union of Soviet Architects]. *Izvestiia*, no. 167, July 18, 1932.
Announces the creation of the SSA. Lists the newly elected officers of the Union's administrative board. Reproduced in *Iz istorii sovetskoi arkhitektury, 1926-1932* (**no. 139**), p. 163, with commentary on p. 164.

2. First Congress of Soviet Architects (1937)

675. Arkin, David E. "Tvorcheskie uroki" [Creative Lessons]. *Arkhitektura SSSR*, nos. 7-8, 1937: 51-53.
Focuses upon the new role of the "client" in Soviet architecture. Provides an illuminating and penetrating analysis of the emerging concepts of socialist realism as they emerged in various debates and discussions at the Congress.

676. Bylinkin, N. P. "Voprosy zhilishchnoi arkhitektury na s'ezde" [Questions of Housing Architecture at the Congress]. *Arkhitektura SSSR*, nos. 7-8, 1937: 54-55.

677. Bulganin, Nikolai A. "Rekonstruktsiia gorodov, zhilishchnoe stroitel'stvo i zadachi arkhitektora" [Reconstruction of Cities, Housing Construction, and the Problems of the Architect]. *Arkhitektura SSSR*, no. 9, 1937: 13-18.

Keynote speech delivered to the Congress by the chairman of the Moscow Soviet (city council) and newly elected chairman of the Council of People's Commissars. Propagandizes the plan for the reconstruction of Moscow, praises Lazar M. Kaganovich for his role in developing it, and outlines its general provisions, which Soviet architects are encouraged to implement with all deliberate enthusiasm and speed.

678.   "Delegatsiia s'ezda v sovnarkome SSSR" [Delegation of the Congress at the Council of People's Commissars of the USSR]. *Arkhitektura SSSR*, nos. 7-8, 1937: 4-6.

A résumé of the proceedings between the delegates of the Congress and the Council of People's Commissars at a meeting held on June 23, 1937. Focuses upon the new challenges which are seen by the Council to face Soviet architects, as well as upon the former's concern for their successful resolution.

679.   "Diskussiia na s'ezde: Tvorcheskie voprosy" [Discussion at the Congress: Creative Questions]. *Arkhitektura SSSR*, nos. 7-8, 1937: 28-35.

Summarizes the highlights of the responses to speeches given by K. S. Alabian (**no. 411**), A. V. Shchusev, and N. Ia. Kolli (**no. 412**). Among the most significant are V. A. Vesnin's defense of constructivism in rebutting Kolli's remarks, M. Ia. Ginzburg's studied attempt to outline viable criteria for socialist realism, G. P. Gol'ts's comments on Leonidov (favorable) and Mel'nikov (unfavorable) and his discussion of formalism, as brought up by Kolli and Alabian, and D. E. Arkin's condemnation of the superficial attempts by Soviet architects to date to utilize the classical heritage in design. An important source for insight into the thinking of the period.

680.   "Dnevnik s'ezda" [Diary of the Congress]. *Arkhitektura SSSR*, nos. 7-8, 1937: 14, 16, 18, 20, 22, 24, 26, 28, 30, 32, 34, 36, 38, 40, 42, 44.

A summary of the proceedings on a day-by-day basis. Also includes summaries of speeches by those outside the architectural community. A list of the newly elected officers of the Union of Soviet Architects is appended.

681.   "Dnevnik s'ezda. Arkhitektura soiuznykh respublik" [Diary of the Congress. The Architecture of the Union Republics]. *Arkhitektura SSSR*, nos. 7-8, 1937: 14-27.

A review of architectural practice in the constituent republics:
Ia. A. Shteinberg on the Ukrainian SSR, S. A. Dadashev on the
Azerbaizhan SSR, V. Mukhamedov on the Uzbek SSR, G. B.
Kochar on the Armenian SSR, M. K. Shavishvili on the Georgian
SSR, T. K. Basenov on the Kazakh SSR, Kh. Z. Tairov on the
Tadzhik SSR, and V. I. Kuznetsov on the Turkmen SSR.

682.   "Pervyi vsesoiuznyi s'ezd sovetskikh arkhitektorov tt. Stalinu,
Molotovu, Kaganovichu, Voroshilovu" [First All-Union Congress
of Soviet Architects to Comrades Stalin, Molotov, Kaganovich,
and Voroshilov]. *Arkhitektura SSSR*, nos. 7-8, 1937: 1-3.
      Letters sent by the Congress to each of the above-named party
functionaries. Significant for the tone of servility typical of what
later was to be recognized as a manifestation of Stalin's cultivation
of the "cult of personality." For similar evidence, though not
relating to the Congress, see the letter signed by the leading
personalities of the Soviet architectural community, "Tovarishchu
Stalinu" [To Comrade Stalin], *Arkhitektura SSSR*, no. 5, 1935:
1. See also **no. 724.**

683.   "Inostrannye arkhitektory na tribune s'ezda" [Foreign Architects on
the Podium of the Congress]. *Arkhitektura SSSR*, nos. 7-8,
1937: 45-50.
      Speeches by Manuel Sanchez Arcas of Spain (p. 45-46), Francis
Jourdain of France (p. 47-49), and Frank Lloyd Wright of the
United States of America (p. 49-50). For impressions of the
Congress by American delegates, see articles by Simon Breines,
"First Congress of Soviet Architects" (**no. 433**), and Frank Lloyd
Wright, "Architecture and Life in the USSR" (**no. 444**).

684.   "Rezoliutsiia s'ezda po dokladam o zadachakh sovetskoi arkhitektury" [Resolution of the Congress on the Speeches Concerning
the Problems of Soviet Architecture]. *Arkhitektura SSSR*, nos. 7-
8, 1937: 4-6.
      Speaks of the need to overcome formalism and eclecticism, to
assimilate the classical and the "contemporary" heritage alike,
and to rally around the goals envisioned by the party and the
state. A useful résumé of official positions and thinking reflected
at the Congress.

3. Second Congress of Soviet Architects (1956)

a. Monographs

685.   Union of Architects of the USSR. *Vtoroi vsesoiuznyi s'ezd sovetskikh
arkhitektorov* [Second All-Union Congress of Soviet Architects].
See no. 141.
An abridged stenographic account of the proceedings. An
important historical document of current official thinking and
policy in Soviet architecture.

b. Articles

686.   "Tsentral'nomu komitetu kommunisticheskoi partii sovetskogo soiuza
i sovetu ministrov Soiuza SSR" [To the Central Committee of the
Communist Party and to the Council of Ministers of the USSR].
Arkhitektura SSSR, no. 1, 1956: 2-3.
Resolution sent by the Congress to the party and state organs,
outlining their commitment to implement the various goals outlined for the architectural community. A useful record of problem areas on which special emphasis was officially placed in the
deliberations of the Congress.

687.   "Dnevnik s'ezda" [Diary of the Congress]. *Arkhitektura SSSR*, no. 1,
1956: 4-15.
A comprehensive record of the proceedings of the Congress,
held November 26-December 3, 1955, on a day-by-day basis. An
excellent source for abstracts of major speeches and proceedings.

4. Third Congress of Soviet Architects (1962)

a. Monographs

688.   Union of Architects of the USSR. *Tretii vsesoiuznyi s'ezd sovetskikh
arkhitektorov* [Third All-Union Congress of Soviet Architects].
See no. 142.
An bridged stenographic account of the proceedings.

b. Articles

689.   "Tret'emu vsesoiuznomu s'ezdu sovetskikh arkhitektorov" [To the
Third All-Union Congress of Soviet Architects]. *Arkhitektura
SSSR*, no. 5, 1961: 2-3.

A message from the Central Committee of the Communist Party and the Council of Ministers of the USSR, outlining the major areas of concern that it hopes will be given special attention by the Congress. Focuses on improving construction and resolving the housing problem.

690.   "Tretii vsesoiuznyi s'ezd sovetskikh arkhitektorov" [Third All-Union Congress of Soviet Architects]. *Arkhitektura SSSR*, no. 5, 1961: 1.

Announces the opening of the Congress on May 18, 1961.

691.   "Tsentral'nomu komitetu kommunisticheskoi partii sovetskogo soiuza i sovetu ministrov SSSR" [To the Central Committee of the Communist Party of the Soviet Union and to the Council of Ministers of the USSR]. *Arkhitektura SSSR,* no. 6, 1961: 1-2.

Resolution passed and sent by the Congress to the party and state organs. Outlines the priorities established by the Congress in tackling the problems· confronting Soviet architects. A useful reference.

692.   "Rezoliutsiia III-go vsesoiuznogo s'ezda sovetskikh arkhitektorov" [Resolution of the Third All-Union Congress of Soviet Architects]. *Arkhitektura SSSR,* no. 6, 1961: 3-5.

Provides a résumé of what are seen to be the highlights of the proceedings and the decisions reached by the Congress. An important source.

VI. Trends in Soviet Architecture after 1932

A. GENERAL AND THEORETICAL WORKS

1. Monographs

693. Academy of Architecture of the Ukrainian SSR. Institute of the History and Theory of Architecture. *Arkhitekturnoe tvorchestvo* [Architectural Creativity] . Kiev, Akademiia arkhitektury UkSSR, 1953. 165 p. illus.

An important collection of essays on the current theory of Soviet architecture, including the problems of assimilating the classical heritage and socialist realism in Soviet architecture.

694. Lagutin, K. K. *Arkhitekturnyi obraz sovetskikh obshchestvennykh zdanii. Kluby i teatry* [Architectural Image of Soviet Civic Buildings, Clubs, and Theaters] . See **no. 212.**

An analysis of Soviet civic architecture and the architectural tenets of composition and form reflected in the designs of selected clubs and theaters.

695. Matsa, I. L. *Besedy ob arkhitektury* [Discussions about Architecture]. See **no. 213.**

Though a popular account, of significant value for making clear the emerging philosophy of a Soviet "socialist" architecture, as formulated by a prominent contemporary Soviet art historian and theoretician.

696. ——. *Za khudozhestvennoe kachestvo sovetskoi arkhitektury* [For an Artistic Quality of Soviet Architecture] . See **no. 214.**

A theoretical work important for developing four conditions as the basis for the development of a socialist architecture.

697. Sushkevich, I. G., ed. *Tvorcheskie voprosy sovetskoi arkhitektury* [Creative Questions of Soviet Architecture]. See **no. 410.**

A collection of addresses by Moscow and Leningrad architects on current architectural practices in, and on the differences between, the styles developed by the two respective cities.

698. Tsapenko, M. P. *O realisticheskikh osnovakh sovetskoi arkhitektury* [Concerning the Realistic Foundations of Soviet Architecture]. See no. 233.

Provides an assessment of achievements in Soviet architecture clearly from the viewpoint of current official Soviet ideological doctrines in architecture, which are articulated and documented in the work.

699. The Ukrainian Academy of Construction and Architecture. *Formuvanniia stiliu sotsialistichnoi arkhitekturi* [Formulation of the Style of Socialist Architecture]. Kiev, Derzhavne vidavnitsvo literaturi z budivnitstva i arkhitekturi URSR, 1961. 221 p.

A collection of scholarly essays analyzing the developments of style in Soviet architecture; concentrates on those aspects which are considered to determine best a socialist style. Reflects an updated interpretation of tectonic problems in Soviet architecture, reflecting a contemporary point of view.

700. Union of Soviet Architects. *Arkhitektura. Sbornik statiei po tvorcheskim voprosam* [Architecture. A Collection of Articles on Creative Questions]. Moscow, Gosarkhizdat, 1945. 124 p.

Coverage includes artistic problems, the problem of implementing the country's architectural and planning heritage in the postwar period of reconstruction and in current design. An important barometer of current official attitudes in Soviet architecture.

701. *Voprosy ot teoriata na sovetskata arkhitektura* [Questions on the Theory of Soviet Architecture]. Sophia, Izd-vo na Bolgarska Akademiia Naukite, 1950. 49 p.

An analysis and résumé of Soviet scholarship on the theory of Soviet architecture. Contains two essays: Karo S. Alabian, "Osnovy voprosi i teoriata na sovetskata arkhitektura" [Basic Questions on the Theory of Soviet Architecture], and Ivan L. Matsa, "Izuchavane istoriata na arkhitekturnite teorii i teoriata na sovetskata arkhitektura" [The Study of the History of Architectural Theory and the Theory of Soviet Architecture]. A valuable synopsis of current Soviet theoretical scholarship on the subject.

2. Articles

702. Alabian, Karo S. "Protiv formalizma, uproshchenchestva, eklektike"
      [Against Formalism, Vulgarization, and Eclecticism] .*Arkhitektura
      SSSR*, no. 4, 1936: 1-6.
          Supports *Pravda*'s attack on formalism, vulgarization, and
      eclecticism in Soviet architecture. Focuses criticism especially on
      the designs submitted by K. Mel'nikov and I. Leonidov to the
      competition for the Commissariat of Heavy Industry Building on
      Red Square; holds these two designs to be the epitome of the
      above three "sins." Argues for the application of socialist realism
      in architecture.

703. Angarov. "O nekotorykh voprosakh sovetskoi arkhitektury" [Con-
      cerning Some Questions of Soviet Architecture]. *Arkhitektura
      SSSR*, no. 4, 1936: 7-11.
          A speech delivered to the All-Moscow Conference of Architects
      on February 27, 1936. Discusses three topics: 1) planning new
      Soviet cities on the model of Stalinogorsk, 2) implementing a
      synthesis of the various realms of art in Soviet architecture, and
      3) experimenting with new formulas of form and content in Soviet
      architecture. Defines the currently sanctioned styles and con-
      demns all others as deviations.

704. "Arkhitektura v bor'be za kachestvo" [Architecture in the Struggle
      for Quality] . *Arkhitektura SSSR*, no. 2, 1933: 3-8.
          Discusses the current struggle for redefining architectural
      quality, for a socialist direction in Soviet architecture, and for a
      more decisive participation of the Soviet architectural community
      in the socialist reconstruction of Soviet cities. Concludes with a
      timely assessment of buildings currently nearing completion in
      Moscow, the criticism reflecting the new standards defined earlier
      in the article.

705. Brunov, Nikolai I. "Etapy razvitiia mirovoi arkhitektury. Za kritiches-
      koe ispol'zovanie arkhitekturnogo naslediia proshlykh epokh"
      [Stages in the Development of World Architecture. For a Critical
      Use of the Architectural Heritage of Preceding Epochs] . *Stroitel'-
      stvo Moskvy*, no. 10, 1932: 25-30.
          A review of the principal historical styles. Assesses the essence
      of each style, characterizing its most enduring tectonic aspects,
      but cautions against a superficial copying of historical forms.

706. ——. "Monumental'nost' v arkhitekture" [Monumentality in Architecture]. *Stroitel'stvo Moskvy*, nos. 2-3, 1933: 22-28.

An analysis of monumentality as a tectonic entity interpreted in various historical styles. Observes that it was a means of an epoch but warns against resorting to superficial attempts at monumentality.

707. "Itogi vsesoiuznogo tvorcheskogo soveshchaniia arkhitektorov" [Results of the All-Union Creative Conference of Architects]. *Arkhitektura SSSR*, no. 7, 1935: 1-4.

An assessment of the deliberations of current problems in Soviet architecture. Useful for defining the major categories in the areas of current polemic and deliberation.

708. Kriger, E. "Obrashchenie k arkhitektoru" [Turning to the Architect]. *Arkhitektura SSSR*, no. 1, 1934: 8-11.

Deals with the general level of propaganda waged in the streets of Moscow in October 1933 for the improvement of the quality of Soviet architecture, or, more precisely, for a move away from modernism to a revival of familiar classical styles. The propaganda included exhibits and banners adorning the streets and architectural displays in store windows.

709. Matsa, Ivan L. "Novaia arkhitektura" [New Architecture]. *Arkhitektura SSSR*, no. 1, 1934: 8-11.

Deals with the general level of propaganda waged in the streets of Moscow in October 1933 for the improvement of the quality of Soviet architecture, or, more precisely, for a move away from modernism to a revival of familiar classical styles. The propaganda included exhibits and banners adorning the streets and architectural displays in store windows.

710. ——. "O prirode arkhitektury" [On the Nature of Architecture]. *Arkhitektura SSSR*, no. 3, 1935: 7-9.

Argues that, in addition to its obvious and apparent nature, architecture is distinguished from other forms of building by its practical problems, which are bound wholly and consciously to the broader socio-political, cultural, and ideological problems of a given society. Deals with the interrelationship among science, technology, and art in architecture and explores the circumstances in which this interrelationship was developed and cultivated in the past.

711.   Mikhailov, B. "Stil' v arkhitekture" [Style in Architecture]. *Arkhitektura SSSR*, no. 12, 1953: 28-32.

Argues that only one style can reflect the unity of form and content expressive of the proletarian class struggle. Develops the ideological presuppositions by which classical and Renaissance design were viewed as appropriate foundations for the Soviet monumental style in the late Stalinist period. Defines the Renaissance as the art of the rising bourgeoisie, which assumed a large number of popular elements in the struggle against feudalism and medieval theology. Affirms socialist realism as a method based on the assimilation of both the "classical" and the "national" heritage.

712.   Miliutin, Nikolai A. "Osnovnye voprosy teorii sovetskoi arkhitektury" [Basic Questions Concerning the Theory of Soviet Architecture]. *Sovetskaia arkhitektura*, Part 1, no. 2, 1933: 6-12; Part 2, no. 3, 1933: 1-13; Part 3, no. 5, 1933: 17-21; and Part 4, no. 6, 1933: 2-11.

A comprehensive theoretical work suggesting basic theses for a new doctrine of Soviet architecture. Distinguishes between "idealistic" and "mechanistic" theories on the one hand and "opportunistic misinterpretations" of Marxist-Leninist dialectics on the other in previous theories of Soviet architecture. The first reasoned argument for defining criteria for a new Soviet philosophy of architecture. Critical analysis provides illuminating insight into both the modern and proletarian episodes of Soviet architecture.

713.   ——. "Osnovnye vorprosy zhilishchno-bytovogo stroitel'stva SSSR i programa proektirovaniia domov perekhodnova tipa i domov-kommun" [Basic Questions of Housing Construction in the USSR and a Program for Designing Transitional Types of Housing and Communal Housing].*Sovetskaia arkhitektura*, nos. 1-2, 1931: 2-7.

A comprehensive analysis of current trends in housing design and construction in the USSR. Includes a systematic proposal for a program to improve the approach to solving the housing problem, focusing upon "transitional" housing and the "dom-kommuny."

714.   ——. "Vazhneishye zadachi sovremennogo etapa sovetskoi arkhitektury" [The Most Important Problems in the Current Period of Soviet Architecture]. *Sovetskaia arkhitektura*, nos. 2-3, 1932: 3-9.

Develops a preliminary set of prerequisites for the social and political consciousness that Soviet architects must assume personally, as well as reflect in their work, as suggested by the Party resolution of June 15, 1931, on city management, which implied imminent changes in the orientation of Soviet architecture (see **no. 158**). Important as one of the first and most reasoned of such proposals.

715. Milonov, Iu. K. "Uroki proshlykh oshybok" [Lessons of Past Errors]. *Akademiia arkhitektury*, no. 2, 1936: 3-8.

A review of all recent theoretical work on Soviet architecture, especially that by the modernist movements, in light of the official call for the negation of modernism and the revival of classicism. Assesses the positions of the former movements and provides an explanation of the reasons for which they are now considered substantially incorrect. Urges a vigorous campaign of self-criticism and discussion of all problems in Soviet architecture. Very useful as an index to the official reaction to architectural problems during this period.

716. "Nashi Zadachi" [Our Problems]. *Arkhitektura SSSR*, no. 1, 1933: 1-2.

An editorial in the first issue of this magazine. Explains the basis for the reorganization of the architectural front, from the abolition of the former architectural movements to the creation of the Union of Soviet Architects, citing speeches by L. Kaganovich, Chairman of the Moscow Soviet, outlining the scope of this reorganization, and referring to the Party decree of April 23, 1932, which made this reorganization official. Argues that the "sterile" modern style must be eliminated and that Soviet architecture must henceforth be embellished with "artistic" forms.

717. "Opyt primeneniia metoda materialisticheskoi dialektiki k postroeniiu uchebnoi programmy po arkhitekturnomu proektirovaniiu" [Applying the Experience of the Method of Dialectic Materialism to the Development of a Program of Instruction in Architectural Design]. *S.A.*, no. 5, 1930: inside front cover and both sides of back cover.

Provides a general outline for a curriculum that superimposes dialectic materialism upon architectural design. Sections include: 1) the rejection of "negation," 2) the unity of form and content, 3) quality and quantity, 4) unity of opposites, 5) movement, and 6) the general relationships among architectural phenomena. According to R. Ia. Khiger (**no. 614**, p. 14), this program was

drafted by Aleksandr A. Vesnin, although it was published un-
signed. Suggests a growing recognition of the coming new framework for elaborating all theoretical and pedagogical work in Soviet
architecture.

718. Perchik, L. "Gorod sotsializma i ego arkhitektura" [The Socialist
      City and Its Architecture]. *Arkhitektura SSSR*, no. 1, 1934: 3-7.
          An essay injected with ideological polemic and employing ex-
      cerpts from speeches by L. M. Kaganovich to establish a basis for
      rejecting modern Soviet architecture as the product of "capitalist
      exploitators."

719. Rempel', L., and T. Vainer "O teoreticheskikh korniakh formalizma
      v arkhitekture" [On the Theoretical Roots of Formalism in
      Architecture]. *Arkhitektura SSSR*, no. 5, 1936: 8-13.
          A concise survey of the development of "formalism" in Soviet
      architecture, intended here to mean not the current expressionism
      practiced by ASNOVA, but all forms of modern idioms grouped
      generically into one such classification on the basis of ideological
      consideration alone. Important for revealing both the criteria for
      such a classification and the current attitudes amid official circles
      that made necessary such a category.

720. "Tvorcheskaia diskussiia soiuza sovetskikh arkhitektorov—tvorcheskie
      puti sovetskoi arkhitektury i problema arkhitekturnogo nasledstva"
      [Creative Discussions at the Union of Soviet Architects—Creative
      Directions of Soviet Architecture and the Problem of Architectural
      Heritage]. *Arkhitektura SSSR*, nos. 3-4: 4-25.
          An important documentary résumé of the views of all major
      architects on the topic under discussion, one which occupied the
      spotlight at this time. The introduction is a comprehensive analysis
      reflecting the official view of the developments of the preceding
      fifteen years. N. S. Nessis speaks mainly of anticonstructivism.
      M. Ia. Ginzburg speaks of the three alternatives facing Soviet
      architecture: 1) restore monuments of the past academically,
      2) produce a collage of various styles, and 3) not imitate the past
      blindly, but only its laws of composition; he suggests the latter.
      A. A. Vesnin speaks against mere copying and for a more intelli-
      gent study of architecture in order to glean and apply the
      fundamentals, rather than employ superficial decorative motifs.
      I. A. Fomin speaks of architectural nihilism, the functionalist
      upswing, and stops finally on Greco-Roman classicism as a univer-
      sal style which lends itself well to a new appropriation and use for

Soviet architecture today. V. S. Balikhin cites planning principles as a frame of reference for classicism. I. L. Matsa treats dialectic materialism and applies it to the current architectural scene. A. V. Vlasov argues that proletarian culture can be built only through a critical assimilation of the heritage of the past and chides functionalists for having so isolated themselves from it. K. S. Alabian rejects the notion that the results of the competition for the Palace of Soviets confused Soviet architects: he argues that the direction has been established and that those who do not see it are simply blind; he views constructivism as insufficiently concerned with public reaction. He states that architecture, once mighty in Greco-Roman times, should again be mighty in the socialist society. D. Arkin provides, in effect, a summary by responding to the various speeches, particularly those by Vesnin and Ginzburg and the functionalists.

721. "Smotr arkhitektury" [A Review of Architecture]. *Arkhitektura SSSR*, no. 5, 1934: 1-3.

An editorial discussing the second exhibit of architectural projects held along Gorky Street in Moscow over the May Day holiday in 1934 in an effort to popularize architecture among the masses. Speaks also of the need to generate discussion of the results of such exhibits among Soviet architects.

722. "Uroki maiskoi arkhitekturnoi vystavki—tvorcheskaia diskussiia v soiuze sovetskikh arkhitektorov" [Lessons of the May Architectural Exhibit—Creative Discussion at the Union of Soviet Architects]. *Arkhitektura SSSR*, no. 6, 1934: 4-17.

A review in the Union of Soviet Architects on May 17 and 22, 1934, of the May Day architectural exhibits. Includes statements by numerous architects in response to the exhibit. Important for indicating the changing trend and the need initially to seek public opinion of the most popular style.

723. "Uroki vsesoiuznogo tvorcheskogo soveshchaniia"[Lessons of the All-Union Creative Conference]. *Arkhitektura SSSR*, no. 6, 1935: 1-5.

Discusses the conference, whose main purpose was to evaluate the architectural practice of recent years, and to evaluate those creative positions and methods in force in Soviet architecture. Among the major topics considered were the understanding of socialist realism in architecture, the relationship of the classical heritage to the understanding of classicism, the evaluation of constructivism as an architectural system, the methods of the architectural organization of urban ensembles, the reworking of national motifs in architecture, the problem of the relationship of architecture and nature, the methods of the architectural mastery of technology, and the theme of socialist man and his relationship to architecture.

724. "Vsesoiuznoe soveshchanie sovetskikh arkhitektorov" [All-Union Conference of Soviet Architects]. *Arkhitektura SSSR*, no. 11, 1934: 1-5.

An editorial discussing the conference. Includes letters sent by the conference to Stalin, Kaganovich, and Molotov recanting past errors and promising to upgrade the efforts of the architectural community.

725. "Za boevuiu marksistkuiu kritiku" [For an Active Marxist Criticism]. *Arkhitektura SSSR*, no. 12, 1934: 2-3.

Editorial discussing the need for a system of Marxist criticism in Soviet architecture.

B. THE COMPETITION FOR THE PALACE OF SOVIETS (1932-34)

1. Monographs

726. All-Union Academy of Architecture. *Dvorets Sovetov* [Palace of Soviets]. Moscow, Izd-vo Vsesoiuznoi Akademii arkhitektury, 1939. 48 p.

727. Atarov, N. S. *El palacio de los Soviets*. 2d ed. Montevideo, Ediciones Pueblos Unidos, 1945. 165 p.

Provides a useful architectural, scientific, and engineering review of the final design by Iofan, Shchuko, and Gel'freikh. Includes an overall-account of the development of the competition Includes an overall account of the development of the competition. Contains much useful material in a highly accessible format.

728. Prokofiev, A. *The Palace of Soviets*. Moscow, Foreign Languages Publishing House, 1939. 32 p.

Gives a concise description of the final design, as well as a brief background of its evolution. Reveals that it was Stalin's idea to place the statue on top of the building.

729.   Union of Soviet Architects. *Arkhitektura Dvortsa Sovetov* [Architecture of the Palace of Soviets]. Moscow, Izd-vo Akademii arkhitektury SSSR, 1939. 112 p. illus.

An abridged stenographic account of the work of the Fifth Plenum of the Administration of the Union of Soviet Architects, with the participation of artists and sculptors. Devoted to questions on the Palace of Soviets and, especially, on the increased striving for a synthesis of the arts in Soviet architecture. Also contains the resolutions passed by the Plenum and photographs on exhibit during the plenary meeting.

730.   —— and the All-Russian Cooperative Union of Artists. *Dvorets Sovetov: Vsesoiuznyi konkurs 1932 g.* [Palace of Soviets: The All-Union Competition in 1932]. Moscow, Vsekokhudozhnik, 1933. 132 p. illus.

Contains excellent reproductions of all major entries in the first stage of the competition, categorized by the level of recognition and prizes. Also includes the resolution of February 28, 1932, by the Palace Competition Committee, as well as its resolutions of May 10 and June 4, 1933. Analytical texts include a discussion of Boris Iofan's revised design. A. V. Shchusev's brief history of the competition, G. B. Barkhin's account of the foreign architects participating in the competition, and a section dealing with reviews of the competition published in the Soviet press.

2. Articles by Soviet Writers

731.   Arkin, David E. "Put' k Dvortse" [Course toward the Palace]. *Sovetskoe iskusstvo*, Dec. 20, 1931.

Groups participants in the first phase of the competition into four general categories: 1) those who revert to "representational symbolism" of pure graphics rather than express an integral architectural concept, 2) those who borrow specific architectural or structural themes from various sources, 3) those who attempt a wholesale revival of preceding architectural styles, and 4) those who continue employing the contemporary, "purely constructive" styles of architecture. Extracted in *Dvorets Sovetov: Vsesoiuznyi konkurs 1932 g.* (no. 730), p. 113-114. For Arkin's observations on apparent trends in the use of the architectural heritage, see his article in *Vechernaia Moskva*, May 3, 1932, abstracted in *Dvorets Sovetov...*, p. 107-108.

732.   "Construction of a Palace of Soviets in Moscow," *Soviet Culture Bulletin*, nos. 6-7, 1931: 30

A brief announcement of the competition and description of the scope of the project. Identifies the Commission for the competition and refers to current negotiations with foreign architects to participate in the competition.

733.   D., S. "Pervye proekty Dvortsa Sovetov" [First Projects for the Palace of Soviets]. *Stroitel'stvo Moskvy*, no. 8, 1931: 2-7.
       A review of the projects submitted to the first phase of the competition and a general discussion of the results.

734.   "Dvorets Sovetov" [Palace of Soviets]. *Arkhitektura SSSR*, no. 1, 1933: 3-15.
       Important for its discussion of the initial phase of the design by Iofan which was accepted for first prize. Text discusses only his design, while photographs show other designs that were submitted.

735.   "Dvorets Sovetov" [Palace of Soviets]. *Sovetskaia arkhitektura*, no. 5, 1933: 1-16.
       Discussion of the third and fourth phases of the competition, with illustrations of the projects developed during these phases. A highly useful source.

736.   "Eskiznyi proekt Dvortsa Sovetov" [A Preliminary Project for the Palace of Soviets]. *Arkhitektura SSSR*, no. 3, 1934: 1-7.
       Text and photographs describing the revision of the prize project by B. M. Iofan, under the supervision of V. G. Gel'freikh and V. A. Shchuko.

737.   "Itogi velichaishego arkhitekturnogo konkursa" [Results of the Great Architectural Competition]. *Stroitel'stvo Moskvy*, no. 3, 1932: 13-16.
       Contains the two decrees issued by the Commission for the Competition. They are 1) "Concerning the Results of Work on the All-Union Open Competition on Composing a Project for the Palace of Soviets of the USSR" and 2) "Concerning the Organization of Work on the Final Composition of the Project for the Palace of Soviets of the USSR in Moscow," both dated February 28, 1932.

738. Khiger, R. Ia. "Dvorets Sovetov" [Palace of Soviets]. *Izvestiia*, Aug. 22, 1931.

Speaks of the significance of sculpture in designing the Palace of Soviets, as well as the need to synthesize sculpture and architecture in the Soviet experience. Abstracted in *Dvorets Sovetov: Vsesoiuznyi konkurs 1932 g.* (no. 730), p. 114.

739. Kut, A. "Dvorets Sovetov" [Palace of Soviets]. *Sovetskoe iskusstvo*, Jan. 26, 1932.

Paraphrases Lunacharsky's speech on the subject to a VOPRA meeting (no. 190). Abstracted in *Dvorets Sovetov: Vsesoiuznyi konkurs 1932 g.* (no. 730), p. 106-107.

740. Lunacharsky, Anatoli V. "Sotsialisticheskii arkhitekturnyi monument" [Socialist Architectural Monument]. *Stroitel'stvo Moskvy*, nos. 5-6, 1933: 3-10.

Comments on the designs submitted to the initial phase of the competition for the Palace of Soviets. Condemns functionalist designs for their bourgeois efforts to divest architecture of its substance. Maintains that eclecticism does not offer a solution to the search for a suitable monumental Soviet style, but praises the design submitted by Zholtovsky. An important insight to one aspect of official attitudes at this time. Reproduced in Lunacharsky, *Stat'i ob iskusstve* [Statements on Art] (Moscow, "Iskusstvo," 1941), p. 624-631; also in *A. V. Lunacharskii ob izobrazitel'nom iskusstve* [A. V. Lunacharsky on the Fine Arts], v. 1 (Moscow, "Sovetskii Khudozhnik," 1967), p. 477-479.

741. ———. "Tezisy doklada Lunacharskogo o zadachakh proletarskoi arkhitektury v sviazi so stroitel'stvom Dvortsa Sovetov" [Theses in Lunacharsky's Speech on the Problems of Proletarian Architecture in Conjunction with the Construction of the Palace of Soviets]. In *A. V. Lunacharsky ob izobrazitel'nom iskusstve* [A. V. Lunacharsky on the Fine Arts]. v. 1. Moscow, "Sovetskii khudozhnik," 1967. p. 479-488.

Twenty-six theses developed by Lunacharsky in response to the initial competition for the Palace of Soviets. An elaborate argument and criteria for the development of a new architectural style that can reflect adequately and appropriately the greatness of the new socialist state. A vital document for illuminating clearly official posture, as interpreted by Lunacharsky, on matters affecting the further development of Soviet architecture.

742. Mikhailov, A. I. "O vystavke proektov Dvortsa Sovetov" [Concerning the Exhibit of the Projects for the Palace of Soviets]. *Za proletarskoe iskusstvo*, no. 9, 1931: 14-19.

An interpretive review of the projects submitted to the first phase of the competition. Critique of projects reflects the proletarian point of view promulgated by VOPRA, restating objections to the constructivist and rationalist approaches to design as expressed in the projects submitted to the competitions by members of the respective groups.

743. Mikhailov, D. "Dvorets Sovetov dolzhen byt' proizvedeniem bol'shogo iskusstva bol'shevizma" [Palace of Soviets Must Be the Product of a Great Bolshevik Art]. *Stroitel'stvo Moskvy*, no. 9, 1931: 3-5.

Surveys the projects submitted to the first phase of the competition and argues against both "eclectic revivalism" and "technical formalism." The former tendency is seen to be exemplified by Boris Iofan's project; the latter, by the work of members of ASNOVA and the ARU.

744. Novitsky, P. "Problema proletarskogo stilia" [Problem of a Proletarian Style]. *Brigada khudozhnikov*, no. 3(10), 1932.

Views the competition as providing valuable material for assessing the current state of Soviet and world architecture. Concludes that none of the projects submitted—either by Soviet or by foreign architects—provides adequate solutions to the vital problems confronting the design of the Palace complex. Is most critical of foreign and especially of Soviet constructivist designs and finds those by VOPRA members to be the most acceptable. Reaches four basic conclusions regarding the implications of the competition for Soviet architecture: 1) the Palace of Soviets must solve the problem of a new class style, architectural image and expressiveness, 2) it must solve anew the problem of monumentality 3) it must solve the problem of the mass character of Soviet architecture, and 4) as the product of socialist art, it cannot rely upon either the revival or the stylization of bourgeois styles but demands the active search for new forms expressing the struggle and world outlook of the proletariat. Abstracted in *Dvorets Sovetov: Vsesoiuznyi konkurs 1932 g.* (**no. 730**), p. 109-111.

745. "Ot zadaniia k proektu. Khronika Dvortsa Sovetov" [From the Assignment to the Project. The Chronology of the Palace of Soviets]. *Stroitel'stvo Moskvy*, no. 3, 1934: 10-11.

A concise chronology of events in the competition from 1922 to 1934. Contains much useful references to important material.

746.   Deleted.

747.   "Postanovlenie Soveta Stroitel'stva Dvortsa Sovetov 19 fevralia
        1934 g." [Resolution of the Soviet on the Construction of the
        Palace of Soviets, dated February 19, 1934]. *Arkhitektura SSSR*,
        no. 2, 1934: 1.
            Reproduction in full of this resolution.

748.   Tolstoi, Aleksei N. "Poiski monumental'nosti" [Quests for Monu-
        mentality]. *Izvestiia*, Feb. 27, 1932.
            Reviews the projects submitted to the first phase of the
        competition and condemns the "sterile, lifeless" contemporary
        styles in evidence. Asserts that the Palace of Soviets must be the
        "House of the World" and that its architecture must thus utilize
        the cultural heritage in accordance with a dialectic philosophy.
        On that basis, examines the various historical styles of world
        architecture and concludes that only the Greco-Roman styles
        provide suitable precedents for the development of a socialist
        Soviet architectural style befitting the Palace of Soviets. One of
        the principal lines of argumentation in the middle thirties. Ab-
        stracted in *Dvorets Sovetov: Vsesoiuznyi konkurs 1932 g.*
        (no. 730), p. 101-105.

749.   Voblyi, I. "Dvorets Sovetov i arkhitekturnoe nasledstvo" [Palace of
        Soviets and the Architectural Heritage]. *Brigada khudozhnikov*,
        no. 3(10), 1932.
            Outlines four apparent trends in the utilization of the archi-
        tectural heritage: 1) utilization of isolated compositional and
        spatial elements, 2) direct application of classical idioms without
        readapting them to the current conditions, 3) a mechanical appli-
        cation of architectural and decorative details, and 4) an outright
        affirmation of reviving archaic architectural forms *in toto*. Ab-
        stracted in *Dvorets Sovetov: Vsesoiuznyi konkurs 1932 g.* **(no.
        730)**, p. 104-105.

750.   Zapletin, N. P. "Arkhitekturno-tekhnicheskii proekt Dvortsa Sovetov
        Soiuza SSR" [Architectural-Technical Project for the Palace of
        Soviets of the USSR]. *Arkhitektura SSSR*, no. 6, 1937: 26-33.
            A detailed analysis of the structural and mechanical solutions
        for the design finally developed by architects Iofan, Shchuko,
        and Gel'freikh.

751.   ——. "Dvorets Sovetov SSSR" [Palace of Soviets of the USSR].
        Sovetskaia arkhitektura, nos. 2-3, 1932; 10-121.
          An exhaustive survey and assessment of the first phase of the
        competition. Includes illustrations of the designs submitted.

752.   ——. "Perelomnyi etap proletarskoi arkhitektury (po materialam
        komisii tekhnicheskoi ekspertizy)" [Turning Point in Proletarian
        Architecture (After the Materials of the Commission on Technical
        Expertise)]. *Stroitel'stvo Moskvy*, no. 3, 1932: 17-34.
          A comprehensive review of projects submitted to the first
        phase of the competition. Sees Soviet architecture undergoing a
        "political reexamination" in search of an appropriate expression.
        Conclusions reflect the changing pattern of demands placed upon
        Soviet architecture. Abstracted in *Dvorets Sovetov: Vsesoiuznyi
        konkurs 1932 g.* (**no. 730**), p. 108, 112.

                    3. Articles by Non-Soviet Writers

753.   Letter of May 13, 1932, from Le Corbusier to A. V. Lunacharsky.
        Published in: *A. V. Lunacharsky ob izobrazitel'nom iskusstve*
        [A. V. Lunacharsky on the Fine Arts]. v. 1. Moscow, "Sovetskii
        khudozhnik," 1967. p. 488-492.
          Letter sent to Lunacharsky in Geneva, where he was a member
        of the Soviet delegation to the disarmament conference at the
        League of Nations. Le Corbusier attacks the decision by the
        competition jury, headed by Viacheslav Molotov, to accept Boris
        Iofan's design for the construction of the Palace of Soviets and
        award it the grand prize. Argues that such action would seriously
        set back the dynamic progress made by Soviet architecture, urges
        serious reconsideration of the matter, volunteers to come to
        Moscow to discuss the matter further, and lectures Lunacharsky
        on the intrinsic advantages of modern architecture in expressing
        the particular spirit of the contemporary age. Of paramount im-
        portance in articulating the great hopes of Western architects that
        the Soviet Union would, by its very revolutionary nature, provide
        the optimum haven for the development of modern architecture.

754.   "The Palace of Soviets, Moscow," *Architectural Review*, v. 71, May
        1932: 196-200.
          A review of the first phase of the competition. Text provides
        general description of the scope of the facility; plates are of a few
        of the designs submitted by leading Western and Soviet architects.
        Includes designs by Hamilton and Iofan.

755. Piacentini, Marcello. "Un grande avvenimento architettonico in Russia. Il Palazzo dei Soviet a Mosca." *Architettura*, v. 13, March 1934: 129-40.

An illustrated review and good analysis of the competition. Excellent plates of designs submitted by Western and Soviet architects, with Boris Iofan's submission covered extensively with superb plates.

C. ECLECTICISM

756. A., D. (Probably Arkin, David). "Protiv eklektike" [Against Eclecticism]. *Arkhitektura SSSR*, no. 2, 1934: 7-9.

Chastises architects who earlier had venerated Le Corbusier's five theses, but who now, having heard the terms "assimilation of heritage" and "artistic quality," have interpreted them to mean simply a restoration of old styles and superficial decoration of façades.

757. Matsa, Ivan L. "O prirode eklektisizma" [On the Nature of Eclecticism]. *Arkhitektura SSSR*, no. 5, 1936: 5-7.

A brief essay on ecleciticism, which the author defines not as a style but an unprincipled "comfortable" approach. A scholarly analysis of eclecticism and the circumstances that engender it both in architecture in general and in Soviet architecture in particular.

758. Vesnin, Viktor A. "Eklekticheskaia retseptura" [An Eclectic Pre-scription]. *Arkhitektura SSSR*, no. 12, 1934: 5-6.

A critique of prevalent practice of simply copying old architectural forms with no consideration either of the functions contained or even of elementary principles of good design.

759. ——. "Men'she 'akademizma'!" [Less "Academism"!]. See **no. 426**.

D. CLASSICISM

1. Monographs

760. Ignatkin, Ivan A. *Sovetskaia arkhitektura i klassicheskoe nasledie* [Soviet Architecture and the Classical Heritage]. Kiev, Gosstroiizdat UkSSR, 1958. 71 p.

Supports the use of the classical heritage in Soviet architecture. Argues that the problem of the classical heritage is one of evaluating critically the work of architects in preceding epochs and proceeds with a cursory evaluation within the framework of current Marxist dialectics. A general restatement of current theoretical pronouncements that innovation in architecture is based upon a unity of structural technology, functional requirements, and artistic forms; argues that the canons of classical architecture, which have consistently embodied such a unity in the past, are therefore still applicable to current requirements in Soviet architecture.

761. Savitsky, Iu. *Russkoe klassicheskoe nasledie i sovetskaia arkhitektura* [Russian Classical Heritage and Soviet Architecture]. Moscow, Gosstroiizdat, 1953. 63 p. illus.

Assesses the directions in the implementation of the Russian classical heritage by Soviet architects by analyzing outstanding works of Soviet architecture. Attempts to show that the creation of a highly ideological and nationalistic Soviet architecture is related to the study and creative utilization of the traditions of classical Russian art. An excellent source for illuminating the argument.

2. Articles

762. Borisovsky, I. "O nepravilnom otnoshenii k naslediiu" [Concerning the Incorrect Attitude toward the Heritage]. *Voprosy teorii arkhitektury*. v. 1, 1955: 94-108.

Criticizes the blind copying of the classical heritage which stresses only the artistic, and not the material, realm of consideration. Assesses the various statements made on this subject. Cites the more original and ideologically appropriate applications of the classical heritage.

763. "K voprosu o 'neklassicheskom' arkhitekturnom nasledii" [To the Question of the "Unclassical" Architectural Heritage]. *Akademiia arkhitektury*, no. 3, 1935: 42-43.

Notes the preference expressed by a majority of Soviet architects at that time for the Greco-Roman classical styles. Warns against overextending this veneration and suggests turning to other systems of architectural expression of the past.

764. Matsa, Ivan L. "O klassike i klassichnost'i" [On Classicism and the Essence of Classicism]. *Akademiia arkhitektury,* nos. 1-2, 1935: 35-38.

   An important theoretical formulation of the early tectonic and ideological conditions for the assimilation of the classical heritage in Soviet architecture. Important for providing the ideological rationale for sanctioning the assimilation of the Greco-Roman style.

765. Rzianin, M. I. "Ob osvoenii klassicheskogo naslediia v sovetskoi arkhitekture" [Concerning the Assimilation of the Classical Heritage in Soviet Architecture]. *Sovetskaia arkhitektura,* no. 3, 1952: 23-34.

   A studied analysis of this problem, as well as of the work of those who best applied it (Shchusev, Zholtovsky, et al.). Includes a gleaning from the Communist "classics" on the subject. For a review of the same problem, see his article: "Ob osvoenii klassicheskogo naslediia v sovetskoi arkhitekture" [Concerning the Assimilation of the Classical Heritage in Soviet Architecture], *Arkhitektura·SSSR,* no. 12, 1952: 16-22.

766. Shchusev, Aleksei V. "Sovetskaia arkhitektura i klassicheskoe nasledstvo" [Soviet Architecture and the Classical Heritage]. *Arkhitekturnaia gazeta,* June 18, 1937.

   Speech at the First All-Union Congress of Soviet Architects. Argues for the implementation of local forms and traditions in the architecture of the republics of the USSR.

767. Vesnin, Viktor A. "Tvorcheskie puti sovetskoi arkhitektury i problema arkhitekturnogo nasledstva" [Creative Directions of Soviet Architecture and the Problem of Architectural Heritage]. *Arkhitektura SSSR,* nos. 3-4, 1933: 14-15.

   Reviews earlier developments of Soviet architecture and argues against the literal copying of classical styles, suggesting tempering the classical idioms with the recent advances made by modern architecture and technology.

E. NATIONALISM

768. Antipov. I. "Russkoe arkhitekturnoe nasledstvo i ego razvitie v noveishei arkhitekture" [Russian Architectural Heritage and Its Development in the Newest Architecture]. *Arkhitektura SSSR,* no. 2, 1941: 46-52.

Discusses the emergence of the Slavic Revival styles in Russian architecture and their subsequent revival by the architects Shchusev, Fomin, and Shchuko during the Soviet period.

769.   Ginzburg, Moisei, Ia. "Natsional'naia arkhitektura narodov SSSR" [National Architecture of the Peoples of the USSR]. See no. 604.
Interesting in contrasting the earlier Constructivist approach to the problem, renouncing so-called "national" styles, with the nationalist forms subsequently advocated by official circles.

770.   Iaralov, Iu. "Ob osvoenii natsional'nogo naslediia v usloviakh indus-trializatsii stroitel'stva" [Concerning the Assimilation of the National Heritage under the Conditions of the Industrialization of Construction]. *Voprosy teorii arkhitektury*, v. 1, 1955: 75-93.
Condemns the mass assimilation of the national and classical heritage at the expense of an insufficient appreciation of socialist content or concern for satisfying the material and cultural needs of the Soviet people. Reviews the various statements, works, and references to the assimilation of the classical heritage. A good reference to the debate on the problem.

771.   Novikov, I. "Traditsii natsional'nogo zodchestva v tvorchestve A. V. Shchuseva" [Traditions of National Architecture in the Practice of A. V. Shchusev]. *Arkhitektura SSSR*, no. 5, 1953: 15-21.
An analysis of Shchusev's design for the Kazan Railway Terminal in Moscow and his use of 16th- and 17th-century Muscovite decorative motifs.

772.   "Problemy natsional'noi arkhitektury sovetskogo vostoka" [Problems of National Architecture in the Soviet East]. *Arkhitektura SSSR*, no. 1, 1934: 1-3.
Editorial in an issue devoted to the question of national architecture. Signals the introduction of nationalistic elements into designs that were heretofore purely neoclassical; rationalizes the need to look not only to the classical but also to the national heritage of all the constituent republics.

773.   Rzianin, M. "Voprosy osvoeniia klassicheskogo naslediia v arkhitek-turnoi praktike natsional'nykh respublik" [Questions on Assimi-lating the Classical Heritage in the Architectural Practice of the National Republics]. *Arkhitektura SSSR*, no. 4, 1953: 17-19.

Reviews what are regarded as leading works in the national architecture of the constituent republics. Condemns "formalistic" and "cosmopolitan" attempts by the left to submerge the national architectural styles and develops criteria for the continued treatment of national themes in the architecture of the Soviet republics.

774. "Voprosy arkhitekturnoi kompozitsii v natsional'nykh respublikakh" [Questions Concerning Architectural Composition in the National Republics] . *Arkhitektura SSSR*, no. 8, 1934: 8-21.

Statements by Moscow architects involved in designing large civic buildings for the national provinces and republics of the Union. Testifies to the serious consideration being given to the problem of creating an architecture "socialist in content, nationalist in form" in the various republics.

Included are statements by A. V. Shchusev on his Tbilisi Institute, V. D. Kokorin on his Palace of Government in Georgia, A. N. Fedorov on his Palace of Culture and Science in the Buriato-Mongol Autonomous Republic, S. N. Kozhin on the Palace of Culture in Nal'chik, M. P. Parusnikov and I. N. Sobolev on the Palace of Soviets in Nal'chik, and N. Selivanov, V. Sergeev, and N. Petrov on the University of Alma-Ata.

F. SOCIALIST REALISM

1. Monographs

775. Brodsky, I. *Za sotsialisticheskii realizm* [For Socialist Realism]. Leningrad, Lenizdat, 1938.

Statements and speeches concerning questions of artistic education and the means of implementing the method of socialist realism in Soviet architecture and art.

776. Kucherenko, Georgii A. *Esteticheskoe mnogobrazie iskusstva sotsialisticheskogo realizma* [Aesthetic Diversity in the Art of Socialist Realism] . Moscow, "Sovetskii khudozhnik," 1966. 232 p.

A theoretical discussion of manner, style, and method implicit in the approach to art as viewed through the current understanding of socialist realism. Important for clarifying the new theoretical premises underlying current changes in the understanding of what constitutes socialist realism, brought about through the introduction of great latitude in interpreting tenets heretofore rigidly defined.

777.   *Za sotsialisticheskii realizm v izobrazitel'nom iskusstve* [For Socialist
        Realism in the Fine Arts]. Moscow, "Sovetskii Khudozhnik," 1958.
           A tendentious defense of the guiding principle of Socialist
        Realism against the ideology of "revisionism" in Marxist-Leninist
        aesthetics. D. Osipov recalls Lenin's dicta and pronouncements;
        A. Mikhailov attempts to refute efforts to view socialist realism
        as simply the product of a fundamental struggle between modern-
        ism and traditionalism in the Soviet visual arts, including
        architecture.

2.   Articles

778.   Fedorov-Davydov, A. A. "Nekotorye voprosy arkhitekturnoi teorii i
           praktiki v svete truda I. V. Stalina 'Ekonomicheskie problemy
           sotsializma v SSSR' i reshenii XIX s'ezda partii" [Some Questions
           of Architectural Theory and Practice in Light of I. V. Stalin's
           work, "The Economic Problems of Socialism in the USSR" and
           the Decisions of the Nineteenth Party Congress]. *Arkhitektura
           SSSR*, no. 3, 1953: 1-6.
              An attempt to relate applicable directives contained both in
           Stalin's recent work and in the decisions of the Nineteenth Party
           Congress to the present theory and practice of Soviet architecture.
           Interprets Stalin's and Malenkov's admonitions to be vigilant in
           the struggle for communism and the cause of socialism as a
           mandate to condemn the "idealistic" and "liberal" tendencies in
           the Soviet architectural community which hamper the acceptable
           depiction of the lofty aims and qualities of socialism, realism, and
           the aspirations of the Soviet society in Soviet architecture. Views
           Shchusev, Fomin, and Zholtovsky as the founders of socialist
           realism in Soviet architecture and measures their achievements
           affirmatively against pronouncements by Lenin and Stalin for the
           purpose of reaffirming the official doctrine of socialist realism.
           A lengthy polemical discourse, valuable for the insight it pro-
           vides to current views and interpretations of developments in
           Soviet architecture.

779.   Kaufman, R. "Sotsialisticheskii realizm i mnogobrazie tvorcheskikh
           individualnost'ei" [Socialist Realism and the Diversity of Creative
           Individuality]. *Tvorchestvo*, no. 3, 1960: 3-4.
              Suggests a more diversified approach to socialist realism, not
           as a predetermined formula for applying the classical idiom, but
           rather as a general aesthetic framework for satisfying contem-
           porary social needs. A new outlook exemplifying current thought.

780. Lebedev, P. I. "Iz istorii bor'by za realizm v sovetskom iskusstve" [From the History of the Struggle for Realism in Soviet Art]. In *Bor'ba za realizm v izobrazitel'nom iskusstve 20-kh godov* [Struggle for Realism in the Fine Arts during the Twenties]. Moscow, "Sovetskii khudozhnik," 1962. p. 7-52.

A comprehensive survey of the artistic activity of the given period, including the work of the "left artists," as well as of the response by Soviet officials and the subsequent official decrees and pronouncements that formed the basis for the official policy in the Soviet arts. Although no specific reference is made to architectural activity, the work is valuable for illuminating more precisely the context within which modernism—including parallel developments in Soviet architecture—fell into official disfavor. See this book also for a very useful collection of documentary material, recollections by important contemporary personalities, and contemporary articles in the press.

781. Minervin, Georgii. "Leninskaia teoriia otrazheniia i voprosy teorii sovetskoi arkhitektury" [Lenin's Theory of Reflection and Questions on the Theory of Soviet Architecture]. *Arkhitektura SSSR*, no. 1, 1953: 1-8.

Analyzes the development of the Marxist theory of cognition as developed in Lenin's work, *Materializm i empiriokrititsizm* [Materialism and Empiriocriticism], 1909. Argues that in developing the materialist theory of reflection, Lenin set forth criteria for the reflection of the objective world in the consciousness of man, thereby positing the philosophical basis for socialist realism. A highly theoretical though important ideological discourse on the foundations of socialist realism in Soviet architecture. For German version of this article, see G. Minervin, "Die Leninische Theorie der Wiederspiegelung und die Fragen der Theorie der socialistischen Realismus," *Deutsche Architektur*, nos. 3-4, 1953: 198-202.

782. Nekrasov, Aleksei I. "Arkhitekturnoe nasledstvo; problema realizma v arkhitekture" [Architectural Heritage; the Problem of Realism in Architecture]. *Arkhitektura SSSR*, no. 1, 1934: 52-60.

Argues that the essence of realism in architecture lies in the very style of creation. Surveys the classical styles to analyze the various aspects of reality or unreality of their compositions. A theoretical essay intended to suggest criteria by which the new Soviet style may appropriately be implemented.

783. Tsapenko, M. P. "Sotsialisticheskii realizm—metod sovetskoe arkhitektury" [Socialist Realism—Method of Soviet Architecture]. *Arkhitektura i stroitel'stvo*, no. 11, 1949: 2-11.

Discusses the method of socialist realism and its applications in Soviet architecture. A forerunner of the author's book, *O realishcheskikh osnovakh sovetskoi arkhitektury* (**no. 233**), which furthers his argument.

784.   Vesnin, Aleksandr A. "O sotsialisticheskom realizme v arkhitekture" [Concerning Socialist Realism in Architecture]. *Sovetskaia arkhitektura*, no. 8, 1957: 69-80.

An interview with the architect discussing the manner in which the content of Soviet reality can best be expressed in architectural forms. Discusses also tradition and innovation in Soviet architecture, the utilization of sculpture and painting in architecture, the organization of the internal components of an architectural facility, the importance in architecture of striving for a unity of content, form, construction, and building materials. For translation into English by Johan Huijts, see "On Socialist Realism in Architecture," *Architectural Design,* no. 1, 1959: 3-6.

785.   Vesnin, Viktor A. "Ot konstruktivizma k sotsialisticheskomu realizmu" [From Constructivism to Socialist Realism]. *Arkhitekturnaia gazeta,* June 23, 1937.

An illuminating discussion of those architectural principles endemic to constructivism that may be applied to socialist realism. Includes author's analysis of the positive potentials of socialist realism in Soviet architecture.

G. SYNTHESIS OF THE ARTS

1. Monographs

786.   Mordvinov, A. G., ed. *Khudozhestvennye problemy sovetskoi arkhitektury* [Artistic Problems of Soviet Architecture]. Moscow, Gosarkhizdat, 1944, 31 p.

A collection of essays that assesses past efforts and reaffirms the policy to synthesize the arts in Soviet architecture in order to reflect a high degree of artistic expressiveness.

2. Articles

787.   Alekseev, G. I. "Sushchnost' khudozhestvennogo sinteza v sovremennoi arkhitekture" [Essence of Artistic Synthesis in Contemporary

Architecture]. In *Voprosy arkhitektury: teoriia, istoriia i praktika sovetskogo zodchestva* [Questions of Architecture: The Theory, History, and Practice of Soviet Architecture]. Leningrad, Leningradskii inzhenerno-stroitel'nyi institut, 1962: 104-106.

A general statement of the synthesis of the arts in Soviet architecture, its earlier repudiation by modernists, its subsequent return, and the particular direction of its development. An important survey of the problem.

788. Alpatov, Mikhail V. "Problema sinteza v khudozhestvennom nasledstve" [Problem of Synthesis in the Artistic Heritage]. *Arkhitektura SSSR*, no. 2, 1935: 21-26.

Speech delivered at the Conference on the Question of Synthesis of the Arts, December 1934. Treats the problem of comparative incompatibility between the spaces and effects created in painting and sculpture and those in architecture. Cites examples and discusses the ways in which these relative incompatibilities have been resolved throughout the history of art and architecture.

789. Arkin, David E. "Problema sinteza v sovetskoi arkhitekture" [Problem of Synthesis in Soviet Architecture]. *Arkhitektura SSSR*, no. 2, 1935: 8-11.

Opening speech delivered at the Conference on the Question of Synthesis of the Spatial Arts, held on December 25, 1934. By citing examples, develops the theme that sculpture and painting can: 1) render a further illumination of the concepts underlying the architectural creation, as in ancient Greece; 2) play an independent though coordinated role with the architectural theme, as in the Italian Renaissance; and 3) provide a decorative and plastic treatment for the architectural form.

790. Balikhin, V. S. "Arkhitektura i skul'ptura" [Architecture and Sculpture]. *Arkhitektura SSSR*, no. 2, 1935: 16-17.

Speech delivered at the Conference on the Questions of the Synthesis of the Arts, December 1934. Argues that sculpture in urban spaces must assume an architectural quality and fulfill architectural functions in order to become part of the architectural ensemble, while not losing its own expressiveness. The synthesis of sculpture and architecture must be understood as the synthesis of the architectural and sculptural space and the activity of the masses that it should depict.

791.   ——. "Sintez iskusstv v praktike sovetskikh arkhitektorov" [Synthesis
       of the Arts in the Practice of Soviet Architects]. *Arkhitektura
       SSSR*, no. 7, 1935: 20-26.
          Uses current projects to explain and analyze the use of the
       various forms of art in current architectural practice.

792.   Bassekhes, A. I. "Itogi tvorcheskogo soveshchaniia" [Results of the
       Creative Conference]. *Arkhitektura SSSR*, no. 2, 1935: 3-7.
          An assessment of the first conference on the question of
       spatial arts called by the Union of Soviet Architects in Moscow,
       December 25-28, 1934.

793.   Bubnova, Ol'ga. "Za ili protiv ornamenta" [For or Against Orna-
       ment]. *Arkhitektura SSSR*, no. 2, 1933: 35.
          In view of the recent decisions to revive the role of ornamenta-
       tion in Soviet architecture, several Western architects were asked
       to comment on their preference for the use of ornamentation in
       contemporary architecture. Among those who responded were
       Adolph Loos, Le Corbusier, and August Perret. Concludes with
       the statement that this question will now have to be seriously
       reconsidered in the Soviet Union in efforts to upgrade its
       architecture.

794.   Favorsky, V. A. "Arkhitektura i zhivopis'" [Architecture and Paint-
       ing]. *Arkhitektura SSSR*, no. 2, 1935: 13-15.
          Speech delivered at the Conference on the Questions of the
       Synthesis of the Arts, December 1934. Analyzes primarily the
       High Renaissance and its use of the various forms of painting to
       heighten and attenuate the architectural treatment and expres-
       sions of masses and surfaces. Feels that constructivism, because of
       its complete lack of painting on wall surfaces, was unable to
       achieve depth.

795.   Fomin, Ivan A. "O sotrudnichestve arkhitektora so skul'pterom i
       zhivopistsem" [Concerning the Collaboration of the Architect
       with the Sculptor and Painter]. *Arkhitektura SSSR*, no. 2, 1933:
       32.
          Argues for synthesis of the arts in Soviet architecture, begin-
       ning necessarily with the initial conceptual phase of design.
       Concludes that such a synthesis would go far in enriching the
       style of Soviet architecture.

796.   Khvoinik, I. E. "Skul'ptura i arkhitektura" [Sculpture and Architecture]. *Arkhitektura SSSR,* no. 2, 1935: 18-21.
       Speech delivered at the Conference on the Questions of the Synthesis of the Arts, December 1934. A sculptor, the author argues that sculptors now must and want to become creators of a concrete, architectonically validated, visual image, since they must answer to the problems of architectonics and the organization of spaces.

797.   Matsa, Ivan L. "K voprosu o khudozhestvennom obraze v arkhitekture" [Concerning the Question of the Artistic Image in Architecture]. *Arkhitektura SSSR,* no. 5, 1933: 36-41.
       A theoretical analysis which attempts to posit the means of materially improving the expressiveness of the architectural object through the correct understanding of architectural tectonics in order to achieve a more organic synthesis of the arts in Soviet architecture.

798.   ——. "Osnovy sinteza" [Bases of Synthesis]. *Arkhitektura SSSR,* no. 2, 1935: 31-34.
       Argues that the period of waiting is over and that there must now begin a close and inseparable collaboration between Soviet architects and artists in order to create the type of architectural forms and facilities that befit the new socialist way of life. Summarizes the program for the implementation of such a synthesis.

799.   Shchusev, Aleksei V. "Arkhitektura i zhivopis'" [Architecture and Painting]. In *Voprosy sinteza iskusstva* [Questions on the Synthesis of Art]. Moscow, 1936. p. 34-41.
       Initially, a speech delivered at the Conference on the Questions of Synthesis of the Arts, December 1934. Argues that it is not only possible but necessary to effect a synthesis of the three plastic arts. Seeks to validate employing painting in architecture. For an initial outline of his ideas in this regard, see his article, same title, in *Arkhitektura SSSR,* no. 2, 1935: 12-13.

800.   "Tvorcheskaia diskussiia o sinteze iskusstv" [Creative Discussion on the Synthesis of the Arts]. *Arkhitektura SSSR,* no. 2, 1935: 27-30.
       An assessment of the discussions held among the participants and attendants at the Conference on the Questions of the Synthesis of the Arts. A very interesting and valuable record.

801.   "Tvorcheskaia tribuna—o sotrudnichestve arkhitektora so skul'ptorom
        i zhivopistsem" [Creative Tribune—Concerning the Collaboration
        of the Architects with the Sculptor and Painter].*Arkhitektura
        SSSR*. no. 2, 1933: 32-33.
            The first discussions on such a collaboration, including state-
        ments by the architects I. A. Fomin and F. D. Friedman and the
        artists V. A. Favorsky and B. D. Korolev. An interesting record of
        the initial dialogue on this subject.

H. BUILDING TECHNOLOGY AND CONSTRUCTION

1. Monographs by Soviet Writers

802.   Academy of Construction and Architecture of the USSR. *Stroitel'stvo
        v SSSR, 1917-1957* [Building in the USSR, 1917-1957]. See
        no. 228.
            Includes authoritative material on the development and subse-
        quent mechanization of the Soviet building industry.

2. Articles by Soviet Writers

803.   "Arkhitektor—na lesa" [Architects—to the Scaffolding]. *Arkhitek-
        tura SSSR*, nos. 3-4, 1933: 61.
            An editorial containing a reproduction of the complete text of
        the resolution by the Moscow committee of the Communist Party
        concerning improvements in construction and a record of the
        discussion, led by L. M. Kaganovich, secretary of the Moscow
        Soviet, concerning the need for the architects to supervise
        thoroughly all phases of construction.

804.   Burov, Andrei K. "Pravda materiala" [Truth of the Material].
        Arkhitektura SSSR, no. 3, 1934: 36.
            Argues that new building materials have not been created for
        the purpose of imitating and creating illusions and that the
        principle of socialist realism must be applied with clarity through
        the honest use of these materials. Condemns efforts to assimilate
        the classical heritage simply by using ferro-concrete structures
        and modern building materials to simulate the architecture of
        antiquity.

805.   Ginzburg, Moisei Ia. "Arkhitekturnye vozmozhnosti sovremennoi
        industrii" [Architectural Possibilities of Modern Industry}. See
        no. 598.

Argues that Soviet architecture has not exploited the possibilities afforded by the newly developing building technology. A concise, penetrating analysis of the problem.

806.   Fomin, Ivan A. "Protiv fetishizma materiala" [Against the Fetishism of Material]. *Arkhitektura SSSR*, no. 3, 1934: 28-29.
       Warns against being carried away with a fetish for building materials at the expense of a more pleasing architecture that would answer not only to the needs but also to the spirit of the new socialist times.

807.   Kolli, Nikolai I. "O materiale i stile" [Concerning Material and Style]. *Arkhitektura SSSR*, no. 3, 1934: 34-35.
       Argues that building materials dictate architectural forms and that building technology determines new ways in which the materials can be applied, thus changing the forms that can be defined with materials. Speaks also of standardization of details as the only means for industrial production in building technology.

808.   Kovel'man, I. A. "Bolezni zdanii" [Infirmities of Buildings]. *Arkhitektura SSSR*, no. 5, 1933: 48-49.
       Cites the various defects of newly constructed buildings. Interesting for revealing the problems causing many of the negative visual characteristics that precipitated the popular rejection of modern architecture in the Soviet Union.

809.   Leonidov, Ivan I. "Palitra arkhitektora" [Palette of the Architect]. *Arkhitektura SSSR*, no. 3, 1934: 32-33.
       Argues that one of the decisive factors determining the style and general composition of an architectural facility, together with the social conditions, is the technology of building materials and construction exploited aesthetically to best advantage.

810.   Liubosh, A. A. "Zadachi arkhitektury v sviazi s industrializatsiei stroitel'stva [Problems of Architecture in Conjunction with the Industrialization of Construction]. In *Tvorcheskie problemy sovetskoi arkhitektury. Sbornik statiei* [Creative Problems of Soviet Architecture. A Collection of Essays]. Moscow and Leningrad, Gosstroiizdat, 1956: p. 107-122.
       A review of the problems of industrializing the building industry and employing prefabricated concrete structural and architectural materials in construction following the decree of

November 14, 1955, ordering the elimination of excesses in design and construction. A useful review of officially identified and defined problems.

811.   Matsa, Ivan L. "Arkhitektura i tekhnika" [Architecture and Technology]. *Arkhitektura SSSR*, no. 3, 1936: 5-8.

A review of the major cause-effect relationships ·between architecture and technology and the manner in which these relationships must continue to develop and diversify under the new formula of socialist realism.

812.   Mel'nikov, Konstantin S. "Arkhitekturnoe osvoenie novykh materialov"[Architectural Assimilation of New Materials]. *Arkhitektura SSSR*, no. 3, 1934:37.

Argues briefly that it is not so much up to the architect to participate in the manufacture of building materials as it is up to the industry to develop unified details and materials that the architect can then artistically utilize to best advantage.

813.   "Ot proekta k ego realizatsii" [From the Design to Its Realization]. *Arkhitektura SSSR*, No. 1, 1933: 33-35.

Treats the architect's responsibility in participating in every phase of construction. In response to the poor quality of construction in the Soviet Union and to the architect's general lack of concern with this problem, a number of leading architects prepared statements on the problem and how to solve it. An illuminating analysis of current problems in Soviet construction.

814.   Shchusev, Aleksei V. "Arkhitektor i stroitel'naia tekhnika" [Architect and Building Technology]. *Arkhitektura SSSR*, no. 2, 1936: 4-5.

Argues that it is the architect's responsibility to be mindful of those building trades with which he must deal for the construction of any given building, and to develop its design accordingly.

2. Monographs by Non-Soviet Writers

815.   Percival, David, and Alex Massie. *The Building Industry in the USSR*. London,   Lawrence & Wisehart, 1943. 47 p.

A résumé of the Soviet building industry reflecting the country's economic, social, and technological growth. Observes that the Soviet government, faced with a terrible housing shortage, was forced to devise new measures and techniques to cope with the problem. Useful for assessing the correlation between design developments in Soviet architecture and the capacity of the Soviet building industry to execute them.

3. Articles by Non-Soviet Writers

816. "La Construction en URSS." *La Construction moderne,* April 1957: 152-54.

A survey of recent developments in the Soviet building industry, with emphasis on prefabricated construction.

817. Coulon, Jean-Jacques. "Les Problèmes techniques en Russie soviét- que." *L'Architecture d'aujourd'hui,* v. 2, no. 8, 1932: 66-69.

A study of industrialization in the Soviet Union, the problems of its building industry, and the effects on modern Soviet architecture.

I. ALL-UNION CONFERENCE OF BUILDERS AND ARCHITECTS (DECEMBER 1954)

1. Monographs

818. Khrushchev, Nikita S. *O shirokom vnedrenii industrial'nykh metodov, uludshenii kachestva i snizhenii stoimosti stroitel'stva* (Concern- ing a Broad Introduction of Industrial Methods, the Improvement of Quality and the Lowering of the Cost of Construction]. See **no. 150.**

Speech delivered by Khrushchev to the Conference. Provides the basis upon which policy reorientation was promulgated in Soviet architecture.

2. Articles

819. "Ob ustranenii izlishestv v proektirovanii i stroitel'stve" [Concerning the Elimination of Excesses in Design and Construction]. See **no. 155.**

Decrees that all further efforts in the country's architectural and building activity be directed toward increasing the utility and comfort of all buildings. Incorporates the conditions set forth by Khrushchev in his speech to the Conference of Builders and Architects **(no. 150).**

820.   "Obrashchenie uchastnikov Vsesoiuznogo soveshchaniia stroitelei, arkhitektorov, rabotnikov promyshlennosti stroitel'nykh materialov, stroitel'nogo i dorozhnogo mashinostroeniiz, proektnykh i nauchno-issledovatel'skikh organizatsii, sozvannogo TsK KPSS i Sovetom Ministrov SSSR, ko vsem rabotkikam stroitel'noi industrii" [An Appeal to the Participants of the All-Union Conference of Builders, Architects, and Workers of the Building Materials Industry, the Building and Highway Machinery Industry, and the Design and Research Organizations called by the Central Committee of the Communist Party of the Soviet Union and the Council of Ministers of the USSR—to All Workers in the Building Industry]. *Arkhitektura SSSR*, no. 1, 1955: 1-5.

Reminds the entire building community that it is now obliged by the Party and the Council of Ministers to implement those improvements set forth in recent official decrees and pronouncements.

821.   "Vsesoiuznoe soveshchanie stroitelei, arkhitektorov i rabotnikov promyshlennosti stroitel'nykh materialov, stroitel'nogo i dorozhnogo mashinostroeniia, proektnykh i nauchno-issledovatel'nykh organizatsii" [All-Union Conference of Builders, Architects and Workers of the Building Materials Industry, the Building and Highway Machinery Industry, and the Design and Research Organizations]. *Arkhitektura SSSR*, no. 12, 1954: inside front cover.

A brief summary of the proceedings.

J. EVALUATIONS AND DEBATES FOLLOWING DE-STALINIZATION

822.   "Diskussiia o novatorstve i nasledii v sovetskoi arkhitekture" [Discussion of Innovation and the Heritage in Soviet Architecture]. *Arkhitektura SSSR*, no. 1, 1956: 46-68.

A summary of the discussion held on this subject, sponsored by the Union of Soviet Architects and the Institute of the History and Theory of Architecture. Contains synopsis of the speech by G. Gradov on innovation and the heritage in Soviet architecture and the one by Iu. Iaralov on the national peculiarities of Soviet architecture in view of the current efforts to industrialize construction. Concludes with a summary of the discussion of these speeches. A useful record of an important aspect of the current debate.

823.   Ivanov, K. A. "O materialisticheskom ponimanii prirody i spetsifiki arkhitektury" [Concerning the Materialistic Understanding of the Nature and Specific Character of Architecture]. *Voprosy teorii arkhitektury*, v. 2, 1957: 21-40.

A speech by the then head of the sector of the theory of architecture within the Institute of the History and Theory of Architecture in the Academy of Architecture of the USSR at a discussion of current problems in Soviet architecture. Argues that the essence of architecture is an indivisible unity of material and ideological determinants, with a preemptive role by the former. Criticizes a one-sided aesthetical view of architectural problems that ignores the technological requirements of construction. Views the main function of architecture to be one of providing for the production of material wealth, and architectural mastery as the ability to incorporate all aspects of the architectural spectrum of considerations—including function, materials, construction, economics, and aesthetic canons—in the solution of every given concrete problem. For a restatement of this task, see same title in: *Arkhitektura SSSR*, no. 10, 1955: 26-32.

824.   ——. "O novatorstve v arkhitekture na osnove sovmestnoi tvorcheskoi raboty arkhitektorov i stroitelei" [Concerning Innovation in Architecture as the Basis of the Simultaneous Creative Work by Architects and Builders]. *Voprosy teorii arkhitektury*, v. 4, 1958: 6-29.

Stresses the importance of collaboration between the architect and the builder in all phases of architectural and construction work as a direct condition for its successful completion. Analyzes the proper correlation of innovation and tradition in architecture and construction, providing valuable insight into the debate on the various aspects of this problem.

825.   ——. "Osnovnye trebovaniia k sovetskoi arkhitekture na novom etape ee razvitiia" [Basic Requirements of Soviet Architecture at the New Stage of Its Development]. See **no. 122.**

Argues that these requirements must: 1) provide a comprehensive approach to solving architectural problems, including simultaneously the combination of material demands and artistic consideration with the economic demands and technological prerequisites, 2) pay particular attention to mass construction, 3) provide foremost for the industrialization of the construction processes, and 4) provide for the fidelity of artistic forms as derived on the basis of Socialist Realism to the material and idological bases of the country.

826.   ——. "O sotsialisticheskom arkhitekturnom stile" [On the Socialist Architectural Style]. *Voprosv teorii arkhitektury*, v. 6, 1960: 9-25.

A speech in July 1959 by the then Director of the Institute of the Theory and History of Architecture and Building Technology under the Academy of Construction and Architecture of the USSR. Develops socio-historical criteria for the Soviet architectural style. Views style as an ideological phenomenon expressing in material and aesthetic form the great diverse nature of Soviet architecture. The prerequisites for a socialist architectural style are: 1) that it satisfy the demands of the entire population, not just of a minority, 2) that architectural affairs be affiliated with the society-at-large and the government, rather than with limited interests, 3) that a materio-technical base be developed and perfected for architecture, and 4) that it employ the progressiveness of socialist ideology, based upon the tenets of Marxism-Leninism. See also p. 172-178 of the same journal for a summation of his views.

827.   Kazarinova, V. "Tektonika zdaniia" [Tectonics of a Building]. *Arkhitektura SSSR*, no. 11, 1954: 36-42.

Observes that tectonic systems are qualitatively distinguished from constructive systems. Asserts on the one hand that the constructive basis should be reflected not independently but as part of the artistic image, while on the other, that the negation and ignorance of tectonic methods has led to the decorative excesses and eclecticism in Soviet architecture. One of the first attempts in this period to reformulate constructive considerations as an integral aspect of the Soviet architectural aesthetic; a precursor of the new "materialist" aesthetic, posited in 1955-56.

828.   Khan-Magomedov, Selim O. "Novatorstvo i konservatizm v tvorchestve arkhitektora" [Innovation and Conservatism in the Practice of the Architect]. *Voprosy sovremennoi arkhitektury*, no. 1, 1962: 31-48.

A theoretical work that posits criteria for defining innovation in architectural design, postulates and analyzes the theoretical continuity in the development of Soviet architecture, attempts to distinguish between conservatism, restorationism, and eclecticism in architecture, and proposes a basis for evaluating the assimilation of the heritage in Soviet architecture. An illuminating study of the problems, supplemented by documented references to major Soviet theoretical works. Highly recommended.

829.   ——. "O sotsialno-eticheskikh problemakh arkhitektury" [Concerning the Socio-Ethical Problems of Architecture]. *Voprosy teorii arkhitektury*, v. 5, 1960: 88-93.

Argues that, in the current struggle for a new creative direction in Soviet architecture, insufficient attention is paid to the ideological and social—or the socio-ethical—significance of architecture, bound closely to the element of style. Observes that architecture is, by its very nature, a social phenomenon and that all its aspects are therefore bound closely to the social conditions characteristic of the particular society in which it is created.

830. ——. "Stil' i khudozhestvennye problemy arkhitektury" [Style and Artistic Problems of Architecture]. *Voprosy teorii arkhitektury*, v. 6, 1960: 44-64.

A comprehensive theoretical study that develops the relationship between style and the artistic problems of architecture. Views style as an ideological, aesthetic, and artistic phenomenon in which the socio-economic conditions of society, the progress of building technology, and the ideology and aesthetic ideals of the society become objective prerequisites for its development. Also develops an affirmative appraisal of modern Soviet architecture in the twenties, viewing that period as having provided a dynamic basis for a progressive socialist style. The stylistic period, 1933-54, is characterized as lacking an organic unity between social essence and the image-bearing expressiveness of a building, with the use of antiquated systems of composition and design—all a regressive step as compared to the preceding period. Views the present period as taking up where the experiments of the twenties ended. A highly recommended source.

831. ——. "Znachenie narodnogo zodchestva dlia massogo stroitel'stva i tipovogo proektirovaniia" [Significance of National Architecture for Mass Construction and Standardized Design]. *Voprosy teorii arkhitektury*, v. 4, 1958: 183-208.

Argues that, with a proper rational attitude by Soviet architects toward traditions of national architecture, this heritage can become a significant tool for solving the pressing problems of mass construction. Argues further that a thorough understanding of architecture and a profound study of its heritage serve as an essential basis for architectural practice and scholarship.

832. Matsa, Ivan L. "O prirode i spetsifike arkhitektury" [Concerning the Nature and Specific Character of Architecture]. *Voprosy teorii arkhitektury* v. 2, 1957: 10-20.

A highly theoretical statement that argues for a division of the customary understanding of architecture into two independent phenomena: 1) architecture as art and 2) simple construction.

The art of architecture, while it takes into account both economics and technology, is distinguished fundamentally from
simple construction by its concentrated emphasis on the development of an integral, systematic artistic image. This argument was
attacked for seeming to negate the architectural importance of
mass prefabricated construction, as compelled by recent official
decrees and pronouncements.

833.   Minervin, Georgi. "Khudozhestvennye problemy massovogo stroitel'-
        stva" [Artistic Problems of Mass Construction]. *Voprosy teorii
        arkhitektury,* v. 4, 1958: 155-182.
            Argues for the interdependence between the public designa-
        tions and social processes that a building is called upon to serve
        and the artistic quality of its design. Provides a comprehensive
        analysis of the problem of the artistic image in the architecture
        of mass construction. A useful source.

834.   Nikolaev, I. "Voprosy ekonomiki i estetiki v sovetskoi arkhitekture"
        [Questions of Economics and Aesthetics in Soviet Architecture].
        Arkhitektura SSSR, no. 11, 1954: 32-35.
            An initial attempt to postulate theoretical foundations for the
        decree set forth by the 19th Party Congress concerning the
        increased use of prefabrication and precast concrete elements.

835.   Rudnev, Lev V. "Arkhitektura dolzhna sluzhit' narodu" [Architec-
        ture Must Serve the People]. *Arkhitektura SSSR,* no. 11, 1955:
        33-34.
            Superficial polemic by a prominent architect supporting the
        campaign to condemn past excessive ornamentation in design and
        construction, especially through the use of the classical idiom.

836.   ——. "O formalizme i klassike" [On Formalism and Classicism].
        Arkhitektura SSSR, no. 11, 1954: 30-32.
            Condemns excessive architectural ornamentation. Suggests the
        reasons for the development of this gravitation toward unprinci-
        pled ornamentation and condemns the classical Zholtovsky school,
        though is careful to avoid negating the personal efforts of the
        architect himself.

837.   Stupin, V. "Arkhitekturnoi teorii nuzhen pravil'nyi metod" [Archi-
        tectural Theory Requires a Correct Method]. *Arkhitektura SSSR,*
        no. 11, 1955: 51-54.

Largely a rebuttal to the article by K. Ivanov, "O materialisticheskom . . ." (no. 823). Illustrates the lack of clarity apparent
in several of the sections in Ivanov's essay, though offers little in
the way of alternate postulations. Valuable for illuminating the
context of the theoretical polemic being waged at this time.

838.   Tasalov, V. "Diskussiia v Akademii arkhitektury SSSR po voprosu
        prirody i spetsifiki arkhitektury" [Discussion at the Academy of
        Architecture of the USSR on the Nature and Specifics of Archi-
        tecture]. *Arkhitektura SSSR*, no. 6, 1955: 41-44.
            An account of the keynote speeches delivered by Ivan Matsa
        and K. Ivanov and the responses and rebuttals from those present.
        Matsa argued that simple construction ought to be distinguished
        from the more complex tectonic essence of architecture. The
        majority of those present, however, supported Ivanov's thesis that
        architecture represented an organic fusion of material culture
        (technology) and art and was an activity whose purpose was to
        create buildings and complexes to house the working, living, and
        cultural processes of the Soviet citizenry. Provides an excellent
        summary of the change in emphasis implicit in the post-1955
        reorientation of Soviet architecture.

839.   ——. "Za pravil'noe ponimanie arkhitektury" [For a Correct Under-
        standing of Architecture]. *Arkhitektura SSSR*, no. 3, 1955: 2-4.
            Suggests that, on the basis of dialectic materialism, the true
        nature of architecture may be perceived as a specific phenomenon
        which both satisfies the material demands of society and achieves
        a high degree of realistic art. Asserts that, while the ideological
        and artistic substance of the architectural image remains deter-
        mined by the criteria of realism, it must also reflect the
        utilitarian and constructive aspects of the problem.

840.   Volodin, P. A. "Stil' v sovetskoi arkhitekture" [Style in Soviet
        Architecture]. *Voprosy teorii arkhitektury*, v. 6, 1960: 26-43.
            Establishes a historical periodization in the development of
        socialist architecture in the Soviet Union. Views style in archi-
        tecture not as a purely ideological and aesthetic phenomenon but
        as a more complicated synthesis of basic material and ideological-
        aesthetic specifics. Especially useful for its stylistic assessment of
        the various periods in the development of Soviet architecture.
        See his summation, p. 165-171.

841.   "Za podlinnoe novatorstvo v arkhitekturnom tvorchestve" [For
       Authentic Innovation in Architectural Creativity]. *Arkhitektura
       SSSR*, no. 10, 1955: 2-4.

       An editorial viewing mass construction through industrialized
       methods as the progressive new development in Soviet architec-
       ture. Argues that this development can be exploited to the fullest
       only through the continuing innovation in design and construction
       and the simultaneous rejection of the accepted archaic canons of
       architectural design. Urges that an intensive campaign be launched
       within the entire architectural community for the optimum
       realization of this goal.

VII. Works by and about Soviet Architects

A. GENERAL ACCOUNTS

1. Monographs by Soviet Writers

842. Academy of Architecture of the Ukrainian SSR. Institute of the History and Theory of Architecture. *Mastera sovetskoi arkhitektury ob arkhitekture* [Masters of Soviet Architecture on Architecture]. Kiev, Gosstroiizdat UkSSR, 1953. 176 p. illus.

A collection of articles and pronouncements by leading Soviet architects on questions of architecture. V. A. Vesnin writes about the stages in the first thirty years of Soviet architecture; G. P. Gol'ts relates his personal experience and discusses the role of ideology in architecture. The articles by I. V. Zholtovsky, which form the major part of the book, thereby reflecting the favor with which the architect was regarded during this period, are oriented toward discussing his own principles of architectural practice and the problems of classicism. The articles by I. A. Fomin assess the problems of the classical heritage and innovation in Soviet architecture and outline the architect's proposal for a new classical style. The articles by A. V. Shchusev articulate the architect's thoughts on the role national forms play in the development of Soviet architecture, citing his own work which implemented the Russian national architectural heritage.

843. Bartenev, I. A. *Zodchie i stroiteli Leningrada* [Architects and Builders of Leningrad]. Leningrad, Lenizdat, 1963. 308 p. illus.

An account of the leading architects and their work in the city from its founding in 1703 to the early 1960s. Of value for information on architects in the Soviet period.

844. Kornfel'd, Ia. A. *Laureaty stalinskikh premii v arkhitekture, 1941-1950* [Laureates of the Stalin Awards in Architecture, 1941-1950]. Moscow, Gosstroiizdat, 1953. 235 p. illus.

A record of the recipients of the prize, including biographical data and a description of the projects that earned this recognition. Profusely illustrated. An excellent source for documenting sanctioned projects.

845.   *Raboty arkhitekturno-planirovochnykh masterskikh za 1934 g.* [Work
of the Architectural and Planning Ateliers in 1934]. Moscow,
Gosstroiizdat, 1936. 112 p. illus.

A review of the newly reorganized studios under the supervision
of the Moscow Soviet. Includes the work completed in 1934 and
part of 1935 by the studios of I. V. Zholtovsky, A. V. Shchusev,
and I. A. Fomin. The architectural work is conveyed almost
exclusively through elevations and perspectives, with few sections
and interior views.

2. Monographs by Non-Soviet Writers

846.   Institute for the Study of the USSR. *Biographic Directory of the
U.S.S.R.* See **no. 111.**

Provides brief biographical data on prominent Soviet personalities and functionaries. Architects include P. V. Abrosimov (p. 5),
K. S. Alabian (p. 12), G. B. Barkhin (p. 62), Ia. B. Belopolsky
(p. 72), A. B. Boretski (p. 93-94), D. N. Chechulin (p. 113-114),
S. I. Chernyshev (p. 117), A. N. Dushkin (p. 148), A. I. Gegello
(p. 172), V. G. Gelfreikh (p. 173), B. M. Iofan (p. 222), A.
F. Khriakov (p. 273), A. G. Kurdiany (p. 331), B. S. Mezentsev
(p. 401), M. A. Minkus (p. 410), A. A. Mndoiants (p. 414) ,
A. G. Mordvinov (p. 417-418), L. M. Poliakov (p. 503-504),
M. V. Posokhin (p. 509-510), I. E. Rozhin (p. 540), E. V.Rybitsky
(p. 547), N. P. Severov (p. 571), M. A. Useinov (p. 689), S. V.
Vasilkovsky (p. 698), A. A. Vesnin (p. 706), A. V. Vlasov (p. 713),
A. P. Voinov (p. 715), V. I. Zabolotny, G. A. Zakharov (p. 746),
and I. V. Zholtovsky (p. 764). Most useful for identifying official
positions held and party affiliation. Lists major works, but
erratically.

3. Articles by Soviet Writers

847.   Georgievsky, M. "Vsesoiuznyi smotr tvorchestva molodykh masterov
arkhitektury" [All-Union Review of the Work of the Young
Masters of Architecture]. *Arkhitektura SSSR*, no. 16, 1947: 8-13.

A review of the work of young Soviet architects, especially
interesting for the revealing framework within which the criticisms
and evaluations are made, reflecting current attempts to eliminate
any reappearing traces of modernism in Soviet architecture.

848.   "God raboty proektnykh i planirovochnykh masterskikh Mossoveta"
[One Year of Work in the Design and Planning Studios of the
Moscow Soviet]. *Arkhitektura SSSR*, no. 9, 1934: 8-17.

A review of the first year's work by the studios organized within the Moscow Soviet on the initiative of L. M. Kaganovich for the purpose of implementing the reorganization of the architectural profession. Includes reports by N. Ia. Kolli, K. S. Mel'nikov, A. V. Shchusev, N. A. Ladovsky, M. I. Siniavsky, and M. Ia. Ginzburg on the work of the studios which they head.

849. Khiger, R. Ia. "Mastera molodoi arkhitektury" [Masters of the Young Architecture]. *Arkhitektura SSSR*, no. 9, 1934: 33-38.
      Assesses the careers of the young architects A. Vlasov, I. Leonidov, M. Barshch, and M. Siniavsky. Provides a good insight into the transitional aspect inherent in the early thirties, especially in the discussion of the former controversial constructivist Leonidov.

850. Levina, E. "Zodchie Leningrada v dni blokady (dnevniki i pis'ma)" [Leningrad Architects during the Days of the Blockade (Diaries and Letters)]. *Sovetskaia arkhitektura*, no. 18, 1969: 125-132.
      Revealing accounts of the activity of the Leningrad architectural community and the manner in which they endured the trials and tribulations of the blockade.

851. Loktev, V. "Nestareiushchee nasledie" [An Ageless Heritage]. *Arkhitektura SSSR*, no. 10, 1970: 11-12.
      Focuses upon the creative genius underlying all noteworthy architectural achievement by way of extracting quotes on the subject by leading Soviet architects. These architects are L. V. Rudnev, I. A. Fomin, I. V. Zholtovsky, A. V. Shchusev, I. A. Golosov, M. Ia. Ginzburg, N. A. Ladovsky, Georgi P. Gol'ts, A. K. Burov, and A. S. Nikol'sky.

852. Perlin, V. M. "Mastera sovetskoi promyshlennoi arkhitektury" [Masters of Soviet Industrial Architecture]. *Arkhitektura SSSR*, no. 7, 1967: 44-52.
      Reviews the careers of Aleksandr V. Kuznetsov, Vladimir Ia. Movchan, Vladimir A. Myslin, Ivan S. Nikolaev, Georgi M. Orlov, Evgeni M. Popov, and Anatoli S. Fisenko.

853. Sokolov, N. "Mastera sovetskoi arkhitektury" [Masters of Soviet Architecture]. *Arkhitektura SSSR*, nos. 17-18, 1947: 79-96.

A review of the work of the leading Soviet architects in commemoration of the thirtieth anniversary of the Bolshevik Revolution of 1917. The nature of the particular evaluations of individual architects provides a valuable insight into the current official assessment of their role and place in the history of Soviet architecture.

B. WORKS BY AND ABOUT INDIVIDUAL ARCHITECTS

1. Pavel V. Abrosimov

854. "Pavel Vasil'evich Abrosimov." *Arkhitektura SSSR*, no. 4, 1961: 59-60.
      A biographical obituary highlighting the architect's career.

2. Karo S. Alabian

855. "Arkhitektory—izbranniki naroda" [Architects—the Choice of the People] . *Arkhitektura i stroitel'stvo*, no. 2, 1946: 3.
      A brief biographical sketch on the occasion of Alabian's having been selected as deputy to the Soviet of Nationalities of the Supreme Soviet of the USSR from the Mikoian region in Armenia.

856. "Arkhitektory—kandidaty v Verkhovnyi sovet SSSR" [Architects— Candidates to the Supreme Soviet of the USSR] . *Arkhitektura SSSR*, no. 11, 1937: 10.
      A condensed but useful biography of the architect, nominated from Erevan, Armenia, as a deputy to the Soviet of Nationalities of the Supreme Soviet of the USSR.

857. Kolli, N. Ia. "Karo Semenovich Alabian." *Arkhitektura SSSR* No. 2, 1959: 63-64.
      An obituary, one of the more descriptive of the available biographies of the architect's career and work.

858. "Pamiati K. A. Alabiana" [To the Memory of K. S. Alabian] . *Arkhitektura SSSR*, no. 12, 1967: 24-25.
      A biography of late architect on the occasion of his seventieth birthday. More in the nature of recollections by colleagues and associates, but contains useful data.

859. Savitsky, Iu. "Karo Alabian." *Sovetskaia arkhitektura*, no. 18, 1969: 92-94.

A highly deferential account of the architect's administrative acumen. Provides great, but subtle, insight into his unquestioned authority and *modus operandi* in administering and supervising the Soviet architectural community through a variety of official positions.

3. Pavel F. Aleshin

860. Iasevich, V. "Pavel Aleshin." *Sovetskaia arkhitektura,* no. 18, 1969: 85-87.

A succinct, informative summary of the architect's career and principal work in the Ukrainian SSR. Only one plate.

4. Grigori B. Barkhin

861. Barkhin, Grigori B. "Tvorcheskie otchety" [Creative Accounts]. *Arkhitektura SSSR*, no. 7, 1935: 39-43.

An autobiographical account of the architect's career. Views his career as emerging in parallel with the development of constructivism in Soviet architecture from 1923 to 1933, and thus provides an excellent synopsis of the major influences affecting the rise of constructivism. Sees the competition for the Palace of Labor, the 1923 Agricultural Exhibit in Moscow, and the 1924 exhibit of Revolutionary German Artists, including the architects Gropius, Meyer, Mendlesohn, Mies van der Rohe, and others, as greatly affecting the evolution of constructivism in Soviet architecture. Barkhin enumerates his work for the period covered and gives his views on the recent proclamation for the reorganization of the Soviet architectural community. A number of excellent plates. An important source.

862. ——. "Osnovnye zadachi nashei masterskoi" [Basic Tasks of Our Studio]. *Stroitel'stvo Moskvy,* no. 9, 1933: 10.

Views the principal task of the studio placed under his supervision to be that of designing large architectural complexes, rebuilding major streets and thoroughfares, and planning green areas. Outlines the approach to be employed.

863. Barkhin, M. G. "G. B. Barkhin, 1800-1969." *Architectural Design,* no. 2, 1970: 88-90.

An authoritative account of the architect's career and principal work by his son, also an architect, who collaborated with his father during the twenties. Contains much useful information.

864.　Kokorin, V. "Zodchii, Pedagog, uchenyi" [Architect, Teacher, Scholar]. *Arkhitektura SSSR*, no. 8, 1955. 47.
　　　　A biographical sketch on the occasion of the architect's seventy-fifth birthday. Although brief, contains useful information, especially relating to the more recent years of his career.

865.　"Pamiati G. B. Barkhina" [To the Memory of G. B. Barkhin]. *Arkhitektura SSSR*, no. 7, 1969: 63.
　　　　An obituary with a capsule biography.

866.　"Zodchii—pedagog—obshchestvennyi deiatel'" [Architect, Teacher, and Public Figure]. *Arkhitektura SSSR*, no. 7, 1960: 55-57.
　　　　A biographical account of the architect on the occasion of his eightieth birthday. Condensed, but very useful; contains much important information and includes useful plates.

5. Mikhail Barshch

867.　Khazanova, V. E. "M. Barshch." *Architectural Design,* no. 2, 1970: 95-96.
　　　　A concise review of the architect's career, with an emphasis on his earlier work during the modernist period in the twenties. Includes a number of important plates. Contains much useful information.

868.　Khiger, R. "Mastera molodoi arkhitektury" [Masters of the Young Architecture]. See **no. 849.** p. 37-38.
　　　　An authoritative characterization of Barshch's work in the constructivist idiom and the subsequent transition into the classical idiom prescribed through official pronouncements. A highly useful source.

6. Andrei E. Belogrud

869.　"A. E. Belogrud." *Stroitel'stvo Moskvy,* no. 8, 1933: 36.
　　　　A brief obituary synopsis of the architect's career.

870. M., S. "A. E. Belogrud." *Arkhitektura SSSR*, no. 3, 1933: 63.
Obituary and brief résumé of his career.

871. Stepanov, V. V. "Arkhitektor A. E. Belogrud" [Architect A. E.
Belogrud]. *Arkhitektura Leningrada*, no. 5, 1938: 33-41.
A comprehensive study of the career and work of an architect
who was among the pioneers of apartment house design in prerevolutionary Russian architecture, and who continued his practice
into the Soviet period until his death in 1933. Interesting for
illuminating yet another aspect of the transition from the architecture of prerevolutionary Russia to the Soviet period.

7. Iakob B. Belopol'sky

872. Morev, N. "Iakob Belopol'sky." *Sovetskaia arkhitektura*, no. 18,
1969: 115-122.
A survey of the architect's career and principal work. Focuses
upon his rise as a leading Soviet architect in the late fifties. Good
illustrations.

8. Leonti N. Benois

873. Munts, O. P. "Arkhitektor, Khudozhnik, stroitel'i pedagog" [Archi-
tect, Artist, Builder, and Teacher]. *Arkhitektura Leningrada*,
no. 3, 1938: 60-70.
A comprehensive study of an architect who, prior to the
Revolution, was a leader in the Mir Iskusstva (World of Art) and
in the Society of Architects-Artists, as well as professor of architecture at the Academy of Fine Arts. Illuminates the transition of
the Leningrad architectural community from the prerevolutionary
to the Soviet period. Contains much useful material and is the
only known published source on Benois.

9. Boris N. Blokhin

874. Belousov, V. "Stroitel', pedagog, uchenyi" [Builder, Pedagogue,
Scholar]. *Arkhitektura SSSR*, no. 6, 1966: 58-59.
A summary of the architect's career and principal work.

10. Dmitri I. Burdin

875. Pekareva, N. "Dmitri Burdin." *Sovetskaia arkhitektura*, no. 18,
1969: 107-114.

A survey of the architect's career and principal work, focusing upon his emergence as a prominent Soviet architect in the postwar period.

11. Andrei K. Burov

a. Monographs

876.   Burov, Andrei K. *Ob arkhitekture* [About Architecture]. See no. 204.
       Provides a brilliant exposition of the architect's highly personal philosophy of architecture. Includes an assessment of his own work and an interpretation of the various periods and problems in the evolution of Soviet architecture. Highly recommended.

b. Articles

877.   Blashkevich, R., K. Zhukov, and O. Rzhekhina. "Tvorchestvo Andreia Konstantinovicha Burova" [Creativity of Andrei Konstantinovich Burov]. *Arkhitektura SSSR*, no. 7, 1958: 13-18.
       An account of the architect's career and principal work, dealing almost exclusively with the postmodernist period. A number of good plates. A useful source.

878.   Burov, Andrei K. "Na putiakh k novoi russkoi arkhitektury" [On the Way to a New Russian Architecture]. See no. 458.
       A scathing denunciation of recent efforts to revive the classical idiom. Argues for a profound renewal of Soviet architecture on the basis of recent Western technological achievements and the recent Constructivist experience.

878a. ——. "Obraz i masshtab. Material i forma" [Image and Scale. Material and Form]. *Arkhitektura SSSR*, no. 12, 1946: 28-36.
       Deals with the new aspects in the problems of image and scale posed by the use of new industrial materials and methods of construction.

879.   ——. "Pravda materiala" [Truth of the Material]. See no. 804.
       Calls for the truthful use of contemporary building materials and condemns superficial efforts to assimilate the classical heritage.

880.　——. "Problemy fasada zhilogo doma" [Problems of the Façade in an Apartment House]. *Arkhitektura SSSR*, no. 5, 1938: 32-34.

An analysis of his apartment house on the Leningrad Prospect in Moscow and the problem of façade design in precast panel construction.

881.　——. "Vtoraia proizvodnaia zolotogo secheniia" [A Second Derivative of the Golden Section]. *Arkhitektura SSSR*, no. 3, 1935: 57.

Explains a second derivative of the Golden Section—the ratio of 528:472—uncovered by the architect, which the architect Zholtovsky called the "function of the Golden Section."

882.　Khazanova, V. E. "A. Burov, 1900-1957." *Architectural Design*, no. 2, 1970: 101-104.

A comprehensive survey of the architect's career, with an analysis of his philosophy and assessment of his principal works, with emphasis on the modernist movement in the twenties. Contains numerous useful plates, though at a small scale, and much useful information here published for the first time.

883.　Zhukov, K. "Andrei Burov." *Sovetskaia arkhitektura*, no. 18, 1969: 95-98.

An impressionistic reflection upon the architect's career and principal concerns in his approach to architectural practice. A useful source.

12.　Iakob G. Chernikhov

a. Monographs

884.　Chernikhov, Iakob G. *Arkhitekturnye fantazii* [Architectural Fantasies]. See no. 205.

Outlines technical and compositional methods for designing architectural fantasies. Richly illustrated with color plates.

885.　——. *Konstruktsiia arkhitekturnykh i mashynnykh form* [Construction of Architectural and Machine Forms]. See no. 206.

Analyzes the design and tectonic basis of constructivism and its relationship to art. Focuses upon the techniques for developing form-rendering constructions. Richly illustrated.

886.   —. *Osnovy sovremennoi arkhitektury* [Foundations of Contempo-
        rary Architecture]. See no. 207.
            Provides a comprehensive analysis of both the tectonic basis
        and the philosophical concepts of modern architecture. Supple-
        mented with plates.

                        b. Articles by Soviet Writers

887.   Mikhailov, [A.?]. "O khlestakovshchine i burzhuaznom vreditel'stve
        na arkhitekturnom fronte" [Concerning Unrestrained Boasting
        and Lies and the Bourgeois Sabotage on the Architectural Front].
        Sovetskaia arkhitektura, nos. 5-6, 1931: 26-29.
            A vituperative attack of Chernikhov's theoretical postulations
        as developed in his two books, *Osnovy sovremennoi arkhitektury*
        (**no. 886**) and *Konstruktsiia arkhitekturnykh i mashinnykh form*
        (**no. 885**). Condemns the constructivist roots of the modern
        architectural theory promulgated by Chernikhov and calls for the
        complete negation of their harmful influence upon Soviet archi-
        tecture.

                      c. Articles by Non-Soviet Writers

888.   Sprague, Arthur R. "Chernikov [*sic*] and Constructivism." *Survey*,
        no. 39, 1961: 69-77.
            A review of Chernikhov's published works. Speculates about his
        place in the general constructivist ambiance.

                            13. Ivan A. Fomin

                              a. Monographs

889.   Dzhandieri, M. *I. Fomin*. Moscow, Gosstroiizdat, 1954. 48 p. illus.
            Part of the Masters of Soviet Architecture series. A general
        account of the architect's career and major work in the pre-
        revolutionary and especially in the Soviet period. A few plates.

890.   Il'in, M. A. *Ivan Aleksandrovich Fomin*. Moscow, Izd-vo Akademii
        arkhitektury SSSR, 1946. 51 p. illus.
            A concise analytical assessment of Fomin's prerevolutionary
        and Soviet career, with a survey of his major work, an analysis of
        his formula for the new classicism, and an evaluation of his role in
        the development of Soviet architecture. Includes a list of the
        architect's projects and buildings.

891. Minkus, M. M., and N. Pekareva. *I. A. Fomin*. Moscow, Gosstroiizdat, 1953. 310 p. illus.

    Analytical and historical narrative divided into the prerevolutionary and postrevolutionary practice. A general assessment of the architect's career and contributions to the development of Soviet architecture. Includes a list of architectural projects, graphic work, and bibliography of published material by and about the architect. Contains excellent plates of the architect's work.

b. Articles

892. Alekseev, B. I. "Monograficheskaia vystavka akademika arkhitektury I. A. Fomina" [Monographic Exhibit of I. A. Fomin, Academician of Architecture]. *Akademiia arkhitektury*, no. 4, 1936: 69-76.

    A review of the exhibit of Fomin's work, organized by the Academy of Architecture during the first part of 1936, and an analytical study of his architectural career. A useful study with a number of good plates.

893. Aranovich, D. "V masterskoi arkhitektora: tvorchestvo I. A. Fomina" [In the Architect's Studio: The Practice of I. A. Fomin]. *Arkhitektura SSSR*, no. 9, 1934: 28-32.

    A reflective account of the architect's practice and experience. Contains useful information on his background and highlights in his career.

894. Ern, I. V. "Iz arkhitekturnogo nasledstva I. A. Fomina" [From the Architectural Legacy of I. A. Fomin]. *Arkhitekturnoe nasledstvo*, no. 12, 1960: 208-209.

    A description of Fomin's project, with illustrations, for the Borodinsky Bridge in Moscow in 1911.

895. Fomin, Ivan A. "Iz moego tvorcheskogo opyta" [From My Creative Experience]. *Arkhitektura SSSR*, no. 5, 1933: 32-33.

    Cites prominent influences in the architect's career. Reviews his work, general approach to design, and difficulties encountered in a practicing studio. Important for revealing the manner of influence exerted by constructivism on Fomin's work and for providing a personal critique of his major projects.

896. ——. "Printsipy tvorcheskoi raboty arkhitekturnoi masterskoi no. 3" [Principles of the Practice of Studio No. 3]. *Akademiia arkhitektury*, nos. 1-2, 1934: 83-91.

An analysis of the conditions which have dictated the reorganization of the architectural profession and which now require critical assimilation of the architectural heritage. Cites the accomplishments of modern Soviet architecture worthy of incorporation in succeeding work and outlines Fomin's dynamic proposal for a new classicism to serve as a basis for the new style of Soviet architecture. An important document which makes clear the architect's philosophy and method of design. Amply illustrated.

897.   Gegello, A. "Iz vospominanii ob I. A. Fomine" [From the Recollections of I. A. Fomin]. *Arkhitektura SSSR*, no. 11, 1962: 61-62.
A brief review of the highlights of Fomin's career by an architect who worked first for, and then with, Fomin during the period of his practice in Leningrad.

898.   Grabar', Igor' E. "Ivan Aleksandrovich Fomin." *Arkhitektura SSSR*, no. 8, 1936: 52-53.
Personal reflections on the architect's career on the occasion of his death.

899.   "I. A. Fomin." *Akademiia arkhitektury*, no. 4, 1936: 68.
An obituary and concise résumé of Fomin's career. A useful reference.

900.   Il'in, Lev A. "Tvorcheskii put' I. A. Fomina" [Creative Journey of I. A. Fomin]. *Arkhitektura Leningrada*, no. 3, 1937: 36-48.
An analytical and interpretive study of Fomin's career from the prerevolutionary period to the Soviet period. Contains much useful information illuminating the roots of Fomin's philosophy and development as an architect and assessing his work, method of design, and role in the development of Soviet architecture. Contains good plates. Highly recommended.

901.   "Ivan Aleksandrovich Fomin." *Arkhitektura Leningrada*, no. 2, 1936: 43.
An obituary and succinct biographical sketch of the architect's career.

902.   Kornfel'd, Ia. "Ivan Aleksandrovich Fomin." *Arkhitektura SSSR*, no. 7, 1936: 77-80.
A review of the architect's career, principal work, and philosophy.

903. Munts, V. "Vydaiushchiisia zodchii" [An Outstanding Architect].
Arkhitektura SSSR, no. 11, 1962: 59-60.
A synopsis of the architect's career on the occasion of the
90th year from his birth.

904. Rudnev, Lev V. "Pamiati uchitelia i druga (k smerti I. A. Fomina)"
[To the Memory of a Teacher and a Friend (On the Death of I. A.
Fomin)]. *Arkhitektura SSSR*, no. 8, 1936: 59-60.
Personal reflections, focusing upon that phase of Fomin's
career in Leningrad with which Rudnev was associated. Provides
some useful insights.

905. Sokolov, N. "Mastera sovetskoi arkhitektury" [Masters of Soviet
Architecture]. See **no. 853**. p. 76, 83.
Includes an assessment of Fomin's role in the development of
Soviet architecture. Provides little in the way of substantive
material or analysis but useful for indicating current official
assessment of Fomin's career.

906. Strigalev, A. "Tema monumental'noi propagandy v tvorchestve I. A.
Fomina" [Theme of Monumental Propaganda in the Work of I.
A. Fomin]. *Arkhitektura SSSR*, no. 5, 1968: 37-42.
Analyzes those projects developed by Fomin specifically for
Lenin's program of Monumental Propaganda in Petrograd. Valua-
ble for illuminating an important phase of Fomin's work during
the earliest postrevolutionary years.

14. Aleksandr I. Gegello

a. Monographs

907. Gegello, Aleksandr I. *Iz tvorcheskogo opyta: vozniknovenie i razvitie
arkhitekturnogo zamysla* [From My Creative Experience; the
Origin and Development of Architectural Conception]. Leningrad,
Gosstroiizdat, 1962. 376 p. illus.
An informative autobiographical account of the architect's
career. Highly useful also for its wealth of personal impressions,
evaluations, and interpretations of developments in Soviet architecture.

b. Articles

908. "Aleksandr Ivanovich Gegello." *Arkhitektura SSSR*, no. 4, 1965: 63.
An obituary and brief review of the architect's career.

909.   Khomutetsky, N. F. "Tvorchestvo A. I. Gegello" [The Practice of
        A. I. Gegello]. *Arkhitektura Leningrada*, no. 3, 1939: 53-72.
        An analytical and interpretive study of Gegello's career. Amply
        illustrated, contains much useful information.

15. Vladimir G. Gel'freikh

910.   Korabel'nikov, A., and B. Sokolov. "Vladimir Georgievich Gel'freikh."
        Arkhitektura SSSR, no. 6, 1965: 48-53.
        A survey of the architect's career, highlighting major develop-
        ments. Contains useful plates. Helpful in illuminating the initial
        phases of his career.

911.   Pekareva, N. "Vladimir Georgievich Gel'freikh." *Arkhitektura SSSR*,
        no. 6, 1960: 51-54.
        A concise review of the architect's career, with emphasis on
        the period following the death of his associate, V. A. Shchuko,
        in 1939.

912.   "V. A. Shchuko i V. G. Gel'freikh." *Stroitel'stvo Moskvy*, nos. 5-6,
        1933: 35.
        A biographical sketch of the architects' careers, with illustra-
        tions.

16. Moisei Ia. Ginzburg

a. Monographs

913.   Ginzburg, Moisei Ia. *Arkhitektura sanatoriia NKTP v Kislovodske*
        [Architecture of the NKTP Sanatorium in Kislovodsk]. Moscow,
        Izd-vo Akademii arkhitektury SSSR, 1940. 88 p. illus.
        An introduction by N. Ia. Kolli, a textual and photographic
        description of the completed complex, and a discussion of
        Ginzburg's particular solutions to the problems in the project.

914.   ——. *Ritm v arkhitekture* [Rhythm in Architecture]. See no. 208.
        Provides an excellent insight into the architect's approach to
        design.

915.   ——. *Stil' i epokha* [Style and Epoch]. See no. 209.
        A lyrical exposition of the architect's creative manifesto.
        Essential to an understanding of his subsequent promulgation of
        constructivism and functionalism in Soviet architecture.

916.   ——. *Zhilishche. Opyt piatiletnei raboty nad problemoi zhilishcha*
         [Housing. The Experience of Five Years' Work on the Problem of
         Housing]. See **no. 210**.
             An authoritative review of housing in Soviet architecture up to
         1932, as well as a record of Ginzburg's 5 years' work on this
         problem. Many good illustrations, many of which are of the
         architect's own work and taken from the periodical *S.A.* Highly
         recommended.

b. Articles

917.   Administration of the Union of Soviet Architects. "Pamiati M. Ia.
         Ginzburga" [In Memory of M. Ia. Ginzburg]. *Arkhitektura SSSR*,
         No. 12, 1946: 53.
             An obituary and concise biographical account of the major
         developments in the architect's career. Significant for its objective
         treatment of the architect's involvement and position of leadership
         in the constructivist movement. A valuable synopsis.

918.   Ginzburg, Moisei Ia. "Arkhitekturnye vozmozhnosti sovremennoi
         industrii" [Architectural Possibilities of Contemporary Industry].
         See **no. 598**.
             Calls for utilizing the latest technological achievements in
         construction and design of mass housing, as well as for the greater
         industrialization of the building processes.

919.   ——. "Estetika sovremennosti" [Contemporary Aesthetics]. *Arkhitek-*
         tura, nos. 1-2, 1923: 3-6.
             An editorial which argues that, although prerevolutionary
         Russian architecture could presumably still afford superficial
         experimentation with idioms of classicism and the Renaissance,
         the years following the Revolution have made clear the need to
         shirk such an empty approach and to develop an architectural
         idiom that exploits to maximum advantage both the means and
         the needs of present times. An important document that reveals
         the first formulations of Ginzburg's personal philosophy.

920.   ——. "Funktsional'nyi metod i forma" [Functional Method and
         Form]. See **no. 599**.
             Develops the philosophy of functionalism and provides great
         insights into the architect's personal convictions and views. For
         other articles by the architect that provide similar insight, *see*

especially "Konstruktivizm kak metod laboratornoi i pedagogicheskoi raboty" **(no. 601)**, "Konstruktivizm v arkhitekture"
(no. 602),"Novye metody arkhitekturnogo myshleniia" **(no. 605)**,
and "Tselevaia ustanovka v sovremennoi arkhitekture" **(no. 606)**.

921.   ——. "Nad chem rabotaiut arkhitektory. Akad. arkh. M. Ia. Ginz-
          burg"[Current Projects of Architects. Academician of Architecture
          M. Ia. Ginzburg. *Arkhitektura SSSR*, no. 2, 1940: 73.
          A brief review by the architect of his current projects, includ-
          ing planning for the southern shores of the Crimea.

922.   ——. "Osvobozhdennoe tvorchestvo" [Liberated Creativity]. *Arkhi-
          tektura SSSR*, no. 9, 1934: 15-16.
          A review of the work of one of the new studios under the
          Moscow Soviet of which the architect is in charge. Valuable for
          articulating the architect's philosophy and making clear that his
          associates in this studio are former members of the OSA who
          have long been proponents of the constructivist philosophy.

923.   ——. "Put' sovetskogo arkhitektora" [Path of a Soviet Architect].
          Arkhitektura SSSR, no. 10, 1937: 71-72.
          Reflects on the circumstances surrounding the evolution of
          Soviet architecture, the principles that motivated his work during
          those years, and the requirements set forth in applying socialist
          realism in Soviet architecture.

924.   ——. "Staroe i novoe" [The Old and the New]. *Arkhitektura*, nos. 3-
          5, 1923: 3.
          An editorial lamenting the endless division of the artistic
          community into various "isms," which may be divided essentially
          into two categories: 1) those who prize the cultural heritage of
          the past but who are unable to escape its pervasive influence, and
          2) those who are bent on negating the heritage. Views both
          extremes as wrong. An important document that reveals the first
          formulations of Ginzburg's personal philosophy.

925.   ——. "Tvorcheskie ochety. M. Ia. Ginzburg" [Creative Accounts. M.
          Ia. Ginzburg]. *Arkhitektura SSSR*, no. 5, 1935: 8-12.
          An autobiographical assessment of the major influences and
          stages in the development of the architect's career, with an analysis
          of his work. Includes plates. An important document.

926.   ——. "Voprosy tektoniki i sovremennaia arkhitektura" [Questions of Tectonics and Contemporary Architecture]. See **no. 220**.
       The last theoretical statement by Ginzburg before his death.

927.   ——. "Za arkhitekturnyi ansambl' zavodskogo raiona" [For an Architectural Ensemble in a Factory Region]. *Stroitel'stvo Moskvy*, no. 9, 1933: 10.
       Views "horizontal" planning as an ineffectual substitute for the complex considerations that make up architectural planning and design. Cites regional planning as his future concern.

928.   ——. Viktor A. and Aleksandr A. Vesnin. "Tvorcheskaia tribuna: problemy sovremennoi arkhitektury" [Creative Tribune: Problems of Contemporary Architecture]. See **no. 420**.
       A call for prudence in the new trend toward the classical heritage. Reassert the essence of their earlier platforms, though divested of constructivist rhetoric.

929.   Khan-Magomedov, Selim O. "M. Ia. Ginzburg." *Arkhitektura SSSR*, no. 10, 1962: 38-46.
       An analytical and interpretive study of the architect's career. Describes the subsequent course of the architect's career from the eclipse of modernism to his death in 1946, illuminating the thrust of his philosophical method in each of his major projects throughout the latter portion of his practice. Particularly useful for illuminating the evolution of his career in study abroad and through his theoretical writings during the constructivist movement and the OSA. Highly recommended.

930.   ——. "M. Y. Ginzburg, 1892-1946." *Architectural Design*, no. 2. 1970: 92-94.
       A review of the architect's theoretical and professional activities, with much useful information, some of which appeared in the author's earlier article, in the Russian language (**no. 929**). Contains numerous plates.

931.   Khiger, R. "M. Ia. Ginzburg. Put' teoretika i mastera" [M. Ia. Ginzburg. The Way of the Theoretician and Master]. *Sovetskaia arkhitektura*, no. 15, 1963: 117-136.
       A valuable account and assessment of Ginzburg's career by an architect and writer who worked closely with him in the OSA.

Suggests influences most prominent in shaping Ginzburg's philosophy, tracing his development through both the substance of his theoretical writings and his architectural work. Also important for clarifying the circumstances in which the OSA was founded and for providing an analytical survey of the architect's published projects. An indispensable work.

932.   "M. Ia. Ginzburg." *Arkhitektura i stroitel'stvo,* no. 2, 1946: 23.
        An obituary, with a biographical synopsis of the architect's career. Brief, but significant for citing the theoretical works produced by the architect during his constructivist years and for a notable restraint of any polemical condemnations of this phase of his activity, especially at a time when reappearances of modernist currents in Soviet architecture were coming under increasingly heavy attack.

933.   Sokolov, N. "Mastera sovetskoi arkhitektury" [Masters of Soviet Architecture]. See **no. 853.** p. 84-85.·
        Includes a general assessment of Ginzburg's career; criticism and negation of Ginzburg's constructivist activities indicates the continuing disfavor in which the modernist movements were viewed officially at this time.

17. Il'ia A. and Panteleimon A. Golosov

934.   Golosov, Il'ia A. "Moi tvorcheskii put'" [My Creative Course]. *Arkhitektura SSSR,* no. 1, 1933: 23-25.
        A general statement by the architect of his philosophy and method of design, which gives evidence of yielding to the ascendancy of the new doctrine of socialist realism.

935.   ——. "Novye puti v arkhitekture" [New Directions in Architecture]. See **no. 290.**
        A lecture delivered before the Moscow Architectural Society on December 13, 1922. Discusses the reasons for the current search for new architectural forms, the value of old architectural forms for contemporary practice, and the possible diversified architectural forms for present and future styles, based on both artistic and structural necessities. Argues that, although classicism proved to be a rigid formula of forms and proportions that stifled inventiveness, some of the fundamental principles inherent in this formula are ageless and therefore applicable in an abstract manner

to contemporary design. An argument akin to the one developed by M. Ia. Ginzburg in his *Ritm v arkhitekture* (no. 208), and one which illuminates the architect's personal philosophy.

936.   ——. "O bol'shoi arkhitekturnoi forme" [Regarding the Grand Architectural Form]. *Arkhitektura SSSR*, no. 5, 1933: 34.
        Speaks of the constructivists' (himself included) earlier notions that the façade was but a function of the graphics of movement, rather than an integral compositional element. Important for revealing the architect's formal rationalization of the new trends officially prescribed for assimilating the classical heritage.

937.   ——. "Tvorcheskie otchety. I. A. Golosov" [Creative Accounts. I. A. Golosov]. *Arkhitektura SSSR*, no. 4, 1935: 49-51.
        An autobiographical account most valuable for illuminating the architect's personal motives behind, first his work in the contemporary constructivist idiom, and secondly, his move toward utilizing the classical idiom. Reaffirms the architect's high regard for the classical heritage.

938.   Golosov, Panteleimon A. "Pristupaiu k rabote s radostiu" [I Approach My Work with Delight]. *Stroitel'stvo Moskvy*, no. 9, 1933: 9.
        Placed in charge of Studio No 9, one of several new studios formed under the jurisdiction of the Moscow Soviet, Golosov welcomes this reorganization, maintaining that it is a more efficient way of working.

939.   Khiger, R. Ia. "V masterskoi arkhitektora. Arkhitektor I. A. Golosov" [In the Studio of the Architect I. A. Golosov]. *Arkhitektura SSSR*, no. 1, 1933: 22.
        A brief analysis of the architect's philosophy and method of design as viewed in the work of his constructivist period. A highly useful reference.

940.   Kyrilov, V. V. "The Golosov Brothers: Panteleimon, 1882-1945; Ilya, 1883-1945." *Architectural Design*, no. 2, 1970: 98-100.
        Two separate studies of the brothers, which analyze the methods and philosophy of each and review their principal works, concentrating on the modernist period. Contains numerous illustrations. A useful source.

941.   Levina, A. "Arkhitektor Panteleimon Golosov" [Architect Pantelei-
        mon Golosov]. *Arkhitektura SSSR*, no. 11, 1968: 52-57.
        A concise review of the architect's career and major work.
        Amply illustrated; contains much useful material.

18.   Georgi P. Gol'ts

942.   Administration of the Union of Soviet Architects. "G. P. Gol'ts."
        Arkhitektura SSSR, no. 13, 1946: 48.
        An obituary and brief capsule of the architect's career.

943.   Bykov, V. "Konstantin Mel'nikov i Georgi Gol'ts." [Konstantin
        Mel'nikov and Georgi Gol'ts]. *Sovetskaia arkhitektura*, no. 18,
        1969: 59-67.
        A review of Gol'ts's work and his approach to the classical
        heritage as a source of design. See especially p. 66-67. Good illus-
        trations.

944.   Bylinkin, N. P. "Mastera sovetskoi arkhitektury. Put' zodchego"
        [Masters of Soviet Architecture. The Path of the Architect].
        Sovetskaia arkhitektura, no. 3, 1952: 67-79.
        An interpretive account of Gol'ts' career; characterizes his
        work in the constructivist idiom as momentary deflection, still
        possessing qualities ultimately worthy of subsequent develop-
        ments in Soviet architecture. Emphasis on his work after 1932
        and the eclipse of modernism. Article contains useful information
        but reflects the strong official antipathy to modernism that
        persisted to this period.

945.   ——."Pamiati G. P. Gol'tsa" [Memories of G. P. Gol'ts]. *Arkhitektura
        SSSR*, no. 14, 1947: 5-8.
        Reflects on the highlights of the architect's career, dealing
        exclusively with the postconstructivist period. Of general interest,
        with a few useful plates.

946.   "Georgi Pavlovich Gol'ts." *Arkhitektura i stroitel'stvo*, no. 5, 1946:
        inside front cover.
        An obituary, with a synopsis of the architect's career.

947.   Gol'ts, Georgi P. "Nad chem rabotaiut arkhitektory. G. P. Gol'ts"
        [Architects' Current Work. G. P. Gol'ts]. *Arkhitektura SSSR*,
        no. 2, 1940: 73-74.
        A brief summary by the architect of his current work.

948. ——. "Tvorcheskie otchety. G. P. Gol′ts" [Creative Accounts. G. P. Gol′ts]. *Arkhitektura SSSR*, no. 5, 1935: 17-20.

An autobiographical account of the major influences and events in the architect's career, including work with Shchusev and Zholtovsky.

949. Savitsky, Iu. "Mastera sovetskoi arkhitektury. G. P. Gol′ts" [Masters of Soviet Architecture. G. P. Gol′ts]. *Arkhitektura SSSR*, no. 7, 1940: 39-50.

An analytical study of the architect's background, career, major work, and influences which shaped his professional development. Particularly useful for illuminating the earlier years of the architect's career. Amply illustrated.

19. Lev A. Il′in

950. Bunin, A. "Pamiati L′va Aleksandrovicha Il′ina" [To the Memory of Lev Aleksandrovich Il′in]. *Arkhitektura SSSR*, no. 9, 1945: 39-40.

An obituary résumé of the architect's career.

951. Il′in, Lev A. "Moi tvorcheskii put′" [My Creative Course]. *Arkhitektura Leningrada*, no. 2, 1938: 58-65.

An informative, lucid autobiographical account of the highlights of the architect's career. Although then chief architect of Leningrad, he focuses upon the prerevolutionary phase of his work.

20. Boris M. Iofan

a. Monographs

952. *Pavil′on SSSR na Mezhdunarodnoi vystavke v Parizhe. Arkhitektura i skul′ptura* [USSR Pavilion at the World's Fair in Paris. Architecture and Sculpture]. Moscow, Izd-vo Akademii arkhitektury SSSR, 1938. 56 p. illus.

Devoted to the discussion of the USSR Pavilion at the 1937 Paris World's Fair. Includes Iofan's article, "Arkhitekturnaia ideia i ee osushchestvlenie" [The Architectural Idea and Its Realization], explaining his approach to the design for the Pavilion.

b. Articles

953.   "Arkhitektor B. M. Iofan" [Architect B. M. Iofan]. *Stroitel'stvo Moskvy*, nos. 5-6, 1933: 34.
       A biographical sketch of the architect and his career.

954.   Iofan, Boris M. "Oformit' ves' raion dvortsa sovetov" [Designing the Entire Region of the Palace of Soviets]. *Stroitel'stvo Moskvy*, no. 9, 1933: 9-10.
       Seeks to develop the entire area in which the Palace of Soviets is to be situated and to incorporate the positive aspects of projects submitted to the competitions.

955.   ——. "Tvorcheskie otchety" [Creative Accounts]. *Arkhitektura SSSR*, no. 6, 1935: 22-29.
       An autobiographical account of the architect's career, especially useful for illuminating the early years.

956.   ——. "Kak ia rabotaiu nad proektom Dvortsa Sovetov" [How I Work on the Project for the Palace of Soviets]. *Arkhitektura SSSR*, no. 5, 1933: 30-32.
       A progress report by the architect on his work on the competition design for the Palace of Soviets, which was earmarked for further development by the Commission. Observes that his personal study and measurements of various architectural monuments in Italy helped him to assimilate the best principles in classical architecture and apply them to his design for the Palace of Soviets.

957.   Mel'nikov, E. "Boris Mikhailovich Iofan." *Arkhitektura SSSR*, no. 5, 1971: 39-42.
       An informative account of the architect's life and work. Illuminates his years in Rome.

958.   Sokolov, N. "Mastera sovetskoi arkhitektury" [Masters of Soviet Architecture]. See **no. 853.** p. 85.
       Includes a brief synopsis of the architect's career.

959.   Tsipirovich, D., and I. Eigel'. "B. M. Iofan." *Arkhitektura SSSR*, no. 11, 1940: 35-52.

An analytical study and assessment of Iofan's career and major projects. Profusely illustrated. An important source for material on the architect.

21. V. D. Kokorin

960. "V. D. Kokorin." *Arkhitektura SSSR*, no. 6, 1935: 34-36.
An autobiographical account of the architect's philosophy and work. Illustrated.

22. Nikolai I. Kolli

961. "Arkhitektor N. Ia. Kolli" [Architect N. Ia. Kolli]. *Arkhitektura SSSR*, no. 1, 1967: 63.
An obituary, surveying the architect's career.

962. Kolli, Nikolai Ia. "K 75-letiiu Korbuz'e (Le Korbuz'e v Moskve)" [On Le Corbusier's Seventieth Birthday (Le Corbusier in Moscow)]. *Arkhitektura SSSR*, no. 12, 1962: 36-42.
Reminiscences of Le Corbusier's work and activity in Moscow by an architect who collaborated with him on the Centrosoiuz Building. Much useful information and a useful source.

963. ——. "Mobilizatsiia sposobnost'ei" [Mobilization of Resources]. *Arkhitektura SSSR*, no. 9, 1934: 9-10.
Calls for mobilizing all of the country's architectural and building forces to the full implementation of the tasks facing Soviet architecture.

964. ——. "Sozdanie masterskikh povysit kachestvo produktsii" [Creating Studios will Elevate the Quality of Production]. *Stroitel'stvo Moskvy*, no. 9, 1933: 8.
Expresses support for the creation of the architectural studios under the jurisdiction of the Moscow Soviet. Sees the result as one of increasing the effectiveness of Soviet architects.

965. ——. "Tvorcheskie printsipy i rabota arkhitekturno-proektnoi masterskoi no. 6" [Creative Principles and Work of Architectural Design Studio No. 6]. *Akademiia arkhitektury*, nos. 1-2, 1935: 77-84.

A review by the architect of the work being done by the studio of which he is head. Suggests his general approach to design and planning. Contains useful illustrations.

966.   ——. "Tvorcheskii itog. Rabota proektnoi masterskoi no. 6 Mossoveta" [Creative Results. The Work of the Moscow Soviet's Studio No. 6]. *Arkhitektura SSSR*, no. 3, 1935: 39-46.

An account of the work performed and in progress at the studio. See **no. 965** for similar material.

23. Vladimir F. Krinsky

967.   Krinsky, Vladimir F. "Prislushivat'sia k golosu mass" [Listening to the Voice of the Masses]. *Arkhitektura SSSR*, no. 10, 1937: 73.

A brief autobiographical highlight of the architect's career. Appears to recant his modernist "transgressions," while advocating accession to the new order.

968.   ——. "Vozniknovenie i zhizn' Assotsiatsii novykh arkhitektorov (ASNOVA)" [Emergence and Life of the Association of New Architects (ASNOVA)]. See **no. 560**.

Personal recollections of the organization of the movement by one of its founding members. Provides much useful insight and information concerning the movement's formative years.

24. Nikolai A. Ladovsky

969.   Khan-Magomedov, Selim O. "N. A. Ladovsky, 1881-1941." *Architectural Design*, no. 2, 1970: 86-87.

A condensed adaptation of the author's earlier article (**no. 970**). Summarizes the architect's career. Many good illustrations, some of which are published for the first time.

970.   ——. "Nikolai Ladovsky." *Sovetskaia arkhitektura*, no. 18, 1969: 51-58.

Examines Ladovsky's career and theoretical thought and asseses his place in the development of Soviet architecture. Provides much useful information on one of the important personalities in modern Soviet architecture.

971.   Krutikov, G. "Arkhitekturnaia Nauchno-issledovatel'skaia Laboratoriia pri arkhitekturnom fakul'tete Moskovskogo Vysshego Khud.

Tekhnich. Instituta" [Architectural Scientific Research Laboratory in the Architectural Faculty of the Moscow Higher Artistic-Technical Institute]. *Stroitel'naia promyshlennost'*, no. 5, 1928: 372-375.

An outline of Ladovsky's experiments and work. Includes a description of the apparatus which he constructed to test the perceptive faculties of students and architects: the "Liglazometr" (measuring perception of linear magnitudes), the "Ploglazometr" (surfaces), "Oglazometr" (volume and mass), "Uglazometr" (incidence of normal lines), and "Prostrometr" (spatial phenomena). For another discussion of these experiments, undertaken also at VKHUTEIN, see no. 537.

972. Ladovsky, Nikolai A. "Baza tvorcheskoi raboty" [Basis for Creative Work]. *Arkhitektura SSSR*, no. 9, 1934: 13-14.

A general view of the architect's method and work, especially under the professional structure recently established by the Moscow Soviet. Identifies individuals working with the architect and the particular projects with which they are involved.

973. ——. "Osnovy postroeniia teorii arkhitektury" [Bases for the Construction of a Theory of Architecture]. See no. 561.

Outlines the theoretical assumptions and applications of Ladovsky's "rational" aesthetics and approach to architectural production. Focuses upon the development of formal criteria for the articulation and perception of architectural forms in space.

974. ——. "Pis'mo v redaktsiu" [Letter to the Editor]. See no. 544.

Outlines briefly the circumstances in which Ladovsky and his followers broke away from ASNOVA and founded the ARU.

975. ——. "Planirovka Avtostroia i Magnitogorska v vuze" [Planning Autostroi and Magnitogorsk in the institutions of higher learning"]. *Sovetskaia arkhitektura*, nos. 1-2, 1931: 21-28.

Outlines the principles of designing socialist cities as taught by Ladovsky in VKHUTEIN (1929) and the ASI (1930). Richly illustrated.

25. I. G. Langbard

976. "Raboty I. G. Langbarda v Belorusskoi i ukrainskoi SSR" [Projects of I. G. Langbard in the Belorussian and the Ukrainian SSRs]. *Arkhitektura Leningrada*, no. 1, 1940: 35-41.

A review of the architect's projects in the two republics during the thirties, with illustrations. Contains some useful background material on his background and approach to design.

26. Nikolai E. Lansere

977.   Petrov, A. "Nikolai Lansere." *Sovetskaia arkhitektura*, no. 18, 1969: 80-84.
        A succinct, informative account of the architect's career and principal work. Contains numerous useful plates.

27. Ivan I. Leonidov

978.   Aleksandrov, P. "Arkhitektor-novator" [Architect and Innovator]. *Arkhitektura SSSR*, no. 1, 1968: 31-42.
        An introductory section of biographical data, followed by an analytical and interpretive study of Leonidov's career, work, and impact upon Soviet architecture. Excellent plates. Highly recommended.

979.   Ginzburg, Moisei Ia. "Itogi i perspektivy" [Results and Perspectives]. See no. **600.**
        A review of the constructivist movement in Soviet architecture, with significant attention devoted to the work of Leonidov, especially his design for the Lenin Institute.

980.   Khan-Magomedov, Selim O. "I. I. Leonidov." *Architectural Design*, no. 2, 1970: 104-107.
        A review of the architect's career, amply supplemented with illustrations. An adaptation of the author's earlier, more comprehensive article in Russian (no. **981**).

981.   ——. "Ivan Leonidov." *Sovetskaia arkhitektura*, no. 16, 1964: 103-116.
        Assesses Leonidov's place in the development of Soviet architecture, in view of the fact that the architect was first a progressive symbol of constructivism in the twenties, only to become a condemned symbol of "formalism" in the thirties and forties. Excellent plates. Contains much useful information. Highly recommended.

981a.   ——. "Kluby Leonidova" [Clubs by Leonidov]. *Dekorativnoe iskusstvo SSSR*, no. 11, 1967: 17-22.

An incisive examination of Leonidov's designs for workers' clubs, intended also to stimulate current work by Soviet architects. Offers an interesting discussion of Leonidov's particular approach to design.

982. Khiger, R. Ia. "Mastera molodoi arkhitektury." [Masters of the Young Architecture]. See no. 849. p. 35-37.

An analysis of the architect considered to be the *enfant terrible* of Soviet architecture and made the object of particularly bitter criticism and attacks accusing his architecture of being representative of a petit-bourgeois current in Soviet architecture. A valuable insight.

983. Kuz'm, A. "Protiv bezotvetstvennoi kritiki. K napadkam na proektu I. Leonidova" [Against Irresponsible Criticism. Regarding the Attacks on the Project of I. Leonidov]. See no. 636.

A rebuttal to attacks on Leonidov.

984. Mordvinov, Arkadi G. "Leonidovshchina i ee vred" [Leonidovism and Its Dangers]. See no. 639.

One of the more pointed attacks on Leonidov.

985. "Rezoliutsiia Sektora arkhitektorov sotsialisticheskogo stroitel'stva o tak nazyvaemoi 'Leonidovshchine'" [Resolution of the Sector of Architects of Socialist Construction Regarding the So-called "Leonidovism"]. *Sovetskaia arkhitektura*, nos. 1-2, 1931: 102.

Responds to the latest wave of criticism and asserts that accusations against all of SASS are actually aimed specifically at Leonidov. Reiterates statements made earlier by the former OSA applauding Leonidov's profound and inventive approach to design, as well as his thorough scientific grounding and social consciousness. Admits that his presentation techniques are highly schematic and that he pays insufficient attention to economic aspects. But does not feel that this is unique to Leonidov or that it justifies his being singled out for such vicious attacks.

986. "Rezoliutsiia sektsii IZO instituta LIIa Komakademii po dokladu t. Mordvinova o 'Melkoburzhuaznom napravlenii v arkhitekture (Leonidovshchine)' priniata 20, XII 1930g." [Resolution of the Section of the Fine Arts Department of the Institute of Literature, Art, and Language of the Communist Academy on the Speech by

Comrade Mordvinov, "Concerning the Petit-bourgeois Direction in Architecture (Leonidovism)," passed on December 20, 1930]. See **no. 659**.

A sixteen-point resolution upholding Mordvinov's contentions as developed in his speech (**no. 639**); text of resolution adapted from the speech. Maintains that "Leonidovism" represents the synthesis of everything negative in the theory and practice of Soviet architecture. Condemns the abstractionism, indifference to program and economic demands, and the contradiction and negation of dialectic materialism in the "Leonidovist" approach to design. Calls for bringing this trend to a close.

28. Evgeni A. Levinson

a. Monographs

987.   Levinson, Evgeni A., and I. I. Fomin. *Arkhitektura i stroitel'stvo zhilogo doma Leningradskogo soveta* [Architecture and Construction of the Apartment House for the Leningrad Soviet]. Moscow, Izd-vo Akademii arkhitektury SSSR, 1940. 28 p. illus.

An account of the project, from the initial design to the final construction. Interesting for the architects' explanation of their search for a design for a large housing complex that would not reflect a false sense of monumentality.

b. Articles

988.   Leiboshchits, N. "Evgeni Levinson i Igor' Fomin" [Evgeni Levinson and Igor Fomin]. *Sovetskaia arkhitektura*, no. 18, 1969; 100-106.

An illuminating examination of the architects' notable but largely unpublicized careers, focusing upon their long partnership and their particular approach to design.

989.   Levinson, Evgeni A. "Iz praktiki arkhitektora" [From the Architect's Practice]. In *Tvorcheskie problemy sovetskoi arkhitektury. Sbornik statiei* [Creative Problems in Soviet Architecture. A Collection of Essays]. Moscow and Leningrad, Gosstroiizdat, 1956. p. 35-58.

An autobiographical account of the architect's career, supplemented by observations on the methodology employed by other Soviet architects. Contains much useful information.

990.   Svirsky, Ia. "Tvorchestvo E. A. Levinsona" [Practice of E. A. Levinson]. *Arkhitektura SSSR*, no. 4, 1965: 51-54.

A record of the highlights of the architect's career. Useful for clarifying his associates in the various stages of his career. A number of good plates.

991. "Tvorchestvo arkhitektorov E. A. Levinsona i I. I. Fomina" [Practice of the Architects E. A. Levinson and I. I. Fomin]. *Arkhitektura Leningrada*, no. 1, 1939: 39-51.

A concise record of the work done by E. A. Levinson in partnership with I. I. Fomin. Contains much valuable information and numerous plates.

29. Lazar M. (El) Lissitzky

a. Soviet Writers

(1) *Monographs*

992. Lissitzky, Lazar M. (El). *Russland: Architektur für eine Welterevolution.* See **no. 268.**

A new edition of Lissitzky's earlier work **(no. 269)**. Plates are of poor quality.

993. ——. *Russland: die Rekonstruktion der Architektur in der Sowjetunion.* See **no. 269.**

Outlines a manifesto for a new Soviet architecture and cites own work to illustrate the applications of the manifesto. Also an authoritative and detailed account of modern architecture in the Soviet Union. Valuable photographs of excellent quality included of major buildings and projects. Highly recommended.

994. Lissitzky-Küppers, Sophie. *El Lissitzky, Life, Letters, Texts.* Trans. from the German by Helene Aldwinckle and Mary Whittall. London, Thames and Hudson, 1968. 407 p. 278 plates.

Introduction by Herbert Read. A comprehensive biography of Lissitzky by his wife, richly supplemented by Lissitzky's personal correspondence. In addition to innumerable references and discussions of architecture in the text, four of Lissitzky's articles on architecture are appended (p. 365-373), as is an article by Mart Stam on Lissitzky's conception of architecture (p. 388-389). Numerous valuable plates of excellent quality, many of which have never before been published. An invaluable document both for clarifying Lissitzky's role as intermediary between Western and Soviet architects and for attempting to clarify and document the influence that quite likely may have been exerted by Soviet artists and architects upon their Western counterparts. Highly recommended. For the original in German, see: *El Lissitzky. Maler, Architekt, Typograf, Fotograf* (Dresden, Verlag der Kunst, 1967).

(2) *Articles*

995.   Lissitzky, Lazar M. (El). "Arkhitektura zheleznoi i zhelezo-betonnoi
ramy" [Architecture of the Steel and Ferro-concrete Frame].
Stroitel'naia promyshlennost', no. 1, 1926.

Argues that most contemporary architects confuse construction
per se with those forms in which it is expressed. Maintains that
the new so-called structural skeletons are all too often applied to
the façade in much the same superficial manner as were the
classical orders and similar motifs presently decried by contemporary architects everywhere. Analyzes the tectonic and
structural essence of the new structural systems, calling for their
synthesis in architectural design.

996.   ——. "Baukhauz v Dessau" [Bauhaus in Dessau]. *Stroitel'naia
promyshlennost'*, no. 1, 1927: 53-54.

A brief review of the history of the Bauhaus. Observes that
activity within the VKHUTEMAS and other Soviet artistic circles
penetrated into the Bauhaus but does not elaborate.

997.   ——. "Funktsional'naia arkhitektura" [Functional Architecture].
Stroitel'naia promyshlennost', no. 1, 1927: 55.

A brief commentary on the railway trade building in Rotter-
dam. Suggests a continuity from the "Moderne" style (the Russian
Art Nouveau) to constructivism and thence to functionalism but
does not elaborate.

998.   ——. "Glaz arkhitektora (izlozhenie knigi E. Mendel'sona)" [Eye of
the Architect (A Review of the Book by E. Mendelsohn)].
Stroitel'naia promyshlennost', no. 2, 1926: 144-146.

Uses the format of a book review to render personal observations on the architecture of New York, Chicago, Detroit, and the
"elevators of Buffalo" upon which Mendelsohn focuses in his
work (*Amerika*) and which represented the objects of special
Western interest during the twenties. An illuminating article.

999.   ——. "Idoly i idolopoklonniki" [Idols and Idol Worshippers].
Stroitel'naia promyshlennost', nos. 11-12, 1928: 854-858.

Criticizes the apparent emulation of Le Corbusier by the Soviet
functionalists. Asserts that, unlike the architect in the West who
is simply a buffer between the "corporate client and the un-
assuming consumer," the Soviet architect has the primary responsibility for structuring the physical environment and thus shaping

the new social order (socialism) that it is designed to contain. Provides rich insight into Lissitzky's attitudes toward both Western and Soviet architecture.

1000. ——. "Katastrofa arkhitektury" [Catastrophe of Architecture]. See no. 312.

1001. ——. "Kul'tura zhil'ia" [Culture of Housing]. *Stroitel'naia promyshlennost'*, no. 12, 1926: 877-881.

Suggests criteria for developing the kind of housing that will respond specifically to Soviet needs and reviews that aspect of contemporary western experience with housing that should be considered by Soviet architects. Concludes that both furnishings and finishing materials ought to be built simultaneously with the housing unit as a whole in order to simplify the means and thus decrease the cost while increasing architectural effectiveness. An early argument for total prefabrication.

1002. Rakitin, V. "El Lissitzky, 1890-1941." *Architectural Design,* no. 2, 1970: 82-83.

A summary of the architect-artist's career and principal works. Provides some useful data and insights on the role played by Lissitzky in the development of modern Soviet architecture and allied arts. Includes numerous illustrations and a bibliography.

b. Non-Soviet Writers

(1) *Monographs*

1003. Richter, Horst. *El Lissitzky. Sieg über die Sonne. Zur Kunst des Konstruktivismus.* Cologne, Galerie Christoph Czwiklitzer, 1958. 86 p. illus.

An authoritative, well-documented essay on Lissitzky's work, though with sparse reference to his architectural activity. Also includes an essay on constructivism, as well as useful notes and a fairly complete bibliography of Lissitzky's writings, including essays published in various periodicals.

(2) *Articles*

1004. Frampton, Kenneth. "The Work and Influence of El Lissitzky." In *Architect's Yearbook 12.* London, Elek Books, 1968. p. 253-268.

A comprehensive survey of Lissitzky's background and professional career in all the phases of artistic activity with which he was occupied, including architecture. Many useful plates.

1005.   ——. "The Work of El Lissitzky." *Architectural Design,* Nov. 1966: 564-566.
A review of Lissitzky's work.

1006.   Gray, Camilla. [El Lissitzky.] In her *Great Experiment: Russian Art 1863-1922.* New York, Harry Abrams, 1962. p. 290, 184, 226, 248, 249, and 252-254.
Includes discussion of Lissitzky, though mostly devoted to his activities in art rather than architecture. For an outline biography, see p. 290.

1007.   Moholy, Lucia. "El Lissitzky." *Werk,* v. 53, June 1966: 229-236.
A synopsis of Lissitzky's influence and work, supplemented with graphic and pictorial material.

1008.   Sharp, Dennis. "El Lissitzky." In his *Sources of Modern Architecture. A Bibliography.* See **no. 32.** p. 22-23.
See indicated pages for a cursory biography and bibliography.

30. Kasimir S. Malevich

a. Monographs by Soviet Writers

1009.   Malevich, Kasimir. *Die gegenstandslose Welt.* Bauhausbucher 11. Munich, A. Langen, 1927. 104 p. illus.
A postulation of the artist's experiments with "architectonics" as the spatial formulation of suprematism, derived from a synthesis of the dynamic diagonal construction and the static composition of art. Argues that this is contemporary art, which is architecture. For English trans., see: *The Non-Objective World,* trans. from the German by Howard Dearstyne (Chicago, P. Theobald, 1959, 102 p., illus.).

1010.   ——. *Essays on Art, 1915-1933.* Trans. Xenia Glowacki-Prus and Arnold McMillia. Ed. Troels Andersen. London, Rapp and Whiting, 1969.
A collection of writings by Malevich on various phases of art, including architecture. A good English language source.

b. Articles by Soviet Writers

1011.   Gan, Aleksei. "Spravka o Kasimire Maleviche" [Information about Kasimir Malevich]. *S.A.*, no. 3, 1927: 104-106.
         A brief account of Malevich's suprematist school, his philosophy, and his work during recent years. Also analyzes the formal and abstract searches in modern Soviet architecture, tracing the roots of Ladovsky's and ASNOVA's work to Malevich's suprematism.

1012.   Malevich, Kasimir. "Arkhitektura kak poshchechina obshchestvennomu vkusu" [Architecture as a Slap in the Face of Public Taste]. *Iskusstvo kommuny*, no. 1, 1918.
         Criticizes attempts in recent buildings in Moscow to render traditional forms with contemporary structural systems and building materials. Eng. trans.: "Architecture as a Slap in the Face to Ferro-Concrete," in Malevich, *Essays on Art* (**no. 1010**), v. 1, p. 60-64.

1013.   ——. "Pis'mo redaktsii" [Letter to the Editorial Board]. *S.A.*, no. 5, 1928: 156.
         Rejects any collaboration with the journal. Includes a brief account of suprematism and Malevich's postulation of "architectonics." An excellent specimen of Malevich's turgid prose.

1014.   ——. "Suprematistische Architektur." *Wasmuths Monatshefte für Baukunst*, v. 11, 1927: 412-414.
         A concise statement by Malevich describing his experiments with suprematist "architectonics." One of few effective published summaries and explanations of his work. Contains excellent plates of his work not readily accessible elsewhere. Article apparently abridged by editors; for corrections by Malevich, see p. 484.

c. Articles by Non-Soviet Writers

1015.   Gray, Camilla. [Kasimir Malevich]. In her *The Great Experiment: Russian Art 1863-1922*. New York, Harry Abrams, 1962. p. 128-140, 291.
         Includes discussion of Malevich's work. For the analysis of his work, see especially p. 128-140; for an outline bibliography, see p. 291.

1016.   Lamac, Miroslac. "Malevich: Le Meconnu / Malevich: The Misunder-
stood." *Cimaise*, nos. 85-86, 1968: 38-45.
A cursory assessment of the artist's theoretical posture.
Suggests that it is much less important than has been believed up
to the present and that it contains numerous "regressions and
contradictions." Article in both French and English.

1017.   Seuphor, Michel. Suprematisme et néoplasticisme." *L'Art d'aujourd'-
hui*, nos. 7-8, 1950.
An illustrated account of suprematism, with references to
Malevich's suprematist "architectonics."

1018.   ——. "Architettura suprematista di Kasimir Malevitsch." *L'Architettura*,
no. 5, 1960: 350-351.
An illustrated review of Malevich's designs for suprematist
"architectonics," with a brief commentary.

31. Konstantin S. Mel'nikov

a. Monographs by Soviet Writers

1019.   Lukhmanov, N. *Arkhitektura kluba* [Architecture of the Club]. See
no. 270.
Devotes the major portion of the work to an analysis of the
numerous clubs designed by Konstantin Mel'nikov, which are seen
as trend setters in Soviet club design.

b. Articles by Soviet Writers

1020.   Bykov, V. "Konstantin Mel'nikov i Georgi Gol'ts" [Konstantin
Mel'nikov and Georgii Gol'ts]. See **no. 943.**
A penetrating analysis of Mel'nikov's brilliant and controversial
career. Reflects a conscious attempt to reassess his place in Soviet
architecture. Provides useful insights into the architect's approach
to design. Symptomatic of the growing admiration of Melnikov in
the West and in the Soviet Union. A few new plates.

1021.   Gerchuk, Iu. "Arkhitektor Konstantin Mel'nikov" [Architect Konstantin Mel'nikov]. *Arkhitektura SSSR*, no. 8, 1966: 51-55.
A review of Mel'nikov's career and major projects. A number
of valuable plates. General, but thus far the only published attempt
at a comprehensive survey of his work.

1022.   Karra, A., and V. Smirnov. "Besprintsipnyi eksperiment" [An Unprincipled Experiment]. *Stroitel'stvo Moskvy*, no. 10, 1929: 20.

Condemns Konstantin Melnikov's work for ignoring the greater questions of economy and social significance. Objects to Melnikov's use of conventional modes of construction.

1022a.   Khan-Magomedov, Selim O. "Kluby segodnia i vchera" [Clubs Today and Yesterday]. *Dekorativnoe iskusstvo SSSR*, no. 9, 1966: 2-6.

A probing assessment of the numerous workers' clubs designed by Mel'nikov. Contains an interesting analysis of the socio-economic nature of workers' clubs as an institution in Soviet life.

1023.   Khiger, R. "Arkhitektor K. S. Mel'nikov" [Architect K. S. Mel'nikov]. *Arkhitektura SSSR*, no. 1, 1935: 30-34.

A synopsis of the architect's philosophy and work and a subtle effort to vindicate Mel'nikov's visionary designs, especially in the competition for the Building of the Commissariat of Heavy Industry on Red Square, from severe criticism. A few valuable plates.

1024.   L-nov. "Neudachnye konstruktsii" [Unsuccessful Constructions]. *Stroitel'stvo Moskvy*, no. 10, 1929: 19-20.

Condemns Melnikov's cylindrical house—because it 1) exemplifies an outmoded manorial type of architecture, 2) produces awkward spaces in plan, and 3) utilizes inefficient and outmoded construction techniques, as well as adopting archaic modes of masonry construction.

1025.   Lukhmanov, Nikolai. "Tsilindricheskii dom" [Cylindrical House]. *Stroitel'stvo Moskvy*, no. 4, 1929: 16-22.

A penetrating analysis of the cylindrical house which the architect, Konstantin Melnikov, designed for himself in Moscow. Examines Melnikov's general philosophy of design. Includes a wealth of graphic and pictorial material on the house.

1026.   Mel'nikov, Konstantin S. "Arkhitekture pervoe mesto" [Architecture to the Forefront]. *Stroitel'stvo Moskvy*, no. 1, 1934: 9-13.

Outlines his philosophy of design and discusses his design for the Palace of Culture at Tashkent. Good illustrations.

1027.   ——. "Arkhitekturnoe osvoenie novykh materialov" [Architectural Assimilation of New Materials] . See **no. 812.**

Argues that it is the building industry's responsibility to develop unified details and materials for the use of the architects. In response to the growing admonition that architects coordinate their work with that of the building industry.

1028.   ——. "Oformlenie proekta" [Formulation of a Project] . *Arkhitektura SSSR*, no. 5, 1933: 35.

Uses his pavilion for the 1925 Paris Exhibit as an example of organizing an architectural project. Speaks also of the need for rapport between the architect and his assistants.

1029.   ——. "Razvivat' svoiu tvorcheskuiu liniiu" [Developing One's Creative Line] . *Stroitel'stvo Moskvy*, no. 9, 1933: 8.

Asserts that each architect must develop his own particular "creative line," and that the newly created studios under the Moscow Soviet will facilitate doing so.

1030.   ——. "Tvorcheskoe samochuvstvie arkhitektora" [Creative Mood of the Architect] . *Arkhitektura SSSR*, no. 9, 1934: 10-11.

Speaks condescendingly of the results of the organization of studios under Mossovet and laments the bureaucratic problems he has faced in attempting to produce work in the studio which he heads. Valuable for identifying his associates and their work.

1031.   "Vos'midesiatiletie Konstantina Stepanovicha Mel'nikova" [Eightieth Birthday of Konstantin Stepanovich Mel'nikov] . *Arkhitektura SSSR*, no. 11, 1970: 68-69.

A succinct, highly informative synopsis of the architect's controversial career and approach to architectural practice during the "modern" period.

1032.   Zheits, V. "O tsilindricheskom dome arkhitektora Mel'nikova" [Concerning the Cylindrical House of Architect Mel'nikov] . *Stroitel'stvo Moskvy*, no. 10, 1929: 18-19.

Condemns what is seen as Konstantin Melnikov's flight of fancy reflecting individual bourgeois standards of the past rather than the needs of the contemporary working masses. Sees the house as failing to provide a proper precedent. Also condemns Lukhmanov's review of the project for failing to point out its profound deficiencies (see **no. 1025).**

c. Articles by Non-Soviet Writers

1033. Starr, S. Frederick. "Konstantin Melnikov." *Architectural Design,* no. 7, 1969: 367-373.

A cursory survey of the architect's career and work, based in part upon the investigation of the architect's personal papers and other material not generally available outside the Soviet Union. Includes a chronological list of buildings and projects completed by Mel'nikov. Contains many useful plates, some of which have never before been published. Another work on Melnikov by the author, entitled *The Drawings of Konstantin Melnikov,* is projected.

32. Nikolai A. Miliutin

a. Monographs by Soviet Writers

1034. Miliutin, Nikolai A. *Sotsgorod. Problema stroitel'stva sotsialisticheskikh gorodov* [The Socialist City. The Problem of Building Socialist Cities]. Moscow, Gosizdat, 1930. 82 p. illus.

A comprehensive systematic study of town planning projects and an analysis of various solutions. Focuses upon the principle of the linear city developed by Miliutin in the Soviet Union during the First Five Year Plan. Theory based on the development of city functions along parallel lines and the rational combination of the units of production, transportation, education, and living. Expresses concern for breaking down distinctions between town and country living by way of fusing the two through the linear scheme. Contains many notions about type of housing and other aspects which were of great concern within the architectural activity of the period.

b. Articles by Soviet Writers

1035. Khan-Magomedov, Selim O. "N. A. Miliutin." *Architectural Design,* no. 2, 1970: 91.

A brief but informative account of Miliutin's career. Cites the various official positions held by Miliutin. The only known published biographical account of this important figure.

1036. Miliutin, Nikolai A. "Konstruktivizm i funktsionalizm: k kharakteristike arkhitekturnykh techenii XX veka" [Constructivism and Functionalism: Characteristics of the Architectural Movements of the 20th Century]. See no. 617.

A comprehensive and illuminating survey of the evolution and aesthetics of constructivism. The last installment of the author's monumental work on the theory of Soviet architecture (**no. 712**).

1037.   ——. "Osnovnye voprosy teorii sovetskoi arkhitektury" [Basic Questions Concerning the Theory of Soviet Architecture]. See **no. 712.**
A comprehensive work presenting a reasoned argument for a new philosophy of Soviet architecture. Based on a critical analysis and assessment of modernist and proletarian philosophies of Soviet architecture in the twenties.

1038.   ——. "Osnovnye voprosy zhilishchno-bytovogo stroitel'stva SSSR i programa proektirovaniia domov perekhodnova tipa i domov-kommun" [Basic Questions of Housing Construction in the USSR and a Program for Designing Transitional Types of Housing and Communal Housing]. See **no. 713.**
Analyzes current trends in housing design and develops a systematic program for the design and construction of housing.

1039.   ——. "Vazhneishye zadachi sovremennogo etapa sovetskoi arkhitektury" [The Most Important Problems in the Current Period of Soviet Architecture]. See **no. 714.**
Focuses upon the problems besetting Soviet architecture in the present transitional period. A perceptive analysis.

c. Monographs by Non-Soviet Writers

1040.   Sprague, Arthur R. "N. A. Miliutin and Linear Planning in the U.S.S.R., 1928-1931." M.A. thesis. Columbia University, 1967. 116 p. illus.
A study of Miliutin's linear planning concepts and schemes. Provides much material on the Russian context of Miliutin's work, and suggests the importance of Western influences.

33. Arkadi G. Mordvinov

1041.   "A. G. Mordvinov." *Arkhitektura SSSR*, no. 5, 1935: 21-24.
An autobiographical account of the architect's work and philosophy.

1042.   "Arkadi Grigor'evich Mordvinov." *Arkhitektura i stroitel'stvo*, no. 2, 1947: 2.

A brief summary of the architect's career on the occasion of his selection as deputy to the Supreme Soviet of the RSFSR.

34. Aleksandr S. Nikol'sky

1043.   Nikol'sky, Aleksandr S. "Iz rabot moei masterskoi" [From the Work in My Studio]. *Akademiia arkhitektury*, nos. 1-2, 1934: 92-97.
A review by the architect of his work from the Revolution to the time of publication, with a statement of his philosophy and an analysis of his major projects. Numerous valuable plates.

1044.   ——. "Tvorcheskie otchety" [Creative Accounts]. *Arkhitektura SSSR*. no. 4, 1935: 52-54.
An autobiographical account of the architect's work, though with emphasis upon speculating about the future of Soviet architecture and proposing ways in which it might develop more effectively along the newly prescribed formula. Argues for appropriating the positive accomplishments of modernism.

1045.   Ol', G. A. "Tvorcheskie vzgliady A. S. Nikol'skogo" [The Creative Views of A. S. Nikol'sky]. In *Tvorcheskie problemy sovetskoi arkhitektury. Sbornik statiei* [Creative Problems of Soviet Architecture. A Collection of Essays]. Moscow and Leningrad, Gosstroiizdat, 1956. p. 85-106.
An analysis of the architect's philosophy, its application in his projects, and an assessment of his career. Contains much useful data and cites numerous unpublished manuscripts prepared by the architect. A recommended source.

1046.   Povelikhin, A. "Arkhitekturnoe dvizhenie v Petrograde-Leningrade v 1920-e gody i masterskaia A. S. Nikol'skogo" [Architectural Activity in Petrograd-Leningrad in the 1920's and the Studio of A. S. Nikol'sky]. *Leningradskii inzhenerno-stroitel'nyi institut. Arkhitektura* [Leningrad Engineering and Building Institute. Architecture]. Leningrad, 1965: 43-62.
Traces the activity of the Leningrad architects who formed a group around Nikol'sky in 1923, later joining the OSA in 1925. Illuminates the initial phases of Nikolsky's career and contains much useful information.

35.   Viacheslav K. Oltarzhevsky

1047.   Arunov, V. "Stareishii sovetskii zodchii (k 80-letiiu V. K. Oltar-
zhevskogo)" [An Elder Soviet Architect (On the 80th Birthday of
V. K. Oltarzhevsky)]. *Arkhitektura SSSR*, no. 5, 1960: 53-54.
A survey of the architect's career. Discusses his stay in the
U.S. in 1924-28, when he received an architectural degree from
New York University.

36.   Dmitri P. Osipov

1048.   "Pamiati D. P. Osipova" [To the Memory of D. P. Osipov].
Arkhitektura SSSR, no. 11, 1934: 72.
An obituary synopsis of the architect's career.

1049.   Vonogradov, N. "K istorii obeliska na sovetskoi ploshchade v Moskve"
[To the History of the Obelisk on Soviet Square in Moscow] .
Arkhitektura SSSR, no. 10, 1937: 69.
A summary of events leading to Osipov's design for the obelisk,
whose construction was completed in late 1918.

37.   Leonid N. Pavlov

1050.   Mel'nikov, E. "Arkhitektor Leonid N. Pavlov" [Architect Leonid N.
Pavlov] . *Arkhitektura SSSR*, no. 2, 1969: 35-41.
An illuminating account of the architect's career and a summary
of his philosophy. Focuses primarily on his more recent work;
contains much useful material.

38.   Mikhail V. Posokhin

1051.   "Mikhail Vasil'evich Posokhin." *Arkhitektura SSSR*, no. 12, 1970:
11-14.
An examination of the architect's career and principal work,
with illustrations.

39.   Boris R. Rubanenko

1052.   "Boris Rafailovich Rubanenko." *Arkhitektura SSSR*, no. 11, 1970:
37-38.
A succinct biographical sketch of the architect's career on the
occasion of his 60th birthday. Includes illustrations of his work.

40. Lev V. Rudnev

a. Monographs

1053. Ass, V. E., P. O. Zinov'ev, et al. *Arkhitektor Rudnev* [Architect Rudnev]. Moscow, Gosstroiizdat, 1963. 127 p. illus.

A collection of essays by the architect's associates treating various stages and aspects of his career. A highly useful, revealing record which illuminates much not only of the architect's career but also the careers of those with whom he worked and the particular circumstances in which they practiced. Contains numerous plates, many of which have never before been published.

1054. Rudnev, Lev V. *Arkhitektura i stroitel'stvo Voennoi Akademii im. Frunze* [Architecture and Construction of the Frunze Military Academy]. Moscow, Izd-vo Akademii arkhitektury, 1940. 32 p. illus.

Introduction by Ia. A. Kornfel'd lauding the building, followed by a brief essay by the architect treating the evolution of the design and construction of the building.

b. Articles

1055. Ass, V., and A. Khristiani. "Lev Rudnev." *Sovetskaia arkhitektura,* no. 18, 1969: 88-91.

A brief, introspective look into the architect's approach to his work by former associates. Contains several plates of his last art work.

1056. Il'in, Lev. A. "Mastera sovetskoi arkhitektury, L. V. Rudnev" [Masters of Soviet Architecture. L. V. Rudnev]. *Arkhitektura SSSR,* no. 3, 1940: 41-49.

A concise analytical study of the architect's career, from his student days through his work in the Soviet period to the time of publication of the article. Contains much useful information not otherwise readily available. A number of good plates.

1057. "Lev Vladimirovich Rudnev." *Arkhitektura SSSR,* no. 5, 1955: 55.

An abbreviated biographical sketch of the architect's career and major projects. A useful synopsis.

1058. "Lev Vladimirovich Rudnev." *Arkhitektura SSSR,* no. 12, 1956: inside front cover.

An obituary and sketch of the highlights of the architect's professional accomplishments.

1059.   Munts, V., and V. Ass. "Vydaiushchiisia sovetskii zodchii" [An
        Outstanding Soviet Architect]. *Arkhitektura i stroitel'stvo Moskvy,*
        no. 1, 1957: 21-25.
            A commemorative account of the architect's career by his
        former associates, on the occasion of his death. Contains useful
        information.

1060.   Rudnev, Lev V. "Printsipy arkhitekturnogo tvorchestva" [Principles
        of Architectural Creativity]. In *Tvorcheskie problemy sovetskoi*
        arkhitektury. Sbornik Statiei [Creative Problems of Soviet Archi-
        tecture. A Collection of Essays]. Moscow and Leningrad, Goss-
        troiizdat, 1956, p. 7-34.
            A detailed discussion by the architect of his philosophy and
        method of design. Supplemented by an analysis of his major
        projects for the purpose of illustrating his method. A bit polemical
        but a useful reference providing much insight into the motives
        behind the architecture of the high Stalinist period.

1061.   ——. "Tvorcheskie otchety" [Creative Accounts]. *Arkhitektura SSSR*,
        no. 6, 1935: 30-33.
            Argues for the use of a guiding concept in design and proceeds
        to review his major projects and explain his method of design. A
        number of excellent plates. A significant article.

1062.   Sokolov, N. "Mastera sovetskoi arkhitektury" [Masters of Soviet
        Architecture]. See no. **853.** p. 83-84.
            Includes a brief assessment of Rudnev's work and contributions
        to Soviet architecture.

41. Aleksei M. Rukhladev

1063.   Krinsky, Vladimir F. "Pamiati A. M. Rukhladeva." *Arkhitektura*
        SSSR, no. 14, 1947: 48.
            A brief obituary account of the architect's career.

42. Anatoli V. Samoilov

1064.   Kolli, Nikolai Ia. "Pamiati Anatoliia Vasil'evicha Samoilova" [To the
        Memory of Anatoli Vasil'evich Samoilov]. *Arkhitektura SSSR,*
        no. 12, 1954: 37.
            A review of the highlights of the architect's career.

1065. Rozenfel'd, Z. "Arkhitektor A. V. Samoilov (k 80-letiiu so dnia rozhdeniia)" [Architect A. V. Samoilov (On His 80th Birthday)]. *Arkhitektura SSSR*, no. 12, 1963: 59-62.

An informative account of the architect's career and principal work.

43. Vladimir N. Semenov

1066. Beloussov (Belousov), Vladimir N. "V. H.[*sic*] Semenov." *Architectural Design*, no. 2, 1970: 84-85.

Contains useful information on the highlights of the architect-planner's distinguished career prior to and following the 1917 Revolution.

1067. Smirnova, O. "Vladimir Semenov." *Sovetskaia arkhitektura*, no. 18, 1969: 77-79.

An informative review of the architect's career, focusing upon a discussion of his philosophy of architectural design and urban planning. A useful source.

1068. "Vladimir Nikolaevich Semenov." *Arkhitektura SSSR*, no. 3, 1960: 63.

A biographical obituary notice.

44. Sergei S. Serafimov

a. Monographs

1069. Rubanchik, Ia., ed. *S. S. Serafimov*. Leningrad, Izd-vo Leningradskogo otdeleniia Soiuza Sovetskikh Arkhitektorov, 1941. 16 p. illus.

A concise biographical record of the architect's career and a chronology of his principal works, 1911-35. A good reference.

b. Articles

1070. "Prof. S. S. Serafimov." *Arkhitektura SSSR*, no. 1, 1940: 74.

An obituary, with highlights of his career.

1071. Rubanchik, S. S. "Mastera sovetskoi arkhitektury. S. S. Serafimov" [Masters of Soviet Architecture. S. S. Serafimov]. *Arkhitektura SSSR*, no. 8, 1940: 61-65.

A concise analytical study of the architect's career and major projects, from the prerevolutionary years to the Soviet period. A useful survey.

1072.   Serafimov, Sergei S. "Tvorcheskie otchety. S. S. Serafimov" [Creative Accounts. S. S. Serafimov]. *Arkhitektura SSSR*, no. 5, 1935: 13-16.

A statement of the architect's views and philosophy of architecture and a review of his major projects. A useful statement.

45. Vladimir A. Shchuko

a. Monographs

1073.   Kaufman, S. A. *Vladimir Alekseevich Shchuko*. Moscow, Izd-vo Akademii arkhitektury, 1946. 67 p. illus., with a list of the architect's projects.

A concise analytical study of Shchuko's prerevolutionary and Soviet career, a survey of his major work, and an assessment of his contribution to the development of Soviet architecture.

b. Articles

1074.   Il'in, Lev A. "Tvorcheskii put' V. A. Shchuko" [Creative Direction of V. A. Shchuko]. *Arkhitektura Leningrada*, no. 2, 1939: 9-25.

An authoritative study of Shchuko's career, his training, and the characteristics of the stages in his development as an architect. Especially significant for articulating the main influences that shaped his career. Amply illustrated with many important plates.

1075.   L-ov. "Novoe zdanie Leninskoi biblioteki, kak monumental'nyi pamiatnik epokhi" [New Building for the Lenin Library as a Monument of the Epoch]. See no. 314.

A review of the second phase of the competition, noting Shchuko's revision from the initial design submitted.

1076.   Minkus, M. "Vladimir Alekseevich Shchuko. Tvorcheskii Put'" [Vladimir Alekseevich Shchuko. His Creative Direction]. *Arkhitektura SSSR*, no. 1, 1939: 31-51.

An analytical and interpretive investigation into the development of Shchuko's career, including the influences and circumstances that affected its evolution and the major projects that the architect produced. Assesses the architect's role in the evolution of Soviet architecture; especially useful for clarifying his transition from prerevolutionary to Soviet times and his gradual ascendancy with the other architects of the Old School. Many excellent and important plates.

1077. "Moskovskie arkhitekturnye organizatsii po povodu konkursa na zdanie Leninskoi biblioteki" [Moscow Architectural Organizations on the Competition for the Building of the Lenin Library]. See **no. 327.**

Declarations of protest against the selection of Shchuko's quasi-classical design from the ARU, the architectural circle in VKHUTEIN, and ASNOVA. The editors of *Stroitel'stvo* . . . petitioned A. V. Lunacharsky, chairman of the competition commission, to explain why Shchuko's design was selected and why the younger architects were excluded from participation (see **no. 336**). This was a clear, though short-lived, victory for the modernist forces in Soviet architecture in the latter twenties.

1078. Shchuko, Vladimir A. "Schastliveishii den' moei zhizni"[The Luckiest Day of My Life]. *Arkhitektura SSSR*, no. 10, 1937: 71.

On the occasion of the 20th anniversary of the Bolshevik Revolution. A synopsis of his spoken response to the new order, as well as a survey of the main stages in his practice.

1079. ——. "Tvorcheskie otchety" [Creative Accounts]. *Arkhitektura SSSR*, no. 6, 1935: 16-21.

An autobiographical account of the architect's own career, and especially of those developments that he considers to have been most influential in shaping and refining it. An important source.

1080. Sokolov, N. "Mastera sovetskoi arkhitektury" [Masters of Soviet Architecture]. See **no. 853.** p. 83-84.

Includes a characterization of Shchuko's work and an assessment of his major projects. Of general interest as an indication of current official opinion of the architect.

1081. " V. A. Shchuko i V. G. Gel'freikh" [V. A. Shchuko and V. G. Gel'-freikh]. See **no. 912.**

A thumbnail biographical sketch of the architects' careers, with illustrations.

46.   Aleksei V. Shchusev

a. Monographs

1082.   Babenchikova, M. V., and N. M. Nesterovoi. *Aleksei Viktorovich Shchusev.* Academy of Sciences of the USSR. Materials for a Bibliography of Scholars of the USSR, Architectural Series. Moscow, Izd-vo Akademii nauk SSSR, 1947. 17 p.

A concise record of Shchusev's career; includes a biographical sketch, arranged chronologically, of the major events in his career, a list of his projects and buildings, and a bibliography of published material by and about the architect. A highly useful reference tool.

1083.   Druzhina-Georgievskaia, E. V., and Ia. A. Kornfel'd. *Zodchii A. V. Shchusev* [Architect A. V. Shchusev]. Academy of Sciences of the USSR, Popular Scholarly Series. Moscow, Izd-vo Akademii nauk SSSR, 1955. 197 p. illus.

A study of his youth and education, his first architectural work, the Kazan Railway Terminal in Moscow, the Lenin Mausoleum, his projects for the center of Moscow, the Marx-Engels Institute in Tbilisi, the Alisher Havo Theater of Opera and Ballet in Tashkent, and the Metro Station at "Komsomol'sky Circle." Includes also a list of projects, scholarly work, and a bibliography of his published work. Contains valuable plates. A good source, though it includes no appreciable discussion of Shchusev's work in the constructivist idiom.

1084.   Grabar', Igor' E., K. N. Afanas'ev, and N. M. Bachinsky. *Proizvedeniia akademika A. V. Shchuseva udostoennye Stalinskoi premii* [Projects of Academician A. V. Shchusev Awarded the Stalin Prize]. Moscow, Izd-vo Akademii nauk SSSR, 1954. 98 p. 54 plates with index.

Introduction by Igor' E. Grabar' (p. 5-8), a concise biography by K. N. Afanas'ev (p. 9-17), and an illustrated review of the Lenin Mausoleum, the Marx-Engels-Lenin Institute, the Tashkent Theater, and the "Komsomol Circle" Metro Station. A highly useful reference both for data on the architect's career and for material on Shchusev's projects that were sanctioned during the height of the Stalin period.

1085.   Shchusev, Aleksei V. *Arkhitektura i stroitel'stvo instituta Marksa-Engel'sa-Lenina v Tbilisi* [Architecture and Construction of the

Marx-Engels-Lenin Institute in Tbilisi]. Moscow, Izd-vo Akademii arkhitektury SSSR, 1940. 40 p. illus.

An introduction by Ia. A. Kornfel'd and a description by the architect of the various phases of design and construction of the building, as well as a description of the facilities and numerous illustrations of the completed building.

1086. Sokolov, N. B. *A. V. Shchusev.* The Academy of Architecture of the USSR, Institute of the Theory and History of Architecture. Moscow, Gosstroiizdat, 1952. 314 p. illus.

Includes an introduction to Shchusev's work and a photographic essay of his major projects, drawings, and buildings. Also included are a list of the major dates in his life, chronological lists of projects and published works, and a comprehensive bibliography of works on Shchusev.

1087. Stoianov, N. N. *Arkhitektura mavzoleia Lenina* [Architecture of the Lenin Mausoleum]. Moscow, Gosstroiizdat, 1950. 103 p. illus.

A history of the three phases of construction and an analysis of Shchusev's design, supported by excellent analytical drawings indicating scale, orientation, and tectonic system of design. An excellent source.

b. Articles

1088. Afanas'ev, K. "Zodchii A. V. Shchusev" [Architect A. V. Shchusev]. *Arkhitektura SSSR*, no. 8, 1967: 29-35.

Analyzes Shchusev's career and attempts to determine the reasons for his widespread popularity. Argues that Shchusev was keenly aware of, and therefore a barometer of, public views and tastes in Soviet architecture. Provides interesting new insights into the architect's work and includes a number of important plates. An important source.

1089. Antipov, I. "Tvorchestvo A. V. Shchuseva" [Creativity of A. V. Shchusev]. *Arkhitektura SSSR*, no. 5, 1941: 29-34.

An assessment of Shchusev's major projects, with an analysis of the sources and inspirations for the respective designs. Includes an evaluation of Shchusev's designs in the constructivist idiom, which are considered here as part of the "fashionable homage" paid to the movement by all Soviet architects in the twenties. Contains highly useful plates and valuable information, though framed in a moderate amount of polemic characteristic of the period.

1090.   Babenchikova, M. V. "Mastera sovetskoi arkhitektury. A. V. Shchusev" [Masters of Soviet Architecture. A. V. Shchusev]. *Arkhitektura SSSR*, no. 5, 1941: 17-28.

A biographical and analytical study of Shchusev's career, his training, his work, and his major projects. Especially useful for its illumination of the early years of Shchusev's career and the circumstances surrounding his transition from the prerevolutionary years to the Soviet period. Contains some excellent plates.

1091.   Council of Ministers of the USSR. "Ot Soveta Ministrov Soiuza SSSR. Ob uvekovechenii pamiati akademika i deistvitel'nogo chlena Akademii arkhitektury SSSR A. V. Shchuseva" [From the Council of Ministers of the USSR. Concerning the Perpetuation of the Memory of Academician and Active Member of the Academy of Architecture of the USSR, A. V. Shchusev]. *Arkhitektura i stroitel'stvo*, no. 5, 1949: inside front cover.

An announcement of Shchusev's death by the Council of Ministers of the USSR and a decree ordering that the Museum of Russian Architecture be named after him, that the Academy of Architecture publish a series of albums of his work, that a number of scholarships be established in his honor in specified architectural schools, that the buildings he designed be so designated by appropriate markers, and that specified pensions be awarded to the immediate members of his family for the rest of their lives. Important because it represents the highest tribute ever paid a Soviet architect by the government.

1092.   Kornfel'd, Ia. "Tvorchestvo akademika A. V. Shchuseva" [Work of Academician A. V. Shchusev]. *Arkhitektura i stroitel'stvo*, no. 9, 1948: 4-9.

A general review of the architect's work on the occasion of his recent death. Lacks objectivity.

1093.   Mikhailov, A. "Vydaiushchiisia zodchii sovetskoi epokhi. Pamiati A. V. Shchuseva" [An Outstanding Architect of the Soviet Epoch. To the Memory of A. V. Shchusev]. *Arkhitektura i stroitel'stvo*, no. 5, 1949: 1-6.

A highly charged account of the highlights of the architect's career on the occasion of his death. Contains some useful information, though framed in a degree both of high emotion commensurate with the occasion and a polemic characteristic of the period that precludes objectivity in the presentation of the material.

1094.   Novikov, I. "Traditsii natsional'nogo zodchestva v tvorchestve A. V. Shchuseva" [Traditions of National Architecture in the Work of A. V. Shchusev]. See no. 771.

An analysis of Shchusev's design for the Kazan Railway Terminal in Moscow and its stylized adaptations of 17th-century Muscovite baroque. Contains a number of useful plates, though of a mediocre quality.

1095.   Shchusev, Aleksei V. "Chto my sozdali, chego nam nekhvataet" [What We Have Created, What We Are Lacking]. *Arkhitektura SSSR*, no. 6, 1937: 22-23.

An idealistic assessment of the course of Soviet architecture. Focuses upon the need to humanize Soviet architecture, to heed the ageless principles of classical architecture, and to create an architecture comprehensible to the masses.

1096.   ——. "Kak budet organizovana nasha rabota" [How Our Work Will Be Organized]. *Stroitel'stvo Moskvy*, no. 9, 1933: 8.

Outlines the manner in which he intends to operate the new Mossovet studio that he will head.

1097.   ——. "Proekt vremennogo mavzolea na mogile Vladimira Il'icha Lenina" [Project for a Temporary Mausoleum on the Grave of Vladimir Il'ich Lenin]. *Stroitel'naia promyshlennost'*, no. 4, 1924: 235.

Cites historical examples serving as inspirations for his design of the mausoleum and discusses his concepts of the project.

1098.   ——. "Shkola mastera" [The Master's School]. *Arkhitektura SSSR*, no. 9, 1934: 12-13.

A review by the architect of the first year's work of the Mossovet studio under his direction. Indicates a growing number of individuals seeking to work under Shchusev, whose work was currently sanctioned by official sources.

1099.   ——. "Stroitel'stvo vystavki" [Construction of the Exhibit]. *Stroitel'naia promyshlennost'*, no. 2, 1923: 5-7.

An illuminating account of the planning and construction of the 1923 Agricultural Exhibit in Moscow, of which Shchusev was in charge with Ivan Zholtovsky.

1100. ——. "Tvorcheskie otchety" [Creative Accounts]. *Arkhitektura SSSR*, no. 4, 1935: 45-48.

An interesting account by the architect of the circumstances that exerted a major influence upon his work. Speaks of his motives in appropriating the functionalist approach and in assimilating the classical heritage and a synthesis of the arts in architecture. A highly useful testament.

1101. Sokolova-Pokrovskaia, Z. K. "Neopublikovannaia rabota A. V. Shchuseva" [An Unpublished Project by A. V. Shchusev]. *Arkhitekturnoe nasledstvo*, no. 12, 1960: 210-211.

A description, with illustrations, of Shchusev's graveside monument for the artist A. I. Kuindzhi in 1914.

1102. Velikoretsky, O. "Aleksei Shchusev." *Sovetskaia arkhitektura*, no. 18, 1969: 68-71.

A reverent assessment of the architect's approach and philosophy of design. Provides some useful insights.

1103. ——. "Tvorcheskii put' mastera. K vystavke rabot akademika A. V. Shchuseva v tsentral'nom dome arkhitektora" [Creative Course of the Master. On the Exhibit of the Work of Academician A. V. Shchusev at the Architects' Central House]. *Sovetskaia arkhitektura*, no. 1, 1951: 77-81.

A review of the exhibit of 400 works by Shchusev and an assessment of the architect's philosophy, method of design, techniques of workmanship, and standards of professional practice. A few plates. Contains useful information

47. Viacheslav A. Shkvarikov

1104. "Viacheslav Alekseevich Shkvarikov. K shestdesiatiletiiu so dnia rozhdeniia" [Viacheslav Alekseevich Shkvarikov. On His Sixtieth Birthday]. *Arkhitektura SSSR*, no. 5, 1968: 62.

A synopsis of the architect's career.

48. Aleksandr I. Tamanian (Tamanov)

a. Monographs

1105. Iaralov, Iu. S. *Tamanian.* The Academy of Architecture of the USSR. Institute of the History and Theory of Architecture. Moscow, Gosstroiizdat, 1950. 164 p. illus.

A concise analytical study of the Armenian architect's career, with illustrations of his designs and buildings, a chronological list of his projects, and a bibliography of material published by and about the architect. An excellent source.

b. Articles

1106. "A. I. Tamanian. Biograficheskaia spravka" [A. I. Tamanian. A Biographical Note]. *Arkhitektura SSSR*, no. 1, 1942: 35.
A condensed biography of the architect and his work.

1107. Alabian, Karo. "Architect A. Tamanian." *VOKS Bulletin,* nos. 5-6, 1942: 40-41.
A brief reflective résumé of Tamanian's architectural career and principal works. Contains some useful insights.

1108. Il'ina, M. "Tvorchestvo Tamaniana" [Creativity of Tamanian] . *Arkhitektura SSSR*, no. 5, 1936: 50-52.
A review of the architect's career and principal work following his death.

1109. Khalpakhch'ian, O. "Aleksandr Tamanian." *Sovetskaia arkhitektura,* no. 18, 1969: 72-76.
An impressionistic exposition of the architect's career by a former associate. Focuses upon his work in the Armenian SSR.

1110. Mushegian, G. "Aleksandr Tamanian." *Arkhitektura i stroitel'stvo,* nos. 3-4, 1946: 7
A synoptic characterization of the contemporary national style and masonry techniques exemplified by Tamanian's major works. A useful source.

1111. "Pamiati A. I. Tamaniana" [To the Memory of A. I. Tamanian] . *Arkhitektura SSSR*, no. 4, 1936: 77.
An obituary biographical overview of the architect's career.

1112. Shchusev, Aleksei V. "A. I. Tamanian." *Akademiia arkhitektury,* no. 2, 1936: 104.
An obituary, with an excellent characterization of the evolution of the architect's career. Specific references to the sources of inspiration and influences in the succeeding stages of his development as an architect make this a valuable source.

1113.   Tamanian, Aleksandr I. "Tvorcheskie otchety" [Creative Accounts].
        Arkhitektura SSSR, no. 5, 1935: 3-7.
        An autobiographical account of the architect's practice. His
        account of developing the stylized order on the basis of traditional
        motifs of Armenian architecture, as exemplified in his design for
        the building of the Armenian Commissariat of Agriculture, is both
        interesting and particularly noteworthy.

49. Vladimir E. Tatlin

a. Soviet Writers

(1) *Monographs*

1114.   Punin, Natan N. *Pamiatnik III Internatsionala* [Monument to the
        Third International]. Petrograd, Izogiz, 1920. illus.
        A descriptive analytical commentary on Tatlin's design for
        the monument, with illustrations.

1115.   ——. *Tatlin. Protiv Kubizma* [Tatlin. Against Cubism]. Petrograd,
        Gosizdat, 1921. 25 p. illus.
        A pamphlet that propagandizes Tatlin's "nonobjectivist" phil-
        osophy that preceded his postulation of constructivism.

(2) *Articles*

1116.   Abramova, A. "Tatlin (1885-1953). K vosmidesiatiletiiu so dnia
        rozhdeniia" [Tatlin (1885-1953). On His Eightieth Birthday].
        Dekorativnoe iskusstvo, no. 2, 1966: 5-7.
        An overview of Tatlin's work and assessment of his impact on
        the Soviet art scene. The first article to be published on Tatlin
        following his death in Moscow in 1953.

1117.   Alekseev, B. "Novoe v tvorchestve V. E. Tatlina" [New Developments
        in the Work of V. E. Tatlin]. *Tvorchestvo,* no. 8, 1940: 14-15.
        Discusses Tatlin's recent work on stage and costume design.

1118.   Arkin, David E. "Tatlin i LeTatlin" [Tatlin and LeTatlin].*Sovetskoe
        iskusstvo,* no. 17, 1932.
        Commentary on Tatlin's design for a man-propelled glider,
        including a discussion of his concepts. Published simultaneously
        with an exhibit of Tatlin's glider in Moscow.

1119.   Artselov, K. "O LeTatline" [On LeTatlin]. *Brigada khudozhnikov,*
        no. 6, 1932: 17-18.
        Reproduction of the catalogue prepared for the exhibition of
        Tatlin's design of the man-propelled glider.

1120.   Ehrenburg (Erenburg), Il'ia. [Tatlin]. In his *A vse-taki ona vertitsa*
        [And Still It Revolves]. Moscow, "Gelikon," 1922: 18-21, 26, 90.
        Includes a penetrating analysis of the "new architecture" which
        Tatlin and his work are seen to have generated.

1121.   Isakov, S. "K kontr-rel'efam Tatlina" [On Tatlin's Counterreliefs].
        Novyi zhurnal dlia vsekh, no. 12, 1915: 46-50.
        An examination of Tatlin's spatial constructions.

1122.   Kronman, E. "Ukhod v tekhniku. Tatlin i 'Le Tatlin' " [Departure
        into Technology. Tatlin and "LeTatlin"]. *Brigada khudozhnikov,*
        no. 6, 1932: 19-23.
        An analysis of Tatlin's concepts and principles of construction
        embodied in his flying machine. A good source.

1123.   Umanskij (Umanskii), Konstantin. [Tatlin]. In his *Neue Kunst in
        Russland.* Potsdam, G. Kiepenheur, 1920: 19-20, 35.
        Includes a discussion of Tatlin's work and its impact and
        following in the Soviet arts.

1124.   ——. "Der Tatlinismus oder die Maschinenkunst." *Der Ararat:* Part I,
        Jan. 1920: 12-14; Part II, Feb.-March 1920: 32-33.
        An analysis of Tatlin's concept of the "Mechanical Image" of
        art.

1125.   Zelinsky, Korneli.   "Tatlin." *Vechernaia Moskva,* Arpil 6, 1932.
        Comments on the strong criticism and interest alike expressed
        in response to Tatlin's ideas and work, especially his "LeTatlin"
        on exhibit in Moscow.

                          b. Non-Soviet Writers

                           (1) *Monographs*

1126.   Andersen, Troels. *Vladimir Tatlin.* Karin B. Lindegren, K. G. P.
        Hultén, and Douglas Feuk, eds. Catalogue no. 75 from Moderna
        Museet. Stockholm, Moderna Museet, 1968. 92 p. illus.

Catalogue for the Tatlin exhibition at the Moderna Museet in July-September 1968. The first published comprehensive presentation and analysis of Tatlin's work. Contains much valuable material by way of extracts from contemporary articles and more recent published assessments of Tatlin's work. Also includes a chronological biographic summary of the artist's life and a selected bibliography or published material by and about Tatlin. Highly recommended.

(2) *Articles*

1127.   Andersen, Troels. [Tatlin]. In his *Moderne russisk kunst, 1910-1925.* Copenhagen: Borgen, 1967: 20-21, 71-74, 111-113, 132-141.
        A systematic analysis of Tatlin's work within the greater historical context of the evolution of modern Russian art.

1128.   Annekov, G. "Tatlin och konstruktivismen." In *Rörelse o konsten.* Stockholm, Moderna Museet, 1961. p. 5-6.
        A survey of Tatlin's theories, supplemented by a brief biographical note, p. 31. Additional comment and illustrations in appended essay by K. G. Hulten.

1129.   Elderfield, John. "The Line of Free Men: Tatlin's 'Tower' and the Age of Invention." See **no. 374.**
        Views Tatlin's Monument to the Third International as the single most significant product of its age and a unique achievement in twentieth century avant-garde art.

1130.   Gray, Camilla. [Tatlin]. In her *The Great Experiment: Russian Art 1863-1922.* New York, Harry Abrams, 1962. p. 142-148, 295.
        Includes a discussion of Tatlin. For an outline and chronological biography, see p. 295. For an analysis of his work and philosophy, see especially p. 142-148.

1131.   Lozowick, L. "Tatlin's Monument to the Third International." *Broom,* no. 3, 1922: 232-234.
        An analysis of Tatlin's monument.

1132.   Rickey, George. [Tatlin]. In his *Constructivism. Origins and Evolution.* New York, George Braziller, 1967. p. 17-34, 296-297.

Traces the development of constructivism through the thoughts of its founders, from its origins in Russia in 1913, to its dissemination in Europe, and its later manifestations in the United States. For discussion of Tatlin and his position in the evolution of constructivism in Russia, see especially p. 17-34. Includes a brief bibliography on Tatlin, p. 296-297.

1133. Seuphor, Michel. [Tatlin]. In his *L'Art abstrait*. Paris, Maeght, 1950. p. 52-56, 226-269, 315.

A historical survey of the background of abstract art. Includes a general discussion of the movements in the Soviet Union. For a discussion relating to the work of Tatlin, see p. 52-56 and 315; illustrations, p. 226-269.

1134. Vallier, Dora. "L'Art abstrait en Russe: ses origines, ses premières manifestations, 1910-1917." *Cahiers d'art*, v. 33-35, 1960: 259-285.

A survey of modern art in the Soviet Union. Includes commentary on Tatlin and his constructivist theories.

1135. Volaková-Skořepa, Z. "Vladimir Jevgrafovič Tatlin." *Výtvarne uměni*, nos. 8-9, 1967: 409-417.

An illustrated survey of Tatlin's work, focusing upon his early periods.

50. Noa A. Trotsky

1136. Arkin, David E. "Pamiati mastera" [In Memory of the Master]. *Arkhitektura SSSR*, no. 11, 1940: 70.

An obituary, with an analytical survey of the architect's career. Though brief, a valuable source of objective analysis and assessment of the architect's major projects and the circumstances which inspired them.

1137. Il'in, Lev A. "Mastera sovetskoi arkhitektury. N. A. Trotsky" [Masters of Soviet Architecture. N. A. Trotsky]. *Arkhitektura SSSR*, no. 2, 1941: 23-33.

An authoritative study of the architect's career, sources of inspiration, and major works. Contains much useful information and numerous plates. An important source.

1138.   ——. "Tvorcheskii put' N. A. Trotskogo" [Creative Direction of N. A. Trotsky]. *Arkhitektura Leningrada*, no. 6, 1940: 11-27.

An authoritative and informative account, complementing the one published by the author early in 1941 (**no. 1137**). Stresses an interpretive analysis of the architect's background, stages of development, and philosophy of design, viewed against the investigation and analysis of the architect's major projects. Many valuable plates. An excellent source.

1139.   "Pamiati vydaiushchegosia sovetskogo zodchego" [In Memory of an Outstanding Soviet Architect]. *Arkhitektura Leningrada*, no. 5, 1940: 79.

An obituary and synopsis of the architect's professional career, with an enumeration of his major projects.

1140.   Trotsky, Noa A. "Tvorcheskii otchet" [Creative Account]. *Arkhitektura SSSR*, no. 4, 1935: 59-63.

An autobiographical account of the architect's training, career, and work, that provides an important insight into his approach to design.

51. Lev M. Tverskoi

1141.   "Lev Mikhailovich Tverskoi (k 80-letiiu so dnia rozhdeniia i 60-letiiu tvorcheskoi deiatel'nosti)" [Lev Mikhailovich Tverskoi (On His 80th Birthday and the 60th Anniversary of His Creative Activity)]. *Arkhitektura SSSR*, no. 5, 1969: 38-39.

A review of the architect's work. Contains much useful information.

52. Leonid A., Viktor A., and Aleksandr A. Vesnin

a. Monographs

1142.   Il'in, Mikhail A. *Vesniny* [The Vesnins]. Moscow, Izd-vo Akademii nauk SSSR, 1960. 192 p. illus.

A biography and penetrating account of the architect brothers from the prerevolutionary years, their training, to their work in the Soviet period. The analysis of their work during the Soviet period is divided into the twenties, the thirties, and their work and administration of the studio under the Commissariat of Heavy Industry. The final coverage discusses Viktor Vesnin's work as president of the Academy of Architecture. Appended sections include the brothers' observations on the various problems of modern architecture and of socialist realism in Soviet architecture. Contains a comprehensive list of all their work, as well as a bibliography of publications by and about the Vesnins. Valuable plates of moderate quality are included. Though discussion of the brothers' dramatic involvement in modern architecture still is guarded, important information is provided. An important source.

1143. Chiniakov, Aleksei G. *Brat'ia Vesniny* [The Vesnin Brothers]. Moscow, Stroiizdat, 1970. 180 p. illus.

Examines the principal work of the Vesnin brothers from the beginning of their architectural and artistic careers, focusing upon the shaping of their philosophy. Illuminates their prerevolutionary activity, as well as their active collaboration with the Soviet avant-garde. Assesses the originality of Soviet constructivism as the principal creative method of the Vesnins. Does not fully supersede Il'in's more comprehensive treatment (**no. 1142**), but rather provides a rich complement by concentrating upon the brothers' role in shaping the constructivist movement in Soviet architecture. Richly illustrated. An important source on both the Vesnins and significant aspects of modern architecture in the Soviet Union.

b. Articles by Soviet Writers

1144. Administration of the Union of Soviet Architects. "Pamiati L. A. Vesnina" [Memories of L. A. Vesnin]. *Arkhitektura SSSR*, nos. 3-4, 1933: 64.

An obituary and short biographical account.

1145. "Aleksandr Aleksandrovich Vesnin (1883-1959)." *Arkhitektura SSSR*, no. 12, 1959: 54.

An obituary with a capsule biography, signed by Gosstroi, the Academy of Architecture, the Union of Soviet Architects, the Moscow Architectural Institute, and the Studio of V. A. Vesnin.

1146. "Arkhitektory—izbranniki naroda" [Architects—the Choice of the People]. See **no. 855**.

A brief commemorative biography on the occasion of V. A. Vesnin's having been among the architects selected as representatives to the Soviet of Nationalities. Cites his receipt of the Gold Medal from the Royal Institute of British Architects in 1945.

1147.   "Arkhitektory—kandidaty v Verkhovnyi sovet SSSR. Viktor Alek-
         sandrovich Vesnin" [Architects' Candidates for the Supreme
         Soviet of the USSR]. See **no. 856.** p. 9-10.
             A biography to commemorate the architect's nomination to
         the Supreme Soviet of the USSR. Contains valuable data to
         identify the individuals under whom V. A. Vesnin studied and
         for whom he worked upon completion of his architectural train-
         ing, as well as details concerning his first years of practice. An
         important source for details regarding the architect's professional
         background.

1148.   Chiniakov, Aleksei G. "Le Korbuz'e i Vesniny" [Le Corbusier and
         the Vesnins]. *Sovetskaia arkhitektura*, no. 18, 1969: 133-143.
             Provides much invaluable insight into the relations and exchange
         between Le Corbusier and the Vesnins by an architect who was
         associated with both. An important source.

1149.   ——. "Mastera sovetskoi arkhitektury. Brat'ia Vesniny" [Masters of
         Soviet Architecture. The Vesnin Brothers]. *Sovetskaia arkhitektura*,
         no. 13, 1961: 97-118.
             An authoritative account of the principal stages in the work of
         the Vesnin brothers, from travels in their youth through their
         careers as the leading modern Soviet architects. An attempt to
         vindicate the Vesnins' dynamic association with, and contribution
         to, modern architecture and constructivism in the Soviet Union.
         A number of good plates; much important material. Highly
         recommended.

1150.   ——. "U istokov sovetskogo zodchestva. Arkhitektory—brat'ia Vesniny"
         [At the Sources of Soviet Architecture. The Vesnin Brothers,
         Architects]. *Arkhitektura SSSR*, no. 3, 1967: 41-54.
             An excellent synopsis of important developments in the careers
         of the Vesnin brothers. A continuation of the author's earlier
         efforts **(no. 1149)** to reevaluate objectively the history of modern
         Soviet architecture and among its most prominent exponents, the
         Vesnin brothers. Contains a number of important drawings of
         excellent quality never before published in available sources.
         Highly recommended.

1151.   Ginzburg, Moisei Ia. "Leonid Aleksandrovich Vesnin." *Arkhitektura
         SSSR*, nos. 3-4, 1933: 64.
             A brief, poignant obituary note reflecting on the loss suffered
         by the surviving Vesnin brothers and by Soviet architecture at the
         death of Leonid A. Vesnin.

1152.   —, Viktor A. and Aleksandr A. Vesnin. "Tvorcheskaia tribuna: problemy sovremennoi arkhitektury" [Creative Tribune: Problems of Contemporary Architecture]. See **no. 420.**

   A new manifesto reasserting the essence of their previous platform, though divested of constructivist rhetoric.

1153.   Il'in, Mikhail A. "Mastera sovetskoi arkhitektury. Brat'ia Vesniny" [Masters of Soviet Architecture. The Vesnin Brothers]. *Arkhitektura SSSR*, no. 1, 1940: 33-49.

   An authoritative, balanced study of the Vesnin's career and an analysis of their major work. Highly useful for discussing projects about which little information is available elsewhere. Of great value in rounding out other available sources. All plates important and well reproduced. An important source.

1154.   Khiger, R. Ia. "V masterskoi arkhitektora. Tvorchestvo brat'ev Vesninykh" [In the Architect's Studio. The Practice of the Vesnin Brothers]. *Arkhitektura SSSR*, nos. 3-4, 1933: 46-51.

   A synopsis of the Vesnins' work during the period of modernism in the twenties. Especially valuable for shedding light on the Vesnins' reaction to the official eclipse of modern architecture and tracing their initial steps in capitulating to the new demands as reflected in their designs for the first projects that followed this turn of events.

1155.   "L. A. Vesnin." *Stroitel'stvo Moskvy*, no. 9, 1933: 34.

   An obituary biographical sketch. Contains useful references.

1156.   Sokolov, N. "Mastera sovetskoi arkhitektury" [Masters of Soviet Architecture]. See **no. 853.** p. 84.

   A general assessment of the Vesnins' work; of little value save for indicating the manner in which they were officially regarded at this time.

1157.   Vesnin, Aleksandr A. "O sotsialisticheskom realizme v arkhitekture" [Concerning Socialist Realism in Architecture]. See **no. 784.**
   An enlightening interview with the architect.

1158.   —. and Viktor A. "Forma i soderzhanie" [Form and Content]. See **no. 623.**

   Argues for integrating form and content in Soviet architecture rather than superficially copying classical styles.

1159.   ——. "Tvorcheskii otchet" [Creative Account]. *Arkhitektura SSSR*,
          no. 4, 1935: 40-44.
              A valuable autobiographical account of the brothers' work
          which reveals their personal philosophy and approach to design,
          as seen especially in their discussion of several of what they
          regarded to be their most important projects. Good plates. An
          important source.

1160.   ——, and Moisei Ia. Ginzburg. "Problemy arkhitektury" [Problems of
          Architecture]. See no. 624.
              A succinct restatement of arguments developed in a prior
          article (no. 420).

1161.   Vesnin, Viktor A. "Ot konstruktivizma k sotsialisticheskomu realizmu"
          [From Constructivism to Socialist Realism]. See no. 785.
              Observes those constructivist principles that can be applied to
          the promulgation of socialist realism.

1162.   ——, and Moisei Ia. Ginzburg. "Dostizheniia sovremennoi arkhitek-
          tury" [Accomplishments of Modern Architecture. See no. 351.
              Focuses upon the achievements of the constructivist movement.

1163.   "Vydaiushchiisia sovetskii zodchii i uchenyi" [An Outstanding Soviet
          Architect and Scholar]. *Arkhitektura i stroitel'stvo*, no. 10,
          1950: 21.
              An obituary and biographical essay on the death of Victor A.
          Vesnin; contains important information, though significant for
          omitting any reference to the architect's work in the constructi-
          vist movement; typical for the period.

                          c. Articles by Non-Soviet Writers

1164.   "Academician Victor Vesnin." *RIBA Journal*, 3d ser., v. 48, Dec.
          1944: 31-32.
              A brief biographical sketch and commentary on the occasion
          of the architect's selection as the recipient of the 1945 RIBA
          Royal Gold Medal.

1165.   Gray, Camilla. [Alexander Vesnin]. In her *The Great Experiment:
          Russian Art 1863-1922*. New York, Harry Abrams, 1962. p. 142,
          146, 190, 226-227, 245-248, 296.

Includes a discussion of Vesnin's work, mostly in realms of art other than architecture. Provides an outline chronological biograpy. Contains some useful plates.

1166. "The Royal Gold Medalist." *The Builder,* Jan. 5, 1945: 13.
A brief commentary on the architect's selection as the 1945 recipient of the RIBA Royal Gold Medal.

1167. "Victor Vesnin." *AIA Journal,* v. 4, Aug. 1945: 47.
A brief biographical sketch on the occasion of the architect's election as honorary corresponding member of the AIA on April 26, 1945.

53. Aleksandr V. Vlasov

1168. "A. V. Vlasov." *Arkhitektura SSSR,* no. 10, 1962: 55.
An obituary; useful for detailing the varied official posts held by the architect throughout his career.

1169. "Aleksandr Vasil'evich Vlasov." *Arkhitektura i stroitel'stvo,* no. 2, 1947: 3.
A short commemorative biography on the occasion of the architect's selection as deputy to the Ukrainian Supreme Soviet. A review of his official posts and awards.

1170. Andreev, P., and Iu. Iaralov. "Mastera arkhitektury. Aleksandr Vlasov" [Masters of Architecture. Alexander Vlasov]. *Sovetskaia arkhitektura,* no. 16, 1964: 89-102.
An analytical biography and study of the architect's career and major work. Includes a number of important plates. Loosely organized but contains important information.

1171. Khiger, R. Ia. "Mastera molodoi arkhitektury" [Masters of the Young Architecture]. See **no. 849.** p. 33-38.
An interesting and revealing account of the young architect; especially valuable for revealing his transition from constructivist functionalism to the method of the Zholtovsky school.

1172. Sokolov, N. "Mastera sovetskoi arkhitektury" [Masters of Soviet Architecture]. See **no. 853.** p. 95.
A brief, favorable reference to the architect and his work, indicating the favor with which he was officially regarded at the time.

1173. Vlasov, Aleksandr V. "Tvorcheskii otchet" [Creative Account].
Arkhitektura SSSR, no. 4, 1935: 55-58.

An autobiographical account of the architect's early career.
Clarifies his association and work with VOPRA and articulates his
philosophy and approach to design and to the notion of an
architecture suitable for the Soviet state. An important statement.

54. Ivan V. Zholtovsky

a. Monographs

1174. Oshchepkov, G. O., ed. *I. V. Zholtovsky. Proekty i postroiki* [I. V.
Zholtovsky. Projects and Buildings]. Moscow, Gosstroiizdat, 1955.
165 p. illus.

A brief essay on Zholtovsky's work, followed by a profusion
of plates. A useful source of illustrations.

b. Articles

1175. Arkin, David E. "O lozhnoi 'klassike,' novatorstve, i traditsii"
[Concerning False "Classicism," Innovation and Tradition].
Arkhitektura SSSR, no. 4, 1939: 12-19.

A spirited criticism of Zholtovsky's eclectic method of appropriating Palladian motifs in a manner that totally ignores contemporary demands and building materials. Cites the architect's
administration building in Sochi as an example of this unfortunate
trend.

1176. Arkin, David E. "Razgovor o Zholtovskom" [Conversation about
Zholtovsky]. *Arkhitektura SSSR*, no. 5, 1940: 54-58.

An assessment of Zholtovsky's method of design and the
works which exemplify the architect's approach. An illuminating
commentary on the eclectic nature of Zholtovsky's work.

1177. Bylinkin, N. P. "O teorii kompozitsii I. V. Zholtovskogo" [Con-
cerning the Theory of I. V. Zholtovsky]. *Arkhitektura SSSR*,
no. 5, 1940: 51-53.

An analysis of the architect's method and theory of composition and philosophy of architecture. Seen as 1) employing traditions of folk art in a rural setting, 2) employing the forms and

tectonic means of the Renaissance in the urban centers, with an
emphasis upon Renaissance forms and decorative motifs, and 3)
stressing the ensemble in synthesizing urban design. An important
source, still the only such analysis of Zholtovsky's architectural
theory of design.

1178.   Council of Ministers of the USSR. "Ot Soveta Ministrov SSSR"
         [From the Council of Ministers of the USSR]. *Arkhitektura
         SSSR*, no. 8, 1959: 53.
              An obituary followed by a brief survey of the architect's
         career, signed by several of the official organs of the Soviet
         architectural community.

1179.   Khiger, R. Ia. "Zodchii I. V. Zholtovsky" [Architect I. V. Zholtovsky].
         Arkhitektura SSSR, no. 2, 1968: 44-51.
              An authoritative analysis of the architect's work, from his
         training and prerevolutionary work through his practice in the
         Soviet period. Focuses on the profound contradictions evident
         between the architect's theoretical aspirations and his achieve-
         ments in actual projects; includes an analysis of the sources from
         the High Renaissance, especially the Palladian motif, evident in
         his designs. A change is noted in the last phase of the architect's
         career, when his designs for apartment buildings become far more
         simplified. Perhaps the single most penetrating, objective study
         published thus far on Zholtovsky, reflecting the growing trend by
         Soviet architectural historians to analyze dispassionately. Highly
         recommended.

1180.   Kruglov, M. "O kompozitsii inter'era v novykh rabotakh I. V.
         Zholtovskogo" [Concerning the Composition of the Interior in
         the New Projects by I. V. Zholtovsky]. *Arkhitektura SSSR*, no.
         10, 1952: 22-26.
              A survey of Zholtovsky's postwar work, with emphasis on an
         analysis of the architect's method of interior design, as seen in his
         most recent buildings. A few plates.

1181.   ——, G. Lebedev, and N. Sukoian. "Ivan Vladislavovich Zholtovsky."
         Arkhitektura SSSR, no. 12, 1957: 21-28.
              Written by Zholtovsky's former associates. Surveys his career
         and approach to design. Contains useful information, though
         colored by an understandable sense of enthusiasm.

1182.   Lazarev, V. "Problemy zhilishchnoi arkhitektury v tvorchestve I. V. Zholtovskogo" [Problems of Housing in the Practice of I. V. Zholtovsky]. *Arkhitektura SSSR*, no. 10, 1952: 14-21.

An analysis of Zholtovsky's current work in housing design. Includes measured drawings of moldings and decorative details employed by the architect.

1183.   Lebedev, G., and N. Sukoian. "Vydaiushchiisia sovetskii zodchii (k 85-letiiu I. V. Zholtovskogo)" [An Outstanding Soviet Architect (In Honor of I. V. Zholtovsky's 85th Birthday)]. *Arkhitektura SSSR*, no. 1, 1953: 17-26.

A brief record of Zholtovsky's career by two of his associates (see **no. 1181** for a later article by the same authors). Though displaying an obvious bias, provides important information in substantially dependable form. Of special value for its account, with supplementary illustrations, of the later stages in Zholtovsky's career.

1184.   Sokolov, N. "Mastera sovetskoi arkhitektury" [Masters of Soviet Architecture]. See **no. 853.** p. 85.

A general assessment of Zholtovsky, indicating his current prominence in official circles.

1185.   Vlasov, Aleksandr V. "Zodchii, uchenyi, pedagog (k vos'midesiatipiatiletiiu akademika arkhitektury I. V. Zholtovskogo)" [Architect, Scholar, Teacher (In Honor of I. V. Zholtovsky's Eighty-Fifth Birthday)]. *Sovetskaia arkhitektura*, no. 4, 1953: 46-69.

A comprehensive study of Zholtovsky's architectural background, development from the formative years to the height of his practice in the Soviet period, philosophical and theoretical antecedents, and major work throughout his career. A balanced treatment of the various periods of the architect's work providing significant insight into his approach and method. Analysis of major projects is amply supplemented with illustrations. Contains much useful information. A good source.

1186.   Zal'tsman, A. "Tvorchestvo I. V. Zholtovskogo" [Practice of I. V. Zholtovsky]. *Arkhitektura SSSR*, no. 5, 1940: 35-50.

Analyzes the development of Zholtovsky's career and assesses the major influences upon his work, most notably the architect's passionate attraction to the High Renaissance in general and the Palladian idiom in particular. Treats also the architect's views on the role of architecture in society and of the architectural ensemble in urban centers. Contains much useful information.

1187. Zholtovsky, Ivan V. "Printsipy zodchestva" [Principles of Architecture]. *Arkhitektura SSSR*, no. 5, 1933: 28-29.

A statement by the architect of his approach to design. Speaks of his central conceptual orientation toward the architectural ensemble of a city and the harmony among its parts and of a unity of all the components within an architectural design. Discusses also coordinating various aspects of professional practice in order to be able to achieve one's fundamental aims in design. A highly useful testament.

Index

Includes names of authors, compilers, editors, sponsoring organizations, and titles of publications. Numbers refer to entries, not pages.

262   Index